CONTENTS

T0386009

Focus 4 Workbook walkthrough

UNITS (pp. 4–131)

UNITS 1–8

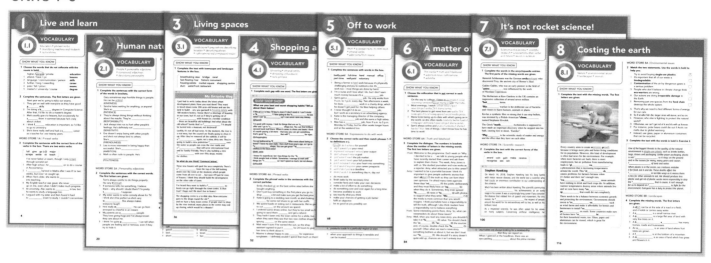

BACK OF THE BOOK (pp. 132–190)

The VOCABULARY BANK is a topic-based word list including vocabulary from all units. It is followed by exercises which provide more vocabulary practice.

Focus 3 Grammar Review contains grammar explanations and revision of the grammar taught in level 3.

The GRAMMAR: Train and Try Again section provides more grammar activities for self-study.

The WRITING BANK provides a list of the useful phrases from the WRITING FOCUS boxes in the Student's Book.

The answer keys to the Self-check, Focus 3 Grammar Review and GRAMMAR: Train and Try Again sections support self-study and promote student autonomy.

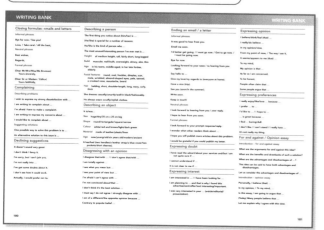
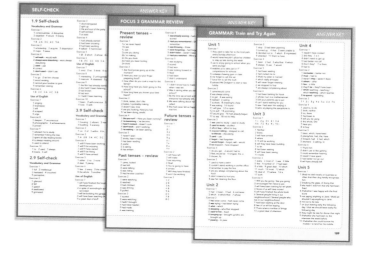

2

DON'T MISS

The SHOW WHAT YOU KNOW tasks in the Vocabulary and Grammar lessons serve as a warm-up and revise vocabulary or grammar students should already know.

The SHOW WHAT YOU'VE LEARNT tasks in the Vocabulary and Grammar lessons help students to check their progress and be aware of their own learning.

The SHOW THAT YOU'VE CHECKED section in the Writing lessons is a useful checklist that accompanies the final writing task.

SHOW WHAT YOU KNOW

1 Add one of the phrases in the box to each sentence to make it more emphatic.

absolutely   at all   on earth   own
so   the question is

It's your fault you are busy now. You should've done more work last week. _own_

1 If you don't do any exercise, I'm not surprised you feel unwell so often. _____
2 I'm sorry I was rude to you. I've had a difficult day. _____
3 Are you going to do it again? _____
4 I don't know why you didn't call me first to check. _____
5 I am convinced she is telling the truth. _____

SHOW WHAT YOU'VE LEARNT

5 Find and correct the mistakes.

She won't buy anything that doesn't cost a fortune, ~~won't~~ she?   _will_
1 The pizza's ready. Take it out of the oven, do you? Sorry to ask, but I've got my hands full. _____
2 Don't get ripped off, do you? _____
3 Let's withdraw another 100 euros, will we? _____
4 Nothing broke when you dropped your bag, was it? _____
5 A: They're going to splash out on a new car.
  B: Will they? _____
6 That's Ella over there, isn't she? _____

| | /6 |

GRAMMAR: Train and Try Again page 174

SHOW THAT YOU'VE CHECKED

In my review ...

• I have used the opening paragraph to attract the reader's attention, mention the name of the TV show and state my overall opinion of it. ☐
• I have used the main paragraphs to give more details about the plot and characters and say what I liked / didn't like about the show. ☐
• I have summarised my review and made a recommendation in the conclusion. ☐
• I have used a formal style. ☐
• I have checked my spelling. ☐
• my handwriting is neat enough for someone else to read. ☐

The SPEAKING BANK lists the key phrases from the Speaking lessons.

The REMEMBER THIS boxes focus on useful language nuances.

The star coding system shows the different levels of difficulty of the activities in the Grammar lessons.

SPEAKING BANK

Beginning your answer

I firmly believe/
I'm not convinced
they do because ...   _____

One obvious/clear advantage /
disadvantage is that ...   _____

I think I'd emphasise/
explain that/how ...   _____

It's absolutely vital / quite
important, I think, because ...   _____

As well as (avoiding fur
products), other
(things that can help)
include ...   _____

I think the main/one/
a significant reason is that ...   _____

**Expressing opinions
tentatively**

It could be argued that ...   _____

I don't feel particularly
strongly about ...   _____

I don't have a strong
opinion about ...   _____

I suppose you could
say that ...   _____

REMEMBER THIS

The noun *chance* can be used to describe:

The possibility that something will happen, especially something you want, e.g.
There's an element of chance when you buy a suitcase.
There's a good chance the contents will be valuable.

An opportunity to do something, e.g.
I haven't had the chance to look in the suitcase yet.
He missed the chance to make a lot of money.

The REMEMBER BETTER boxes provide tips on learning, remembering and enriching vocabulary.

REMEMBER BETTER

On a separate piece of paper, make a list in English of products or services that you have paid for that fit the categories below. Look at the list later or tomorrow and see if you can remember what the categories were.

A product/service that you got for **a bargain price**.
A product/service that you **paid out** for.
A product/service you **shopped around** for.
A product/service which you found through **online shopping**.
A product/service that you got in **a chain store**.
A product that was **an impulse purchase**.

4 ★ ★ Change the underlined words so that the tense is correct in the second sentence.

If only I <u>was more outgoing</u>.
If only I <u>had been more outgoing</u> when I was at school.
1 I wish I <u>could go on holiday</u>.
  I wish I _____ last summer.
2 If only we <u>lived in a big city</u> now.
  If only we _____ when we were children.
3 I wish I <u>hadn't lived alone</u> at university.
  I wish I _____ now.
4 If only I <u>hadn't been so tired</u> that night.
  If only I _____ now.

5 ★ ★ ★ Complete the messages with the correct forms of the words in the box.

begin   can   explore   invest   make   spend

If you love the sea, then **Ocean Fans** is the website for you.

Sea not Space – jellyfish99 writes:

It's high time we <u>explored</u> the world's oceans more thoroughly. Amazingly, 95 percent of our waters remain unseen by human eyes. I would rather governments ¹_____ in this than in developing weapons, for example.

I wish we ²_____ concentrate on learning more about what is here on Earth and how to preserve it. The answer to many of our environmental problems could lie beneath the waves – if only we ³_____ the effort to look.

1 Reply – ocotboy8 writes:

I couldn't agree more, jellyfish99. I wish we ⁴_____ the billions it took to fight the wars of recent years on preserving the planet and its oceans instead. If only we ⁵_____ developing clean energy alternatives earlier, the Earth might now be in a much better state.

Skills Reviews with speaking, reading and writing tasks in the exam format help students to prepare for their exams.

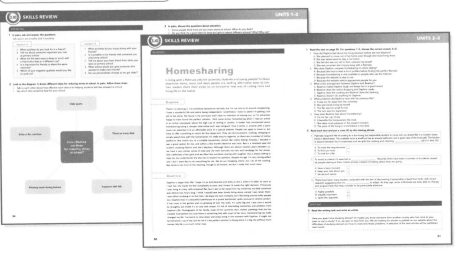

1 Live and learn

VOCABULARY

1.1

Education • phrasal verbs
• describing teachers and students
• collocations

SHOW WHAT YOU KNOW

1 Choose the words that do not collocate with the nouns in bold.

higher / (people) / private	**education**
1 attend / have / go	**lessons**
2 language / communication / person	**skills**
3 further / long / rewarding	**career**
4 pass / fail / prove	**exams**
5 master's / university / course	**degree**

2 Complete the sentences. The first letters are given.

Next year we're going to **t**_ake_ our exams.

1 They get on well with everyone as they have good **p**_____ skills.

2 I'm doing a **b**_____ degree in Computer Science. After that, I'd like to do a master's degree.

3 Matt usually goes to lessons, but occasionally he **s**_____ them in summer because he's crazy about cricket.

4 I think **f**_____ education is important, so I'd like to go to university.

5 She's done really well and had a **s**_____ career as a teacher for over twenty years.

WORD STORE 1A | Phrasal verbs

3 Complete the sentences with the correct form of the verbs in the box. There are two extra verbs.

> fall   give   go (x2)   major
> ~~scrape~~   settle   sit   teach

I've never failed an exam, though I only _scrape_ through sometimes!

1 After high school, he _____ on to do a course in Accountancy.

2 I _____ behind in Maths after I was ill for two weeks, but now I've caught up.

3 When Yen's older, she wants to _____ into teaching.

4 My English teacher was great, she never _____ up on me, even when I didn't make much progress.

5 At university, Alex wants to _____ in law, but he wants to study a language too.

6 I argued with my sister and then found it hard to _____ down to study. I couldn't concentrate.

4 Complete the tips with the correct form of the phrasal verbs in Exercise 3.

TIPS
FOR SUCCESSFUL STUDY

● Have a long-term plan. What do you want to _go into_ after you finish your studies? Working towards a goal can inspire you to work hard now.

● Motivate yourself. If you find it hard to ¹_____ and study at home, then give yourself a treat _after_ you finish. For example, listening to music or having a hot chocolate.

● Talk to your teachers and find out how you are doing. If you have ²_____ the other students, ask for help to catch up.

● Make a study plan. Only ³_____ the second task when you have finished the first, and so on. That way you will complete all your work.

● Take responsibility for your learning. If you have taken an exam or test and just ⁴_____ , then focus on how you can improve. Passing isn't enough, try to get good marks!

● Choose subjects you enjoy to ⁵_____ . You'll work harder if you like a subject – and be more likely to ⁶_____ the subject if you hate it.

WORD STORE 1B | Describing teachers and students

5 Match the definitions with the words in the box.

> bully   ~~disruptive~~   dyslexic   gifted   lenient
> self-disciplined   strict   swot

causing problems and preventing something from continuing in its usual way _disruptive_

1 having a natural ability to do things well _____

2 not strict in the way you punish someone or the standards you expect _____

3 able to make yourself do the things you know you have to do _____

4 someone who uses their strength or power to frighten or hurt someone weaker than them _____

5 someone who spends a lot of time studying and seems to have no other interests _____

6 expecting people to obey rules or do what you say _____

7 having a condition that makes it difficult to read or spell _____

6 Complete the text with the correct form of the words that describe teachers and students in Exercise 5.

HAVE YOUR SAY!

Students say ...

Our teachers are always telling people off, they should be more _lenient_! I don't often get into trouble because I'm ¹_____ and I always do my work. I'm not a ²_____ though; I don't spend all my time studying. But not everyone's like me. Teachers should help students develop their learning skills and critical thinking, not just tell us facts!

I really struggle with reading because I'm ³_____ , but all my teachers have been brilliant! They've taught me different ways to improve my reading skills and supported my learning both at school and at home using online tools.

Teachers say ...

I'm quite a ⁴_____ teacher and I think pupils should do what they're told. It annoys me when ⁵_____ students interrupt, shout and mess around. I also dislike ⁶_____ who threaten other students physically or verbally. I don't tolerate it in my classroom. I enjoy teaching all my students, but it's a real pleasure to teach ⁷_____ students who make strong academic progress.

WORD STORE 1C | Collocations

7 Complete the text with the correct collocation. The first letters are given.

Hi Erin,

I'm really enjoying my philosophy course! I've attended all my l_ectures_ so far and I'm learning a lot. I'm glad I don't have to ¹g_____ any lectures, though, I'd forget what to say ☺. I'm reading a lot too, it's a great way to deepen my ²k_____ of the subject. I've chosen my option for this year – logic! I don't have to ³s_____ an exam at the end of the course, but I have to write a long essay. I've also discovered I have a ⁴p_____ for surfing and I'm going to ⁵e_____ on a course in summer. I know you love water sports – would this be of any ⁶i_____ to you? We could do it together!

What about you? Have you finished writing your ⁷d_____ yet? Do you still want to work in the ⁸f_____ of computer technology?

Oh, good news! My brother is still at school, he didn't get ⁹e_____ after all. In fact, he's really changed! He's studying hard now and he got a ¹⁰s_____ to study in France for three months.

Write soon,

Karl

┌─────────────────────────────────────┐
│ SHOW WHAT YOU'VE LEARNT │
└─────────────────────────────────────┘

8 Choose the correct answers A–C.

1 Maria is very ___ at art. She can draw and paint extremely well.
   A strict   B self-disciplined   C gifted

2 At the end of my university course, I have to write a ___ of 10,000 words. I've never written such a long essay before!
   A dissertation   B degree   C diploma

3 After I've finished my degree in Medicine, I'd love to work in the ___ of medical research.
   A field   B area   C course

4 I need to study harder for my next History exam as I only just ___ through this one. Two marks less and I would've failed!
   A passed   B scraped   C fell

5 I'm not sure yet which subject I'm going to major ___ . I've got to decide soon.
   A at   B in   C on

6 I've been off school for 10 days, so I've fallen ___ the rest of the class, but I'm sure I'll soon catch up.
   A after   B off   C behind

7 The professor ___ the lecture extremely fast, so it was hard to take notes.
   A attended   B gave   C spoke

8 All he does is study and he's even asked the teacher for some extra work – what a ___ !
   A dyslexic   B bully   C swot

9 It's time to ___ and do your homework now. You've got to calm down!
   A settle down   B give up   C go on

10 This summer I'd like to ___ on a course to learn all about filming and how to edit films.
   A pass   B deepen   C enrol

                                        /10

5

GRAMMAR

1.2
Present and past habits

SHOW WHAT YOU KNOW

1 Complete the sentences about present and past habits with one word.

Graham always _used_ to pay attention in Physics lessons. It was his favourite subject. ☐

1 Didn't you _____ to skip lessons occasionally when you were at school, Dad? ☐

2 The security guard does _____ unlock the school gates until exactly 7:30 a.m. ☐

3 Our French teacher from primary school _____ only speak Italian in class. No wonder we didn't learn much! ☐

4 Lucy didn't _____ to get on with her brother, but things are better now that they are older. ☐

2 Which sentence in Exercise 1 describes a present habit? Tick the appropriate box.

3 ★ Complete the dialogues with _always_ and the correct form of the verbs in the box.

(hang   play   put   talk   ~~tease~~)

Dad: Why can't you two just get on with each other?

Melanie: Because he _'s always teasing_ me. Why can't he just leave me alone?

1 Alice: Well, it's good to be studious, but Luke _____ about schoolwork. I don't think he has a social life at all.

Max: Yes, I can see how annoying he is.

2 Amber: Why did you split up with Richard then, Erin?

Erin: Oh, he and his friends _____ computer games or talking about them. I hardly ever saw him, and when I did, the conversation was boring.

3 Paul: I'll do it tomorrow, OK?

Gemma: Oh, Paul. You _____ things off until tomorrow, or next week, or whatever. Why don't you just get it out of the way now?

4 Butcher: Why _____ around here, little dog? Can you smell those sausages? I don't know how someone so small can eat so much. Come on then, boy, come here! It's your lucky day!

---

4 ★ ★ Choose the correct option to complete the text.

● ○ ○

Educate Yourself

Results a mess? Try not to stress. You can still find success.

Teachers and parents [1]_will / are_ always telling young people how important it is to work hard at school. Of course, this is good advice, but some very successful people [2]_performed / were always performing_ very poorly as students and still went on to achieve great things.

Deep thinker Albert Einstein [3]_used / use_ to get poor grades in French at school. Though brilliant in other subjects, he struggled to master French and failed his college entrance exams as a result.

Actor Orlando Bloom [4]_didn't use to / wouldn't_ find school easy and [5]_would / will_ struggle with many subjects as a result of his dyslexia.

It is important to do your best at school of course, but there are clearly other routes to success.

5 ★ ★ ★ Complete the second sentence so that it has a similar meaning to the first. Use the word in capitals.

I didn't have a large circle of friends at school, but now that I'm at university I know lots of people. **USE**

I _didn't use to have_ a large circle of friends at school but now that I'm at university I know lots of people.

1 Holly bites her nails constantly. **IS**
Holly _____ her nails.

2 Ms Wilson, our neighbour, was very curious – she would always ask us a lot of questions. **TO**
Ms Wilson, our neighbour, _____ very curious – she would always ask us a lot of questions.

3 Stephen leaves everything until the last minute and then panics. **WILL**
Stephen _____ everything until the last minute and then panic.

4 We picked and ate fresh fruit from the garden when we were kids. **WOULD**
We _____ fresh fruit from the garden when we were kids.

SHOW WHAT YOU'VE LEARNT

6 Choose the correct answers A–C.

1 Naomi didn't ___ to suffer from allergies when she lived in the countryside.
   A use   B used   C would

2 Scott is not very bright. He ___ raise his hand in class even when he has no idea of the answer.
   A would   B always   C will

3 Whenever I stayed at Auntie Freda's, she ___ always make pancakes for breakfast.
   A will   B would   C used

4 ___ you use to watch that funny show with the puppets? I can't remember its name now.
   A Did   B Would   C Were

5 When they were younger, Ben and Jamie ___ to walk to school together. Now Jamie drives.
   A will   B used   C enjoyed

6 Summer holidays ___ to last forever when I was in primary school.
   A would   B seem   C used

/6

GRAMMAR: Train and Try Again page 171

1 Choose the correct option to complete the extract from the recording.

Extract from Student's Book recording 🔊 **1.8**

Speaker 1

My earliest memory? I have / 'm having a vague memory of the Christmas before I was three, but I **¹**have / had very vivid memories of my third birthday party, and I can remember other events very clearly from when I was three years old. Some people say I must **²**have / had to confused a memory with photos **³**I'll see / I've seen of the same events. But **⁴**I'd / I've asked my mum about it and she agrees that my memories are accurate. For some of them, there's no photographic evidence or anything that **⁵**could / could have jogged my memory, so I believe they're real.

---

2 Complete the extract from the recording with the words in the box. There are two extra words.

confused   jogged   losing   manages
~~memories~~   remember   recall   vague

Extract from Student's Book recording 🔊 **1.8**

Speaker 2

Most people in my family have rubbish *memories* , but my grandfather's amazing. He's not like other old people who are **¹**_____ their memory and get **²**_____ – he's really switched on. He remembers dates and names and places. He can even **³**_____ in detail events that happened 50 years ago – and he's 77! I'm 16 and I can't **⁴**_____ what I did yesterday! I wish I had his memory – it would help me a lot in my exams. I asked him how he **⁵**_____ to remember things so well, and he says it's because he drinks green tea! I think it's because he reads a lot and stays active. He walks every day – he's much fitter than I am.

REMEMBER THIS

Different phrases can be used to talk about memory:

- for remembering – *bear something in mind, learn by heart, think back to something, ring a bell.*
  We're studying the table of elements in Chemistry and we have to learn it by heart.
- for forgetting – *slip your mind, escape you, draw a blank.*
  I'm sorry I didn't call you – it slipped my mind.

---

3 Read REMEMBER THIS. Complete the phrases with the words in the box.

back   bear   bell   draw   escape   heart   slip

to *slip* sb's mind	– to forget about sth
1 to think _____ to sth	– to try to recall an event
2 to _____ you	– to try to think of something but not be able to
3 to learn by _____	– to memorise sth
4 to _____ sth in mind	– to remember sth
5 to _____ a blank	– to be unable to remember sth
6 to ring a _____	– to sound familiar

4 Complete the sentences with the correct form of the words and phrases in Exercise 3.

I should be able to remember his address, but it *escapes* me.

1 Can you _____ to that day and tell me what happened?
2 _____ that it'll take a few hours to drive there, so leave early.
3 Actors need to _____ their lines _____ before filming can begin.
4 I'm sure I've seen him somewhere before, but I'm _____ at the moment.
5 Her name didn't _____ , but when I saw a photo, I remembered who she was.
6 Oh no! I didn't do my homework; it completely _____ .

WORD STORE 1D | Memory

5 Complete the sentences with the words in the box.

earliest   ~~good~~   jogged   lost
photographic   sieve   vague   vivid

I have a *good* memory for faces. I forget people's names, but never their faces.

1 I can remember all the details of my holiday in Prague. I have such _____ memories of it.
2 Joe has a _____ memory. He can read a page of any book and then remember everything on it.
3 In my _____ memory, I'm in the garden. I must have been about two years old.
4 After his accident, he _____ his memory completely. He didn't even remember his own name.
5 Sara has a memory like a _____ . You tell her something and the next minute she's forgotten it!
6 I've only got a _____ memory of our old house. I can remember my bedroom, but not much else.
7 I'd forgotten about his birthday, but when I read the note it _____ my memory, so I bought him a present.

1 Read the text quickly and choose the best title for it.
1 The Real Rain Man
2 The Biggest Slice of Pi
3 The Man with the Amazing Mind

Daniel Tammet is a linguistic and mathematical genius. He speaks eleven languages, performs complex mental arithmetic in seconds, and on March 14, 2004 publicly recited pi from memory to 22,514 decimal places. It took him five hours and nine minutes. However, since childhood, despite his phenomenal mental abilities, Daniel has struggled to learn the personal skills that most of us take for granted: communication, empathy and the ability to see the big picture.

Daniel's skills and limitations are the result of Asperger's syndrome, a form of autism. He is a high-functioning autistic savant who possesses similar abilities to those of the character played by Dustin Hoffman in the film *Rain Man*. ¹__ 'I'm lucky,' he says, 'because most others who have rare abilities are also seriously disabled.'

Life is easier for Daniel now that he is in his thirties, but growing up with autism was tough for him and his family. As a baby, he used to cry constantly and only repetitive motion would stop him. ²__ As a result, he never played with other children, or even with toys. 'Numbers were my toys,' he says.

To him, numbers have colours, shapes, textures* and personalities. He has described his visual image of 289 as particularly ugly, and 333 as particularly attractive. Three is green, five sounds like a clap of thunder, and thirty-seven is lumpy*. This cross-connection between unrelated senses is known as synaesthesia, and in Daniel's case it allows him to 'experience' numbers rather than calculate them. As he explains, 'When I multiply numbers together, I see two shapes. The image starts to change and evolve, and a third shape appears. That's the answer.'

It was this unique ability that helped him to remember pi to so many decimal places, back in 2004. ³__ 'To me, it is as beautiful as the Mona Lisa,' he explains.

Daniel has many gifts often associated with autism. He can copy a picture so accurately that it could have been traced*, and he planned his autobiography *Born on a Blue Day* without taking a single note. Nevertheless, he is more aware of the many things he can't do. He knows, for instance, that he is difficult to live with because he cannot understand what others are feeling. He admits that most of the time, he has to pretend to show emotions. ⁴__ He reveals that when his cat died, he cried and understood grief* for the first time.

In 2004, Daniel met Kim Peek, the savant on whom *Rain Man* was actually based. Unlike Daniel, Peek, who passed away in 2009, was unable to manage daily life independently. ⁵__ 'We swapped facts and figures like others swap gossip,' says Tammet. With the help of his father, Peek travelled America spreading the message that difference is not necessarily a negative thing.

Like Peek, Daniel is putting his gifts to good use. He gives regular lectures, has written three successful books, and been the subject of numerous studies and documentaries. Much of his work involves helping scientists understand how the brain works. 'I used to long* to be like other people,' he says. 'But they tell me that I have the same effect on them as Professor Stephen Hawking. That in the contradiction* between ability and disability, they see humanity.'

GLOSSARY

texture (n) = the way a surface or material feels when you touch it
lumpy (adj) = covered with or containing small solid pieces e.g. *a lumpy mattress*
trace (v) = copy a drawing by putting a very thin piece of paper over it and then drawing the lines you can see through the paper

grief (n) = extreme sadness caused by the death of someone you love
long (v) = want something very much, especially when it seems unlikely to happen
contradiction (n) = a difference between two statements, beliefs or ideas that means they cannot both be true

2 Read the text. Complete gaps 1–5 with sentences A–F. There is one extra sentence.

A Despite these limitations, he is slowly extending his emotional range. ☐

B At school, he struggled to read body language or make eye contact, finding it impossible to interpret how other people were feeling. ☐

C *Born on a Blue Day* was named 'Best Book for Young Adults' in 2008 by the American Library Association. ☐

D Remarkably, though, he was able to read two pages of a book at once, one with each eye, and remember every single word. ☐

E There are only about fifty savants in the world (all men), but Tammet is unique in being able to describe how his mind works. ☐

F Tammet describes seeing the number as a landscape through which he travelled in his mind. ☐

3 Read the text again. Are statements 1–7 true (T) or false (F)?

1 The film *Rain Man* is partly based on Daniel's life story. ☐

2 Unlike other savants, Daniel is able to explain his remarkable abilities. ☐

3 At school, Daniel didn't find interacting with others easy. ☐

4 Daniel claims he can see, hear and feel numbers. ☐

5 Daniel may not actually be experiencing the emotions he shows to other people. ☐

6 Kim Peek and Daniel Tammet wrote a successful book together. ☐

7 Daniel says that people sometimes confuse him with Professor Stephen Hawking. ☐

4 Complete the collocations with the verbs in the box. There are two extra words. Then match the collocations with the meanings a–e.

> find   have   involve   make   put
> read   see   take

take something for granted ☐ f

1 _____ something to good use ☐

2 _____ eye contact with someone ☐

3 _____ an effect on someone ☐

4 _____ someone's body language ☐

5 _____ the big picture ☐

a to influence someone to change their ideas or behaviour

b to understand the most important facts about a situation rather than the details

c to look directly into someone's eyes

d to understand physical communication such as gestures

e to make the most of something or use it to your advantage

f to expect something to be available all the time and forget that you are lucky to have it

---

REMEMBER BETTER

When learning a new collocation, remember that it may include words that have multiple meanings, e.g. in the collocation *to see the big picture*, the word *picture* refers not to a painting, drawing or photograph, but to a situation.

Complete the sentences with the collocations in Exercise 4. Change the form if necessary.

On this week's show, how to *read* your partner's *body language*.

1 Ellen was so embarrassed she couldn't even _____ the nurse.

2 Julia has _____ her bilingualism _____ working as an interpreter in the European Parliament.

3 The doctor's warning obviously _____ Kelly. She has started going to the gym again.

4 Ten hours into the power cut, Damien realised just how much we all _____ electricity _____ .

5 The chairman accused the union leader of focusing on minor details and failing to _____ .

WORD STORE 1E | Collocations

5 Complete the collocations. The first letters are given.

Man in accident

Sam Green, 23, was **f**ound unconscious in his car which had hit a tree in a storm. It is believed that during the crash he hit his head, causing him to ¹**l**_____ consciousness, and subsequently ²**f**_____ into a coma. Doctors have confirmed that he ³**r**_____ consciousness and ⁴**c**_____ out of the coma a week later. Fortunately, Mr Green didn't ⁵**s**_____ any other injuries and he has now fully ⁶**r**_____ and left hospital. Nobody knows how the accident happened – it will ⁷**r**_____ a mystery. Mr Green believes that his car might have been ⁸**s**_____ by lightning as the engine suddenly stopped working, which is known to happen when lightning hits a vehicle.

Learn with us!
We have fully qualified tutors for all ages and subjects. Do you ⁹**f**_____ the urge to ¹⁰**a**_____ a new skill or ¹¹**s**_____ an old one? We have a teacher for you! Phone Jill on 0712 384576.

VOCABULARY PRACTICE | Expressions with *brain*

6 Look at the vocabulary in lesson 1.4 in the Student's Book. Complete the second sentence so that it means the same as the first. Use expressions with *brain*.

I can't stop thinking about that song.
I've got that song *on the brain*.

1 Suddenly, Mark had a great idea.
Suddenly, Mark had a _____ .

2 Jackie was responsible for inventing that machine.
Jackie was _____ that machine.

3 I'm trying hard to remember that actor's name.
I'm _____ to remember that actor's name.

4 Shall we try and think of some new ideas?
Shall we _____ some new ideas?

5 She's very intelligent.
She's very _____ .

9

GRAMMAR

1.5

Verb patterns

---

1 Tick the correct sentences. Sometimes both are correct.

1   a   The extension to the tram line allows me to travel all the way home without walking.   ☐
    b   The extension to the tram line allows me travel all the way home without walking.   ☐
2   a   Many families can't afford sending their children to private schools.   ☐
    b   Many families can't afford to send their children to private schools.   ☐
3   a   Jay likes to ask his teachers difficult questions.   ☐
    b   Jay likes asking his teachers difficult questions.   ☐
4   a   My parents won't let me to miss school unless I'm really sick.   ☐
    b   My parents won't let me miss school unless I'm really sick.   ☐

2   ★ Complete the sentences with the correct forms of the verbs in brackets.

Do you fancy _going_ (go) to Jim's birthday party with me next Sunday?

1   The teacher told a joke which caused the whole class _____ (laugh).
2   We've arranged _____ (meet) after school today to talk about the end of term party.
3   We feel the school should do more to encourage students _____ (recycle) their rubbish.
4   Please keep _____ (work) on Exercise 6. I'll be back in a moment.
5   Chloe! You spend too much time _____ (talk). Please be quiet and focus on the lesson.

3   ★ ★ Match the sentences with the correct meanings a or b.

1   A   I remember putting my wallet in my back pocket but now it's gone!   ☐
    B   I remembered to zip my purse safely in my bag.   ☐
    a   *Remember something, then do it.*
    b   *Remember that you did something earlier.*
2   A   I forgot to mention that I'm vegetarian.   ☐
    B   I'll never forget meeting the Prime Minister.   ☐
    a   *Forget that you need to do something.*
    b   *Forget something that happened earlier.*
3   A   Eva stopped to tie her shoelace.   ☐
    B   Please stop looking at your phone when I'm trying to talk to you.   ☐
    a   *Stop doing one thing in order to do something else.*
    b   *No longer do something.*
4   A   For a better night's sleep, try drinking more water and less coffee throughout the day.   ☐
    B   We tried to persuade our guests to stay a little longer.   ☐
    a   *Make an effort to do something difficult.*
    b   *Do something as an experiment to see what happens.*

4   ★ ★ ★ Complete the text with the correct forms of the verbs in the box.

forget/do   hear/Mum and Dad/talk ~~remember/fall~~   stop/think   try/count   try/get

When I was little, I _remember falling_ asleep as soon as my head hit the pillow most nights. I recall the comfort of [1] _____ downstairs and how the faint sound of their voices used to send me to sleep almost immediately. These days, I find it a lot more difficult. To my mind, there is nothing more frustrating than lying in bed [2] _____ to sleep. Sometimes, I can't [3] _____ about school and exams. I worry that I might have [4] _____ some homework for one of my subjects or some other trivial thing. I [5] _____ sheep once, but it didn't work. I ended up worrying about my Maths test the next day.

5   Find and correct the mistakes in the sentences.

There are a number of reasons why girls tend ~~doing~~ better at languages than boys. _to do_

1   Brianne clearly remembers to meet her boyfriend for the first time. _____
2   After the recent thefts, we would like to advise students not leave valuables in their lockers. _____
3   We were tired and thirsty, so we stopped having a drink at the café. _____
4   I saw the boys breaking the window then run away. _____
5   If your computer freezes, try to turn it off and on again and see if that helps. _____
6   Our teacher always makes us to switch our phones off before the lesson. _____

/6

GRAMMAR: Train and Try Again page 171

1 Translate the phrases into your own language.

SPEAKING BANK

Speculating about people

Based on …, I'd say he's/
she's/it's …

_____

_____

Judging by …, I (don't) think …

_____

It looks/seems as if/
as though …

_____

_____

He/She/It appears/
doesn't appear to be …

_____

_____

The chances are (that) he's/
she's/it's …

_____

_____

Showing certainty

Clearly, (there's a problem/
something is wrong.)

_____

_____

It's obvious/clear (from the
expression on his/her face)
that …

_____

_____

_____

He/She/It is definitely/
certainly (not) …

_____

_____

Showing uncertainty

It's hard to be sure
(whether/if …)

_____

_____

It's not easy to say
(whether/if …)

_____

_____

I can't really tell
(whether/if …)

_____

_____

**Speculating about the
situation**

He/She could/might have
('ve) just + Past Participle
(recent past)

_____

_____

_____

He/She could/might be + -ing
(present)

_____

_____

He/She could/might be about
to + infinitive (near future)

_____

_____

2 Match the beginnings of the sentences with the endings.

	It's obvious	(g)
1	It seems	( )
2	It appears as	( )
3	Based	( )
4	It's not	( )
5	She might have	( )
6	It's hard	( )

a on his appearance, I'd say he's fit and healthy.
b easy to say exactly why he's upset.
c just started at a new school, or moved into a new class.
d though the little boy is very excited about something.
e to be autumn, judging by the colour of the leaves.
f to be sure whether they are related, but they look similar.
g from her uniform that she's in the army.

3 Choose the correct option to complete the description.

This photo shows a martial arts class of some sort. I can't really ¹_sure / tell_ whether it's karate, or judo, or some other combat sport, but judging ²_by / on_ his black belt, the man in the middle is an expert. ³_Personally / Clearly_, he's the instructor and the other people watching him are students. The ⁴_chances / chance_ are they are fairly new students as some of them aren't wearing suits or belts. In fact, they could be ⁵_having / have_ their very first class because it looks as though he is demonstrating a fairly simple move. They are ⁶_surely / definitely_ watching closely – perhaps they might be ⁷_about / just_ to have a go themselves.

4 Complete answers 1–4. The first letters are given. Then match them with questions a–d.

1 P̲ersonally̲, I t̲hink̲ they should be able to inspire less sporty students to get involved.
F_____ t_____ r_____ I f_____ it is important to make PE lessons fun, and not too competitive.

2 T_____ b_____ h_____ , although I'd like to keep fitter, I don't have time. Walking to school is the only exercise I get.

3 Combat sports and motor sports, I suppose.
ᵃI_____ m_____ o_____ though, if the people involved know the risks, then it's up to them if they want to put themselves in danger.
ᵇT_____ w_____ I t_____ campaigns to ban things like boxing or motorcycle racing are a bad idea.

4 Definitely 'doing'. I love sport and I ᵃi_____ to keep swimming and playing football until I'm old and grey. ᵇA_____ , I also enjoy watching sport, but if I had to choose, then 'doing'.

a Which sports do you think are the most dangerous? ☐
b Is regular exercise important to you? Why? Why not? ☐
c In your opinion, what characteristics should good PE teachers have? ☐
d Given the choice, do you prefer doing sport, watching sport, or no sport at all? ☐

1 ★ Mark the sentences as formal (F) or informal (I).

a Hi John, **[I]**
b Dear Mr Johnson, **[F]**

1 a Has the principal been informed about the incident? ☐
  b Has anyone called the principal and told her what happened? ☐

2 a If you want to know more, drop me a line. ☐
  b Should you require more information, do not hesitate to contact me. ☐

3 a Applicants for the scholarship should have a strong interest in jazz. ☐
  b You need to be into jazz to get the scholarship. ☐

4 a When was the university set up? ☐
  b Do you happen to know when the university was established? ☐

5 a There's no way I'll finish the essay tonight – there isn't enough time. ☐
  b I am afraid there is too little time for me to complete the assignment tonight. ☐

6 a This study has been conducted annually for five years. ☐
  b Someone has carried out this study every year for five years now. ☐

7 a Sometimes people think that teenagers are childish and don't take them seriously. ☐
  b Sometimes teenagers are thought to be too immature to be taken seriously. ☐

8 a Students caught using a mobile phone during the exam will be removed from the room. ☐
  b If a teacher catches you using a mobile during the exam, he/she'll ask you to leave the room. ☐

2 ★★ Complete the second sentence with the word in the box so that it has a similar meaning to the first. There are two extra words.

accessible   additional   dressed   ~~evaluated~~
graduated   judging   return   unlikely

You won't get any marks if you hand in your project late.
Projects submitted after the deadline won't be _evaluated_.

1 After your lunch break, go back to the classroom.
Please _____ directly to the classroom after your lunch break.

2 Before going to school, make sure you are wearing the right clothes.
Before leaving, check you are suitably _____ .

3 I don't think that the government will postpone the educational reform by a year.
It is _____ that the government will postpone the educational reform by a year.

4 If you need more information, please talk to the school secretary.
_____ information can be obtained from the school secretary.

5 My sister was awarded a degree in Physics last year.
My sister _____ in Physics last year.

3 ★★★ Read the note and the library rules. Then use the information in the text to complete the student leaflet. Use no more than two words in each gap. The words you need do not appear in the note.

Alex,
Thank you for agreeing to write the new library leaflet for first-year students. Here are the rules we need to explain. Can you make them more student-friendly?

University Library
Rules and regulations

Access to the library

• A valid library card is required to access the library.
• Library cards are personal and non-transferable.
• In the case of loss or theft of a library card, the library should be notified immediately and a new card will be issued.
• Library cards need to be renewed annually.

Borrowing books

• Students are allowed to borrow up to 10 books at a time.
• The maximum loan period for books is three weeks.
• Books returned after the due date will be charged at 25 pence per day.

Opening times

• Standard opening times:
  Monday to Friday   8:00 a.m. to 8:00 p.m.
  Saturday and Sunday   9:00 a.m. to 2:00 p.m.
• The library reserves the right to change opening times on bank holidays.
• The latest news and current opening times for the library can be consulted on our website.

Library
Important information for new students

You need a valid library card to [1]_____ the library. Please remember that all cards are personal – you mustn't let [2]_____ use yours. If your card is lost or [3]_____ , please [4]_____ know as soon as possible and we'll give you a new one. You will have to renew your card [5]_____ , so talk to a librarian at the beginning of the next academic year about this.

As a student, you may borrow a maximum [6]_____ 10 books for three weeks. Please make sure you [7]_____ them _____ on time. If you return them [8]_____ , you'll have to pay a fine (25 pence per day).

The Library is usually open from 8 a.m. to 8 p.m. on [9]_____ and from 9 a.m. to 2 p.m. at the weekend. Please remember that the opening times [10]_____ be different on bank holidays. Don't forget to [11]_____ our website for the latest news.

4 ★ **Complete the dialogues with one word in each gap.**

A: Was Barry a gifted child?
B: I think so, but he was also rather lazy. He often fell _behind_, but always managed to catch up.

1 A: Who was your favourite teacher?
   B: Mr Harrison. He taught us not to give _____ on anything important in life.

2 A: Why do you drink so much coffee on Wednesdays?
   B: In _____ to stay awake during the history lecture! It's so boring.

3 A: Is it true that patients sometimes _____ out of a coma after months, even years?
   B: It's not common, but it's definitely possible.

4 A: How did you travel to school, Dad?
   B: Well, we lived in the suburbs, so I _____ to take the bus to school every day.

5 A: Have you managed to fix your computer yet?
   B: Yes, it seems as _____ everything's in order!

6 A: Can you tell me something about your plans for the future?
   B: I hope to work in the _____ of education and training one day.

5 ★ ★ **Choose the correct answers A–D.**

Getting ideas

Do you sometimes find it really difficult to _B_ ideas for school projects? Most of us know the problem. It ¹___ to be easy when we were younger – we had great imaginations and loads of creativity. But it gets harder and harder. So, you're sitting at home trying to think of interesting things to put in an essay or a story. Or you ²___ your brains all day, but you can't remember that great idea you had last night. You're ³___ and your mind is empty. So what do you do? You ⁴___ trying, of course! However, this may be entirely the wrong approach.

Experts say that one of the best things to do is to stop ⁵___ about the problem completely. Change the space you're in. Move into another room or go outside. Another answer is to ⁶___ worrying about it for a while. Go for a walk or take a shower and think about something completely different. Ideas or the answer to your problem will pop into your head like magic!

It's also important to keep your ⁷___ sharp and train it to be creative! If you regularly ⁸___ lots of things, the mental exercise can help when you really need to access those ideas quickly.

	A	B	C	D
	A make	(B) get	C come	D learn
1	A would	B will	C used	D was
2	A jog	B lose	C rack	D work
3	A frustrated	B thrilled	C relieved	D enthusiastic
4	A urge	B keep	C force	D intend
5	A think	B to think	C to thinking	D thinking
6	A set off	B hand in	C catch up	D put off
7	A skills	B mind	C vision	D consciousness
8	A remind	B search	C familiarise	D memorise

6 ★ ★ ★ **Complete the sentences using the prompts in brackets. Do not change the order of the words. Change the forms or add new words where necessary. Use up to six words in each gap.**

Look at this article. It _might be of interest to_ (might/be/interest) you.

1 Jane's teacher _____ (try/convince/she/change) her study routine, but she didn't listen.

2 My dad and his friend _____ (always/cause/trouble) at school and were often punished by the head teacher.

3 It's hard to say why the scientists in the photo look so excited, but they _____ (might/just/make) a very important discovery.

4 I _____ (not/help/bite/nail) when I'm really stressed.

5 When I was at primary school, pupils _____ (use/stand up) when a visitor came into the classroom.

6 It took Helen weeks _____ (recover/injury) she got in a PE lesson.

7 ★ ★ ★ **Complete the second sentence so that it has a similar meaning to the first. Use between two and five words, including the word in capitals.**

I didn't pack my lunch, so I paused at a small café and bought a tuna sandwich. **STOPPED**
I didn't pack my lunch, so I _stopped to buy_ a tuna sandwich at a small café.

1 I can use my brother's tablet when he doesn't need it. **LETS**
   My brother _____ his tablet when he doesn't need it.

2 George struggled at school because he had a poor memory. **SIEVE**
   George struggled at school because he had _____ .

3 I think Daniel is responsible for organising this campaign. **BRAINS**
   I think Daniel _____ this campaign.

4 Doctors say people should walk for at least twenty minutes a day. **ADVISE**
   Doctors _____ for at least twenty minutes a day.

5 Did you do science experiments with your previous teacher? **TO**
   Did you _____ science experiments with your previous teacher?

13

WRITING

A CV and a covering email

1 Read Robert's notes for writing a CV. Which are correct? Correct the incorrect statements.

1 A CV should be 3–4 pages long.
2 Use headings and bullet points to organise the CV.
3 Always use full sentences.
4 Never include a photo.
5 Include referees that are linked to your education and work experience.
6 Describe your skills and experience using positive language.

2 Read Robert's CV. Complete it with the expressions in the box.

> dedicated member   excellent command
> ~~experience~~   proven ability
> relevant knowledge   skills

Robert Wilkinson
253 Oxford Road,
Manchester, M1 4LB
Mob: 07188 326623
r.wilkinson@mail.com
DOB: 14.03.01

Personal profile

Bright and responsible sixth-former with practical _experience_ of sports coaching for children and a ¹_____ to work well in a team.

Skills and achievements
• excellent time management and organisation skills
• ²_____ of German
• well-developed leadership ³_____

Education and qualifications

Currently: Astley Sixth Form College, Manchester
2010-2017: Astley College, Manchester
GCSEs: Combined Science (grades 5-6), Maths (grade 5), English Language (grade 7), English Literature (grade 6), Sports Studies (grade 8), D&T Product Design (grade 5), Geography (grade 6), Spanish (grade 7)

Employment history

Summer 2017 Work experience: Aston Primary School summer camp
• ⁴_____ of activities team (sports and crafts)
• ⁵_____ of health and safety regulations and first aid
2015-2017 Assisting in coaching of local Under 10s football team

Interests

Skateboarding, computer programming, design and technology, film

Referees

Ms T. Smith
Office Manager,
Aston Primary School
t.smith@astonprimary.com

Mr G. Brown
Sports Coach
g.brown@sportforall.co.uk

3 Choose the correct option.

I am a bright sixth former with practical experience of commanding /(helping) tourists. I am a student with a proven ability to ¹meet / experience deadlines. I have an excellent ²command / use of Spanish and German and well-developed communication ³skills / abilities. I am also a competent ⁴speaker / user of most computer software and a dedicated member ⁵of / to a French club.

4 Rewrite the sentences in Exercise 3 to make them suitable for a CV.

Bright sixth-former with practical experience of helping tourists.

_____
_____
_____
_____
_____
_____
_____
_____

5 Match the beginnings of the sentences with the endings to make tips for organising a covering email.

Use full sentences [b]
1 Say why you are writing and ◯
2 Give details about yourself and explain ◯
3 Explain more about your ◯
4 Mention availability for an interview and ◯

a relevant skills and experience. Don't just repeat what's on your CV.
b and a variety of positive language.
c why you want the job.
d any attachments you are sending.
e which job you are applying for.

6 Complete each gap with the words in the box. Then match the sentences with tips 1–4 in Exercise 5.

> apply   attend   confident   consideration
> experience   ~~passionate~~   response
> suited   welcome

I am an eighteen-year-old student and I am _passionate_ about working with animals. Tip ②

1 I have attached my CV for your _____ . Tip ◯
2 I feel _____ I possess relevant skills and would be well _____ to the position. Tip ◯
3 I am writing in _____ to your online advertisement for volunteers at an animal hospital. Tip ◯
4 I would be delighted to _____ an interview at your convenience. Tip ◯
5 I would _____ the opportunity to work with professional vets. Tip ◯
6 I wish to _____ for the position of sports coordinator. Tip ◯
7 Additionally, last summer I gained work _____ at a local vet's. Tip ◯

7 Read the task below. Then complete the email with sentences a–f. There are two extra sentences.

◉◎◎

Sports camp staff
Are you keen on sports? We are looking for young people to work at our summer sports camps. You must be able to teach 6–12 year-olds different sports and have work experience in this area.

Send your CV and covering letter to:
Mrs King, r.king@rees-sports.com

Write a covering email to accompany your CV.

- Say which job you are applying for and where you saw the ad for it.
- Explain why you want the job.
- Explain more about your skills and experience.
- Say what you are including with your letter.

From: r.wilkinson@mail.com
Subject: Robert Wilkinson – summer work application
Attachments: Robert Wilkinson CV

Dear Mrs King,

I am writing in response to your advertisement seeking staff for a sports camp for young people aged 6–12 years old. *e*

I am a nineteen-year-old student and a keen athlete. ¹___ I passionately believe in the benefits of sport for young people. I feel strongly that I would learn a lot from the experience of working with a successful organisation, such as Rees Sports Camps and would welcome this opportunity.

Last year, I was lucky enough to work as a volunteer on a sports programme in local primary schools. ²___ As part of my responsibilities, I coordinated a successful football tournament and sat in on planning meetings. I gained considerable work experience and feel confident I possess all the relevant skills and would be well suited to the position.

I would be delighted to attend an interview at your convenience. ³___ Please do not hesitate to contact me if you require any further information.

Yours sincerely,

Robert Wilkinson

a I have attached my CV for your consideration.
b My ambition is to pursue a career as a sports coach when I finish my education.
c I regularly contribute ideas for a sports magazine.
d I worked alongside several experienced sports coaches and supervised the children during activities.
e I wish to apply for the position of assistant sports coach.
f I have many relevant skills for this position, and so I believe I am an ideal candidate.

---

8 Read the advert and do the writing task.

Are you thinking of a career as a vet?

Come and work alongside professional vets this summer! We are looking for enthusiastic young people with good communication skills who are organised and passionate about looking after animals.

Send your CV and covering letter to Alex Barrie – a.barrie@mail.com

---

Write a CV (no photo) and a covering letter to apply for the position.

- Use appropriate headings in your CV.
- Invent any necessary details.
- Explain your relevant skills and experience.
- Say why you want the job.

In my CV:

• I have written 1–2 pages and have avoided using full sentences.	☐
• I have used headings and bullet points to organise the information logically.	☐
• I have described my skills and experience using positive language.	☐
• I have chosen referees linked to my education and work experience.	☐
• I have checked if a photo is required or not.	☐

In my covering email:

• I have used full sentences and a variety of positive language.	☐
• I have said why I am writing and which job I am applying for.	☐
• I have given details about myself and why I want the job.	☐
• I have given more information about relevant skills and experiences and not simply repeated what is on my CV.	☐
• I have mentioned my availability for an interview and any attachments I am sending.	☐

In both my CV and letter:

• I have checked my spelling and punctuation.	☐
• I have checked my handwriting is neat enough for someone else to read.	☐

VOCABULARY AND GRAMMAR

1 Complete the sentences with the words in the box. Change the form if necessary. There are two extra words.

> brain coma conscious disrupt
> distance expel ~~sharp~~ strike

I want to _sharpen_ my design and technology skills.

1 I hit my head and lost _____ . I came round a few minutes later.

2 There are some _____ students in my class. They shout out and mess around all the time.

3 I nearly got _____ from school once. Luckily, the head teacher allowed me to stay.

4 The tree was _____ by lightning and caught fire.

5 Anne's really _____ . She's the most intelligent person I know.

/5

2 Choose the correct answer A–C.

What profession do you want to go _B_ when you finish school?
A up   (B) into   C in

1 I'd like to work in the ___ of engineering as a career.
A area   B field   C course

2 We'll never know the answer; it will ___ a mystery.
A remain   B solve   C recover

3 When I was off school ill, I fell ___ in my studies.
A back   B off   C behind

4 I have a really ___ memory of my fifth birthday party. I can remember everything about it.
A vague   B distant   C vivid

5 Our Maths teacher is ___ . He doesn't mind if we talk in class as long as we do our work.
A lenient   B self-disciplined   C strict

/5

3 Complete the sentences with the missing words. The first letters are given.

My earliest **m**_emory_ is moving house. I was only two years old.

1 I got a **s**_____ to study at university, so I didn't have to pay to go.

2 He learns fast; he can **a**_____ new skills really easily.

3 I've nearly finished my university course. Now I just have to write my **d**_____ . It's supposed to be 10,000 words long!

4 When you study, it's a good idea to **m**_____ in the subject you love most.

5 He forgets everything you tell him. He's got a memory like a **s**_____ !

/5

4 Find and correct the mistakes. One sentence is correct.

He ~~would live~~ a long way from college in his first year, but now he lives 5 minutes away. _used to live_

1 When my sister was younger, she will walk around when she was studying. _____

2 They always were disturbing other students, which was annoying. _____

3 I didn't used to enjoy science, but now I want to study it at university. _____

4 Kate is always asking the teacher for extra homework. What a swot! _____

5 We don't used to pay attention in class, but now we do. _____

/5

5 Complete the sentences using the prompts in brackets.

The rain _caused me to have_ (cause/me/have) an accident.

1 We decided _____ (go) to the library to research our project.

2 His parents _____ (let/he/choose) which subjects he wanted to study.

3 I usually _____ (avoid/revise) for exams until the last moment.

4 Can you _____ (remind/your brother/give) his homework to the teacher?

5 I can _____ (remember/visit) the London Eye. It was fun!

/5

6 Choose the correct answer A–C.

○○○

In the family

Dominic Foster and his dad John both have a _C_ for numbers, which is how they've ended up doing the same apprenticeship in insurance at the same company – at the same time! John, who [1]___ an electrical engineer, had to give up due to bad health and was looking for a new challenge. Meanwhile, his son Dominic had decided [2]___ to university as he didn't want to spend time [3]___ a degree and preferred on-the-job training. Although the pair both chose to [4]___ on the course for different reasons, as soon as people find out, they can't help [5]___ them and wondering who will get better results. Luckily, they are both doing well! After finishing, they both intend to use their studies in different ways. Dominic says he will probably go into web development and John hopes to go into project management.

A urge   B interest   (C) passion

1 A would be   B used to be   C used to

2 A to not going   B not going   C not to go

3 A doing   B do   C to do

4 A sit   B attend   C enrol

5 A to compare   B comparing   C compare

/5

Total /30

7 Choose the correct option.

Politics *didn't use* / *wasn't used* to be of interest to me, but now it is.

1 I can hear them *sing* / *singing* now. They're really loud!

2 We didn't know what to do, but then Sam had a *brainwave* / *brainstorm*. It was a great idea!

3 Jane is so annoying. She *will* / *would* sing quietly while we're studying and it drives me mad!

4 I only just *fell* / *scraped* through my exams, I'll work harder next time.

5 Do you ever feel a(n) *consciousness* / *urge* to learn a new skill?

/5

8 Complete the sentences with the correct forms of the words in brackets

He looks so surprised – *judging* (JUDGE) by his appearance, I'd say he's confused.

1 There's so much information on the Internet that I find researching online a good way to _____ (DEEP) your knowledge of a subject.

2 She was _____ (CONSCIOUSNESS) when the ambulance arrived, but she came round on the way to the hospital.

3 I think I'd make a fantastic spy because I've got a _____ (PHOTOGRAPHY) memory. I wouldn't need a camera.

4 I'm not sure what to put for my personal _____ (ACHIEVE) in my CV. I guess I could include learning to programme.

5 Mark always hands his projects in early or on the day, so has a _____ (PROVE) ability to meet deadlines.

/5

9 Complete the second sentence so that it means the same as the first. Use the word in capitals.

My parents said I could go to the party as long as I went with a friend. **LET**
My parents *let me go* to the party as long as I went with a friend.

1 My teacher thought it would be a good idea for me to study biology. **ADVISED**
My teacher _____ biology.

2 I didn't know how the accident had happened because I had no memory of my car hitting the tree. **REMEMBER**
I didn't know how the accident had happened because I couldn't _____ with my car.

3 When I was younger, I often read books all day. **SPENT**
I often _____ when I was younger.

4 Tom messes around in class all the time. It's so annoying. **ALWAYS**
Tom _____ in class. It's so annoying.

5 They were very keen students and would attend all the lectures, which is why they did well. **TO**
They were very keen students and _____ _____ all the lectures, which is why they did well.

/5

10 Complete the text with one word in each gap.

Tidy desk, better thinker?

If you find it hard to settle *down* to study, you might want to take a good look at your desk. Is it messy with stuff scattered all around? Experts are now encouraging people ¹_____ tidy their desks as the clear space will enable you to think better and I'm a fan of this theory. When I was younger, I ²_____ to leave piles of books and papers on my desk in between cold cups of tea and snack wrappers, so of course I was ³_____ losing things. Each time I sat down to study, I had to search for whatever I needed and inevitably ended up wasting a lot of time and getting frustrated. Finally, after racking my ⁴_____ I came up with a method of organising everything. I bought some bookshelves and big files and then organised the books and put the papers in the files, each file for a separate subject. Now, after studying I ⁵_____ always tidy everything away so, the next time I sit down, my desk is clear. It definitely helps me study!

/5

Total /20

Education for all

We usually associate long and rewarding careers with older people who have had time to go deeply into their subject and have worked in the field for many years, but in fact it's not always the case. **1____** Then, by the time she was seventeen, she was already running a successful foundation, giving lectures and talks at universities and international events as well as making films, all of which focus on education and climate change.

Whilst Oduwole has roots in Africa, she was born and grew up in Los Angeles. Her first trip to Africa came about after she entered a national film-making competition. **2____** In order to film scenes for the documentary, Oduwole travelled to Ghana and was even able to conduct interviews with some of the people involved in transforming the country.

It was during that trip that Oduwole first realised she had a passion for education. She saw many young girls on the streets and realised they were not attending lessons and got the urge to do something to help. **3____** As part of this role, she speaks to young people about the importance of school and getting a good education. She also organises the DUSUSU awards which honour African first ladies and ministers who strongly support education for girls and gender equality.

Whilst these achievements already seem unbelievable for such a young woman, she hasn't stopped there. **4____** When classrooms are flooded and children can't get to school then they quickly fall behind with their studies and many give up altogether. She has met various presidents to discuss this issue and has given speeches to the United Nations and UNESCO on green initiatives.

5____ One of her more recent projects involves giving workshops to girls and women under the age of twenty-five to help them acquire skills in basic film-making techniques, in the hope that it will empower them to share their own stories, and if possible, enable them to make money.

Whilst Oduwole gives much of her attention to helping girls, she believes her work does not exclude boys. **6____** She hopes that by setting an example of what females are capable of achieving, males will gain an understanding of the need for equality and the difficulties their classmates and colleagues can face. She understands, too, that life in parts of Africa can be difficult for everyone. Her focus at the moment is to ensure girls and women experience equal opportunities in life, which is undeniably a big task, especially for someone so young.

1 Read the text on page 18. Complete gaps 1–6 with sentences A–H. There are two extra sentences.

A After her return to the United States she started her foundation, Dream Up, Speak Up, Stand Up (DUSUSU) which signalled the beginning of her mission as a powerful education advocate.

B When she speaks at schools and events, her audiences are made up of all genders and she hopes that her talks make an impact on everyone present.

C Oduwole's group made a film that impressed their teacher so much that they won first prize.

D The project was to create a film about a revolution, and since Ghana saw what is considered to be one of the most successful revolts on the African continent, Oduwole chose it as her subject.

E Oduwole understands the threat that climate change poses to education.

F At the age of nine, Zuriel Oduwole started a successful career as a film-maker which inspired her to look for ways to encourage girls in Africa to attend school.

G She has written to various presidents and governments with ideas about how to encourage children to stay in the classroom when their parents want them to go out to work.

H Despite spending much time speaking at events and campaigning for equality, Oduwole still finds time to develop her own film-making and to share her knowledge with others.

2 Read the text again. For questions 1–4, choose the correct answer, A–C.

1 Why did Zuriel focus on Ghana for her first film?
   A She had met some of the people behind the revolution and wanted to learn more.
   B She had previously travelled to Ghana and wanted to encourage girls to attend school.
   C Ghana's political history was appropriate for the topic of the competition.

2 What is the purpose of the DUSUSU awards?
   A To recognise people who are working to improve the opportunities available to females.
   B To put the wives of African presidents in the spotlight so they can help more women and girls.
   C To enable Oduwole to give speeches to young people about attending school.

3 Why has Oduwole chosen to focus on climate change?
   A She wants to give speeches on the topic to the United Nations.
   B She thinks climate change is misunderstood by young people.
   C She sees a connection between climate change and students dropping out of school.

4 What impact does Oduwole hope to have on boys?
   A That they will campaign for equality in Africa with their classmates and colleagues.
   B That they will understand more clearly the problems young women in Africa have.
   C That they will learn to set a good example for their male friends and family members.

WRITING

3 Read the advert and write a covering email.

Are you looking for an interesting and exciting summer job?

We organise music events, from classical music festivals to big pop concerts, and are looking for enthusiastic, self-disciplined people with excellent communication skills to fill the following roles:

•Waiter/Waitress   •Cleaner   •Social media manager   •Ticket seller

Send your CV and covering email to: paula.smith@eventsforyou.com

Write a covering email to apply for one of the positions advertised.
- Say why you are writing and which job you are applying for.
- Give details of your skills and experience.
- Explain why you are best suited for the post.
- Say when you are available for an interview and what documents you are attaching.

2 Human nature

VOCABULARY

2.1

People • personality adjectives
• compound adjectives
• describing personality

SHOW WHAT YOU KNOW

1 Complete the sentences with the correct form of the words in brackets.

Gary sometimes says horrible things to people. He can be _unkind_. (KINDNESS)

1 Sandra hates waiting for anything, or anyone! She's so _____ . (PATIENCE)
2 They're always doing things without thinking about the results. They're _____ . (RESPONSIBILITY)
3 Jack always tries not to hurt other people's feelings. He's definitely not _____ . (SENSITIVITY)
4 Eva doesn't enjoy being with other people and she's not always kind to others. She's _____ . (FRIENDLINESS)
5 Lisa is more interested in being happy than successful. She's _____ . (AMBITION)
6 Mark is often rude to people. He's _____ . (POLITENESS)

WORD STORE 2A | Personality adjectives

2 Complete the sentences with the correct words. The first letters are given.

Tom's always careful to do things properly. He very **t**_horough_.

1 If someone tells me something, I believe them – why should I doubt them? I'm pretty **t**_____ , I suppose.
2 My sister wants to write comedy shows for TV. I think she'd be perfect as she's very **w**_____ . She always makes everyone laugh!
3 He's really **m**_____ . He can go from annoyed to cheerful in an instant.
4 My parents are **a**_____ people. They love giving hugs and I've always known they care about me.
5 I think I'm quite **p**_____ . I can tell when people are feeling sad or nervous, even if they try to hide it.

---

3 Complete the text with the words in the box.

daring insecure ~~intellectual~~
spontaneous tactful witty

Tell us about you and your BFF! Why do you think you're friends?

My best friend and I are complete opposites! For one thing, he loves studying and is always reading and doing research online because something fascinates him. I suppose he's quite _intellectual_ – and I'm not! I don't mind a bit of homework, but I'd rather be out having fun with friends and meeting new people. When I go out, I'm quite ¹_____ , I don't think it's necessary to plan everything before you do it, I love the fact that I never quite know what I'm going to do or where I'll go. My friend likes to plan every detail, but the thing is, he's not that confident – he's a bit ²_____ and worries all the time about making mistakes, even silly little ones, which is crazy because he's got a brain the size of China! Unlike me, he's not that keen on new experiences, I'll even have a go at tricky or adventurous things – I guess you could say I'm pretty ³_____ . He thinks before he says anything in case he upsets somebody and is very ⁴_____ and good with words. I'm not very ⁵_____ , I seem to say the first thing that comes into my mind and I'm terrible at keeping secrets. Despite our differences, we get on incredibly well. I know he'll always be there for me if I've got a problem, and I'll do the same for him. That's why we're such good friends!

WORD STORE 2B | Compound adjectives

4 Match the words in the box with words 1–7 to make compound adjectives.

back centred conscious critical headed
~~hearted~~ minded natured tempered willed

kind-_hearted_
1 self-_____ , _____ , _____
2 good-_____   5 strong-_____
3 laid-_____   6 level-_____
4 short-_____   7 fair-_____

5 Complete the conversations with the compound adjectives in Exercise 4.

A: What's up?
B: It's my sister. She's decided to start a band, but she's terrible at the guitar. I'm trying to persuade her not to – it'd be a disaster. But once Jane decides to do something it's impossible to stop her.
A: You know your sister, she's so _strong-willed_ I doubt you'll manage to stop her!

1 A: What do you think about social media?
  B: Well, it's got advantages and disadvantages. I mean, it's a great way of keeping in touch and it's fun, but it's easy to spend too long online.
  A: You're very _____ , aren't you?

2 A: I wish I could be as _____ as you. You never seem to be stressed out about anything, not even exams.
  B: Well, doing yoga and getting enough sleep helps me stay calm.

3 A: You've eaten all the biscuits again and left the kitchen in a real mess. How can you be so _____ ? I wish you'd think about the rest of us sometimes!
  B: Sorry! I'll clear it up now.

4 A: Matt's great, isn't he? I was really upset after I'd had an argument and he took me out for coffee and just listened to me. He's one of the most _____ people I know.
  B: Definitely! He'll always help you if he can, and he's really generous, too.

5 A: I wish I was more confident. I never know what to say to people and I feel like they're going to think I'm boring.
  B: Don't be so _____ , you've got a great personality!

6 A: My brother lost his temper again! I don't know what's up with him – he seems to get angry really easily at the moment.
  B: Really? Perhaps there's a reason he's so _____ . Have you asked if anything's wrong?

WORD STORE 2C | Describing personality

6 Find and correct the mistakes.

If you have a love ~~on~~ learning, you'll really enjoy university. _of_

1 The best way to make people feel on ease is to smile, use their name and listen to them. _____

2 We need some new ideas. Can you think out the box and come up with something? _____

3 Alex has a strong personality, she's a bit larger than herself sometimes! _____

4 You don't have to be the soul and life of the party for people to like you, just be yourself. _____

5 The best way to accept a compliment without seeming too full with yourself is to just say 'Thank you' and smile. _____

7 Choose the correct answers A–C.

Personality survey

Please post your answers to the question below. Answers will be anonymous. Thanks!

How would *you* describe yourself to a stranger?

1 The most important thing to know about me is that I'm traditional and very family-oriented. I'm sociable and I ¹__ most at ease in familiar situations. I think I'm ²__ , often thinking of others before myself. I'd do anything for the people I love. I'm definitely ³__ and I don't do things without thinking them through.

2 Everyone describes me as practical! I think it's important to pay attention to the details of everything and be ⁴__ . What's the point of doing something if you don't do it well? I have a ⁵__ of learning, but I wouldn't say I was ⁶__ , I'd rather be repairing my car or building something than writing an essay or doing research.

3 I'm a people person. Everyone says I'm friendly, ⁷__ and have good relationships with others, so it must be true! I wouldn't say I was the 'life and ⁸__ of the party,' though, because I don't always like being the centre of attention. I'd rather be chatting to someone quietly and getting to know them. Strangers are just friends you don't know yet!

4 I'd tell a stranger that my two main qualities are that I'm adventure-loving and ⁹__ , I never know what will end up happening on any specific day because if I suddenly feel like doing something, I'll probably go ahead and do it! Another thing I'd tell them is that I'm not afraid to take risks, though being so ¹⁰__ can cause me problems – once I went climbing and broke my leg!

	A	B	C
1	feel	think	live
2	kind-hearted	self-centred	laid-back
3	self-centred	short-tempered	level-headed
4	tactful	thorough	trusting
5	love	enjoyment	life
6	intellectual	insecure	moody
7	self-centred	moody	affectionate
8	heart	soul	centre
9	perceptive	spontaneous	insecure
10	self-conscious	fair-minded	daring

/10

SHOW WHAT YOU KNOW

1 Match beginnings 1–6 with endings a–g and put the verbs into the Past Perfect Simple. There is one extra ending.

Beth was embarrassed because
she _had put on_ (put on) `h`

1 Dan couldn't order his new trainers online
because they _____ (run out) ◯

2 Lee never found his phone.
It _____ (fall) ◯

3 Jill couldn't claim her lottery win because
someone _____ (steal) ◯

4 John wasn't allowed in the pool because he
_____ (not/bring) ◯

5 Kyle _____ (never/use)
a washing machine before ◯

6 I wish we _____ (not/book) ◯

a of his size.

b the winning ticket out of her handbag.

c out of his pocket while he was lying on
the grass.

d and had no idea how they worked.

e a swimming cap.

f the car from his dad.

g cinema tickets for 5 p.m. We won't have time
for dinner.

h odd socks by mistake that morning.

2 ★ Complete the texts with the verbs in the box.

> had been cycling   had been
> had been feeling
> had been looking forward to
> had done (x2)   had eaten   had failed
> had he set off   hadn't worked

1 Avril's face was rather a funny green colour. She
said she _had eaten_ a whole tub of ice cream an
hour earlier and ᵃ_____
rather sick ever since. When I asked why she
ᵇ_____ that, she said that
she ᶜ_____ a test at school
and needed cheering up. Clearly her plan
ᵈ_____ .

2 Jack ᵃ_____ to
school for ten minutes when he noticed
how quiet the streets were and finally
realised it was Saturday. Why on earth
ᵇ_____ for school on
a Saturday? It ᶜ_____ a
long and stressful week and he ᵈ_____
_____ the weekend all week. His family
were going to laugh when they found out what
he ᵉ_____ .

3 ★ ★ Complete the sentences with the Past Perfect Simple or the Past Perfect Continuous forms of the verbs in brackets.

a When we finally landed, the plane _had been flying_ (fly) for
fourteen hours.

b When we finally landed, the plane _had flown_ (fly) over
5,900 miles.

1 a Trevor _____ (live) in this town for 20
years before he found out that his next door neighbour
used to be a famous actress.

b Trevor _____ (know) his next door
neighbour for twenty years before he found out she used
to be a famous actress.

2 a Vladimir _____ (sneak) out of the house
secretly at night for months before he was finally caught.

b Earlier that night, Vladimir _____
(sneak) out of the house without waking his parents.

3 a The security guard _____ (sleep) for
hours when the office was broken into.

b The security guard was fired because he
_____ (sleep) through the burglary.

4 ★ ★ ★ Complete the text with the Past Perfect Simple or the Past Perfect Continuous forms of the verbs in the box.

> always start   correctly predict   do   go off   hear
> look forward   love   put up   receive   snow   ~~wait~~

George and Gina _had been waiting_ for Christmas for roughly 364 days.
Ever since they were children, they ¹_____ everything
about the festive season, especially Christmas dinner. And George and
Gina ²_____ early. By the end of each summer, they
³_____ most of their Christmas shopping, and by late
October, they ⁴_____ their tree. Their friends
⁵_____ Christmas cards in early November for as long
as they could remember.

This year, the weather forecasters ⁶_____ a white
Christmas – George and Gina's absolute favourite. Ever since they
⁷_____ this, they ⁸_____ to Christmas even
more than ever. When George opened the curtains on Christmas morning,
he was greeted by a winter wonderland. Unfortunately, when he went
downstairs, he discovered it ⁹_____ so much that the
electricity ¹⁰_____ . Christmas dinner was a cold ham
sandwich eaten in a dark room next to an unlit tree.

SHOW WHAT YOU'VE LEARNT

5 Choose the most suitable tense to complete the sentences.

1 The mathematician _had attempted_ / _had been attempting_ the problem nearly one hundred times before she finally solved it.

2 By midnight, all the guests _had left_ / _had been leaving_.

3 Claire was given full marks in the speaking test.
She _had revised_ / _had been revising_ all week long.

4 When the police examined all possible causes of the
accident, they discovered that the driver _had probably fallen_ / _had probably been falling_ asleep behind the wheel.

5 Ryan left the room after the exam _had finished_ / _had been finishing_.

6 They _had planned_ / _had been planning_ the wedding for
months when he discovered she was actually in love with
someone else.

_/6_

GRAMMAR: Train and Try Again page 172

2.3

Comparative expressions
• dependent prepositions

1 Read the extracts from the interview. Complete the comparative expressions with the words in the box. There are two extra words.

better   characteristics   just   like   more (x2)
much   same   ~~similar~~   worse

Extracts from Student's Book recording 🔊 **1.24**

RN: [...] love is a powerful neurological condition. When you fall for someone, it's *similar* to hunger or thirst, but ¹_____ permanent.

P: That's not a very romantic image.

RN: Well, no, but it's fascinating. In fact, romantic love has all the ²_____ of addiction. [...] You focus on the person, you obsessively think about them and you will take enormous risks to win this person that you're obsessed with. Also, ³_____ an addict, you need to see them more and ⁴_____ . [...] First, there's an area deep in the centre of the brain – it's a primitive part of the brain which developed 65 million years ago. [...] The more passionate the love, the more activity there was in that area. We also found activity in a second area of the brain that becomes active when people eat chocolate! Chocolate can be addictive, ⁵_____ like romantic love!

P: And what happens when someone is rejected? Does the activity in those areas of the brain stop?

RN: Unfortunately for the broken-hearted, no. The obsession can get ⁶_____ when you're rejected. We put people into the brain scanner just after their partner had split up with them, and we found that there was as ⁷_____ activity, or even more, than when they were in love.

2 Choose the correct words to complete the sentences.

1 Love, it seems, is similar __ chocolate in certain ways.
   A to   B as   C than
2 This new model of the phone has all the characteristics __ the old one, plus several exciting new innovations.
   A from   B that   C of
3 __ many seventeen-year-olds, Monica couldn't wait to be eighteen.
   A As   B Like   C Similar
4 As young adults come of age, they spend __ and more time thinking about romantic relationships.
   A even   B much   C more
5 Every Christmas is __ like the last. Can't we do something different this year?
   A just   B similar   C worse
6 If I had as much money __ them, I'd definitely give some of it to charity.
   A than   B as   C to

3 Read REMEMBER THIS. Find and underline an example of a *the ... the ...* structure in the extracts in Exercise 1.

REMEMBER THIS

Use comparatives with *the ... the ...* to say that things change or vary together:
The longer we are together, the more I love you.
Note the word order in both clauses:
the + comparative expression + subject + verb

Comparative expressions with nouns can also be used:
The longer the relationship, the more partners discover about each other.
Note how the word order in the first clause differs:
the + comparative adjective + the + subject

4 Use the prompts to complete the sentences with *the ... the ...* structures.

(Nice/hotel, money)
The nicer the hotel, the more money you'll have to pay for a room.

1 (fast/car, petrol)
_____ it uses.
2 (long/hike, water)
_____ you'll need to take with you.
3 (big/barbecue, sausages)
_____ we'll be able to cook.
4 (cute/puppy, chance)
_____ there is of finding it a good home.
5 (steep/ski slope, falls and injuries)
_____ there are.

WORD STORE 2D | Relationship phrases

5 Choose the correct option.

Have you ever *tripped / gone /* (fallen) for someone you'd just met?

1 John and Madeleine have been going *out with / out to / up with* each other for two years.
2 Karen has *put / split / finished* up with her boyfriend. She's moving to Australia and he didn't want to go.
3 If you find yourself becoming obsessed *to / for / with* social media, it's a good idea to have a break from sites or only go on them for a set time each day.
4 I was really *attached / attracted / attractive* to him the moment I saw him. He had such a lovely smile!
5 Sam and Lisa are madly *in love with / on love with / in love for* each other and they're getting married in May.

READING

2.4

Young adult fiction • word families

1 Read Texts 1 and 2 quickly. Is the statement true (T) or false (F)?

One of the texts suggests that dystopian novels such as *The Hunger Games* are not as popular as they were in the past.

TEENAGE BOOK FREAK

1

You searched for 'The Hunger Games' – 17 results match your search:

The Hunger Games trilogy by Suzanne Collins started as a series of young adult adventure novels and is now a multimedia franchise worth millions – the film adaptation of the first novel grossed over $400 million and helped launch the career of Oscar winner Jennifer Lawrence. For anyone unfamiliar with the series (where have you been for the last few years?) the story is set in a dystopian* future in the totalitarian nation of Panem. The Hunger Games are an annual event in which two representatives from each of Panem's 12 districts are selected to take part. Unfortunately for the young representatives, the Game's goal is to eliminate their fellow competitors in a brutal fight to the death – and it's all televised for the rest of Panem to enjoy.

Clearly, with a plot like this, both the books and films contain violence and killing. It used to be taboo for children to kill children in stories, but this is evidently no longer the case. And *The Hunger Games* is far from alone in presenting a grim and bloody vision of the future. Among many others, there's Moira Young's *Blood Red Road*, Malorie Blackman's *Noughts and Crosses* and Meg Rosoff's *How I Live Now*, a story of teenage passion in a future England at war, and now a major film starring Saoirse Ronan.

So what is it about these dark tales that attracts teenage readers? Why has dystopia become so fashionable? Are we, today's young adults, perhaps reacting to the negativity caused by economic recession, university fees and the prospect of never getting a mortgage?

Meg Rosoff says older teenagers 'see adulthood on the horizon and that's as scary as the apocalypse.' Imagining that you're living in a place in which millions have starved to death* (The Hunger Games), been killed off because eternal youth* has been discovered (Gemma Malley's *The Declaration*) or are living in a world dried up by climate change (Moira Young's *Blood Red Road*) can help you look at your problems in a different light. Compared to a dystopian nightmare, fears about having spots or taking exams seem considerably less terrifying.

Moira Young expresses a similar idea: 'I think it (Blood Red Road) fits with young people's anxieties about the future, in that it's about a heroic figure triumphing over the odds*.' Gemma Malley suggests that dystopias not only magnify* what teens go through in terms of bullying* and the struggle to make their own decisions, but also feed 'their appetite for adrenaline. These novels are like scary rides in a theme park.'

Fans of young adult fiction, and in particular female ones like me, seem to respond not just to the action-packed plots of these novels but also the realism of the flawed* and complex characters that are found in them. Katniss Everdeen, the heroine in *The Hunger Games*, has hunting skills and a fierce protectiveness towards her little sister that make her, like Meg Rosoff's Daisy, and Moira Young's Saba, the opposite to Bella Swann, the passive, well-behaved vampire lover from Stephenie Meyer's *Twilight* series. One fellow *Hunger Games* fan commented 'If you've got a brain, vampires suck. Girls aren't waiting to be saved any more. Katniss is the kind of strong teenage heroine we were all waiting for.'

Tales of dystopia won't be popular forever. Just like vampires and werewolves before them, they will eventually be replaced by something new. If you, dear readers, are anything like me, then you'll be eager to discover what the next trend in teenage fiction is going to be.

2

The first UK book convention dedicated to young adult (YA) fiction opened in style with charismatic author Malorie Blackman dressed in a Star Trek outfit, addressing the audience in the language of Klingon!

One of the appealing aspects of YA novels and authors is openness to debate. Blackman, who led the two-day event, appeared on a panel discussing the ongoing appeal of dystopia. The panellists discussed the need for YA to be realistic and truthful, even when the truth is painful. 'Teenagers write stuff that is way darker and more hopeless than some of the published stories anyway,' said one panellist. Another suggested that it would be patronising* to teenagers to be told that there are certain subjects they shouldn't be reading about. 'YA has to represent the real world and not just present a rosy image of it.'

The convention was enjoyed by hundreds of young readers and was a great success.

GLOSSARY

dystopia (n) – an imaginary place where life is extremely difficult and unfair things happen
starve to death (verb phrase) – die of hunger
eternal youth (adj + n) – the mythical state of never growing old
triumphing over the odds – succeeding or winning in a very difficult situation

magnify (v) – make larger
bully (v, n) – to threaten or hurt someone, especially someone smaller or weaker
flawed (adj) – having mistakes, weaknesses or damage
patronising (adj) – someone who is patronising talks to you in a way that shows you they think you are less intelligent or important than them

2 Read Text 1 and Text 2 again and choose the correct answers A–D.

1 Text 1
  A recommends a selection of dystopian novels.
  B attempts to explain the appeal of dystopian novels.
  C is critical of dystopian novels.
  D reviews a well-known dystopian novel.

2 Text 1 suggests that dystopian novels
  A are unsuitable for teenagers because they are too violent.
  B are often scarier than novels about vampires or werewolves.
  C can help teenage readers to put the problems of adolescence into perspective.
  D are an escape from the realities of teenage life.

3 The author mentions the character Katniss Everdeen as an example of
  A a new kind of female heroine.
  B a traditional female character.
  C a passive, well-behaved heroine.
  D a unique character in young adult fiction.

4 In Text 2, the quote 'Teenagers write stuff that is way darker and more hopeless than some of the published stories anyway' was intended as
  A a criticism of teenage authors.
  B an example of possible negative effects of reading dystopian novels.
  C praise for current teenage authors.
  D justification of the dark nature of dystopian novels intended for teenagers.

5 In both texts, it is suggested that
  A old taboos are being broken in new young adult fiction.
  B certain subjects are unsuitable for teenage readers.
  C realism is an important aspect of successful young adult fiction.
  D dystopian novels will eventually become unfashionable.

REMEMBER BETTER

When you are reading authentic texts, such as the novels mentioned in the article above, look out for typical endings used to form nouns and adjectives. Try to work out the meaning of unfamiliar words using context and your knowledge of common patterns of word formation.

Complete the table with the correct forms.

Noun	Verb	Adjective
nation nationalist nationalism	*nationalise*	national
competition competitiveness 1 _____	compete	competitive
darkness	2 _____	dark
3 _____ responsibility	respond	responsive
triumph	triumph	4 _____
protection protector 5 _____	protect	protective
6 _____	dedicate	dedicated

---

3 Complete the sentences with the correct words from the REMEMBER BETTER table.

The government is planning to *nationalise* the postal system using taxpayers' money.

1 Here we see the _____ Chinese gymnastics team – the new Olympic champions and the pride of their nation.
2 Jane is absolutely _____ to her job. She is the most creative and caring teacher I know.
3 Successful retailers are _____ to customers' desires. They identify needs and try to meet them as quickly as possible.
4 Aid workers treating Ebola patients must wear masks, gloves and full _____ clothing at all times.
5 My uncle has always been very _____ . He can't stand losing at anything, but especially cards.

VOCABULARY PRACTICE | Physical actions

4 Look at the vocabulary in lesson 2.4 in the Student's Book. Complete the sentences with the correct form of the words and phrases in the box.

> crouch down   flicker across   flinch
> give a wave   grimace   grip   hesitate
> let out a groan   manipulate   ~~swallow~~

I chewed my food slowly and then *swallowed* it.
1 I _____ to speak to the little boy so my face would be at the same level as his.
2 He _____ at the thought of having so much work to do before the exam.
3 After I hurt my hand, I found it hard to _____ objects firmly, and especially hard to _____ a computer mouse.
4 I wasn't sure what to say, so I _____ before speaking. 'Hello,' I finally whispered.
5 Simone knew they were too far away to hear her, so instead she _____ with her hand.
6 When the teacher gave us extra homework, we all _____ . We weren't pleased at all!
7 Mike was thinking about being on holiday, so he _____ when the alarm bell went off.
8 A smile _____ Josh's face, but he managed not to laugh.

WORD STORE 2E | Ways of looking

5 Complete the text with the correct form of the words in the box.

> gaze   glance   glimpse   ~~peep~~   peer   stare

Starting high school is hard, but changing to a new school when everyone else has already been there for a year is even harder. I walked behind the headmaster. He opened the classroom door a little and I *peeped* inside. When we walked in, everyone ¹_____ at me for what seemed like forever. I could feel all thirty teenagers looking at me. I kept my eyes on the floor. 'Sit here, Max,' the teacher said. Quickly I ²_____ up and then looked down again as I walked to the desk. When the other students had gone back to work, I ³_____ at the board, but I was feeling so stressed that I just couldn't concentrate – and I definitely wasn't going to explain that to the teacher. I ⁴_____ out of the window when I suddenly saw some hockey players outside. I only ⁵_____ them for a second as they walked round the corner of the building, but it was enough. If there was a hockey team, school was going to be fine.

GRAMMAR

2.5

Relative clauses

SHOW WHAT YOU KNOW

1 Read the situations and choose which sentence, *a* or *b*, is correct.

1. We didn't open all the gifts immediately.
   a. The gifts which we opened immediately were left on a table in the restaurant. ☐
   b. The gifts, which we opened immediately, were left on a table in the restaurant. ☐

2. I have one cousin.
   a. My cousin whose husband is from London got married in England. ☐
   b. My cousin, whose husband is from London, got married in England. ☐

3. All the guests danced.
   a. The guests who danced all evening got a bit hot and sweaty. ☐
   b. The guests, who danced all evening, got a bit hot and sweaty. ☐

4. Not all the coffee was delicious.
   a. The coffee which was served after dinner was delicious. ☐
   b. The coffee, which was served after dinner, was delicious. ☐

5. There are two village churches.
   a. The village church where we got married is over 200 years old. ☐
   b. The village church, where we got married, is over 200 years old. ☐

2 Underline the relative pronouns that can be replaced by *that* in Exercise 1.

3 ★ Match the main clauses 1–4 with the most suitable comment clauses a–e.

During the Thai festival of Loy Krathong, floating paper lanterns are released into the night sky, (e)

1. My grandad gave me £100 when I graduated from university, ☐
2. Many Australians spend Christmas Day on the beach, ☐
3. Fazal isn't eating during the day because of the festival of Ramadan, ☐
4. Dad forgot my parents' wedding anniversary, ☐

a. which didn't go down well with Mum.
b. which was generous considering his only income is his pension.
c. which seems strange to those of us celebrating in the cold European winter.
d. which means he's very hungry by the time the sun finally sets.
e. which is a truly spectacular sight.

4 ★ ★ Complete the sentences with relative pronouns. If a pronoun is unnecessary, leave the gap blank. Add commas where necessary.

The one place _where_ I feel most relaxed is home.

1. This is the temple _____ Hindus built to worship Hanuman, the monkey god.
2. Maddie is the cousin _____ went to live in Australia.
3. Alison _____ boss was really rude and short-tempered has finally decided to quit her job.
4. It's an ancient machine _____ our ancestors used to predict the future.
5. She called us selfish _____ we think was very hypocritical.

5 ★ ★ ★ Rewrite the sentences with reduced relative clauses. Which sentence cannot be rewritten?

The house which overlooks the valley has gorgeous views.
The house overlooking the valley has gorgeous views .

1. Prince William Bridge, which was built in 2012, is the newest in the city.
   _____
2. There's a Japanese death metal band that is playing at the club on Saturday.
   _____
3. Most of the buildings that were destroyed in the war have been rebuilt.
   _____
4. Pupils who live in the hills have to walk several hours to get to school.
   _____
5. Jim finally proposed to Tina, which was what we've all been waiting for.
   _____

SHOW WHAT YOU'VE LEARNT

6 Choose the correct option to complete the text.

What is Generation Z?

Generation Z refers to people ¹*who / whose* were born between 1995 and 2010. They have a lot in common with the previous generation, ²*who / Ø* known as millennials, but they also differ in many ways.

Whereas millennials are said to be idealistic, Gen Z are more sensible and realistic. They do care about the world, but the things ³*Ø / that* really concern them are money and security.

Millennials do well in situations and places ⁴*which / where* everybody works together to achieve goals. Gen Z, on the other hand, are independent. They want to complete tasks on their own rather than in a team, ⁵*that / which* is something that makes them more competitive. It's also the generation ⁶*who / whose* members are more likely to start their own business and succeed at an earlier age than millennials.

Do you agree with these characteristics? Do they describe you?

/6

GRAMMAR: Train and Try Again page 172

SPEAKING

Telling a personal anecdote

1 Translate the phrases into your own language.

SPEAKING BANK

Introducing the anecdote

(Right, so) I'm going to tell you about (a great day out.)

(OK, so) this is a story about (a day I'll never forget.)

This took place about (a month ago.)

Sequencing events in the anecdote

As soon as/When/Just after (we got there, the sun came out.)

Initially/To begin with, (we were the only people there …)

As/While (we were sitting there …)

Suddenly/All of a sudden, (the weather changed.)

Describing events vividly

Predictably/As expected, (other people soon started …)

Unexpectedly/Out of the blue, (it started pouring with rain.)

Luckily/Fortunately, (after it stopped raining, the sun came out again.)

Finishing the anecdote

Without a doubt, it was (one of the best days I've had in ages.)

When I look back (on that day) now, I feel …

It turned out to be (an unforgettable day out.)

Strangely/Funnily enough, (the best days are often the ones you don't really plan.)

2 Put the words in order to complete the sentences.

1 a great day out / I'm going / about / to tell you
   Right, so *I'm going to tell you about a great day out* .
2 the presentation / expected / was lengthy and tedious
   As _____
3 look back / I always / on that day now / I / smile to myself
   When _____
4 and there she was / sudden / of a / we turned a corner
   All _____
5 the / a car appeared on the horizon / of / blue
   Out _____
6 to be / worth / turned / all the effort / out / in the end
   It _____
7 we left / as / it started snowing heavily / soon
   As _____

3 Match the sentences in Exercise 2 with their functions.

1 introducing an anecdote   [1]
2 sequencing events in an anecdote   ☐ and ☐
3 describing events vividly   ☐ and ☐
4 finishing an anecdote   ☐ and ☐

4 Complete the anecdote using the words in the box. There is one extra word.

> enough   fortunately   initially   just   place
> predictably   ~~story~~   unexpectedly   without   when

OK, so this is a *story* about a weekend I'll never forget. It took ¹_____ last summer in Staffordshire, in England. I was visiting my cousin and we both love cycling, so we decided to go on a trip. We packed up our stuff, got on our bikes and cycled about 50 miles to a campsite very near the famous theme park, Alton Towers. ²_____ after we set off, it started raining and, ³_____ for England, it didn't stop all day. We arrived at the campsite like a pair of drowned rats. ⁴_____ , we managed to get the tent up quickly and began the long process of drying out. Or so we thought.
⁵_____ we woke up the next morning, we discovered that the tent had ⁶_____ leaked in the night and all our things, including our clothes were still wet through. There was nothing we could do, so we pulled on wet jumpers, jeans and shoes and headed for the theme park. Funnily ⁷_____ , it turns out that the fastest and most exciting way to get dry is to ride a rollercoaster with 14 loops at 50 miles per hour.
⁸_____ a doubt, that weekend was one of the wettest and funniest I've ever had.

5 Read the anecdote in Exercise 3 again and put the following parts in order.

A What happened step by step   ☐
B Where and when the anecdote took place,
   and other background information   ☐
C What the anecdote is going to be about and
   background information   [1]
D Why the day was so memorable   ☐
E Who was involved in the day   ☐

USE OF ENGLISH

Collocations

1 ★ Choose the correct answers A–D.

JUDGING PEOPLE

It is extremely <u>A</u> to avoid forming an opinion about people we don't know at all. Most of us have a nasty ¹__ of judging people by their appearance. Still, it is useful to remember that our perception might be wrong. A normally cheerful person might ²__ miserable on a particular day for a number of reasons. Maybe they ³__ badly the night before? Or maybe they have a toothache?

Since we can't help forming opinions about each other, it's a good idea to try to make a great first impression on others. So, when you are introduced to someone new, make sure you ⁴__ politely and say your name clearly. A good handshake is ⁵__ important. Sometimes your body language can say more about you than your words.

	A	B	C	D
	(A) difficult	B neat	C normal	D casual
1	A trend	B routine	C habit	D tradition
2	A feel	B set	C keep	D look
3	A slept	B went out	C turned up	D expected
4	A roar	B smile	C glance	D laugh
5	A healthy	B equally	C painfully	D bitterly

2 ★★ Complete the sentences with the correct form of the words in brackets.

The main aim of this project is to challenge commonly held *beliefs* (BELIEVE) regarding education.

1 The stand-up comedian's performance was so funny that, after a few minutes, the public was roaring with _____ (LAUGH).

2 Brad is very relaxed and good at making people feel at _____ (EASY), even strangers.

3 In a conflict, both sides need to give up something to reach an _____ (AGREE).

4 Without her vivid _____ (IMAGINE), the filmmaker wouldn't have created such a fascinating world.

5 It was surprising to find out that Glenn and I shared an _____ (INTERESTING) in psychology and wanted to become therapists.

6 I'm pretty sure my application will be rejected as I don't meet some of the _____ (REQUIRE).

3 ★★★ Replace *very* with the correct adverb form of the words in the box.

(bitter~~ter~~ deep high painful perfect supreme)

He must have been **very** disappointed when his application was rejected. *bitterly*

1 Maggie is quite outgoing, but her twin sister, Carol, is **very** shy. _____

2 Don't worry. It's **very** normal for people to feel a bit nervous about school life. _____

3 After moving towns and changing schools in the same month, Rick felt **very** depressed. _____

4 In my opinion, Sophia is a **very** intelligent and well-liked student. _____

5 The rock band seems **very** confident on stage even though they've never played in front of so many people. _____

4 ★★★ Complete each pair of sentences with the same answer A–C.

My parents taught me to share so I didn't mind when my sisters <u>B</u> with my toys.
His acting career started when he <u>B</u> the part of a teenage boy in a popular TV series.
A took   (B) played   C had

1 There are __ bedrooms now that David's guests have left.
Their parents encouraged them to be __ spirits, which meant they were often in trouble at school.
A spare   B free   C unoccupied

2 During the storm, the lights went __ and the room was in complete darkness.
It is common for folk traditions to die __ when people move to the city.
A off   B down   C out

3 Our next full-time __ starts on February 3rd. The price of the tour includes a three-__ meal in a local restaurant.
A course   B dish   C part

4 Regular exercise is an important part of a __ lifestyle.
Nuts and seeds are a great __ snack for your lunchbox.
A healthy   B organic   C vegetarian

5 Have you worked for an international __ before?
My brother is good __ . People enjoy spending time with him.
A firm   B team   C company

5 ★ Circle the best answers to complete the letter.

Dear Professor Brown,

I apologise for the (delay in responding to your letter) / getting back to you so late. We have been ¹badly / extremely busy over the last few months.

I am ²delighted / over the moon to let you know that ³we want to publish your book / your book proposal has been accepted for publication.

We believe that your book, ⁴which / whose message is ⁵loud and clear / neat and tidy, will be well-received.

⁶Please find attached / Here comes a draft contract. Could you check that your personal details are up-to-date and ⁷return / send back two signed copies as soon as possible?

Please do not hesitate ⁸contact / to contact me should you require any further information.

⁹Best, / Yours sincerely,

Raphael Morgenstern
Senior Editor

6 ★ ★ Complete the sentences using the prompts in brackets. Do not change the order of the words. Change the forms or add new words if necessary. Use up to six words in each gap.

The committee hasn't reached an agreement yet – _the voting has been postponed till_ (voting/postpone) next week.

1 I was waiting for the bus when I realised that I _____ (forget/lock) the front door.

2 My car has _____ (nasty/habit/break down) when I have a morning meeting.

3 My brother and I _____ (not/use/share) bedroom when we were small.

4 Mark had a terrible headache because his neighbour's dog _____ (bark/ages).

5 I _____ (raise/parents) in a small ski resort in the mountains.

6 I don't spend much time with Connor because he

_____ (always/complain) his personal problems.

7 ★ ★ ★ Complete the second sentence so that it has a similar meaning to the first. Use between two and five words, including the word in capitals.

I haven't got enough money to go to the concert. **CAN'T**
I _can't afford to go_ to the concert.

1 I ran faster than this when I was younger. **USE**
I _____ run this slowly when I was younger!

2 First we made some sandwiches, and then we watched the film. **HAD**
We watched the film _____ some sandwiches.

3 The teacher let us leave early yesterday. **PERMISSION**
The teacher _____ early yesterday.

4 Dave had started planning the wedding ten months before he married Kate. **HAD**
Dave _____ for ten months before he married Kate.

5 Where did you grow up? **TELL**
Could _____ you grew up?

6 My sister was angry with me for borrowing her dress. **OFF**
My sister _____ borrowing her dress.

7 You shouldn't eat chocolate if you're trying to be healthy. **AVOID**
You _____ chocolate if you're trying to be healthy.

8 ★ ★ ★ Complete the text with one word in each gap.

Marry me!

A proposal of marriage is _an_ important moment and in the past it ¹_____ to be a very private one. However, today some people make it an extremely public event. Some men have proposed ²_____ their girlfriends on big screens at football matches or on TV programmes in front of millions of people. One man ³_____ proposed in front of the crowd at Glastonbury music festival also organised the wedding at the site. Others have got married after putting the words 'Will you marry me?' into crossword puzzles ⁴_____ their girlfriends to solve.

One of the most unusual proposals happened in 2015, when a Japanese man decided to cover 7,000 kilometres around Japan on foot, by car, ferry, and bicycle. He ⁵_____ planned his trip very carefully, recording each step with GPS technology, ⁶_____ is used to monitor the location of things and people. At the end of his journey, the GPS drawing spelt out an enormous 'Marry me!' Was it worth the effort? Judging ⁷_____ the fact that he's a married man now, it turned out well! This was probably the world's most extraordinary proposal. Having said that, no doubt someone will soon try to make an ⁸_____ crazier one!

WRITING

2.8 An article

1 Complete the tips for writing an article with the words in the box.

> anecdote ~~attention~~ define develop formal
> personal question summarising think

Title: attract the reader's *attention* by asking a ¹_____ , using rhyme or wordplay or ² _____ the topic.

Introduction: should ³_____ the topic and make the reader want to continue by asking a question, telling an ⁴_____ , or giving an interesting fact, statistic or quote.

Main paragraphs: ⁵_____ the topic and discuss the issues.

Conclusion: give your ⁶_____ opinion and leave the reader with something to ⁷_____ about.

Remember: make your writing more ⁸_____ by avoiding informal phrases, colloquial language or contractions.

2 Match the beginnings and the endings of possible titles for the article in the writing task below. Then match the titles to the techniques for attracting a reader's attention A–D.

> Write an article for your school website describing how you met a close friend and explaining why friends are so important for young people growing into adulthood.

	Is There Anything More	⟨f⟩
1	A Fortunate	☐
2	How I Lost a Wallet	☐
3	The Time I Spend	☐
4	Where Would We Be	☐
5	Fantastic Friends and	☐

a	and Gained a Best Friend
b	Marvellous Mates
c	Without Our Friends?
d	and Life-changing Meeting
e	With My Greatest Friend
f	Important Than a Friend?

A	Ask a question	C	Summarise the topic
B	Use vivid adjectives	D	Use rhyme/wordplay

3 Group these eight sentences into four possible introductions to articles.

A Have you ever thought about the festive season on an industrial scale?

B The vast majority of young people meet their friends through school.

C Every year, nearly sixty million Christmas trees are grown in Europe and between ten and twenty million turkeys are killed for Christmas dinner in the UK alone.

D So, why are friends so important for young people? Well, besides sharing sweet snacks, there are, in my opinion, three main reasons.

E As someone once said, a possible answer to that question is 'A good friend knows all about you and still loves you.'

F However, I met my closest friend through an act of kindness and honesty, followed by a fortunate coincidence. And I do feel fortunate because I believe every young person needs a close friend.

G What exactly does it mean to be a good friend?

H Someone once said 'The only thing better than a friend is a friend with chocolate.'

A followed by *C*
1 __ followed by __
2 __ followed by __
3 __ followed by __

4 Read the extract and decide which combination of sentences in Exercise 3 would make the best introduction to this article.

__ followed by __

> Shaun and I met for the first time in ¹totally weird circumstances. ²I'd taken a taxi back from town one Saturday night and, ³stupidly, left my wallet on the back seat. Shaun had been the next customer in the taxi, and had found the wallet and my contact details. Being an honest person, he got in touch. The next day we met and he ⁴gave me back my wallet. I ⁵said thanks, and said goodbye. ⁶Ages after that, I joined an English class and guess who was sitting there in the classroom? Shaun! It took us a moment to work out where ⁷we'd met before, but we soon remembered and became ⁸best mates in no time at all.

5 Replace the underlined parts with phrases from the box to make the paragraph in Exercise 4 more formal. There are two extra phrases.

> I had ☐   I would ☐   mistakenly ☐
> nearly a year later ☐   returned ☐
> thanked him ☐   the best of friends ☐
> very unusual ⟨1⟩   we had ☐   we would ☐

6 Rewrite the underlined parts of the sentences using participle clauses.

Our friends understand best how we feel <u>because they have experienced many of the same things as us.</u>
Having experienced many of the same things as us, our friends understand best how we feel.

1 <u>Because I had never had a female friend before,</u> I didn't know what to expect when our friendship began.

_____
I didn't know what to expect when our friendship began.

2 Close friends often seem to know what is on each other's minds <u>because they spend so much of their time together.</u>

_____
close friends often seem to know what is on each other's minds.

3 Friends can share secrets <u>because they have gained each other's trust.</u>

_____
friends can share secrets.

4 <u>Because they are often interested in the same things,</u> friends always have something to talk about.

_____
friends always have something to talk about.

7 Read the task and the article below. Then choose the correct option.

This week's competition

**Technology and teenagers go hand in hand nowadays. However, this isn't necessarily a good thing. Do you think technology is overused or used well by adolescents? If you are a teenager, we want to hear your views. Send us an article in which you describe the very best things about using technology and discuss the challenges it poses.
A selection of the best articles will be printed in the upcoming edition of Psychology Magazine.**

SHOW WHAT YOU'VE LEARNT

8 Complete the writing task in Exercise 2. Before you start, follow steps 1–3 below.

1 Think about where your article will appear and who will read it.
2 Make notes on the role of friendship. Think of at least two points.
3 Decide which techniques you are going to use to attract and hold the reader's attention.

SHOW THAT YOU'VE CHECKED

In my article:

- I have used one of the techniques to come up with an interesting title. ☐
- in the first paragraph, I have presented the topic and attracted the reader's attention. ☐
- in the main part, I have developed the topic. ☐
- in the last paragraph, I have given my personal opinion and given the reader something to think about. ☐
- I have used formal or neutral language. ☐
- I have checked my spelling and punctuation. ☐
- I have used at least one participle clause to express reason. ☐
- my handwriting is neat enough for someone else to read. ☐

Technology:
controlled or in control?

Have you ever wondered why teens are so keen on technology? [1]*Growing up | Having grown up* with it, we are digital natives – people who are at ease with everything from the Internet to smartphones, apps and computer games. However, I can report that while technology plays a huge role in my life, I do not overuse it.

Using technology has many benefits. For many of us, the Internet is a valuable tool which allows us to research information and educate ourselves easily through access to different cultures and perspectives. In addition, keeping in touch with friends using smartphones and social media gives us a sense of community and helps us maintain supportive relationships and develop our identities. Finally, online games allow us to share interests with people we would never normally meet.

As we all know, the benefits of technology are not without risk. A recent survey showed some shocking statistics. [2]*Spending | Having spent* up to nine hours a day on social media, some teens are becoming isolated from the real world; [3]*checking | having checked* their phones more than ten times a night, 10 percent of young people have serious sleep problems. Furthermore, learning how to be a good digital citizen and being able to analyse content for its accuracy and value can be a struggle.

Despite the challenges, as far as I am concerned, once you learn to establish sensible boundaries and use technology safely, the benefits are endless. I believe that most teens are aware of this and that they are in control of technology, not controlled by it.

VOCABULARY AND GRAMMAR

1 **Complete the sentences with the correct forms of the words in the box. There are two extra words.**

> ~~attract~~   crouch   fill   grip   hesitate
> intellect   mood   perceive

Have you ever been really _attracted_ to someone because you loved their personality?

1 John thinks everything he does is wonderful – I don't know why he's so _____ of himself.

2 Jamie loves learning and studying complex things. He's really _____ .

3 Sandra _____ for a few seconds before opening the door and entering the room.

4 I _____ down so I could see the object on the floor better.

5 I hadn't said anything, but Jake's pretty _____ and he realised something had upset me.

/5

2 **Complete the sentences with the missing words. The first letters are given.**

Being very **s**_pontaneous_, Jan booked a holiday abroad and left the very next day!

1 He **g**_____ quickly at the magazine cover and then put it down.

2 I **f**_____ for my husband the first time I met him. It was love at first sight!

3 The painting was amazing and I **g**_____ at it for a long time.

4 This was it! I **s**_____ nervously but my mouth was very dry. I walked on stage to sing in front of hundreds of people.

5 When she tasted the coffee, she **g**_____ , because she'd added salt instead of sugar.

/5

3 **Complete the sentences with the missing words or phrases. Use the definitions in brackets to help you.**

When a spider suddenly ran out from under the bed, I _flinched_ (moved my face in fear)!

1 Do you know why Josh has been so _____ (becoming angry very easily) recently?

2 Maggie _____ (broke up) with Tim last week, so he's really upset.

3 Ella's really outgoing. She's always the _____ of _____ (someone exciting to be with).

4 If you weren't so _____ (thinking only about yourself), you would have more friends.

5 I didn't know anyone at the party, so Rob came to talk to me and made me feel _____ (comfortable).

/5

4 **Choose the correct option.**

I didn't know J.K. Rowling wrote /(had written)/ had been writing a new book. I only saw it in the shop last week.

1 By the time I arrived at the theatre, the play already started / had already started / had already been starting. I was late!

2 There was lots of snow on the ground because it snowed / had snowed / had been snowing all night long.

3 Although Dave worked / had worked / had been working hard all day, he still hadn't finished his report.

4 Last night, I talked / had talked / had been talking to my parents about my problem because it had been worrying me for weeks.

5 Diane knew / had known / had been knowing Matt for months before she started going out with him.

/5

5 **Complete the sentences with _who, which, where, whose_ or _Ø_ (no pronoun). Omit the relative pronoun where possible.**

My father, _who_ was born in Scotland, has travelled all over the world.

1 I've got two friends _____ living in the same street as me.

2 My brother often invites friends round without asking, _____ is irritating.

3 I love writers _____ books give you an understanding of people's characters and motivation.

4 My cousins are the people _____ I spend most time with, apart from my friends.

5 Children _____ brought up speaking two languages are better at solving problems.

/5

6 **Choose the correct answers A–C.**

Recently, Sarah Elliot _A_ with Paul Edwards at the airport to fly to Las Vegas. They were on their way there to get married – nothing unusual about that, you might think. However, the couple **¹**___ in person before! Sarah and Paul met online and **²**___ for a few days when they decided to get married. Sarah was a fan of a TV show called _Married at First Sight_, about couples who meet for the first time on their wedding day. Experts work hard to make the best matches between people depending on their personality and values, and the show follows how successful the marriages are. Sarah had watched an episode of the show recently and **³**___ Paul about it for days, describing it in detail. Paul **⁴**___ of _Married at First Sight_, but when Sarah explained the concept, he immediately proposed! They **⁵**___ that Las Vegas was the perfect place for their ceremony and made arrangements for the wedding.

	A met up	B had met up	C had been meeting up
1	A didn't meet	B hadn't met	C hadn't been meeting
2	A were only chatting		B had only chatted
	C had only been chatting		
3	A told	B had told	C had been telling
4	A didn't hear	B hadn't heard	C hadn't been hearing
5	A agreed	B had agreed	C had been agreeing

/5

Total /30

7 Complete each pair of sentences with the same word.

Jane's going to _have_ a baby next month.
If you can't _have_ a laugh about your problems, things must be bad.

1 I have really _____ memories of my trip to Canada. I remember everything perfectly.
Jack has a _____ imagination. He writes stories about amazing creatures that he invents.

2 When he heard the terrible news, he _____ out a groan.
I wanted to help her and finally she _____ me.

3 It's so noisy in here I can't _____ .
We need original ideas, so let's _____ outside the box.

4 Our house is quite hard to _____ from the city centre. You have to take two buses to get there.
They argued about it for ages and then finally managed to _____ an agreement.

5 She smiled at him across the room and then gave a _____ .
The surfer managed to catch the _____ and ride it all the way to the beach.

/5

8 Complete the sentences with the correct form of the words in brackets.

Saying that girls gossip a lot is a _stereotype_ (STEREOTYPICAL).

1 I don't know Mark well, but he's a really _____ person. He's travelled all over the world. (INTEREST)

2 I'll always remember my first dance competition. Performing was so exciting, it was an _____ day. (FORGET)

3 A lot of people feel _____ about their appearance and don't think they look good enough. (SECURITY)

4 Tom is completely _____ (OBSESSION) with Ariana Grande. He listens to her music all the time.

5 We arrived at the café early, so we were the only people there for a while. Then, _____ , (PREDICTION) lots of people arrived around 11 a.m. for a coffee.

/5

9 Complete the sentences using the prompts in brackets. Change the forms or add new words where necessary. Use up to six words in each gap.

I was tired because _I had been running_ (I/run) for nearly an hour without stopping.

1 We set off a bit late and, by the time we finally arrived at the cinema, _____ (the film/already/start).

2 Maria didn't know what to do because _____ (she/have/not/listen) to the teacher for the last five minutes.

3 I _____ (have/know) Jack's brother for years before I met Jack.

4 Yesterday I was happy because I _____ (have/win) a prize the previous day.

5 When I went to Madrid on holiday, _____ (I/have/not/learn) Spanish for long. Luckily, I somehow managed to make people understand me.

/5

10 Complete the text with one word in each gap.

Top 5 things that make humans special

#1 **Our brains.** Humans are _highly_ intelligent. Although our brain is only about 2.5 percent of our body weight, we are able to think and work out ideas far better than any other mammal and have developed sophisticated information exchange systems of languages. We had ¹_____ communicating with music and art for hundreds of years before language developed, but the way we communicate with words is an incredible achievement that has put humans on a different level.

#2 **Self awareness.** Unlike most animals, we are aware of ourselves and our thoughts. The advantage of this is improved social interaction, but the downside, of course, is that people can become ²_____ and worry or get embarrassed about what others think of them.

#3 **Rules and laws.** Although some animals follow basic rules in order to live in groups, we have been able to develop complex laws ³_____ everyone has to follow. These laws govern everything from defining criminal behaviour to how we can trade, from education to the environment.

#4 **Education and learning.** Humans have the longest childhood of any species, which gives our brains lots of time to develop. It takes us far longer to learn things, such as how to walk or feed ourselves, than other mammals. However, we learn far more complex things than how to simply survive and have formal education systems which aim to cultivate a ⁴_____ of learning that can last throughout our lives.

#5 **Love.** Last but not least, we are very romantic and perhaps the only animal that falls madly in love ⁵_____ another member of the species!

/5

Total /20

SPEAKING

1 **In pairs, ask and answer the questions.**

Talk about personality and friendship.

Student A

1 What qualities do you look for in a friend?
2 Tell me about someone important you met at primary school.
3 What are the best ways to keep in touch with a friend who lives in a different city?
4 Is it important for friends to share the same interests?
5 Which of your negative qualities would you like to work on?

Student B

1 What activities do you enjoy doing with your friends?
2 Is it possible to be friends with someone you only know online?
3 Tell me about your best friend from when you were at primary school.
4 What advice would you give someone who wanted to make new friends?
5 Do our personalities change as we get older?

2 **Look at the diagram. It shows different ideas for reducing stress at school. In pairs, follow these steps.**

• Talk to each other about how effective each idea is for helping students feel less stressed at school.
• Say which idea would be best for your school.

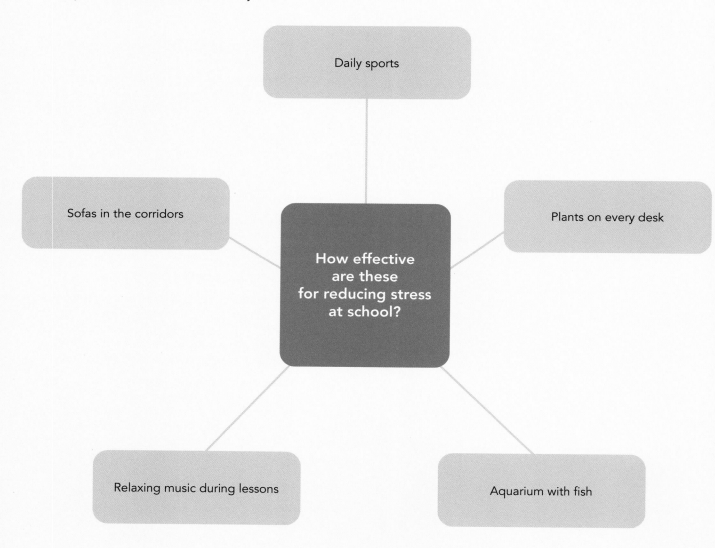

Daily sports

Sofas in the corridors

Plants on every desk

How effective are these for reducing stress at school?

Relaxing music during lessons

Aquarium with fish

3 In pairs, discuss the questions about education.

1 Some people think there are too many exams at school. What do you think?
2 Do you think it's a good idea for boys and girls to attend different schools? Why?/Why not?
3 Should higher education be free for everyone?
4 In what ways does technology help students at school?
5 Should students be given more choice about the subjects they study? Why?/Why not?

4 Do the task in pairs.

Student A
Look at the photos. They show people explaining problems. Compare the photos and say what the disadvantages of each method of communication are.

Student B, how do you prefer to communicate with your friends? Why?

Student B
Look at the photos. They show teenagers doing different activities. Compare the photos and decide what they say about the people in them.

Student A, which photo best represents teenagers today? Why?

3 Living spaces

3.1 VOCABULARY

Landscapes • prepositions describing location • describing places • collocations and compound nouns

SHOW WHAT YOU KNOW

1 Complete the text with townscape and landscape features in the box.

> breathtaking view   bridge   canal
> fast-flowing river   historic monument
> ~~housing estate~~   market square   shopping centre
> slum   waterfront restaurant

My Everyday Blog

I just had to write today about the latest urban development plans. Have you read them? They want to knock down some 200-year-old houses and use the land to build ... yes, you guessed! A _housing estate_ with 100 modern homes. I know there's a shortage of housing in our town, but it's not as if they're getting rid of a ¹_____ with houses in a terrible condition – these are beautiful old buildings! And what about the old school? Surely that's a ²_____ ? It should be turned into a museum, not destroyed!

Luckily, it's not all bad news. At the moment, the river is a real mess, but the council are finally going to clean it up. After they've removed all the rubbish, it will be a ³_____ again, not a slow, dirty one. They're going to build a new pedestrian ⁴_____ over the water so people can cross the river easily and a ⁵_____ that will serve international food and be family-friendly. They're also building a new ⁶_____ with over fifty shops, mostly for clothes.

<u>So what do you think? Comment below!</u>

These new houses will spoil the area completely. There's a ⁷_____ from the top of the hill looking down over the town at the moment, which people come from all over to see ... but soon it'll just be rows of houses. I think they should build the development on the other side of town.
....
I've heard they want to build a ⁸_____ so boats can go right through the town centre. Is that true? I hope not! We don't live in Venice!
....
The shopping centre is a terrible idea. Now everyone goes to the shops round the old ⁹_____ , and we have a busy town centre. If people start to shop by the river instead, many places in the centre may end up closing, which would be a disaster!

WORD STORE 3A | Prepositions describing location

2 Choose the correct option.

Turn right (at)/ in / on the roundabout.
1 We live at / in / on the coast near Dover.
2 Luckily, I live in / within / by walking distance of the town centre so I never take the bus.
3 We often play football at / on / in the park.
4 The local shops are at / in / within easy reach of our house, they're only five minutes away.
5 It's easy to get to the countryside because we live at / on / in the outskirts of town.
6 We don't live at / on / in the suburbs, we live at / on / in the city centre.
7 You can get lots of tourist information at / on / in the town hall.
8 My school is in / within / at 500 metres of my house so it doesn't take long to get there.

WORD STORE 3B | Describing places

3 Circle the word that does NOT collocate with the adjective given.

	urban	area / space /(town)/ development
1	quaint	space / backstreet / town / neighbourhood
2	bustling	market / square / nightlife / streets
3	shabby	building / city centre / architecture / house
4	vibrant	square / atmosphere / nightlife / colours
5	medieval	architecture / colours / castle / centre
6	picturesque	old town / scenery / village / development

4 Read the extracts from city guides and choose the correct answers A–C.

> Brazil's cities combine some of South America's most beautiful beaches with vibrant culture and _B_ streets.

> Get lost in the quaint little ¹__ of Seville's Santa Cruz district.

> Many of Amsterdam's budget hotels are located in the ²__ area close to Central Station.

> Visit the ³__ old town in Lisbon and enjoy its many wonderful buildings.

> Bilbao's centre has undergone huge urban ⁴__ and is now home to the Guggenheim Museum.

> For ⁵__ architecture, visit Carcassonne in France. The town is built on a hillside, surrounding an old castle.

> Ibiza's ⁶__ nightlife includes some of the largest and most famous nightclubs in the world.

	A	B	C
	A inner	(B) bustling	C nightlife
1	A backstreets	B cities	C nightlife
2	A square	B urban	C neighbourhood
3	A urban	B building	C picturesque
4	A scenery	B development	C neighbourhood
5	A medieval	B shabby	C quaint
6	A delicious	B charming	C vibrant

5 Match the beginnings of the sentences with the endings.

The city centre is great for biking because there are a lot of cycle (f)

1 There's a pedestrian ◯
2 In the old town there are plenty of cobbled ◯
3 Bangkok isn't a quiet city, there's noise ◯
4 There isn't any on-street ◯
5 The town is surrounded by rolling ◯
6 When I go into the city centre, I leave my car in an underground ◯
7 I don't drive in the city because there's a reliable ◯
8 We live in the suburbs so I have a short daily ◯

a parking where I live, so I leave my car at my parents' house.
b car park while I go shopping.
c zone where no cars are allowed.
d streets which make it picturesque.
e commute to my office in the city centre.
f lanes that you can use.
g hills where you can go hiking.
h pollution day and night.
i network of buses and trams.

6 Complete the text with the words in the box.

cobbled lanes network on-street
rolling ~~underground~~ zones

○○○

●●●●

WHERE ON EARTH?

Have you visited somewhere interesting?
We'd like to hear about it. Post your comments below:

York, England

York is about halfway between London and Edinburgh and it's a fascinating place to visit. We left our car in an _underground_ car park and explored the city on foot because there is very little ¹_____ parking in the centre. It's a very bike-friendly city and there are many cycle ²_____ . There are also some car-free pedestrian ³_____ .

The city was built by the Romans and within the ancient walls there are some traditional ⁴_____ streets (rather bumpy for cyclists!) with medieval buildings. The centre is quaint and picturesque, but there are plenty of modern shops, thirty world-class museums as well as the beautiful Minster (the cathedral).

When you've had enough of the city, there's plenty more to explore – York is surrounded by the ⁵_____ hills of the Yorkshire Dales and North York Moors, with a reliable ⁶_____ of buses to get there. It's definitely worth a visit!

---

7 Complete each pair of sentences with the correct words A–C.

1 That book up there on the shelf is just out of my ___ . Could you pass it to me?
School's not far away, it's within easy ___ .
A access B distance C reach
2 The nightlife is great, but it creates a lot of noise ___ .
___ is a serious environmental problem in big cities.
A parking B pollution C contamination
3 There's a ___ atmosphere in the town centre.
All the fishing boats on the island are painted ___ colours.
A vibrant B bustling C picturesque
4 I use the train for my ___ commute to work.
It's a ___ newspaper, so there's a new edition every morning.
A short B regular C daily
5 There's a children's play area in our local ___ that we often go to.
Let's leave the car in the new underground car ___ while we have lunch.
A zone B parking C park

/5

8 Find and correct the mistakes in the sentences.

There's a ~~relying~~ bus network in our town. _reliable_
1 Would you rather live in a busy city centre or on the suburbs where it's quieter? _____
2 The centre of Amsterdam is great for cyclists because there are plenty of cycling lanes.
_____
3 We visited a lovely market town at the border of England and Wales. _____
4 Although I haven't lived there for a long time, Dundee is my house town – I was born there and often go back to visit family. _____
5 Our town attracts a lot of tourists – it's full of quaint backstreets and historical monuments.
_____

/5

GRAMMAR

3.2

Future forms including the Future Perfect Continuous

SHOW WHAT YOU KNOW

1 Choose the correct option to complete the dialogue.

Joel: Make sure you don't miss the last episode, Liz.

Liz: I wouldn't miss it for the world. I ¹*'ve watched / 'll be watching* at 8 o'clock. Don't worry.

Joel: By the end, we ²*'ll be finding out / 'll have found out* who the killer is.

Liz: Finally! I reckon it's the detective himself.

2 ★ Complete the sentences with the structures in the box.

> ~~will have been climbing~~   will have been living
> 'll be eating   'll have been waiting   'll have finished
> will have started   won't have been

By the time he reaches the peak, Whittaker and his team *will have been climbing* for nearly two weeks.

1 At the rate that Alicia reads, she _____ every book in the library soon.

2 If we don't book something for this summer, we _____ on holiday for three years in a row.

3 Come on, traffic lights?! The party _____ if we don't get there soon.

4 In five minutes we _____ exactly two hours for the pizza delivery. I'm going to phone them and complain.

5 By the time their house is finally finished, the Jones family _____ in a caravan in the garden for over two years.

6 I know you're hungry, sweetheart. I promise we _____ in no more than twenty minutes.

3 ★ ★ Use the prompts to make three sentences about each sign.

1

> **GREENVALE SHOPPING CENTRE OPENING 1st JULY**

By / June / builders / finish / build
By June, the builders will have finished building
the new shopping centre.

a In / July / people / shop
_____ there.

b By / Christmas / centre / operate
_____ for _____ months.

2

> **HORROR** MOVIE MARATHON TONIGHT
> 8 p.m. – 4 a.m.

a At / 11 p.m. / first horror film / finish
_____

b By / midnight / audience / watch
_____ the second film.

c By / 4 a.m. / audience / sit in the cinema
_____ for _____ hours.

---

4 ★ ★ ★ Complete the text with the Future Continuous, Future Perfect Simple, or Future Perfect Continuous forms of the verbs in brackets.

2050 — Cities of the Future

By 2050, human beings <u>will have been building</u> (build) and living in cities for around 10,000 years. It is estimated that, by this date, more than 70 percent of the world's population ¹_____ (live) in urban environments. In preparation for this, developers in the US alone ²_____ (construct) nearly ninety million new homes by 2050.

The cities of the future are likely to be much cleaner places than those we inhabit today. By then architects ³_____ (design) buildings that use smart materials to help reduce air pollution and we ⁴_____ (use) less fossil fuel and more alternative energy for decades, making cities considerably less polluted than they are today. Solar panels ⁵_____ (become) the norm on most buildings by 2050, and we ⁶_____ (recycle) a much larger proportion of our waste than we do today. Where will you be living in 2050? Wherever it is, it is very likely to be in a city.

SHOW WHAT YOU'VE LEARNT

5 Choose the correct answers A–C.

1 By the end of this month, the Green Party ___ for a greener city for four years.
   A will have campaigned   **B** will be campaigning
   C will have been campaigning

2 If we don't repair the bridge now, by this time next year it ___ down.
   A will probably be falling   **B** will probably have fallen
   C will probably have been falling

3 I know you're stressed now, but remember this time next week ___ in a café in Paris.
   A you'll have sat   **B** you'll be sitting
   C you'll have been sitting

4 Before she's 30, Gia hopes she ___ the house of her dreams.
   A 'll have bought   **B** 'll have been buying
   C 'll be buying

5 Skydivers, listen up! In sixty seconds' time, you ___ towards earth at nearly 200 mph.
   A 'll be falling   **B** 'll have fallen
   C 'll have been falling

6 By Friday, I ___ in this hospital bed for two weeks. If only I'd been more careful.
   A 'll have lied   **B** 'll have been lying
   C 'll be lying

/6

GRAMMAR: Train and Try Again page 173

GRAMMAR: Train and Try Again page 173

38

3.3

Prepositions • near antonyms
• collocations and compound nouns

1 Complete Part 1 of the recording extract by adding the preposition *of* in five more places.

Extract from Student's Book recording ◄) **2.5**

Part 1

Welcome to the Lifestyle Programme. Let's start with the shocking results ^of^ a recent survey: 35 percent British people do not know any their neighbours. Well, it's not a problem for residents Springhill co-housing project in the southwest England. Springhill is a new housing development thirty-five homes in a typical residential area.

---

of a recent survey   3 _____
1 _____   4 _____
2 _____   5 _____

2 Match the adjectives with their definitions.

affordable ☐   well-established ☐
neighbourly ☐   communal ☐
daily ☐   latest ☐
sustainable ☐1

1 able to continue without causing damage to the environment
2 inexpensive
3 most recent
4 happening every day
5 existing for a long time and respected or trusted by people
6 behaving in a friendly way towards the people who live near you
7 shared by a group of people who live together

3 Complete Part 2 of the extract with the adjectives in Exercise 2.

Extract from Student's Book recording ◄) **2.5**

Part 2

Residents have their own self-contained flats or houses and gardens but share a common house for *communal* meals. The co-housing idea comes from Denmark where it is ¹_____ and according to the ²_____ government housing figures, tens of thousands of Danish people live in this way. There is growing interest around the world in the model as a provider of ³_____ , sustainable social housing. Building materials are natural or recycled. Springhill is not only ⁴_____ in building terms, but in human terms too, encouraging the ⁵_____ social contact that we know is key to health and happiness. We're sure there'll be a 100 percent improvement in ⁶_____ relations at Springhill.

---

4 Match three near antonyms in the box with each of the adjectives.

cold ~~costly~~ extravagant hostile infrequent irregular occasional overpriced temporary unsociable damaging wasteful

1 affordable *costly*, _____
2 daily _____
3 neighbourly _____
4 sustainable _____

5 In your vocabulary notes, add more near antonyms for these adjectives from this unit.

1 bustling _____
2 historical _____
3 quaint _____
4 reliable _____
5 shabby _____
6 vibrant _____

WORD STORE 3D | Collocations and compound nouns

6 Complete the sentences with the words in the box.

domestic household housing multi-storey residential self-contained second ~~tower~~

The views of the city from our flat are fantastic because we're up on the tenth floor. I never thought I'd enjoy living in a *tower* block, but I do.

1 I think _____ car parks are a great way of providing room for more vehicles in a small space.
2 The traffic will get worse when they finish building the new _____ development of 50 homes.
3 We used to live in the city centre, but we moved out to a quiet _____ area on the city outskirts when we had children.
4 When Sue and Pete retire, their dream is to buy a _____ home in Spain and spend every winter there.
5 I think the washing machine is the best _____ appliance ever. It saves so much time!
6 Having lived in a house with two other people and got fed up with sharing the kitchen and bathroom, Jack's now looking for a _____ flat.
7 Who's responsible for doing the _____ chores, like washing up and cleaning, in your household?

1 Read the text quickly and choose the best summary.

The text aims

1 to persuade people that tiny homes are the most environmentally-friendly accommodation.

2 to inform readers about the reasons why people choose to live in tiny homes.

3 to describe the potential advantages and disadvantages of living in a tiny home.

Tiny houses

Humans have always traditionally lived in tiny homes, such as caves, huts and cabins. However, when homes became more permanent, bigger started to be seen as better. Property was in many ways a measure of wealth and success. In the last decade or so, however, people's priorities have begun to change and there is a growing tiny house movement. Tiny houses, as the name suggests, are very small homes and the reasons for choosing them are as diverse as the buildings themselves.

For some people, the choice is purely financial, as they either can't afford a bigger house or they want to remain debt-free. ¹____ Most owners therefore do not need a **mortgage** or only need a small loan to build them, so they are able to spend their money on other things. For many young people this is a huge attraction. 'I'd just got my first job and money was **tight**,' says Lidia. 'Buying a tiny house was the best option for me since rents were so high.'

Tiny houses are also **considerably** cheaper to run than the average house, since energy bills are far lower. ²____ Although Amanda and Simon struggled to get rid of many of their possessions before moving to their tiny home, they found it had unexpected bonuses. 'Living more **minimally** gave us the financial freedom we sought and enabled us to **prioritise** better and

set new personal goals. We grew as individuals,' they explain.

Others choose tiny living for environmental or well-being reasons, and **shrinking** your home can have a huge impact on both. 'Our entire house was built using recycled materials,' Aleesha reveals, 'and contains fewer things to replace or repair. Our energy consumption has dropped by a **staggering** 98 percent. Because the house is small, we've found ourselves spending more time outdoors and are much fitter – physically and mentally.' ³____ Typical modern homes, in contrast, can make it tougher.

Having a permanent home that is mobile* can also be a big attraction. Tiny homes can be built on trailers*, offering the possibility of living in different places without moving house – your home goes with you. ⁴____ 'I'm retired and spend winter in the south and then head north for the summer. I don't have to maintain two homes and I meet so many fascinating people on the way,' says Marina.

A final advantage is that, compared to standard houses, tiny homes can

be relatively easy to build. You can buy kits online or design your own. Thirteen-year-old Luke did just that – he planned and built his house with the money he earned from doing chores for neighbours and family. It cost $1,500 and is about 1.68 metres wide and three metres long. In the future, he plans to build a mobile tiny home to live in while he studies.

Tiny living might not be for everyone, but it has many attractions. You can live a happier life with more freedom, save money and know you're not doing it at the cost of the environment.

GLOSSARY

mobile (*adj*) – easy to move and use in different places   **trailer** (*n*) – a vehicle used for carrying something heavy

2 Read the text again. Complete gaps 1–4 with sentences A–E. There is one extra sentence.

A The benefits don't stop there, either. Because they live in such a reduced space, people buy less since there is only room for the essentials (things that are important and necessary).

B This is appealing to people who don't want to settle down anywhere and it's also a great option for those who thrive on variety or who have to change location for work.

C The many advantages offered by tiny homes explain why people are increasingly looking into them as a potential solution to the housing crisis.

D Tiny houses, due to their size, require fewer resources to build and maintain and they can be built in far smaller spaces.

E Bearing this in mind, it is easy to see why tiny living could more readily contribute to a sustainable, healthy lifestyle.

3 Read the text again and decide if the sentences are true (T) or false (F).

1 People tend to live in tiny houses for similar reasons. ☐

2 Lidia didn't want to rent somewhere to live because it cost too much. ☐

3 For Simon and Amanda, the main benefit of tiny living was having fewer things. ☐

4 Aleesha used to spend as much time outside as she does now when she lives in a tiny home. ☐

5 Since all tiny homes can be easily moved, owners can live anywhere they choose. ☐

6 A teenager has designed a tiny home which he paid for with his own money. ☐

4 Complete the definitions with the words in bold in the text.

	to a very small degree or amount	*minimally*
1	extremely great or surprising	_____
2	money that you borrow from a bank in order to buy a house	_____
3	with a very limited amount of money	_____
4	becoming smaller	_____
5	put several things/problems in order and deal with the most important ones first	_____
6	much or a lot	_____

5 Complete the sentences with the words in Exercise 4.

The number of young people who live at home has increased *considerably*. There are far more nowadays.

1 I'll have to _____ today's tasks, otherwise I'll never get them all done.

2 Their house cost a _____ five million pounds! Unbelievable!

3 I don't earn much, so things are _____ , but I manage to get by.

4 Most people find that living _____ with fewer possessions is good for their mental health.

5 We'd always wanted a house with a pool, so we took out a really big _____ – we'll be paying it off forever!

6 Most businesses are expanding, not _____ . I hope we can increase our market share as well.

VOCABULARY PRACTICE | Describing houses

6 Look at the vocabulary in lesson 3.4 in the Student's Book. Complete the text with the words in the box. There is one extra word.

> canvas ~~central~~ cramped damp draughty
> en suite fireplace fitted inaccessible
> minimalist running snug

The house where I was born

My grandmother grew up in a house that was practically falling down! I've seen photos and heard all about it. It was freezing in winter as there was no <u>central</u> heating and it was ¹_____ because there were gaps around all the windows where the wind came blowing in. The roof was in poor condition, so the rain came through, making the house very ²_____ . Her family spent most evenings sitting round the big open ³_____ , trying to keep warm. There was no ⁴_____ kitchen, just some old cupboards and a sink and a fridge that made a terrible noise. It wasn't in such bad condition that it didn't have ⁵_____ water, but the water never got particularly hot as the boiler didn't work too well. Of course, there was no such thing as an ⁶_____ bathroom! The bedrooms were small and ⁷_____ . When she was young, she didn't miss these luxuries because she loved being out in the hills and woods. Sometimes when I'm listening to the rain as I lie in my cosy bed in my ⁸_____ modern semi-detached house surrounded by all my bits and pieces, I think about my grandmother's house. I'm glad to live in town and not in an ⁹_____ house in the middle of nowhere, sleeping on an old ¹⁰_____ camp bed!

WORD STORE 3E | Idiomatic expressions

7 Complete the sentences. The first letters are given.

When we were young, there were no rules. The children could run **w**_ild_.

1 In tricky situations, you need to keep your **w**_____ about you and think of solutions quickly.

2 We had a **h**_____ moment when the bedroom ceiling collapsed, but everyone got out safely.

3 I've always enjoyed my own **c**_____ . Spending time by myself allows me to recharge my batteries.

4 Living in the country isn't everyone's cup of **t**_____ but it's perfect for me, as I've always loved nature.

5 It's always been **s**_____ nature to me to set my burglar alarm before going out. I can't believe I forgot yesterday.

6 People notice if you tell them to do things you never do. You need to practise what you **p**_____ .

7 When the house caught fire, Sandra kept a **c**_____ head and called the emergency services. She didn't panic at all.

SHOW WHAT YOU KNOW

1 Choose the correct option to complete the dialogue in an English oral exam between the examiner and candidate.

E: Let's start with a few personal questions. Tell me about the place where you live.

C: OK, well we live in a bright and leafy neighbourhood. It's a safe place with [1]*very little / very few* crime, perhaps because [2]*much / many* of the people living in the area are families with kids. [3]*A few / A lot* of the people who live in the area are from overseas so it's a very multi-cultural place. You can hear all kinds of different languages when you are walking down the street. Most of the time it's pretty quiet although there is always [4]*too much / too many* traffic in the mornings and afternoons and [5]*too much / too many* cars parked on the road at night.

2 ★ Add the missing preposition *of* to three of the sentences below.

 I know plenty ^of^ people who grow tired of working in big companies and decide to quit their jobs and slow down. *plenty of*

1 A couple my friends are deep thinkers, which makes them interesting to talk to about life's ups and downs. _____

2 Though normally confident, many the people on the stage that night were in fact very nervous. _____

3 Not all teenagers are eager to spend time with their friends at the weekends. _____

4 No exam will ever be as hard as the one you have to take at the end of this course. _____

5 Elsa's pen broke, but luckily none the ink spilled out into her handbag. _____

6 Both rooms had been painted a shade of blue that reminded Hannah of her favourite flowers. _____

3 ★ ★ Choose the correct answers A–C.

The Rise of Megacities

Until the mid-20th century, [1]____ people lived in rural areas, but now the majority of the world's population lives in urban areas. Cities have grown dramatically and [2]____ of them have even become 'megacities', the name given to urban areas with more than 10 million inhabitants.

According to the United Nations, there are currently 33 megacities, the largest of which is Tokyo, Japan, with a population of 37 million. Unlike Tokyo, [3]____ the megacities are in poor countries. There, people leave rural areas because there are [4]____ opportunities for work or education, and [5]____ hope of a good life.

When there is rapid population growth, poor countries face [6]____ social, economic and environmental problems. Cities need [7]____ clean water and electricity, as well as hospitals, schools, rubbish removal facilities and transport. But with [8]____ money, it's almost impossible to keep up with the demands of a growing population.

This is why megacities are one of the world's greatest challenges. The question we need to ask is, 'Can our planet survive urban growth?'

4 ★ ★ ★ Complete the second sentence so that it means the same as the first. Use the word in capitals.

 I'd like to raise a toast to all the volunteers who helped out today.
 EACH
 I'd like to raise a toast *to each of the volunteers* who helped out today.

1 In my circle of friends there are a number of only children and one set of twins.
 SEVERAL
 In my circle of friends _____ and one set of twins.

2 I've got two rain jackets so you can borrow whichever of them you like.
 EITHER
 I've got two rain jackets _____ them.

3 Every single person who attended agreed that the concert had been a once in a lifetime experience.
 ALL
 _____ agreed that the concert had been a once in a lifetime experience.

4 None of the students were late for the exam.
 STUDENT
 _____ was on time for the exam.

5 Not one animal was hurt during the making of this film.
 ANIMALS
 _____ were hurt during the making of this film.

SHOW WHAT YOU'VE LEARNT

5 Find and correct the mistakes. One sentence is correct.

 ~~Number of people~~ commented on Lucy's new dress. *A number of people*

1 Most of cafés have free Wi-Fi these days. _____

2 Helen paid more than forty euros for some these cactuses. _____

3 Each the puppies has a different character. _____

4 All priests attended the mass that Sunday. _____

5 Liam couldn't remember the names of either of babies. _____

6 I have little time for rude, self-centred people. _____

/6

GRAMMAR: Train and Try Again page 173

1 A most of	B most	C lots
2 A some	B both	C every one
3 A loads	B none of	C many of
4 A a few	B few	C many
5 A no	B none of	C neither
6 A few	B many of	C a number of
7 A a couple of	B every	C a great deal of
8 A little	B a little	C plenty

SPEAKING

Organising a place to live

1 **Translate the phrases into your own language.**

SPEAKING BANK

Suggesting a course of action

What do you think about
(+ -ing)?

Maybe we ought to
(just) …

What would you say if we
(+ Past Simple)?

Given the choice,
I'd rather …, and you?

Objecting

No way!/Absolutely not!/
You must be joking! (informal)

Fair? I think it's
completely unfair.

(Well yeah, but) Wouldn't it
be better to …?

I know/see what you mean/
what you're saying, but …

I'm not convinced
(we'll be able to afford it/
that's a good idea/
that'll work.)

Compromising

If you agree to (pay more), I'll
(take the smaller room).

We could (split the cost/go
halves/share).

Why don't we compromise/
meet halfway
(and agree that …)?

I guess so./I suppose that
could work.

OK, that seems like
a fair compromise.

Agreeing

True./Right./
Absolutely./Totally.

I fully/completely agree.

You are absolutely right.

OK, that's settled then.

2 **Complete the phrases with the words in the box.
There are two extra words.**

> agree choice compromise convinced halfway
> joking know mean saying settled think

   What do you _think_ about (+ing) ⬜S
1 You must be _____ ! (informal) ⬜
2 Why don't we meet _____ and …? ⬜
3 OK, that's _____ then. ⬜
4 Given the _____ , I'd rather … . And you? ⬜
5 I'm not _____ … ⬜
6 I completely _____ . ⬜
7 OK, that seems like a fair _____ . ⬜
8 I see what you're _____ , but … ⬜

3 **Label the phrases in Exercise 2 as S for suggesting
a course of action, O for objecting,
C for compromising, or A for agreeing.**

4 **Complete the dialogues. The first letters are given.**

1
Jacob: M_aybe_ we o_ught_ to j_ust_ have a joint
        birthday party?
Maddy: [1]N_____ w_____ ! Why have one
        party when we could have two?
Jacob: Well, I [2]k_____ w_____ you
        m_____ , but I don't have much money.
        If we have a joint party, we [3]c_____
        s_____ the cost.
Maddy: Well, I [4]g_____ so. So, what do you
        fancy doing?

2
John: [5]W_____ w_____ you s_____
        i_____ we did some domestic chores this
        evening, Brandon? The place is a real mess.
Brandon: You are [6]a_____ r_____ . The bathroom
        is disgusting and we haven't washed up for days.
John: Totally. [7]I_____ y_____ a_____
        to do the kitchen, [8]I_____ do the bathroom.
Brandon: Right. The only thing is we've only got three
        more episodes of *Game of Thrones* to watch
        to finish the series.
John: That's true. Well, [9]w_____ d_____ we
        c_____ and watch one episode while we
        have dinner and then do the chores?
Brandon: OK, [10]t_____ s_____ then … or we
        could watch two episodes, then clean up and
        save the last one for tomorrow.
John: Good idea. Or, maybe we could finish the
        series today and do the chores tomorrow.
Brandon: I [11]f_____ agree.
John: Shall I order pizza then?
Brandon: Great.

USE OF ENGLISH

3.7

Determiners

1 ★ **Complete the dialogues with the phrases in the box.**

> all the   all of them   another one   both of them
> ~~each of the~~   every one of   every one of them
> one of them   the others   the whole

Tour guide: … and interestingly *each of the* city's three skyscrapers was built by the same company. Now, if you look to your right, you'll see …

Amber: Paige, this tour is so boring.

Paige: I know. Let's wait till they go round the corner then we'll head for the shops instead!

1 Mary: Wow! Your nails are cool.

Lilly: Nice huh? I've painted ᵃ_____ a different colour.

Mary: Where did you get ᵇ_____ different colours from?

Lilly: They were a present from my dad.

2 Ashley: There are two good films on television tonight, look.

Judd: I'm afraid I've already seen _____ .

3 John: Tom! ᵃ_____ house stinks of burnt dinner.

Tom: I know, I'm sorry. I opened ᵇ_____ the windows downstairs, but it didn't make much difference.

4 Val: Well, Bess had six puppies but unfortunately one of them is very ill.

Bill: What a shame. Are ᵃ_____ healthy?

Val: Well, ᵇ_____ is blind in one eye and ᶜ_____ is very small, but apart from that they are OK.

5 Zoe: There are so many expensive designer shops here.

Reece: I know and _____ are empty. Most people can't afford to shop there.

2 ★★ **Complete the second sentence with one word so it means the same as the first. Do not use the same determiners as in the first sentence.**

I've read all the guide books on Berlin that were in the library.
I've read *every* guide book on Berlin that was in the library.

1 He's got bad cuts on each foot.
He's cut _____ his feet badly.

2 Did you eat all of the pizza?
Did you eat the _____ pizza?

3 Give every child a red crayon.
Give a red crayon to _____ child.

4 The club holds salsa nights on the 14ᵗʰ and 28ᵗʰ of each month.
The club holds salsa nights _____ two weeks.

5 What time are our other friends coming to the party?
What time are the _____ coming to the party?

3 ★★ **Choose the correct answers A–D.**

GRAND DESIGNS

Do you live on a housing estate, in a house that is identical to *D*? Perhaps you have an idea for a dream home? *Grand Designs* on Channel 4 tonight might give you just the right inspiration.

Nearly twenty years ago, Channel 4 broadcast the first in a series of programmes that is still continuing today. **1**___ episodes follow a person, or a couple, who have planned to build a house **2**___. Some people have a lot of money and can afford to build eye-catching, ambitious houses, but **3**___ are working on small budgets. What is important for the programme is that the people are passionate about their projects and that **4**___ one of the designs is unusual and clever.

The 140 episodes have covered a wide range of projects, ranging from the amazing restoration of a ruined castle to the construction of a house built from shipping containers on farmland with breathtaking views. **5**___ these new properties are smart houses, and also use environmentally-friendly materials. Could YOUR dream home become a reality on this programme?

	A each other	B the other's
	C one another	Ⓓ everyone else's
1	A Each	B Both
	C All	D Every
2	A for others	B themselves
	C both of them	D each other
3	A others	B the other
	C another	D the other ones
4	A all	B each
	C either	D both
5	A Both of	B Every
	C Each	D Many of

4 ★★★ **Complete the dialogues with one word in each gap.**

1 Andy: There are only two direct trains to Aberdeen on Saturday mornings – at 9 and 11 o'clock. Which one do you want to take?

Beth: I don't mind. *Both* of them sound OK.

Andy: The first train is usually packed, so let's take the _____ one.

2 Carmen: Good to be home at last.

Daniel: Didn't you enjoy your holiday?

Carmen: The en suite room was great, but ᵃthe _____ experience was a bit disappointing. The brochure promised exciting activities ᵇ_____ day, but in fact, I spent a lot time by the outdoor pool, doing nothing.

3 Eddy: Before I hand in my assignments, I usually ask Lucy to check them for mistakes and I do the same with her essays in return.

Mia: It's a fantastic idea for friends to correct each _____ work.

4 Hannah: Isaak finished his grilled cheese sandwich in two minutes and asked if he could have _____ one.

George: He must have been starving!

5 ★ **Complete the sentences with the correct form of the verbs in brackets.**

On my last flight, the flight assistant asked everyone ᵃ*to pay* (pay) more attention to the safety instructions. She didn't even let my younger brother ᵇ*play* (play) a game on his mobile.

1 I turned the key and tried ᵃ_____ (start) the engine, but nothing happened. I wasn't surprised. After all, nobody ᵇ_____ (drive) the car for a few months.

2 Hearing about wars, economic crises, and natural disasters made Wayne ᵃ_____ (feel) so depressed that he stopped ᵇ_____ (watch) the news last week.

3 A few months ago my grandparents decided ᵃ_____ (go) on a trip around Europe. This time next week they ᵇ_____ (stay) in a chalet in the Swiss Alps.

4 Lily and Jack love ᵃ_____ (be) the centre of attention. They ᵇ_____ (always / talk) about their lives.

5 In some countries, anyone ᵃ_____ (enter) an airport has to go through security control, not just passengers ᵇ_____ (depart) from it.

6 ★ ★ **Complete the reviews with one word in each gap.**

YOUR COMMENTS

When we arrived at the B&B, the hosts welcomed us and showed us around. They were so friendly that they made everyone feel at *ease*. Thank you so much, Andy and Harriet!

1 The cottage is set in the picturesque English countryside as advertised, but there was no ᵃ_____ water for a day of our stay. We had to use a hand pump to get water for cooking or washing, ᵇ_____ was a major inconvenience!

2 The flat we stayed in had every household ᵃ_____ you can think of, including a dishwasher and a tumble dryer. It would have been useful to have ᵇ_____ chair in the living room, though. One wasn't enough for the two of us.

3 I fell in love with the town at first sight. I grew up in a similar place, where everything was within ᵃ_____ distance. We didn't even ᵇ_____ to have a car in those days.

4 I highly recommend Josh, ᵃ_____ was our guide last weekend. You'll ᵇ_____ with laughter when you hear his jokes about famous historical figures.

5 The restaurant had a fantastic waterfront location, but we were bitterly ᵃ_____ when the food arrived. We ordered two main dishes and ᵇ_____ was tasty! We left hungry and angry!

7 ★ ★ **Complete the text with the correct form of the words in the box. There are two extra words.**

bitter   equal   health   ~~important~~
notify   other   permit   require

The first months are difficult

Going to university is one of the most *important* events in any young person's life. You rent a room in a different city and, suddenly, you don't have to ask your parents for ¹_____ to do anything anymore. You can go out every night if you want. With dozens of welcome parties for new and exchange students, the first months on campus are particularly busy.

During this time many young people realise that it's difficult to lead a ²_____ lifestyle. Some can't believe that their favourite dish takes more than an hour to make. ³_____ don't want to waste their time in the kitchen. Fast food becomes an attractive alternative and you end up eating it, even though you know it's not good for you.

Luckily, after a few months, things slow down and most students begin to focus on their coursework. If you don't start thinking about your exams in advance and do really badly, you might receive a letter ⁴_____ you that you won't be able to return to the university next year.

Having fun and passing exams are ⁵_____ important in the first year of university. Still, it's useful to remember that you're less likely to be kicked out if you spend some time in the library.

8 ★ ★ ★ **Complete the second sentence so that it has a similar meaning to the first. Use no more than six words, including the word in capitals.**

I haven't got enough money to go to the concert.
CAN'T
I *can't afford to go* to the concert.

1 I tested Anna and she tested me on the new vocabulary.
OTHER
Anna and I _____ on the new vocabulary.

2 Who did you respect most in your family when you were younger?
UP
Who did you _____ most in your family when you were younger?

3 There was an airport strike and many tourists couldn't fly to Spain this morning.
STOPPED
An airport strike _____ to Spain this morning.

4 Are flats more expensive now than last year?
WONDERING
I _____ more expensive now than last year.

5 There were no towels in the bathroom – I think this was strange for a four-star hotel.
FOUND
There were no towels in the bathroom, _____ strange for a four-star hotel.

6 Few people followed the expert's advice, as she didn't do what she advised others to do.
PREACHED
Few people followed the expert's advice, as she didn't really _____ .

WRITING

3.8

A 'for and against' essay

1 Read the model essay and tick the four topics that are mentioned.

1 public transport
2 crime rates
3 air pollution
4 employment and income
5 cultural and social life
6 affordable housing
7 social isolation
8 traffic problems

---

[1]

Since the industrial revolution began in the late 18th century the number of <u>city dwellers</u> has grown and <u>rural</u> populations have <u>shrunk</u>. Although this suggests that life in the city may be superior in some ways, there are definitely pros and cons to metropolitan living.

[2]

Perhaps the strongest argument for living in cities is that there are greater employment opportunities than in the country. **¹E_____** , salaries tend to be higher, meaning that city dwellers often have more <u>disposable income</u>. A **²f_____** benefit of city living is the numerous ways in which this income can be spent to <u>enrich</u> people's lives. For those who manage to achieve a healthy work-life balance, cities can provide a comparatively well-paid job which allows them to enjoy a variety of cultural and social experiences.

[3]   [4]

One of the most **³p_____** arguments against <u>urban</u> life is, ironically, the sense of isolation that living together with so many others can cause. Rural communities frequently enjoy a strong sense of togetherness, but <u>urbanites</u> often feel a lack of connection with others. It is impossible to form a relationship with all the people in a big city, so a common solution is to ignore the vast majority of them. This may also be related to another of the **⁴m_____** of city life, namely high crime rates.

[5]

All things **⁵c_____** , despite the fact that cities can be lonely and dangerous places to live, I feel the benefits outweigh the drawbacks. **⁶P_____** , I enjoy living in the city and wouldn't want to live in the country while I am still young.

[6]

2 Match the following definitions with the underlined words in the essay.

1 <u>*city dwellers*</u> & _____ people who live in cities
2 _____ relating to the city rather than the countryside
3 _____ relating to the countryside rather than the city
4 _____ have become smaller
5 _____ money to spend on non-essential things
6 _____ improve the quality of something

> **REMEMBER THIS**
>
> When used as nouns to mean 'the land that is outside towns and cities', the words *country* and *countryside* are synonyms and are always preceded by the definite article *the*.

3 Complete gaps 1–6 in the essay with the missing words. The first letters are given.

4 Replace the words in Exercise 3 with the words and phrases below.

Likewise   [1]
Another   [ ]
convincing   [ ]
On balance,   [ ]
As far as I'm concerned, [ ]
drawbacks   [ ]

5 Label the different sections (1–6) of the model essay in Exercise 1 using the descriptions below.

A a summarising statement   [5]
B a statement that mentions both sides of the issue [ ]
C arguments for the topic   [ ]
D a personal opinion   [ ]
E general or factual comments on the topic   [ ]
F arguments against the topic   [ ]

6 Underline two sentences which express concession in the model essay.

7 Choose the correct option to complete the sentences expressing concession.

1 *Although / Despite* there are numerous pluses to rural life, there are also considerable minuses.
2 *Even though / Despite* life in the country can be quiet, there is usually a strong sense of community in smaller villages.
3 For those who love the outdoors, there is plenty to do in the countryside *in spite of / although* the lack of clubs, galleries and cinemas.
4 *Although / Despite* the air is clean and the noise minimal, there is little entertainment in the country.
5 Finally, country life allows for clean and healthy living close to nature *despite / even though* the distance from the amenities of the city.

8 Read the task below. Then complete gaps 1–8 with the missing words. The first letters are given.

> Many people feel city centres should be pedestrian zones to improve the quality of life for people living there. Write a 'for and against' essay. Describe the advantages and disadvantages of having car-free city centres.

The idea of banning cars in cities is gaining popularity. Already, cities such as Copenhagen, Milan, Oslo and Madrid either have car-free centres or are working towards this goal. Even ¹t_____ there are several potential drawbacks to pedestrian city centres, there are also numerous benefits.

One of the strongest ²a_____ for pedestrian city centres is that they are far healthier and safer for everybody – the air is cleaner, noise pollution falls and there are fewer accidents. ³S_____ , banning cars encourages people to walk or cycle around the centre, so they get fitter. Yet another benefit is that shops and restaurants there attract more business, since it is easier and faster for people to get around and they are not stuck in endless traffic jams.

⁴D_____ clear advantages, there are also considerable disadvantages. The first drawback is that you need to create and maintain a reliable network of public transport that is cheap and efficient, and this requires serious funding. ⁵L_____ , building 'park and ride'* facilities outside a city centre is costly and only moves the traffic problem to the outskirts – which most residents have chosen precisely to avoid traffic issues. Another ⁶m_____ is that older people, the disabled and families with young children might struggle without a car.

On ⁷b_____ , there are pros and cons to having pedestrian city centres. ⁸P_____ , I feel that having some car-free zones which are bike and pedestrian-friendly are the best solution, but it is not practical or desirable to ban cars entirely.

'Park and ride' schemes aim to reduce urban traffic. Drivers leave their cars in car parks on the outskirts of a town or city and travel into the centre on public transport.

9 Read the task below. Before you start, note down some ideas and plan your essay. Include at least one sentence that expresses concession.

> Despite the fact that the number of city dwellers around the world is rising, many people prefer to live in the country. Write an essay to present arguments for and against living in the country, including examples and your own opinion.

In my 'for and against' essay:

• I have started with a general statement or with facts about the issue.	☐
• in the first paragraph, I have mentioned both the benefits and drawbacks of the issue.	☐
• I have described the benefits of living in the country in one paragraph and its drawbacks in the next paragraph.	☐
• I have included additional comments and examples to support both aspects of the issue.	☐
• I have written at least one sentence which expresses concession, using *although, even though, despite* or *in spite of*.	☐
• I have included phrases which express comparison, e.g. *in the same way, similarly, equally* and *likewise*.	☐
• in the last paragraph, I have summarised both aspects of the issue and presented my opinion.	☐
• I have not used contractions (e.g. *I'm, aren't, that's*).	☐
• I have checked my spelling and punctuation.	☐
• my handwriting is neat enough for someone else to read.	☐

VOCABULARY AND GRAMMAR

1 Complete the sentences with the correct adjectives. The first letters are given.

During the festival this **p**_icturesque_ village attracts many tourists.

1 They're planning a new **h**_____ development here. There will be more homes and a shopping centre.

2 At night, there is a **v**_____ atmosphere in the harbour. It's filled with colour and noise.

3 You can visit the **m**_____ castle in the old centre. Although it was built around 1450, it is still in good condition.

4 Every Tuesday and Saturday, there is a **b**_____ market in the village, where you can buy food and clothes.

5 If the village is beautiful, the **s**_____ around is even more so – the rolling hills and, in the far distance, the mountains.

/5

2 Complete the text with the correct prepositions.

If you're looking for a great place to visit on holiday, then come to Eyemouth, a small town _on_ the border between Scotland and England. It's ¹_____ the coast, and one of the best places to stay is at the Beach Palace Hotel, which offers excellent views of the harbour and is within 100 metres ²_____ the beach. If you don't fancy the beach, the hotel is also ³_____ easy reach of the city centre. ⁴_____ the town centre, you'll find narrow cobbled streets and many traditional buildings. To find the hotel, turn right ⁵_____ the roundabout near the town hall and follow the road towards the harbour.

/5

3 Choose the correct answers A–C.

Is there any _B_ parking where you live?

1 Noise ___ is a big problem in the city centre. Many people don't want to live there for that reason.

2 We used to live in the city centre, but we recently moved to a house on the ___ of town.

3 Although the city now is mostly modern buildings, the centre still has some beautiful ___ architecture which dates back to the 14th century.

4 My daily ___ to the office takes about 40 minutes. I drive to the station and then catch a train into the city centre.

5 Ibiza is known for its ___ nightlife, and many world famous DJs come to the island to work in the clubs.

	A	B	C
	A off-side	Ⓑ on-street	C by-road
1	A pollution	B nuisance	C disturbance
2	A outside	B outskirts	C outdoor
3	A medieval	B ancient	C Middle Ages
4	A trip	B travel	C commute
5	A busy	B quaint	C vibrant

/5

4 Complete the sentences with the Future Continuous, Future Perfect Simple, or Future Perfect Continuous forms of the verbs in brackets.

By the end of next year our local authorities _will have built_ (build) over 100 new houses for the community.

1 The garden is a real mess so Tom's going to deal with it tomorrow, starting at 9 a.m. By lunchtime, he _____ (work) in the garden for over 3 hours.

2 I feel really excited about going on holiday. In a few weeks' time I _____ (enjoy) long walks on the beach.

3 My family has lived in this house for generations. By the end of next year, my family _____ (own) the property for exactly 150 years.

4 We're getting a new carpet. At this time tomorrow, they _____ (fit) it in my bedroom. I can't wait to see it!

5 We're off on holiday tomorrow morning. By 7 p.m. tomorrow evening, we _____ (arrive) at the hotel if the flight is on time.

/5

5 Complete the sentences with the words in the box. There are two extra words.

> any ~~couple~~ deal either
> neither no none plenty

Only a _couple_ of Sarah's friends knew why she was moving house.

1 I'd be happy to live in _____ of the flats because they're both in good condition and the right location.

2 I'm afraid _____ pets are allowed in this tower block.

3 As far as I know, _____ of the houses in the new development have more than three bedrooms.

4 The house is in a great location, but it needs a great _____ of work before we can live in it.

5 Madrid is famous for its squares. There are _____ of them, so you can always find somewhere to sit and enjoy the sunshine.

/5

6 Choose the correct option.

Have you heard that the Wards bought _every_ / _each_ / _either_ of their five children a house?

1 Very _few_ / _several_ / _most_ of our neighbours are originally from this town. Most have moved here in the past five years.

2 In our street, people are proud of their small front gardens – you can tell as _all_ / _either_ / _every_ one of them is well kept.

3 Out of the five students, only two managed to get a place in halls of residence. I don't know if _another_ / _others_ / _the others_ have found somewhere to live yet.

4 I spent _the whole_ / _all the_ / _a couple of_ day sorting my bedroom out, but it was worth it as it looks amazing now!

5 I've looked at so many cookery magazines for recipes that I'm not sure if I can be bothered to read _another_ / _other_ / _no_ one.

/5

Total /30

7 Complete the sentences using the prompts in brackets. Do not change the order of the words. Change the forms or add new words where necessary. Use up to six words in each gap.

I don't think we'll have any problem finding a new house, as *there are plenty of houses* (there/plenty/ house) on the market at the moment.

1 The architects say they _____ _____ (finish/housing development) soon, most likely by the end of the month.

2 I can't believe it – _____ (spite/remind) them three times to buy bread at the supermarket, they still forgot!

3 The builders _____ (build/garage) while we are away on holiday next week.

4 Katia _____ (teach/children) for over thirty years when she retires next month.

5 I've had a clear-out and given away _____ _____ (deal/stuff) so the house is looking much better.

/5

8 Complete each pair of sentences with the same word.

Are there any underground car *parks* near here where I can leave the car?
The hundred largest public *parks* in the UK cover an area equivalent to almost 56,000 football pitches!

1 My _____ town is Manchester, which is where I was born and where I still live.
We live in Madrid, but we have a second _____ on the coast where we spend every summer.

2 Ella is always very _____ . She's never let me down in the past.
I bought a car because there isn't a _____ network of buses where I live.

3 The old cottage didn't have _____ water, so we couldn't have a shower.
I go _____ as a way to get rid of stress. Maybe I'll do a marathon one of these days.

4 In the school holidays, our parents let us run _____ as long as we were home for meals.
You can't get out of the vehicle during the safari, as there will be _____ animals around.

5 There are four people in our _____ , my parents, my sister and me.
When we move, we'll need to buy some _____ appliances, such as a new fridge.

/5

9 Complete the second sentence so that it has a similar meaning to the first. Use the words in capitals.

Although the bigger flat was expensive, we bought it because it was in the right location. **OF**
We bought *the bigger flat in spite of* the cost, because it was in the right location.

1 The burglar won't be here any more when the police arrive. **ESCAPED**
By the time the police arrive, the burglar _____.

2 This house might be worth buying, but other houses had no potential. **OTHERS**
This house might be worth buying, but _____ had no potential.

3 We are moving to our new house on Monday next week. **LIVING**
We _____ in our new house next week.

4 Ruth gave me some ideas on how to go about finding good places to stay in Wales. **COUPLE**
Ruth gave me _____ on how to go about finding good places to stay in Wales.

5 I think both dark red and deep blue would work well. **EITHER**
I like both dark red and deep blue. I think _____ would work well.

/5

10 Complete the text with one word in each gap.

Books, books, books

Sitting down with a good book is second *nature* to me – I'd far rather be immersed in a great story than watch TV. It's true that reading is not everyone's [1]_____ of tea, but it is mine! That's why I love the picturesque town of Hay-on-Wye – it's somewhere all book lovers should visit! It's [2]_____ the border of England and Wales, and it's famous for having nearly 40 second-hand and antiquarian bookshops. Apart from bookshops specialising in particular fields and those offering more general stock, there are a [3]_____ of other places full of books, including pubs, a fire station and a cinema.

What's more, every May and June, thousands of book lovers gather in Hay-on-Wye to take part in the Hay Festival, during which all the streets and parks become a giant reading site. [4]_____ reason to go is the opportunity to meet authors and listen to readings and lectures.

It's also amazing that with advancements in technology and many more people now reading e-books, the town still attracts those who prefer paper versions. Soon, I'll [5]_____ been visiting Hay-on-Wye every May for over twenty years, and I hope I'll be visiting for many years to come.

/5

Total   /20

Homesharing

Is living with a flatmate only for university students and young people? In these expensive times, more and more people are seeking alternative ways to live. Two readers share their views on an innovative new way of cutting costs and living life to the fullest.

Daphne

There's no denying it, I've somehow become an old lady, but I'm not one to sit around complaining. I have a wonderful life and adore being independent, nonetheless I have to admit I'm getting a bit old to live alone. My house is my sanctuary and I have no intention of moving out, so I'm extremely happy to have found the perfect solution. I first came across homesharing when I read an article in an online newspaper about the high cost of renting in London. A reader had commented about homesharing being a cheaper alternative and I was intrigued. How it works is, anyone with a spare room can advertise it at an affordable price on a special website. People can apply to move in, but have to offer something in return for the cheap rent. They can do housework, cooking, shopping or simply spend time with the homeowner. It's really easy to organise, as there are a number of online platforms that match you to a suitable housemate, almost like online dating! Anyway, I decided it was a great option for me, and within a few months Beatrice was here. Bea is a nineteen-year-old student studying fashion and she's fabulous. Although there are almost seventy years between us, we have a very similar sense of style and she even borrows my hats and handbags for her shows. She's definitely a free spirit and we often find ourselves roaring with laughter. She is always willing to help me, but understands she also has to respect my opinions, despite my age. I'm very strong-willed and I don't want Bea to do everything for me. We do our shopping online, but I do all the cooking. Bea tends to do most of the cleaning, though to be honest, we don't make that much mess.

Beatrice

Daphne is larger than life! I hope I'm as kind-hearted and witty as she is when I'm older. As soon as I met her, she made me feel completely at ease, and I knew I'd made the right decision. Previously I was living in a tiny, self-contained flat, but it was so far away from my university my daily commute was almost two hours long. I think I would have been lonely living alone, except I was never there. I was either studying or on the train. I do enjoy my own company, but I like being around other people too. Daphne lives in a beautiful townhouse on a quaint backstreet, quite unusual in central London. It has roses in the garden and ivy growing all over the walls. It's quite big and I was sure it would be draughty, but inside it's so cosy and unique. It's full of interesting mementos and artefacts from Daphne's life. Photographs of her family, maps of the countries she's visited, paintings that she has created. Everywhere you look there is something that tells a part of her story. Homesharing has really changed my life. I've learnt to slow down and enjoy living in the moment with Daphne. It might not be everyone's cup of tea, but for me it's the perfect solution to being alone in a big city without much money. My life is so much richer now.

1 Read the text on page 50. For questions 1–5, choose the correct answer A–D.

1 How did Daphne feel about her living situation before she met Beatrice?
 A She planned to move out of her home even though she loved living there.
 B She was determined to stay in her home.
 C She felt she was too old to find a solution by herself.
 D She was uncertain she'd enjoy living with a flatmate.

2 Why does Daphne compare homesharing to online dating?
 A Because she had to read a lot of profiles before finding the perfect flatmate.
 B Because homesharing is only available to people who use the Internet.
 C Because the website is easy to use.
 D Because the website selects appropriate people for you.

3 What is the arrangement between Daphne and Beatrice?
 A Beatrice makes Daphne laugh and keeps her in a good mood.
 B Beatrice does the online shopping and Daphne cooks.
 C Daphne does the cooking and Beatrice does the cleaning.
 D Beatrice doesn't do anything for Daphne.

4 What problems did Beatrice have with her previous flat?
 A It was too far away from her university.
 B She was lonely living by herself.
 C The flat was too small for her.
 D The rent was too expensive.

5 How does Beatrice feel about homesharing?
 A It's not her cup of tea.
 B It benefits the homeowners the most.
 C She takes more pleasure in the present moment.
 D The pace of life living in a homeshare is too slow.

2 Read each text and put a cross (X) by the missing phrase.

1 Flatmate required! We're looking for a fun-loving but responsible student to move into our shared flat in a modern tower block in Manchester. The available room is small but has an ensuite bathroom and a great view of the local park. The kitchen is shared between four housemates and we split the cooking and cleaning. _____ , call 011 444 792.

 A To meet the requirements ☐
 B To find out more ☐
 C To look for a flat ☐

2 To avoid accidents it's essential to _____ . Recently there have been a number of accidents caused by people staring at their mobile phones instead of looking where they are going.

 A have a hairy moment ☐
 B keep your wits about you ☐
 C be second nature ☐

3 There have been many studies conducted with the aim of discovering if personality is fixed from birth, with recent research suggesting that it's _____ to adapt. As they age, some individuals are even able to change and acquire traits that they consider to be particularly attractive.

 A highly possible ☐
 B equally important ☐
 C quite the opposite ☐

WRITING

3 Read the writing task and write an article.

Have you spent time studying abroad? Or maybe you know someone from another country who has come to your town or city to study? If so, we want to hear from you. We are looking for articles to publish on our website about the difficulties of studying abroad and how to overcome those problems. A selection of the best articles will be published next month.

4 Shopping around

VOCABULARY

4.1

Shopping • phrasal verbs
• shopping collocations
• verb phrases

SHOW WHAT YOU KNOW

1 Complete each gap with one word. The first letters are given.

SHOP SHOP SHOP!

What are your best and worst shopping habits? Tell us about them below!

If the p*rice* is low, I'll buy it, even if I don't need it. I can't resist a ¹b_____ ! I love going to the ²s_____ to see what I can ³p_____ up! I can never save any money.
@Sam23

I'm good with money. I look for things that are on ⁴s_____ offer and I go to ⁵c_____ shops too. You can find brilliant second-hand stuff there. When it comes to shoes and boots I think it's worth paying a bit more – that way you can get something that's good ⁶q_____ that will ⁷l_____ for ages.
@shoppingboy

I'm not bothered by ⁸f_____ . Who cares about being on trend? I have my own style. I love stuff from years ago, so I go to ⁹v_____ shops. You can get great ¹⁰d_____ clothes in the best ones!
@old_style

I know it's superficial, but I buy things for the ¹¹b_____ – I think people look at labels. Sometimes I manage to wait until things are ¹²r_____ so I don't spend so much, but not always.
@Alex929

WORD STORE 4A | Phrasal verbs

2 Complete the phrasal verbs in the sentences with the correct particles.

Emily checked *up* on the best online sites before she bought anything.

1 Don't just buy something in the first place you go to; shop _____ a bit and make sure you get the best price.

2 Katia is going to a wedding next month, so she's looking _____ for some red shoes to go with her outfit.

3 We spend loads on eating out in restaurants. We've got to cut _____ on the amount we spend.

4 I ordered some shoes online, but they're too small so I'm going to send them _____ and get a refund.

5 They hadn't been into the town centre for a while, but when they went they saw that two new clothes shops had sprung _____ on the same street.

6 Matt wasn't sure if he wanted the suit, so the shop assistant agreed to put it _____ for 24 hours to give him time to think about it.

7 Maxine is always happy to pay _____ for expensive sunglasses – I definitely wouldn't spend that much on them!

---

3 Complete the advice with five of the phrasal verbs in Exercise 2. Change the form if necessary.

shopsafely.co.uk

Free advice for careful consumers

Mobile phones

If you are going to *pay out* for an expensive new phone, first ¹_____ on the manufacturer's plans – they may be bringing out a new model soon. You should also ²_____ , as prices vary between companies and your phone might be on special offer somewhere. Before you sign a contract for a new phone plan, ³_____ any potential disadvantages, for example, do you have to stay with the same company for a year or longer? Could you get a cheaper deal if you ⁴_____ the number of messages you send? Finally, remember you can also look online for special offers. If you don't like the phone when it arrives, then ⁵_____ it _____ immediately – the longer you wait, the more likely you will end up having to keep a phone you're not keen on.

WORD STORE 4B | Shopping collocations

4 Match the words in boxes A and B to make collocations. Then complete the definitions.

A | bargain chain ethical impulse local ~~mass-produced~~ online responsible

B | attitude brands prices ~~products~~ purchases shopping store values

things that are made cheaply and in big quantities using machines *mass-produced products*

1 things that you buy without planning to _____

2 one of a group of shops owned by the same company _____

3 buying things from websites _____

4 when the cost of something is less than usual, or very low _____

5 morally correct beliefs about what is right and wrong _____

6 products made in a particular region or area _____

7 when your approach to things is sensible and can be trusted _____

5 Complete the interview with the collocations in Exercise 4.

A: Can I ask you some questions about shopping?
B: Sure.
A: Firstly, do you think it's important to support brands that promote _ethical values_?
B: Definitely. That's why I always buy Fair Trade products – they're environmentally friendly.
A: What about ¹_____ ? Are there any businesses from round here that sell products made in this area?
B: I don't know of any. We mostly have high-street shops, you know, the usual ²_____ . That's why I think ³_____ is so great. There are lots of websites where you can buy cool stuff.
A: But don't you think the Internet encourages ⁴_____ ? I mean, you just have to click and that's it. It's so easy to buy things you weren't intending to.
B: I guess so. I mean, I've definitely bought things I hadn't meant to.
A: Where do you shop for ⁵_____ ?
B: I think you get the best deals online, too. I don't do much shopping in town. The only things you can get there are the ⁶_____ that everyone buys. If you want something more individual, then you have to shop on the Internet.
A: Would you say you have a ⁷_____ to shopping and buying things?
B: I'd like to think so. I don't shop just because I've got money to spend, I buy stuff that I need, rather than things I happen to want.

WORD STORE 4C | Verb phrases

6 Choose A, B or C to complete the sentences.

I'm saving up for my holiday, so I _A_ on a limited budget at the moment.
(A) am   B have   C put

1 When you're ready to pay, ___ your PIN in the machine.
  A type   B enter   C give
2 Some shops ___ a bad reputation, but actually they're pretty good.
  A give   B do   C have
3 You've worked really hard. You should ___ yourself to something nice. It doesn't have to be expensive!
  A pay   B give   C treat
4 There's a great market here on Sunday mornings. It's a brilliant place to ___ bargain-hunting.
  A find   B look   C go
5 It's important to ___ local producers, so I tend to avoid shopping in supermarkets and chain stores.
  A support   B spend   C buy

REMEMBER BETTER

On a separate piece of paper, make a list in English of products or services that you have paid for that fit the categories below. Look at the list later or tomorrow and see if you can remember what the categories were.

A product/service that you got for **a bargain price**.
A product/service that you **paid out** for.
A product/service you **shopped around** for.
A product/service which you found through **online shopping**.
A product/service that you got in **a chain store**.
A product that was **an impulse purchase**.

7 Read the text and complete each gap with one word.

ECO SHOP

| Home | Our story | Products | Promotion | Contact |

OUR STORY

Eco Shop is for people who have a responsible _attitude_ to the planet.

Everything we sell is organic, recycled and environmentally friendly. Shoppers love our ethical ¹_____ ! Buying from our organic range can help you cut ²_____ on the damage you do to the planet. Helping people to reduce this is one of our aims.

We also sell arts and crafts made by people from our area because we believe in ³_____ local producers. All these items are hand-made, they are not ⁴_____ products created in their thousands.

We started our online shop in 2015 and it has been a huge success. We have a guaranteed returns policy – we believe you should be able to send something ⁵_____ for up to 30 days after a purchase if you don't like it. You can also cancel an order up to six hours after it has been made. After all, who hasn't made an ⁶_____ purchase and regretted it later?

Eco Shop prices are very competitive, so if you have a limited ⁷_____ , ours is the website for you. We also understand you may wish to ⁸_____ around. If you find the same item cheaper on another website, we'll refund the difference! It hasn't happened yet because we usually have fantastic, ⁹_____ prices!

We also offer luxury items – why not treat ¹⁰_____ to some hand-made body lotion or soap or one of our fabulous organic cotton or silk shirts?

/10

53

SHOW WHAT YOU KNOW

1 Complete the question tags and reply questions with the correct pronoun.

I am your best friend, aren't _I_ ?

1 You aren't well, are _____ ?
2 Dad is coming, isn't _____ ?
3 Stella and George weren't happy, were _____ ?
4 A: We want to go shopping.
   B: Do _____ ?
5 A: The supermarket was closed.
   B: Was _____ ?
6 A: You and I are going to have a serious talk.
   B: Are _____ ?

2 ★ **Match statements 1–6 to the appropriate reply questions a–g.**

I love your new jeans.   (g)
1 Kelly wanted to come shopping too.   ( )
2 Leo has his haircut every three weeks.   ( )
3 Fran was late again.   ( )
4 The girls have all bought new sports gear.   ( )
5 Mike and Marta are coming for dinner.   ( )
6 It snowed half a metre here yesterday.   ( )

a Does he?   d Did she?   f Have they?
b Was she?   e Did it?   g Do you?
c Are they?

3 ★★ **Choose the correct auxiliary verb to complete each question tag. Then add an appropriate reply question.**

A: We can pay by credit card, _can_ /_can't_ we? I don't have enough cash on me.
B: _Don't you_ ? I've got some cash, so don't worry.
1 A: This isn't going to be enough money for a burger, ᵃ_is_ / _isn't_ it? I'll have a hot dog instead.
   B: ᵇ_____ ? Actually, that's a good idea. Make it two.
2 A: The players were tired, ᵃ_were_ / _weren't_ they? They were really slow in the second half.
   B: ᵇ_____ ? I must say I didn't notice.
3 A: You won't be late, ᵃ_will_ / _won't_ you? The Smiths are arriving at 5 o'clock.
   B: ᵇ_____ ? Oh goodness. OK, I'll try to leave early.
4 A: I haven't been picked for Saturday's team, ᵃ_have_ / _haven't_ I? That's it! I'm not coming to the training sessions anymore.
   B: ᵇ_____ ? Then you'll never be picked.
5 A: They will pay their share, ᵃ_won't_ / _aren't_ they? I can't afford to pay for everyone.
   B: ᵇ_____ ? I thought your dad gave you loads of money for Christmas.

4 ★★★ **Complete the tags with the appropriate auxiliary verbs, then use them in the dialogues.**

a Don't forget them, _will_ you?
b Let's just go, _____ we?
c Nothing bad happened, _____ it?
d That's Mandy's brother, _____ it?
e You do realise that it won't make much difference, _____ you?
f Everybody enjoyed it, _____ they?
g That's a little bit dramatic, _____ it?

Sasha: Ralph, are you going to bring those reusable shopping bags? ___*a*___ I don't want to be responsible for filling the world with plastic shopping bags.
Ralph: OK, OK, got them. ¹_____ There's so much unnecessary packaging in our shopping anyway that a couple of plastic bags fewer won't change much.
Sasha: Ralph, it's that kind of attitude that will lead to the extinction of the human race.
Ralph: ²_____ , Sasha?
Sasha: ³_____ , Ralph?

Mum: How was the party, Adam? ⁴_____
Adam: Yeah, I think so. Well, nearly everybody. Elliot left early.
Mum: Did he? Elliot? ⁵_____
Adam: Yep, the elder one. He was fine at first and then suddenly he apologised, said he wasn't really in a party mood and left.
Mum: Did he? Why? ⁶_____
Adam: Not really. I don't think he was too happy that Emma and I were dancing together.
Mum: Ah-ha! Oh, poor Elliot. Young hearts break so easily. So Emma, huh?
Adam: Er … yeah, well I guess I should be getting on with my homework now, Mum.
Mum: Should you? Well, that's the first time I've ever heard you say that, Adam.

SHOW WHAT YOU'VE LEARNT

5 Find and correct the mistakes.

She won't buy anything that doesn't cost a fortune, ~~won't~~ she?   _will_
1 The pizza's ready. Take it out of the oven, do you? Sorry to ask, but I've got my hands full.   _____
2 Don't get ripped off, do you?   _____
3 Let's withdraw another 100 euros, will we?   _____
4 Nothing broke when you dropped your bag, was it?   _____
5 A: They're going to splash out on a new car.
   B: Will they?   _____
6 That's Ella over there, isn't she?   _____

/6

GRAMMAR: Train and Try Again page 174

1 Choose A, B or C to complete the extract of the interview with Martin.

Extract from Student's Book recording 🔊 **2.20**

I: So, what kind of things do you get?

M: Well, there's an element ¹__ chance when you buy a suitcase ²__ you can't look inside before you bid for it. The better the suitcase, ³__ more likely you are to find designer clothes. But you could be very unlucky with a high-quality bag and just find dirty socks – that's the chance you ⁴__ . Luckily, the auctioneers open the bags and throw ⁵__ anything horrible like food that's gone off or wet stuff that's gone mouldy. When you buy suitcases, you just get clothes. They take ⁶__ electrical goods and shoes and they sell ⁷__ in separate lots.

I: […] It's really surprising how many bags get lost!

1 A of	B in	C to
2 A though	B that	C as
3 A how	B the	C it's
4 A have	B get	C take
5 A away	B up	C down
6 A off	B out	C over
7 A it	B those	C to

REMEMBER THIS

The noun *chance* can be used to describe:

The possibility that something will happen, especially something you want, e.g.
There's an element of chance when you buy a suitcase.
There's a good chance the contents will be valuable.

An opportunity to do something, e.g.
I haven't had the chance to look in the suitcase yet.
He missed the chance to make a lot of money.

2 Read REMEMBER THIS. Complete the collocations using the words in the box.

even   half   ~~high~~   jump   lifetime   million
slim   stand   take

Chance (possibility)

a *high* /**strong chance** – something is very likely to happen
an ¹_____ /**50-50 chance** – an equal chance that something will or won't happen
a ²_____ /**remote chance** – something is not very likely to happen
a **one in a** ³_____ **chance** – something is extremely unlikely to happen
sb doesn't ⁴_____ **a chance (of + -ing)** – it is not possible that sb will be able to do something
sb is in with a chance (of + -ing) – it is possible that sb will be able to do something

Chance (opportunity)

⁵_____ **a chance** – accept an opportunity
⁶_____ **at a chance** – eagerly take an opportunity
the chance of a ⁷_____ – a chance that sb will probably never have again
now's your chance – you have the opportunity to do something right now
given ⁸_____ **a chance** – if there is any opportunity to do something

3 Complete the sentences with words and phrases in Exercise 2. Change the form if necessary.

Both the mother and the father have blonde hair so there is a *high* chance the child will be fair too.

1 Make sure you lock the food away. _____ chance, bears will enter the campsite and eat whatever they can find.

2 The Jamaican skier _____ a chance of winning a medal, but he seems to be enjoying the event.

3 You could win millions! Don't miss _____ . Enter our competition right now.

4 Look, you said you wanted to talk to her. Well, there she is. _____ chance.

5 Claire _____ the chance to earn some extra cash babysitting for her neighbours.

6 Don't worry, there's only _____ chance that something will go wrong. You'll be fine.

7 There are only five kilometres to go in the race and Herriot is definitely _____ a chance of winning if he keeps running at this pace.

8 We'd like to _____ this chance to thank you for everything you've done to help the orphanage.

WORD STORE 4D | Noun phrases

4 Complete the sentences with the words in the box.

~~bag~~   belongings   goods   house
market   property   sale   stall

Have you ever lost a checked *bag* when you've flown somewhere?

1 Every Sunday morning there is a flea _____ near my house that sells second-hand clothes and furniture.

2 Do you know a good auction _____ ? We're considering selling some paintings and looking for recommendations.

3 If you can't find your coat, you should check in lost _____ . That's where everything people have left behind is put.

4 My aunt and uncle have a market _____ where they sell some of the cheese, fruit and vegetables that they produce on their farm.

5 Go early if you want to find the best things at a car boot _____ – or go at the end to get a bargain.

6 I don't have a problem with pre-owned _____ , I rarely buy new things. Almost everything I own has had a previous life somewhere!

7 When you leave the train, be sure to take all your personal _____ with you.

1 **Read texts A–C quickly and choose the best title for each text.**

1 Money to burn?
2 Can I pay with plastic?
3 Have you got change for £100 million?

Text A

In Britain today, there are around three billion banknotes in circulation worth over 58 billion pounds. In 2013 alone, the Bank of England **issued** 760 million new banknotes and **destroyed** 845 million old ones. As well as the £5, £10, £20 and £50 notes commonly found in the nation's wallets and purses, there are just over 4,000 £1m and £100m notes – known as Giants and Titans – not in circulation, with a value of around £8bn. These are used internally by banks and are not legal tender*. Nevertheless, they are carefully locked away.

Text B

The average paper banknote in Britain lasts around 6 months before it becomes damaged or worn and must be removed from circulation. In the UK, old notes used to be burnt, but in a move to be greener, the majority are now **shredded**, **compacted** and then used with other organic materials to **manufacture** agricultural compost. Between 1988 and 1992 at the site where this shredding takes place, £600,000 worth of notes that were intended for destruction were stolen by three couples who worked there. The couples managed to **sidestep** security controls and remove the notes from the site by **concealing** them in their underwear.

Text C

Paper money will soon be a thing of the past in Britain as the Bank of England introduced plastic banknotes from 2016. Australia was the first country to go plastic in 1988, and more than 20 other countries including New Zealand, Mexico and Canada have since **switched**. Plastic notes are highly durable*, lasting for around two years, or four times longer than the average paper note. Crucially*, plastic money is waterproof so it can survive washing machines, rainstorms and dips in the ocean. Although polymer notes are more expensive to produce, their durability makes them cheaper and more ecologically sound* over time.

2 **Match statements 1–4 with texts A–C. One text has two matching statements.**

1 Different countries make their banknotes out of different substances.
2 Not all banknotes are available to the general public.
3 Despite high production costs, new British banknotes will be more cost-efficient in the long run.
4 The way banknotes are disposed of has changed.

3 Read the texts again and answer the questions.

1. Which two texts mention specific amounts of money? ☐ & ☐
2. Which two texts mention environmental factors related to banknotes? ☐ & ☐
3. Which two texts mention the destruction of old banknotes? ☐ & ☐
4. Which two texts mention issues related to the security of banknotes? ☐ & ☐
5. Which two texts mention banks? ☐ & ☐
6. Which two texts mention the average lifespan of paper banknotes in the UK? ☐ & ☐
7. Which is the only text to mention the future? ☐

4 Underline the answers to the following questions in the texts.

1. In which country were plastic banknotes first used?
2. How are Giants and Titans kept secure?
3. What makes plastic banknotes more environmentally friendly than paper ones?
4. For how long is the average British banknote in circulation?
5. What do old banknotes in the UK eventually become?
6. What is the largest amount of money mentioned in the three texts?

5 Complete the definitions with the base forms of the verbs in bold in texts A, B and C.

to damage something so badly that it no longer exists, or cannot be used or repaired – _destroy_

1. to cut or tear something into small, thin pieces e.g. paper, meat or cabbage – _____
2. to hide something carefully – _____
3. to change from doing or using one thing to doing or using another – _____
4. to officially produce something such as new stamps, notes, passports or visas – _____
5. to press something together so that it becomes smaller or more solid – _____
6. to use machines to make goods or materials, usually in large numbers or amounts – _____
7. to avoid dealing with something difficult – _____

6 Complete the sentences with the verbs in Exercise 5. Change the form if necessary.

Many of Port-au-Prince's major buildings were _destroyed_ in the earthquake that struck Haiti in 2010.

1. This salad is easy to make – first _____ the cabbage, then add tomatoes, feta cheese and olive oil.
2. This year the Post Office is _____ Christmas stamps featuring pictures of snowflakes taken under a microscope.
3. This incredible scrapyard machine can _____ a car into a cube that measures just 1m³.
4. The tiny town of Qiaotou in Eastern China _____ 60 percent of the world's buttons and 80 percent of its zips.
5. In my opinion, this company offers the best sports equipment – you will never convince me to _____ brands.
6. The Minister _____ any questions about him running for president in next year's election.
7. There are actually recorded cases of people attempting to escape from prison using tools that were sent to them _____ inside cakes.

VOCABULARY PRACTICE | Making and spending money

7 Look at the vocabulary in lesson 4.4 in the Student's Book. Complete the texts with the correct forms of the verbs in the box.

bid   come   fundraise   hold   ~~increase~~   make (x2)

Business consultant

Contact us if you want to expand your business. We'll show you ways to _increase_ your earnings and ¹_____ the profits you've always dreamed of.

Skills for Life

We are a charity that helps teenagers at risk learn new skills, and we need volunteers to help us ²_____ . All the money goes towards helping young people in need.

Mystery buyer

A mystery buyer recently paid over $2.2 million for a painting at an auction which ³_____ yesterday in New York. The buyer ⁴_____ for the painting by phone and art critics are speculating about their identity.

SUCCESS STORIES

The number of teenage entrepreneurs who have already ⁵_____ a fortune is rising. Many have become millionaires before the age of twenty, showing that young people have what it takes to build a business.

Sotheby's

We are one of the most exclusive and famous auction houses in the world. To find out what is ⁶_____ up for auction, please consult our website.

WORD STORE 4E | Being rich and poor

8 Complete the second sentence so that it means the same as the first. Use the word in capitals.

Simon's dad's got a lot of money. **WELL**
Simon's dad's _well-off_ .

1. Even though they've both got jobs, they never have enough money. **SHORT**
   Even though they've both got jobs, they're always _____ .
2. There is nothing more frustrating than wandering round the shops when you've got no money. **BROKE**
   There is nothing more frustrating than wandering round the shops when _____ .
3. Robert works 40 hours a week and still has only just enough money to buy the things he needs. **ENDS**
   Robert works 40 hours a week and still struggles to _____ .
4. £120 for a pair of sunglasses?! Can you afford to spend so much on things you don't need? **BURN**
   £120 for a pair of sunglasses?! Have you got _____ ?
5. They hardly have enough food and money to live on. **HAND**
   They're living _____ .
6. The Smiths are incredibly wealthy. **ROLLING**
   The Smiths _____ .
7. I've always wanted to be really rich. **LOADED**
   I've always wanted _____ .

GRAMMAR

4.5
Present and past modal structures

1 Choose the correct modal structure to complete the advice.

BEAR SAFETY

Hiking in Black Bear Country

Enjoy the mountains and stay safe with these tips:
1 Bears are wild animals and *should* / *shouldn't* always be treated with respect.
2 If a bear approaches you, you *need to* / *needn't* try and stay calm.
3 You *must* / *mustn't* run as this may cause the bear to chase you.
4 You *ought to* / *ought not to* approach the bear. Instead back away slowly and avoid eye contact.

2 ★ Cross out *to* where it is not necessary.

Everyone should ~~to~~ benefit from money made through the sale of our country's oil.
1 Improvements in education and healthcare need to compensate for the high taxes we are paying.
2 You'd better to avoid the dark backstreets late at night unless you want to get into trouble.
3 If you have a sensitive stomach, you ought not to eat hot chillies.
4 Visitors simply must to experience the vibrant nightlife of Rio during the week of the carnival.
5 With our affordable design ideas you needn't to spend a fortune to make your living room look stylish.
6 We ought to set off early in case there are traffic jams.

3 ★★ Rewrite regrets 1–5 using the modal structures in brackets.

Deathbed Regrets

A former nurse who looked after dying patients has listed the five most common deathbed regrets.
1 I wish I'd had the courage to live a life true to myself, not the life others expected of me.
2 I wish I hadn't worked so hard.
3 I wish I'd had the courage to express my feelings.
4 I wish I hadn't lost touch with my friends.
5 I wish I'd let myself be happier.

1 I *should have had* (should) the courage to live a life true to myself.
2 I _____ (ought/not) so hard.
3 I _____ (ought) the courage to express my feelings.
4 I _____ (should/not) with my friends.
5 I _____ (should) myself be happier.

4 ★★★ Complete the gapped sentences with appropriate modal structures so they have a similar meaning to the prompts.

Why did I bother buying a big bottle of water? Denise already had one.
I *needn't have bothered buying* a big bottle of water because Denise already had one.
1 Rod's luggage went missing, so it was necessary for him to go to the lost property office.
Rod's luggage went missing, so he _____ _____ to the lost property office.
2 Helen wishes she hadn't spent a fortune on a new phone. She found her old one down the back of the sofa.
Helen _____ on a new phone as she found her old one down the back of the sofa.
3 Luckily, someone handed in my wallet so it wasn't necessary to cancel my bank card.
I _____ my bank card because someone handed in my wallet.
4 Dad gave me his old ski goggles, so there was no need to bother wasting money on a new pair.
I _____ wasting money on a new pair of ski goggles because Dad gave me his old ones.
5 It would have been better not to spend so long shopping around as the first shop was the cheapest anyway.
We _____ so long shopping around as the first shop was the cheapest anyway.
6 We didn't bother dressing up smartly because it wasn't necessary. It was a very casual party.
We _____ dressing up smartly because it was a very casual party.

5 Choose the correct option.
1 Talent alone is not enough. Actors *need to have* / *needed to have* determination to make it in Hollywood.
2 Claire *needn't have walked* / *didn't have to walk* far before she found herself in a beautiful leafy neighbourhood.
3 Sarah *shouldn't have* / *didn't need to* put on a party two days before New Year's Eve. Hardly anyone came.
4 You *mustn't have* / *needn't have* bought milk. We like our coffee black.
5 You *ought not to have proposed* / *ought not to propose* a toast unless you know what you are going to say.
6 They *didn't need to* / *shouldn't* bother lighting candles or torches as the moonlight was so bright.

/6

GRAMMAR: Train and Try Again page 174

SPEAKING

Making and justifying choices

1 Translate the phrases into your own language.

SPEAKING BANK

Comparing and contrasting options

X (Going to the market) is …, but Y (shopping online) is …
_____
_____
_____

X is the only one/option that …
_____
_____

When you compare the two/X and Y …
_____
_____

It is (much) more likely that …
_____
_____

X is definitely the cheaper/better/more suitable choice.
_____
_____
_____

Choosing an option and justifying the choice

That's why I'd opt for X.
_____
_____

… and therefore, it's probably/clearly the best choice.
_____
_____
_____

The main/Another reason (why X would be my choice) is that …
_____
_____
_____

I prefer X mainly/simply because …
_____
_____

This option is (clearly) the most/least + adjective … because …
_____
_____
_____

Explaining reasons for rejecting other options

X might (require less effort), but I wouldn't choose it because …
_____
_____
_____

X isn't the best choice if you consider …
_____
_____

The reason I wouldn't go for/pick/choose X is because …
_____
_____
_____
_____

2 Put the words in order to complete the sentences.

only / is / option / that / the
X _is the only option that_ teenagers would identify with.

1 choice / is definitely / suitable / because / the more
X _____
it sells a wider range of goods.

2 why X / main / my choice / reason / would be
The _____
is because, as far as I'm concerned, the design is more eye-catching.

3 much / that / more / is / likely
It _____
young people would shop here.

4 the least / option / because / is clearly / suitable
This _____
it seems to be a store for children rather than young adults.

5 because / might be / but / choose it / cheaper / I wouldn't
X _____
it appears to be really poorly made.

6 choice / if / the best / you / isn't / consider
X _____
how long it will take to learn how to use it.

3 Complete the dialogues. The first letters are given.

1
James: Pizza or burger?
Karen: James, you just don't listen to me, do you?
James: What?
Karen: I told you I've decided to become a vegetarian.
James: Oh right, yes … And therefore …?
Karen: Therefore a burger probably isn't the best c_choice_.
James: Of course. So …?
Karen: So, pizza! That's why I'd ¹p_____ a pizza, James. You're so slow sometimes.

2
Pete: If I had a million euros, I'd buy a sports car.
Ryan: A sports car? Really? Sports cars are pretty common now, ²b_____ speed boats or yachts really turn heads.
Pete: Well, it's not about showing off. I'd prefer a sports car ³s_____ because it's far more practical. Imagine how quickly I could get to work every morning!
Ryan: Work? You already have a million euros in your pocket, remember?

3
Leila: Hey, Else. You look nice. Is that a new top? It's gorgeous.
Else: Thanks. Yeah, it is. I went shopping at the weekend. I love charity shops and second-hand shops.
Leila: Really? Well, I suppose it depends what you are looking for. There's a lot of rubbish, and they aren't always ⁴t_____ b_____ o_____ if you consider how long you need to spend going through all the clothes to find something worth having.
Else: Well, to be honest, that's exactly ⁵w_____ I'd o_____ f_____ shopping there. I love searching for bargains. I've found some great designer stuff for just a few pounds.

1 ★ **Complete the sentences with the missing prepositions.**

At my school, students are allowed <u>to</u> express their opinions freely.

1 Students are forbidden _____ using their mobile phones during the exams.

2 The bakery closes early if they manage _____ sell most of the goods.

3 Under 18s were banned _____ watching that movie as it was too violent.

4 I didn't succeed _____ persuading my parents to buy me a new pair of trainers.

5 You ought _____ save almost all the money you earn if you want to buy a second-hand car.

2 ★ ★ **Write the meaning that the underlined modal verb expresses** *(ability, obligation, probability, prohibition)*. **Then rewrite the sentence using the word in capitals.**

Students <u>may</u> call their teachers by their first name. *permission* **PERMITTED**
Students are permitted to call their teachers by their first name.

1 You <u>can</u> save up to 90 percent if you buy a train ticket in advance. _____ **LIKELY**

_____

2 Job applicants <u>should</u> tell the truth in their CVs. _____ **SUPPOSED**

_____

3 Sorry, but I <u>couldn't</u> withdraw any money from the bank yesterday. _____ **UNABLE**

_____

4 Students <u>may not</u> dye their hair bright colours. _____ **ALLOWED**

_____

3 ★ ★ **Choose the correct answers A–C.**

Sarah was <u>A</u> to take part in the auction because she wasn't 18.
Ⓐ forbidden   B allowed   C bound

1 Kelly is __ to run out of money if she doesn't start earning a salary soon.
   A unlikely   B certain   C required

2 If you have signed a contract, the company is __ to pay you as promised.
   A obliged   B permitted   C unlikely

3 The price of seafood is __ to rise as fish shortages increase.
   A required   B permitted   C sure

4 The bank is __ to lend you any more money until you pay your debts.
   A meant   B unable   C forbidden

5 We __ selling everything we advertised on eBay.
   A managed to   B succeeded in   C were able to

4 ★ ★ **Match the words in the box with the phrases in italics of a similar meaning.**

> aren't able to   bound   ~~forbidden~~   obliged
> permitted   supposed   unlikely

Family Finance Focus

How to survive ... your first car boot sale

Get there early. Sellers are often *banned* / *forbidden* from setting up after a certain time – usually very early in the morning!

1 Take some cash. Sellers are usually *required* / _____ to pay a small fee to the organisers.

2 Check what you can and can't sell. Rules differ. For example, sale of food is often not *allowed* / _____ .

3 Prepare plenty of change. You are *certain* / _____ to be presented with notes by customers.

4 Set realistic prices. It is *not probable* / _____ that customers will pay more than a few pounds for any single item.

5 Don't worry if you *don't manage to* / _____ sell everything – it's rare that anyone leaves with an empty car boot.

6 Don't take it too seriously – car boot sales are *meant* / _____ to be fun!

5 ★ ★ ★ **Complete the sentences using the prompts in brackets. Do not change the order of the words. Change the forms or add new words where necessary. Use between two and five words in each gap.**

We are sorry to inform passengers that, due to weather conditions, we <u>are unlikely to arrive</u> (unlikely/arrive) on time.

1 Patients _____ (ban/wear) outdoor shoes in the hospital building for a long time now.

2 Children under the age of 12 _____ (only/permit/use) the pool when accompanied by an adult.

3 Giant darts! Fun for all the family, folks! Win a pound for every target you _____ (succeed/hit).

4 New students _____ (require/report) to the registration office before 4 p.m. today.

5 _____ (sure/visit) the gift shop and buy a souvenir before you head home.

6 In the morning, the trains are so crowded that sometimes people _____ (unable/board) them.

6 ★ ★ Choose the correct answers A–D.

A good example

Most people _A_ that a 'social business' is a contradiction. Surely, a business ¹__ the owners and not society? However, there is now a ²__ of wonderful sandwich shops in Scotland which show that a business really can help society. It's called *Social Bite* and was launched by a couple, Josh Littlejohn and Alice Thompson in 2012, after Josh ³__ a Nobel Prize winner talking about using businesses to help solve social problems. *Social Bite* has an excellent menu designed by a top chef and serves delicious coffee and food for a good ⁴__ .

Now this is the part ⁵__ it gets interesting. Twenty-five percent of its employees used to be homeless and if the business makes ⁶__ , all the money goes to charity. In addition to this, customers can pay in advance for a meal for homeless people. At the moment, more than 100 homeless people receive a free meal every day through donations from customers. The owners have decided ⁷__ anyone, including managers, more than seven times the salary of the lowest paid worker. Perhaps more businesses ⁸__ follow this example.

(A) would think	B thinks	
C used to think	D are always thinking	
1 A owes	B saves	C benefits	D earns
2 A list	B chain	C range	D store
3 A to hear	B had heard	
C hearing	D had been hearing	
4 A price	B cost	C value	D discount
5 A that	B which	C whose	D where
6 A cash	B a profit	C earnings	D a fortune
7 A not pay	B not to pay	C not paying	D to not paying
8 A should	B ought	C must	D had better

7 ★ ★ ★ Complete the sentences using the prompts in brackets. Change the forms or add new words where necessary. Use up to five words in each gap.

Why don't you go out and meet your friends instead of _wasting time watching_ (waste/time/watch) TV?

1 Do you think _____ (your grandfather/retire) by the time he is 65?

2 You _____ (need/not/call) Anne. I had already texted her to explain where we were meeting her.

3 My little brother has a nasty habit of dropping litter on the street, _____ (make/my neighbours/furious)!

4 I'm really good at picking up bargains, _____ (I/be/not)?

5 You really _____ (should/stop/buy) new clothes. Your wardrobe is full, but you always wear a T-shirt and jeans!

8 ★ ★ ★ Complete the second sentence so that it has a similar meaning to the first. Use between two and five words, including the word in capitals.

Tony spent all his pocket money and didn't want to go out at the weekend.
ALREADY
Tony didn't want to go out at the weekend because _he had already spent_ all his pocket money.

1 We missed the bus and were unable to get to the shopping centre on time.
MANAGE
We missed the bus and _____ to the shopping centre on time.

2 I don't think I'll move to a different city next year.
STILL
I think _____ in the same city next year.

3 We wanted the party to be a nice surprise for Jimmy, but he didn't like it.
MEANT
The party _____ a nice surprise for Jimmy, but he didn't like it.

4 In those days, she worked as a waitress at the weekends, but she doesn't any more.
TO
In those days, she _____ as a waitress at the weekends.

5 The book attracted a lot of attention when it was first published in the UK.
DEAL
The book attracted _____ attention when it was first published in the UK.

9 ★ ★ ★ Complete the text with one word in each gap.

Influences

Have you ever _stopped_ to think what influences our decisions when we buy clothes? Is it what our friends are wearing or is it advertising on social media and TV? Personally, I ¹_____ to admit that I like to be fashionable and, in particular, I look ²_____ for trends that celebrities buy into. My parents think that I ³_____ too much time looking at fashion blogs, but I don't agree. Of course, I don't have enough money to get expensive designer clothes, so I often wait and buy clothes on special ⁴_____ . Luckily, in my part-time job at the clothes shop ⁵_____ I work, I get to see all the new clothes as soon as they come in. And working there enables me to get good discounts, too!

I guess you could say that the clothes in my wardrobe are quite stylish. But I also like clothes that are a ⁶_____ unusual. I believe that it's important to show your personality through what you wear. I have a passion ⁷_____ clothes and want to study fashion design in London. I hope that I ⁸_____ have started my own clothing line by the time I get a degree.

61

1 Complete the advice using the words in the box. There are two extra words.

> begin complain happen ~~incident~~ informal
> narrative tenses reaction reply summarising

When writing a formal email describing an *incident* and making a complaint, ¹_____ the introduction by saying why you are writing and end it by ²_____ your complaint.
In the main body of the email use ³_____ to describe the incident you are complaining about and give your ⁴_____ to it.
In the closing paragraph, say what you would like to ⁵_____ , make a final statement and mention that you expect a ⁶_____ .

2 Match the beginnings with the endings to make phrases.

I am writing …	g	a to reconsider your policies.
1 I am particularly … ⬜	b to treat paying customers in this way.
2 Without doubt … ⬜	c upset because …
3 We urge you … ⬜	d to contact you and complain …
4 It is simply unfair … ⬜	e to your response.
5 We decided … ⬜	f the worst part of the whole incident was …
6 I look forward … ⬜	g to draw your attention to …

3 Complete the email with one word in each gap. The first letters are given.

4 Complete the sentences with *so* or *such + a, an* or Ø (no article).

I have never been *so* embarrassed in my life.
1 I can't remember the last time I received _____ unfriendly service.
2 It is hard to believe that someone working in customer service could be _____ rude.
3 How can you charge nearly £20 for _____ poor product?
4 To be honest, I have never had _____ awful meal.
5 We had waited _____ long to be served that in the end we got up and left the restaurant.

5 Replace the underlined phrases in the sentences with the correct forms of the words in the box. Add any other necessary words.

> accuse behalf disappointment
> fact humiliated ~~threat~~ urge

When we said angrily that we would call the manager, the waiter told us to go ahead and said he didn't care. *threatened to*
1 The manager said we were guilty of trying to leave the restaurant without paying the bill. We couldn't believe it! _____
2 The restaurant was so disappointing that our celebration was ruined. _____
3 What is true is that the restaurant was half empty so the kitchen can't have been as busy as the waiter claimed. _____
4 We strongly recommend that you reconsider your policies when it comes to reservations. _____
5 It was such a humiliating experience that we never want to eat there again. _____
6 I am writing in the name of myself and my friends. _____

Dear Sir or Madam,

I am writing to make a **f**ormal **c**omplaint about an incident that ¹**t**_____ **pl**_____ earlier today at the Westgate Centre branch of your clothing store. I am extremely unhappy with the service I received.

I bought a top from the store last weekend but when I got home, I discovered it had a hole in the sleeve that I had not noticed while I was trying it on. I had kept my receipt and so returned to the store this morning to exchange the top.

At the store, I ²**app**_____ one of the assistants (whose name was Lydia, according to her badge) and explained the situation. She looked at the hole and said there was no way it had been sold like that and ³**acc**_____ me of making it myself! I tried to ⁴**rea**_____ **w**_____ her, but she would not listen. She said it was the customers' responsibility to check for damage before leaving the shop. To ⁵**m**_____ **ma**_____ **wo**_____ , she raised her voice and attracted the attention of several of the other customers in the store. In the end, I left the shop feeling absolutely ⁶**hu**_____ , extremely annoyed and without a new top.

I trust you understand why I have ⁷**de**_____ to **c**_____ you and **c**_____ . I ⁸**a**_____ that you **in**_____ the **ma**_____ and that you replace my damaged top. It is ⁹**s**_____ **unf**_____ to **tr**_____ paying customers in this way.

I ¹⁰**l**_____ **fo**_____ to your **re**_____ .

Yours faithfully,
Emma Jennings

6 Read the task and the letter. Then complete the gaps with the correct form of the words in the box.

> approach   complain   discriminate   ~~draw~~
> humiliate   investigate   reason   respond   threaten

> You recently went to a sports centre with a friend to play tennis. While you were getting changed, you saw four adults making a mess in the changing room, but shortly after you started playing, a member of staff came up to you and your friend and claimed that you had done it. You and your friend were asked to leave. Write a letter of complaint. In your letter explain what happened and say what you expect from the sports centre.

Dear Sir or Madam,

I am writing _to draw_ your attention to an incident that took place at the Harwood Sports Centre last Sunday. My friend and I were treated extremely badly by staff and it was such a ¹_____ experience that we decided to contact you and make a formal ²_____ .

Last Sunday, we had booked a tennis court at the sports centre and had just started playing when one of the staff ³_____ us. Her name was Karen (according to the badge she wore) and she accused us of making a mess in the changing rooms. When we tried ⁴_____ with her and explain that we weren't responsible, she asked us to leave. To make matters worse, she ⁵_____ to ban us from using the sports centre again.

The truth is, the changing rooms were already in a terrible state when we arrived. We noticed a group of four adults there who were dropping rubbish and generally making a mess. When we mentioned this, Karen simply laughed and refused to believe us or even to check the CCTV. In the end, we left the sports centre without being able to play and feeling very annoyed.

We ask that you ⁶_____ the matter and refund the money that we spent booking a tennis court and travelling to and from the sports centre. It is extremely unfair ⁷_____ against young people in this way.

I look forward to your ⁸_____ .

Yours faithfully,

Simon Redman

7 Rewrite the sentences using _so_ or _such_ and make any other necessary changes.

> We were treated very badly. We decided to contact you.
> _We were treated so badly that we decided to contact you._

1 The experience was humiliating. We want to complain.

_____

2 We received terrible service. We won't be coming back to your restaurant.

_____

3 The waiters took a long time to bring the food. It was cold when it arrived.

_____

4 It was unfair. We were annoyed.

_____

8 Read the task below. Before you start writing, note down some ideas and plan your work.

> Last Saturday, you went to Tino's Restaurant to celebrate your birthday, but the food and service were terrible – you had a long wait for your food and when it came some dishes were cold and one order was incorrect. You complained to the waiter but he was rude and refused to do anything. The manager was not there. Write a letter of complaint to the restaurant manager. In your letter explain what happened and say what you expect to happen as a result of the letter.

In my letter:

• in the first paragraph I have explained the reason for my complaint.	☐
• in the main part I have described the situation, including all the information given in the task, and my reaction. I have used a range of narrative tenses.	☐
• in the last paragraph, I have stated my expectations as a result of the letter and that I am expecting a reply.	☐
• I have used formal language.	☐
• I have not used contractions (e.g. I'm, it's, that's).	☐
• I have used an appropriate formal ending (e.g. Yours faithfully).	☐
• I have checked my spelling.	☐
• my handwriting is neat enough for someone else to read.	☐

VOCABULARY AND GRAMMAR

1 Find and correct the mistakes. One sentence is correct.

I'm going to ~~call~~ for that painting in the auction that's on next week. I hope I get it! _bid_

1 I can't understand why that restaurant has such a bad response. Every time we've eaten there the food has been amazing! _____

2 I'd like to get a new winter coat, but it has to be red. I'll look up for something suitable. _____

3 There is a fly market in the city centre at the weekend. If you're lucky, you might find some jewellery you can afford. _____

4 When I've got a bit of extra money, I go bargain hunting at the local markets and then sell my purchases online to make a profit. _____

5 A number of small clothes shops closed down when a new key store opened last year. _____

/5

2 Complete the sentences with the words in the box. Change the form if necessary. There is one extra word.

> broke   burn   cost   fortune
> ~~increase~~   shop   support

Is changing your job the best way to _increase_ your earnings? I think so – I've got two years' experience in this job, so I think I'll apply for something better paid.

1 They've made a _____ setting up beauty centres for pets. It's going so well they can afford to open three new sites.

2 We had to pay for some emergency repairs to our roof, so now we're completely _____ .

3 If you want to encourage people to start new businesses in the area, you should _____ local producers.

4 Before you choose a new laptop, it's a good idea _____ around a bit so that you know what's available.

5 The Collins family must have money to _____ if they go on luxury cruises three times a year.

/5

3 Complete the text with the correct form of the words in brackets.

ME & SHOPPING

I'm not _loaded_ (LOAD), in fact I sometimes find it hard to make ¹_____(END) meet – that's why I'm always careful with my money. I take excellent care of my personal ²_____ (BELONG) so they last as long as possible. When I have to buy something, I take my time. I certainly avoid ³_____ (IMPULSIVE) purchases as far as possible. My favourite thing is something I was fortunate enough to find in a car boot ⁴_____ (SELL). It's a beautiful carpet – it's fairly old, but it's excellent quality and it looks perfect in my bedroom. It's hand-made and I love that – it's definitely not one of the mass-produced ⁵_____ (PRODUCE) you find in the shops these days.

/5

4 Complete the sentences with the correct forms of question tags and reply questions.

A: How about having a picnic by the river?
B: Brilliant! Let's invite Greg and his girlfriend, _shall we_?

1 A: John seems to be having problems with his online shop.
   B: _____? I thought he was a real expert in IT.

2 A: Do you know that Phoebe is going to be the main photographer at Christie's wedding?
   B: _____? That sounds great.

3 A: My computer has broken down and I have to finish my Chemistry project by tomorrow.
   B: Amy has got a new laptop, _____?
   Let's find out if she's willing to lend you hers.

4 A: Don't forget to pay the electricity bill, _____?
   B: I won't. I've already put it in my handbag.

5 A: I've inherited a house with an orchard, but I don't have a clue how to go about it, especially the garden.
   B: Dan used to grow fruit and vegetables in his garden, _____? So maybe ask him for help.

/5

5 Complete the sentences with the correct modal verbs and the correct forms of the verbs in brackets. In some sentences, more than one answer is possible.

I think you _should keep_ (keep) the receipt in case the tablet stops working and you want to get a refund.

1 We _____ (not/hire) a car at the airport because our friends picked us up and then lent us theirs.

2 We're in a theatre. You _____ (use) a mobile phone during the performance.

3 Camilla _____ (not/keep) all her valuables in one place. If she had had them in different locations, the burglar wouldn't have found them so easily.

4 The Burtons _____ (cancel) their holiday at the last minute because Mr Burton fell seriously ill.

5 Diane _____ (not/bring) so many outfits to the wedding. It was only a short reception.

/5

6 Choose the correct option.

You are not _able_ /(supposed) to take more than three items into the changing room.

1 I think in the USA you are _obliged_ / _allowed_ to tip people like taxi drivers. It's expected of you.

2 You can't take a cat to a restaurant. You are _forbidden_ / _certain_ to be asked to leave it outside.

3 Kids under the age of 10 are _banned_ / _required_ from entering the exhibition.

4 Matthew is _unlikely_ / _meant_ to be on time. He never is.

5 Would you believe that James _managed_ / _succeeded_ in getting a bank loan to buy a boat?

/5

Total   /30

7 Complete the text with one word in each gap.

My most memorable visit to a market so far has been to La Boquería in Barcelona. As soon as I crossed the iron gates of the market, I was <u>approached</u> by a stallholder who saw my surprised face and said: 'You've never been here before, **1**_____ you? Come and taste some of my produce.' I treated **2**_____ to some samples of his finest hams, cheeses and seafood. I learnt that many of Barcelona's top chefs buy their produce in the market because the food sold there is good value for money, so you don't have to pay **3**_____ to get high quality. I bought a few things, but regretted not buying more – I definitely **4**_____ have purchased some of the delicious ham, but I didn't.

So, you **5**_____ better plan a visit to La Boquería when you're next in Barcelona. I'm sure it'll be an amazing experience, not only for its incredible food but also for its unique atmosphere.

/5

8 Complete the second sentence so that it has a similar meaning to the first. Use the word in capitals.

I don't think Becca will join us for the weekend trip. She's down with flu and will probably not recover by then.
UNLIKELY
It *is unlikely that Becca will join* us for the weekend trip. She's down with flu and will probably not recover by then.

1 If I were you, I wouldn't spend so much money on clothes every month.
HAD
You _____ so much money on clothes every month.

2 It wasn't necessary for him to pay a deposit on the flat.
PAID
He _____ a deposit on the flat.

3 It's a shame you didn't go to the party.
OUGHT
You _____ to the party.

4 You can't park there for more than an hour.
ALLOWED
You _____ there for more than an hour.

5 I'm sure they'll go to Spain next summer, they always do.
BOUND
They _____ to Spain next summer, they always do.

/5

9 Choose the correct option.

Excuse me, ⟨do you happen to know⟩ / *happen you to know* / *does it happen you know* where the bathroom is?
1 Everyone has left, *hasn't he / haven't they / aren't they*?
2 Mum has just offered to help us buy a flat, so we *don't have to use / shouldn't use / needn't have used* our savings. What a waste of money!
3 After making lots of noise in the café, they were *banned from going / bound to go / supposed to go* there again.
4 I've already had a sandwich, but I'm still hungry. Could I have *another one / others / the other one*?
5 Jenny *ought to have bought / ought not to have bought / should buy* a smaller coat. The one she chose was far too big.

/5

10 Choose the correct answers A–D.

Hitting the jackpot

My friend Johnny had always dreamt of <u>C</u> a fortune, but every business he got involved in failed after a few months. It was harder and harder for him to **1**___ ends meet. One day, he decided to buy a lottery ticket to try his luck. To his utter amazement, he hit the jackpot and won several million pounds. He knew that such a large amount of money would **2**___ him to have a comfortable life for quite a few years. While picking up his prize he was advised by a lawyer to keep quiet about it and put most of the money **3**___ and only spend a little. Of course, Johnny took no notice and told everyone about his win. Some of his family members regarded it as the chance of a lifetime to become a bit better off as well. They started begging him for money because they thought that since he was **4**___ in it, he should help them. He bought himself a car and gifts for all his family and friends. Very soon he realised that his prize was nearly gone. He tried to do something about it, but it was too late. When I last spoke to him, he told me that not listening to the lawyer's advice was a mistake and he **5**___ so much to begin with. Well, I agree. If only he had listened to the advice given to him when he was collecting the money …

	A	B	C	D
	A do	B doing	ⓒ making	D make
1	A take	B get	C make	D have
2	A allow	B let	C oblige	D permit
3	A off	B back	C out	D aside
4	A falling	B rolling	C dropping	D earning
5	A didn't need to spend	B must have spent		
	C shouldn't spend	D ought not to have spent		

/5

Total /20

SPEAKING

1 **In pairs, ask and answer the questions.**

Talk about shopping.

Student A

1 What have you bought recently that was a good bargain?
2 Do you enjoy shopping in chain stores? Why?/ Why not?
3 Is it important to check where the things you buy were made?
4 Would you like to work in a clothes shop? Why?/Why not?
5 Tell me about the last time you bought a present for someone.

Student B

1 Do you enjoy window shopping? Why?/ Why not?
2 What is the most expensive thing you've ever bought?
3 What are the advantages and disadvantages of going shopping alone? Why?
4 Who in your family do you enjoy buying presents for? Why?
5 Do you think you would make a good sales person? Why?/Why not?

2 **Read the instructions on your card and role-play the conversation.**

Student A

The situation:

You and Student B are responsible for organising the food for your end-of-semester party. You have a small budget and want to buy as much food as possible from a big supermarket. Student B wants to buy from the local market which is more expensive. Tell Student B why you think it's better to go to the big supermarket. Think about the price, variety of products and location of the supermarket.

Your goal:

Discuss all the options and decide where to do the shopping for the party.

Student B

The situation:

You and Student A are responsible for organising the food for your end-of-semester party. You have a small budget and want to spend it at the local market where food is produced ethically and is probably healthier. Student A would prefer to buy cheaper food at a big supermarket. Tell Student A why you think it's better to go to the local market. Think about the quality of products and why it's important to support local businesses.

Your goal:

Discuss all the options and decide where to do the shopping for the party.

3 Look at the photos and answer the questions.

Student A
Look at the two photos showing alternative holiday accommodation options. What can you see in the photos? Who might be interested in staying in each of these places? Which of these options would you choose for your own holiday and why?

1

2

Student B
Look at the two photos showing modern ways of living. What can you see in the photos? What are the advantages and disadvantages of each home? Which one would you like to live in?

1

2

4 Discuss this question together. 'The main reason people choose a particular place to live is to be close to the place they study or work.' What do you think?

5 Off to work

VOCABULARY

5.1

Work • expressions to do with work
• phrasal verbs
• adjectives from nouns

SHOW WHAT YOU KNOW

1 Complete the sentences with words in the box.

> badly-paid   full-time   ~~hard~~   manual   office
> part-time   well-paid   voluntary

1 Being a farmer is _hard_ work because it's physically
   challenging and you're outdoors a lot. It's _____
   work too – most things are done by hand.
2 I'm a nurse and I love what I do, but I don't earn
   much money because it's a _____ job.
3 Sam's got a _____ job. He only works from
   9 a.m. to 1 p.m. every day. Two afternoons a week,
   he does _____ work in a charity shop, which
   he doesn't get paid for. He likes helping others.
4 I never thought I'd do an _____ job,
   but I work as a secretary in an advertising agency.
5 Katie is the managing director of the company.
   It's a _____ job and she earns a high salary.
6 Max has a _____ job, from 9 a.m. to 5 p.m.
   Monday to Friday, but he often works longer hours
   and at the weekend too.

WORD STORE 5A | Expressions to do with work

**2 Choose the correct verbs and then match phrases 1–9
to definitions a–j.**

   (think)/ do / achieve for yourself   □ c
1 say / speak / put your mind   □
2 improve / increase / extend your output   □
3 do / achieve / enter a goal   □
4 go / enter / reach the job market   □
5 get / work / reach your full potential   □
6 put / increase / enter your heart into something   □
7 do / reach / improve your career prospects   □
8 work / do / put to a deadline   □
9 think / work / do something day in, day out   □

a do more work
b finish tasks by the necessary time
c consider facts and make your own decisions
d make a lot of effort to do something
e do something over and over again for a long time
f become available to work
g say exactly what you think
h make your chances of getting a job better
i fulfil an objective
j be as good as you possibly can

**3 Complete the advert with the correct forms of the
verbs in Exercise 2.**

Dunham Advertising Agency

Are you about to _enter_ the job market? We're looking for
a talented school-leaver to work in our office as assistant
designer.

* Do you [1]_____ your heart into everything you do?
* Are you able to [2]_____ for yourself and plan your
  own work?
* Do you have opinions and [3]_____ your mind?
* Are you able to organise your time, [4]_____ your
  goals and [5]_____ to tight deadlines?
* Can you [6]_____ something day in, day out and still
  remain enthusiastic and creative?
* Could you [7]_____ your work output if necessary?

If you've answered 'yes' to the questions above and you're
interested in [8]_____ your career prospects and
[9]_____ your full potential, then get in touch!

Contact: Human Resources at Dunham Advertising Agency
for an application form.

(Tel: 0171 111 2222; dunham-h-r@dunhamadvertising.mail)

**4 Complete the article with the missing words. The first
letters are given.**

○○○

THINKING ABOUT A NEW JOB?

Before you **a**_pply_ for a new job, there are many things
you should consider.

* Are you prepared to work [1]l_____ h_____
  or even weekends, or do you want a typical 9 to 5 job?
* Does the job involve a long commute, and if so,
  will you be able to work [2]f_____ h_____
  sometimes and not go into the office every day?
* What is the job environment like? Will you be
  working indoors? If you hate sitting inside, then you
  need to look for a job working [3]o_____ instead.
* What exactly will you be required to do? For example,
  will you have to work with your [4]h_____ to
  make or repair things, or do you need to sit and
  think at your desk?
* If you love travelling, will there be opportunities to
  work [5]a_____ in an office in a different country?
* What is the company's reputation for looking after
  and keeping their employees like? Do people ever
  get [6]f_____ ? Has anyone in the company
  [7]r_____ from their job for any reason recently?
  Why?
* Do you really want to work [8]i_____
  advertising/technology/teaching? Or would another
  field suit you better?

Make sure you've answered all those questions before
you start looking for that dream job!

WORD STORE 5B | Phrasal verbs

5 Choose the correct answers A–C.

It's no good, I can't put _B_ writing this report any longer. I'll start now.
A up   (B) off   C on

1 I don't have to send in the job application form until the end of the month, but I'm going to work ___ completing it this week.
A towards   B to   C for

2 Stop messing about. It's time you ___ down to writing your CV and looking for a part-time job.
A sat   B put   C got

3 Before I write my dissertation, I'm going to ___ out each chapter, so I can plan my research.
A carry   B burn   C map

4 Max was exhausted, but he managed to keep ___ the task until he'd finished and could present it to his boss.
A out   B at   C towards

5 Remember to take breaks while you're studying for your exams or you'll ___ out!
A burn   B carry   C set

6 If you want to succeed, you should ___ out your objectives and think about how to achieve each one. It will motivate you!
A set   B put   C keep

7 You can't rely on Jack, he never ___ out half of what he says he'll do. He gives up when things get tough.
A works   B puts   C carries

6 Complete the text with the correct forms of the phrasal verbs in Exercise 5 so they have the same meaning as the verbs in brackets.

○○○

Pop Gossip! All the latest juice on the stars!

Jarvis leaving No Direction

Poly-fi Records have confirmed that Jarvis Harvey _has carried out_ (has done) his threat to resign as the lead singer of boy band No Direction. Reports say Harvey ¹_____ (has become ill from overwork) from touring and writing two albums in a year. However, he ²_____ (delayed) leaving until the end of the band's current UK tour. Harvey, who writes all the band's songs, struggled to finish the last album, but ³_____ (continued to work on) it and now wants a complete break from music.

New album for Bluster

Katie Bluster has confirmed she will shortly release her long-awaited second album. Bluster ⁴_____ (planned in detail) the album months ago, but didn't ⁵_____ (finally start) recording any songs until last month. She claims she ⁶_____ (has been making progress with) this album for three years. Bluster ⁷_____ (has arranged) a strong marketing campaign for the album, so we can expect to be hearing her latest music everywhere soon!

WORD STORE 5C | Adjectives from nouns

7 Complete the sentences with the correct form of the words in the box.

conscientiousness   enthusiasm   ~~knowledge~~
overwork   punctuality   purpose   single-mindedness

Maria is really _knowledgeable_ about history – you can ask her anything and she'll always know the answer.

1 Mark is one of the most _____ people I know. If you arrange to meet, he'll always arrive on time or early – I've never known him to be late.

2 When Jan gets an idea, that's all she thinks about. She's so _____ about things.

3 I feel really _____ about our new recycling project. I'm so interested in learning more about how to protect the environment!

4 Many doctors are _____ . They have to be in the hospital for such long hours with so few breaks, I don't know how they manage.

5 Steve doesn't like his job much, but he's _____ , so he works carefully and doesn't forget to do anything.

6 I like to have clear aims of what I want to achieve and how I'm going to do it in my work, then I can be more _____ at the office.

8 Choose the correct answers A–C.

1 Polly always ___ tasks, even if they are boring.
A keeps at   B reaches   C improves

2 I don't think I could do a job where I had to do the same thing ___ , day out. I need to have lots of variety or I'd get bored.
A every day   B time in   C day in

3 When you're a journalist, it's important to be able to work to a/an ___ because stories have to be ready very quickly.
A output   B deadline   C potential

4 If you carry on working at this rate, you'll burn ___ ! You need to rest sometimes or your health will suffer.
A out   B off   C up

5 Jim is really passionate about his work. He puts his ___ into it.
A arms   B head   C heart

6 Daisy's teacher expressed concern about her always putting ___ her homework until the last minute.
A in   B off   C on

7 If you aren't ___ and arrive late at the office, the boss will give you a formal warning.
A overworked   B single-minded   C punctual

8 Once I've finished my science degree, I'll be entering the ___ market. It's a scary thought!
A job   B work   C career

9 The company has taken on a huge IT project. We will have to ___ achieving all the objectives bit by bit.
A work towards   B set out   C map out

10 Candidates for this job must be ___ about current scientific research in tropical illnesses.
A conscientious   B purposeful   C knowledgeable

/10

---

1 Complete the sentences with the verbs in the correct form.

1 'I'm babysitting for my neighbours.'
She said she _____ for her neighbours.

2 'I work for my aunt.'
He told me he _____ for his aunt.

3 'Dad's left the office.'
Mum said Dad _____ the office.

4 'The doctor was on duty all night.'
They said the doctor _____ on duty all night.

2 ★ Choose the correct option to complete the conversation.

Zuzu: Welcome to Madam Zuzu's spiritual contacts. Who would you like to contact?

Maud: My poor departed husband, Derek, please.

Zuzu: I can feel a presence. Derek, are you there?

Derek: Yes, I'm standing next to Maud.

Zuzu: He says he [1]*is / was* standing right next to you.

Maud: Ah! Oh my goodness. Is he OK?

Zuzu: Derek, your wife is asking whether [2]*are you / you are* OK.

Derek: Tell her I'm fine. Tell her she should look behind the fridge for the missing key.

Maud: What did he say?

Zuzu: It was hard to tell. I think he said [3]*I am / he was* fine and you should [4]*look / have looked* behind the fridge for the missing key.

Maud: Oh, I was wondering where that had got to.

Derek: Maud, don't forget to put the bin out on Thursday mornings. Tell her, please.

Zuzu: He said [5]*not to / don't* forget to put the bin out on Thursday mornings.

Maud: I thought you'd stop telling me what to do after you died, Derek!

Derek: Tell her I love her.

Zuzu: He says he loves [6]*her / you.*

Maud: Oh, he's so romantic! Tell him I love him too. Wait for me, Derek!

Derek: What was that? What did she say?

Zuzu: She says she [7]*loves / loved* you too and [8]*to wait / wait* for her. Oh, you two are just so sweet!

Director: CUT!!!! OK, that wasn't bad. Zuzu, can you do it once again but be a bit more serious?

3 ★ ★ Put the words in brackets in the correct order to report the questions.

Could you draw up a shortlist?
They asked <u>us if we could draw up</u> (draw up/we/could/if/us) a shortlist.

1 Has the company filled the vacancy?
I asked _____ (whether/him/filled/had/the company) the vacancy.

2 Do you have a sense of adventure?
She asked _____ (me/I/had/if) a sense of adventure.

3 Did you both apply for the same job?
They asked _____ (whether/had/applied/us/we/both) for the same job.

4 ★ ★ ★ Report the comments. Only change the tenses if necessary.

'We employed Tom last month.'
They said <u>they had employed Tom the month before</u> .

1 'The company has been attempting to target the youth market since last year.'
She told me _____

2 'Can I interview you here and now?'
He asked _____

3 'I get a real sense of achievement from my job.'
She says _____

4 'I might miss the meeting tomorrow.'
He said _____

5 'Wait here.'
She told me _____

6 'Don't forget to renew your passport next month.'
She told me _____

7 'How long had you been campaigning for a change in the law?'
The presenter asked _____

5 Complete the gaps in the conversation to report the head teacher's speech.

Does everyone have a seat? OK, be quiet please! Good morning everyone. Last month, you all voted for a new student representative and I am pleased to announce that Philip Coen has been chosen. Some of you might not know Phillip very well, but I'm sure he will make a fine representative.

Mel: I missed the meeting. Tell me what happened.

Sam: The head teacher checked if everyone <u>had</u> a seat then asked us all [1]_____ quiet.

Mel: OK, OK, but what was it about?

Sam: She said that [2]_____ all the students [3]_____ for a new representative …

Mel: I know that! Who won?

Sam: … and that Philip Coen [4]_____ .

Mel: Who? I didn't vote for him.

Sam: Well, she said that some of us [5]_____ not know Phillip very well, but he would make a fine representative.

Mel: Do you know him?

Sam: No, not really, but if the head teacher says he [6]_____ make a fine representative, then hopefully she's right.

/6

GRAMMAR: Train and Try Again page 175

LISTENING LANGUAGE PRACTICE

5.3

Words connected with work
• phrases describing change

1 Choose the correct option to complete the extract from the recording.

Extract from Student's Book recording 🔊 **2.37**

P: Dr Atkins, what do you think the world of work (will)/ *is going to* look like ten years from now?

DA: Well, it certainly won't look the same as now. Technology now enables us ᵃ*to work / working* anywhere and so there's been a steady rise in people working from home and a sharp drop in the number of people <u>commuting</u> to work.

P: As technology takes over tasks that people ᵇ*will do / used to do*, what kind of skills will be useful for people in the future?

DA: People will have to focus on the kind of skills that ᶜ*must / can't* be done by a machine or a robot such as ¹_____ and management jobs or caring for other humans.

P: So you don't think that dentists and teachers should worry about their jobs just yet.

DA: No, definitely not. The need for jobs in the medical and teaching ²_____ will remain constant. Many of the traditional jobs will still be necessary ten or twenty years from now – we'll always need lawyers, politicians, fire-fighters and so on. And we ᵈ*mustn't / won't* forget the ³_____ : we'll always need artists, writers and actors. I also think there will be a marked increase in jobs connected with alternative energy. [...]

P: So which jobs do you think are at risk in the future?

DA: Um, I think there will be a gradual decline in jobs in retail – shop assistants ᵉ*aren't / can't be* required in the days of online shopping. Any office jobs and factory jobs that ᶠ*could have been / can be* done by computers and robots will disappear.

P: Finally, can you name any ⁴_____ that don't exist now and will in the future?

DA: I think we'll see jobs like body-part maker, robot mechanic and space ⁵_____ . But I could be completely wrong!

2 Match the words and phrases with the definitions.

tourist guide	ⓔ	3 job title ☐
1 professions ☐		4 leadership ☐
2 commuting ☐		5 creative industries ☐

a the action of guiding a group of people or organisation
b the journey from home to a place of work and back again
c economic activities which involve making or generating objects and ideas
d a name that describes someone's professional position
e a person who is paid to show visitors around places of interest
f paid occupations that usually involve training and qualifications

3 Complete the extract from the recording with the words and phrases in Exercise 2.

WORD STORE 5D | Phrases describing change

4 Choose the correct words to make sentences about the information in the graphs.

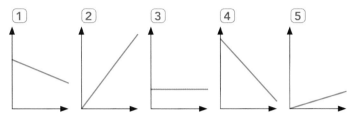

1 There has been *an increase / a drop* in the number of young people out of work.
2 We're expecting a *sharp / steady* rise in the number of teenagers entering higher education.
3 The number of 17-year-olds who work part-time will remain *constant / marked*.
4 There has been a *rapid / gradual* decline in the number of Polish people moving to the UK.
5 A *steady / growing* number of secondary school students are seeking Saturday jobs.

5 Complete the sentences with the words in the box so they describe the graphs in Exercise 4.

gradual decline   marked increase   sharp drop
steady rise   unchanged

1 There has been a _____ in the number of young people out of work.
2 We're expecting a _____ in the number of teenagers entering higher education.
3 The number of 17-year-olds who work part-time will remain _____ .
4 There has been a _____ in the number of Polish people moving to the UK.
5 There has been a _____ in the number of secondary school students seeking Saturday jobs.

REMEMBER BETTER

Search online for 'infographics' plus a topic that interests you and the word 'trends', e.g. 'infographics music trends'. Then practise using the language from this lesson to describe trends presented in any relevant charts, graphs and diagrams you find.

READING

5.4

Young earners • choosing a career
• verb-noun collocations

1 Read Text 1 quickly and choose the website news section that it should <u>not</u> appear in.
1 Education news
2 Technology news
3 Business news
4 Youth news

2 Read Text 2 and choose two sections in Exercise 1 that it could appear in. ◯ & ◯

Text 1

On Sunday afternoon, food delivery rider Jim Adams, 18, was rushed to hospital with a suspected broken leg. He'd been struck by a car while riding his bike. Despite his injury, Jim was most concerned about how he would support himself while unable to work. Jim, like many young adults, is a gig worker and was delivering an order when the accident happened.

A 'gig' is a paid piece of work that people do, especially if they are self-employed. Unlike regular employees, gig workers do not have benefits such as paid sick leave* and a minimum wage*. They have no job security, so their workload, and therefore their pay, is unpredictable. This makes budgeting impossible and means that gig workers can be exploited – when there are bills to pay, any job for any fee will do.

You might think such work conditions would put people off, but it's estimated that almost 25 percent of American workers are now employed in the gig economy and this is expected to rise. It's difficult to wrap your head around such a statistic. So what's the attraction? Well, there are plenty of people like Jim – a university student – whose circumstances don't allow them to work normal hours. They're not happy about their lack of rights, but they have no choice but to do this kind of job. Equally, there are students who choose gig work because of the freedom it gives them to make their own decisions about when to wake up, when to work and how much work to take on. For them, gig work is a great solution.

So is gig work worth it for young people? Well, it's convenient for students trying to balance work and study. It also helps to develop self-discipline* and a work ethic* which will stand them in good stead later in life. But there's a danger that, over time, the gig economy will normalise casual work and employment benefits will then become a thing of the past. And if you're injured on the job, like Jim was, bad luck … help won't be at hand. You'll be on your own.

Text 2

The days of the paper round, once a rite of passage into work for thousands of young people in the UK, appear to be numbered. Newsagents across the country, once inundated with schoolchildren keen to supplement their weekly income by delivering newspapers to homes, are now being forced to cut back because they cannot recruit enough paper boys and girls.

Stefan Wojciechowski, a representative of UK newsagents said: 'Kids don't want to do paper rounds anymore because of increasing pocket money.' This means '[…] there is no longer the incentive to get up at the crack of dawn and [trudge] through rain, sleet and snow. […] It's a shame because not only is a paper round good exercise, it is also a very good way of bridging the gap between school and work. Youngsters get a sense of a good work ethic, which is good preparation for the future, […] but it's no good if they are just getting pocket money from their parents instead of earning independently.'

With its early morning starts in all weathers, back-breaking bags and risk of dog attacks, the paper round has long been seen as a character-building introduction to work for many youngsters. However, the lack of children prepared to take on the job, as well as competition from supermarkets and online media, means that many rounds are being phased out.

GLOSSARY

sick leave (n) – time that you take off work because you are sick

minimum wage (n) – the lowest legal amount an employee can be paid

self-discipline (n) – the ability to control yourself and to make yourself work hard

work ethic (n) – a belief in the value of work

3 Read Text 1 and Text 2 again and choose the correct answers A–D.

1 The nature of gig work means that
  A workers can be taken advantage of.
  B some jobs are more dangerous than others.
  C it is suitable for all kinds of employees.
  D employers are responsible for workers' benefits.

2 A benefit of gig work is that
  A more and more workers are turning to it as a source of income.
  B it is a popular choice with students.
  C workers are in complete control of their workday.
  D work is always available whenever you need it.

3 There is a risk that due to the gig economy
  A more casual positions will become available in the future.
  B people will choose not to work in regular jobs.
  C some workers may need to stop studying.
  D there will be a decline in workers' rights.

4 Young people are not delivering newspapers these days because
  A they are too busy with school work.
  B they are getting regular income from other sources.
  C of the health and safety risks involved.
  D of the harsh weather in the UK.

5 Both texts mention
  A the negative impacts of working while still studying.
  B why earning independently is necessary for young people.
  C how young people can benefit from working while still studying.
  D how young people's attitudes to work have changed.

4 Read the texts again. Are statements 1–6 true (T) or false (F)?

1 Jim considered his injury to be of greater importance than his loss of income. ☐
2 Financial stress is just as great for gig workers as it is for regular employees. ☐
3 In the future, more than a quarter of American workers will be engaged in gig work. ☐
4 When doing gig work, you cannot choose your working hours. ☐
5 Paper rounds have other benefits for young people besides money. ☐
6 More than one reason is given for the gradual disappearance of paper rounds. ☐

5 Complete the collocations from the text with the correct prepositions. Then match them to definitions a–f.

wrap your head _around_ sth [f]
1 stand you _____ good stead ☐
2 become a thing _____ the past ☐
3 help is _____ hand ☐
4 bridge the gap _____ sth and sth ☐
5 phase sth _____ ☐

a when an aspect of life no longer exists
b to reduce or get rid of the difference between two things
c close to you and easy to reach or access
d gradually stop using or providing something
e be useful or helpful to someone
f understand something because it is complex or makes no sense

6 Complete the sentences with the collocations in Exercise 5.

How did he become so successful when he never studied? I just can't wrap _my head around_ it.

1 When Steve set up his first business, he knew his parents' help was always _____ .
2 Get into the habit of saving money from an early age, as it will stand you _____ later.
3 The company is _____ the original version of its software after a rapid decline in sales.
4 The introduction of tablet computers helped to _____ smartphones and laptops.
5 After winning the lottery, their financial worries became _____ the past.

VOCABULARY PRACTICE | Choosing a career

7 Look at the vocabulary in lesson 5.4 in the Student's Book. Complete the emails with words and phrases related to choosing a career. The first letters are given.

Hi Sara,

How are you? How's college? I'm about to do my final exams and then enter the job market! But how are you supposed to choose a c_areer_ p_ath_ at the age of 21? I don't fancy doing the same job for years, in fact I'd like to try a few different things. Maybe I'll look into ¹j_____ -s_____ or a position with ²f_____ , so I'm not working 9–5 every day. Being a ³p_____ -t_____ could work too. That way I could spend some time doing my hobbies every day too.

What about you? Have you applied for any jobs yet?

Tim

Hi Tim,

I'm fine thanks, busy revising at the moment!

Have you thought about seeing a ⁴c_____ to get some ⁵c_____ g_____ ? They should have useful advice about how to ⁶t_____ in different career fields. You could also become a ⁷f_____ .

I know being self-employed sounds scary, but it could be just the solution and your living room could be your ⁸w_____ !

I found out yesterday I've got a job as a research assistant at college, so I'll be joining the ⁹w_____ all too soon!

Sara

WORD STORE 5E | Verb-noun collocations

8 Complete the sentences with the correct form of the verbs in the box.

be (x2) find focus have (x2) lack

My sister _has_ a vocation – she's wanted to train as a vet since she was five years old.

1 I'm going to set up my own business because I want to _____ in charge.
2 Jack doesn't really know what he wants to do and _____ purpose at the moment.
3 Lucy finally _____ her niche last year when she got a job as a tour operator.
4 I was struggling in my role at the company last year as I didn't _____ on my strengths.
5 If you're like me, you _____ wired differently from everyone else, but that can be an advantage.
6 I don't think everyone _____ one true calling, I think most people end up in their jobs by chance.

GRAMMAR
5.5
Reporting verbs

SHOW WHAT YOU KNOW

1 Complete the sentences with the correct forms of the reporting verbs in the box.

(~~add~~   explain   point out   reply   suggest)

'Oh, and one more thing, I think Rachel is really spoilt.'
She _added_ that she thought Rachel was really spoilt.

1 'Why don't we put on a surprise party for Nicky's birthday?'
Alex _____ putting on a surprise party for Nicky's birthday.

2 'The coffee machine isn't working because you've forgotten to put water in it.'
He _____ that I had forgotten to put water in the coffee machine.

3 'Giving a speech at a wedding is easy. I'll tell you how. First say something nice about the newlyweds then propose a toast.'
My brother _____ that first I should say something nice about the newlyweds then propose a toast.

4 Me: 'Who's got the gift?'
Rhys: 'I have.'
Rhys _____ that he had the gift.

2 ★ Choose the correct option to complete the sentences.

1 The manager apologised for *be / being* late for the interview.
2 The company refused *to pay / that they would pay* overtime.
3 Ella begged *them to give / to give* her the job.
4 The boss promised *that he would increase / increasing* their salaries.
5 His wife accused him *of / that* caring more about his job than about her.
6 The interviewer suggested *wearing / to wear* smarter clothes to the second interview.

3 ★ ★ Add a missing word to each sentence.

Mr Jones thanked Kelly ^for babysitting so late and gave her an extra £10.

1 The sergeant ordered his men not shoot unless they were shot at.
2 I begged her to contact my parents, but she ignored me and called my mum.
3 Even though we've been friends for years, they haven't invited to their wedding.
4 Taylor apologised being so grumpy and explained that she was very tired.
5 I only had a couple of pounds, but thankfully the manager insisted paying for my taxi home.
6 Jasmine didn't object spicy food, as long as it wasn't ridiculously hot.

4 ★ ★ ★ Complete the second sentence so that it reports the first. Use the words in capitals and change the time expressions as required. Sometimes more than one answer is possible.

Why don't we close the shop early today?
PROPOSE
He _proposed closing the shop early that day._

1 Don't work for free.
ADVISE / US
She _____

2 You got the job? Well done!
CONGRATULATE / ME
They _____

3 Please, please visit us again next month.
URGE / HER
We _____

4 Remember to count the money tonight.
REMIND / THEM
He _____

5 OK, I forgot to place the order yesterday.
ADMIT
He _____

SHOW WHAT YOU'VE LEARNT

5 Complete the text with the correct forms of the words in brackets.

Legal Laughs

Take a look at these crazy real-life court cases. Do you think the lawyers managed to convince _the judges that they were right_ (the judges/they/be/right)?

A surfer took another surfer to court after accusing him
¹_____ (take) his wave. The judge refused
²_____ (continue) the case after deciding it was impossible to put a price on the 'pain and suffering' caused.

A woman sued a TV station and its weather forecaster for $1,000 after he assured viewers ³_____ (the weather/will be) sunny and in fact it rained. The woman claimed ⁴_____ (the forecast/cause) her to leave home lightly dressed and as a result she became ill.

A woman blamed ⁵_____ (an American supermarket chain/cause) injuries to her feet when canned goods fell from a broken shopping bag. The woman's husband also tried to sue the supermarket chain. He suggested ⁶_____ (he/miss) his wife's 'comfort and attention' while she was recovering.

/6

GRAMMAR: Train and Try Again page 175

5.6 SPEAKING

Problem solving

1 Translate the phrases into your own language.

SPEAKING BANK

Talking about a problem

What's wrong/the matter?

What's up (with it)?

I seem/appear to have lost/
forgotten/broken …

I haven't (got) a clue. / I've
no idea. / I wish I knew.

Every time I try to …, it …

Perhaps there's something
wrong/a problem with the …

Talking about a solution

Have you tried … + -ing?

It's worth a try/a go, I suppose.

I doubt that'll work, but let's
see.

Problem solved!

No, that doesn't/didn't make
any difference.

Expressing annoyance

What are we supposed to do
now?

Why on earth did/didn't you …?

How should I know?

You should've checked/asked
first.

We should've thought about
that earlier.

2 Match the beginnings of the phrases with the endings.

Every time I try to switch it on …	h	a	plugging it in to charge?
1 You should've …		b	solved!
2 Have you tried …		c	with it?
3 It doesn't …		d	wrong?
4 How should …		e	I know?
5 What's the matter …		f	thought about that earlier.
6 Problem …		g	make any difference.
7 What's …		h	it beeps and then nothing happens.

3 Complete the dialogue. The first letters are given.

Zack and Rob are university students sharing a small flat …

Zack: What's up, buddy? How's it going?

Rob: Fine, until 10 minutes ago when the Internet went off.

Zack: Oh no. W*hat's* u*p* w*ith* it?

Rob: ¹I'_____ n_____ i_____ .

Zack: Perhaps ²t_____ a p_____ w_____ the modem. ³H_____ y_____ t_____ switching it off, then switching it back on?

Rob: Of course! It didn't ⁴m_____ a____ d_____ .

Zack: How about the 'troubleshoot' function?

Rob: Ha! I ⁵d_____ that'll w_____ , but I_____ s_____ . It says it is not possible to connect, please contact your service provider.

Zack: Well, we knew that.

Rob: Listen, you did pay the bill this month, right?

Zack: The bill? Oh, erm …

Rob: Zack! ⁶W_____ on e_____ d_____ you remember? What ⁷a_____ we s_____ to do n_____ ?

Zack: Don't panic! I can go to the website and pay it right now.

Rob: Think about it for a second, Zack …

4 Complete the dialogues with the words and phrases that appeared in the lesson.

Conversation 1

Kate: Hello, Mum? Help!

Mum: Kate? What's *wrong*?

Kate: Oh Mum, I need my jeans for tonight, but they are still wet and I can't get the dryer working.

Mum: Well, what's ¹_____ ?

Kate: How ²_____ ? I've never even used it before.

Mum: Well, if you helped me more with the housework, you might know how to use it. I suggest you simply wear something else tonight.

Kate: Mum! Those jeans are the only thing that matches my new top.

Mum: Well you ³_____ about that earlier. All you can do now is put them on the radiator.

Conversation 2

Ollie: Hello, Computer World helpline. This is Ollie. How can I help?

MB: Yes, hello. This is Mr Brown. I've got a problem with the computer I bought from your shop just last week.

Ollie: OK, Mr Brown. What's wrong?

MB: Every ⁴_____ I try to switch the thing on, it beeps and then nothing happens.

Ollie: OK, it sounds like an electrical problem. Perhaps the battery is flat. Have ⁵_____ plugging it in to charge, Mr Brown?

MB: Well, Ollie, of course I have tried that, you know! But it doesn't ⁶_____ !

Ollie: I'm sorry Mr Brown, but I have to check everything. Forgive me for asking, but is the power cable actually plugged into the back of the computer?

MB: What? Of course it … Oh dear. Ollie, I think I owe you an apology.

Ollie: That's OK, Mr Brown. And are you able to switch it on now?

MB: Er … yes. Yes, that's it, problem ⁷_____ . Sorry, Ollie.

Ollie: No need to apologise. We are here to help.

1 ★ **Match the beginnings of the sentences with the endings.**

My boss looks down | [b]
1 I'm tied up |
2 We've run out |
3 After dropping out |
4 I wouldn't put up |
5 We usually come up |
6 His leadership style grew out |
7 He sometimes tries to get out |
8 It's difficult for companies to keep up |

a of attending a dull weekly meeting with his boss.
b on anyone who doesn't have a university degree.
c of his own experiences of working for global companies.
d of paper, so I won't be able to print any documents today.
e with a colleague making negative comments about my work.
f with a lot of marketing ideas, but only show the client two or three.
g of college, he started his own company in his parents' garage.
h with modern work practices if employees are resistant to change.
i with work tonight, so I'll order some food online to eat at the office.

2 ★ ★ **Complete the sentences with phrasal verbs with *up* or *get*.**

1 **GET**
   a Liam had a meeting in central London at noon, but then he had to get *back to* the office.
   b I keep meaning to learn to web design, but I just don't get _____ starting it.
   c My brother doesn't earn very much, but he's happy in his job and he gets _____ his boss well.
   d My mother always knows when I am really ill and when I only want to get _____ going to school.

2 **UP**
   a My younger brother _____ up _____ his physics teacher as a role model.
   b The company will probably _____ up _____ a lot of opposition once the plan to fire 200 workers is made public.
   c If you don't _____ up _____ your rights, nobody will defend them.
   d When I oversleep, I usually skip breakfast in order to _____ up _____ the lost time and arrive at the office on time.

3 ★ ★ **Complete the sentences with the words in the box.**

clear-out   downpour   letdown   off-putting
~~outset~~   run-down   upbringing   warm-up

It's no surprise that the team didn't do well this year, as the new coach had to deal with a lot of problems from the *outset*.

1 This used to be a _____ area, but it's changing quickly to become one of the city's most fashionable districts.
2 Each training session starts with a _____ activity so participants can revise what they learned the week before.
3 The _____ started a few minutes after I got to work, so luckily I didn't get wet.
4 It's a good idea to do a big _____ of your wardrobe every year and get rid of things you no longer use.
5 Sometimes it's difficult to explain my cultural _____ to people who grew up in a different country.
6 Please don't bring strong-smelling food into the office, as it might be _____ for your colleagues.
7 His last business self-help book, *Working Better*, was a complete _____ – it didn't offer any new information.

4 ★ ★ ★ **Complete the text with the missing words. The first letters are given.**

A great job

A few years ago Mike Tilson completed secondary school and **w**_ent_ on to study law, just like his parents expected him to do. However, he wasn't a hard-working student and he [1]**d**_____ out of university a few months later, a great [2]**l**_____ for his parents. He took on some part-time jobs, but they were low-paid and monotonous. It was then that Mike [3]**c**_____ up with a brilliant business idea and asked his family for a loan to start up a company.

Mike's idea [4]**g**_____ out of his love for music. Having always loved performing, he now manages a group of singing waiters. They pretend to be normal waiters at events and celebrations, but then they burst into a song, much to the guests' surprise.

Mike has come up [5]**a**_____ some problems with his business, but the company has still been very popular from the [6]**o**_____. When asked why his idea has been so successful, he always says that it comes [7]**d**_____ to hard work. Although he hardly ever sings himself these days, he is often tied up [8]**w**_____ work at the weekends as he needs to make sure everything is ready for the performances. 'It's brilliant to see people's faces when the waiters start singing!' he says.

5 ★ **Complete the sentences with one word in each gap.**

1 A: And then you *will* never guess what he said next. He ¹_____ her he hadn't been there at all …

   B: Lily, sorry to interrupt. I don't want to be rude, but I have ²_____ of work to do and I really ³_____ get on with it.

2 A: What a day! I'm exhausted! Do you ⁴_____ ordering a pizza and watching a movie?

   B: Have you forgotten that you promised ⁵_____ wash that huge pile of dishes in the kitchen or are you just trying to get ⁶_____ of doing it?

   A: No, of course not. I just don't feel like doing the washing-up today. And I can pay for the pizza.

   B: Well, if you put it like that, I guess we can live with dirty pots for ⁷_____ twenty-four hours. Double salami and cheese?

   A: This is ⁸_____ you're my best friend!

6 ★ ★ **Complete the second sentence so that it has a similar meaning to the first. Use between two and five words, including the word in capitals.**

In my opinion, some bosses push their employees too hard.
PRESSURE
In my opinion, some bosses *put too much pressure on* their employees.

1 My colleague said it was a good idea for us to take a break.
   SUGGESTED
   My colleague _____ take a break.

2 I didn't read the notice carefully.
   SHOULD
   I _____ the notice carefully.

3 My doctor told me that I shouldn't spend too long at the computer every day.
   WARNED
   My doctor _____ too long at the computer every day.

4 I don't think Marty will reply before Friday.
   LIKELY
   I don't think Marty _____ before Friday.

5 House prices usually rise faster than salaries.
   TEND
   Salaries _____ than house prices.

6 I worked for two companies in London – both companies were in the city centre.
   EACH
   I worked for two companies in London – _____ in the city centre.

7 ★ ★ **Complete the sentences using the prompts in brackets. Do not change the order of the words. Change the forms or add new words where necessary. Use up to six words in each gap.**

When employees aren't given enough training, *mistakes are bound to happen* (mistake/bound/happen).

1 We _____ (stop/receive/expensive/gift) from Uncle Pete after he was made redundant.

2 The twins loved it when their big brother made up bedtime stories _____ (they/be/main) characters.

3 I organised a surprise party for Jake's birthday, but he wasn't surprised at all. Somebody _____ (must/tell/he) about it.

4 People _____ (use/look) up to him until he was convicted of stealing.

5 Fiona said she was sure _____ (she/catch/cold) from a man sneezing on the train last Friday.

8 ★ ★ ★ **Complete the text with the correct forms of the words in the box. There are two extra words.**

> ~~advice~~   add   different   enthusiasm
> equal   visit   warn   willing

Stand up, sit down!

Doctors *advise* people to stand up and walk around for at least twenty minutes a day. However, many adults are ¹_____ to change their routines, even though it is common knowledge that sitting down all day is bad for their health. They think they need to become more athletic to notice a ²_____ , which is not true.

Experts believe that healthy habits develop at a young age. For this reason, several primary schools in the UK have started to make physical activity a priority for their students and want them to move at every opportunity. For example, they have to stand up when a ³_____ comes into the classroom or stand up and sit down at certain points during songs. A representative from one of the schools says that the children are very ⁴_____ about this new approach. He ⁵_____ that increased activity like this is also leading to better concentration and more highly motivated students.

Sounds like an excellent idea for all of us! You can start tomorrow by having a stroll at lunchtime.

WRITING

5.8 An opinion essay

1 Complete the advice about writing an opinion essay with the words in the box. There are two extra words.

> aspects   comment   discuss   examples   issue
> ~~main opinion~~   opposing   restate   support
> ~~topic~~   understand

- In the **introduction**, introduce the _topic_ and state your _main opinion_. Then say which points of view or
¹_____ you will discuss.
- In **paragraphs two and three**, ²_____ different aspects of the issue and ³_____ your main opinion. Expand the discussion by giving
⁴_____ .
- In **paragraph four**, acknowledge an ⁵_____ opinion and say why you disagree with it.
- In the **conclusion**, ⁶_____ your main opinion and include a final ⁷_____ .

2 Read the task and Sara's essay. Underline three words or phrases which express certainty and three words or phrases which describe consequences.

> Many jobs have long working hours which lead to stress, burnout and a lack of work-life balance. At the same time, youth unemployment is increasing. In your opinion, should there be a four-day working week to tackle both these problems?
>
> Write an opinion essay on this topic analysing the benefits of a four-day week for work-life balance and employment.

3 Match the beginnings of the sentences with the endings.

To sum up, it is harder for young people   ⓔ
1 It is true that in some cases jobs are harder   ◯
2 When it comes to young people,   ◯
3 I am of the opinion that it is much harder to find ◯
4 It is also important to consider this issue with regard to ◯
5 Some people do not agree and feel that unemployment ◯
6 All in all, entering the job market is tough for young people ◯

a   the effects of long-term unemployment on young people.
b   competition for jobs tends to be stronger.
c   and can seriously affect their motivation.
d   does not seriously affect young people.
e   to find a job today than it was in the past.
f   employment during difficult economic times.
g   to find now because of technological advancements.

4 Choose the option that is **not** correct. In one of the sentences, all the options are correct.

1 The most obvious _result / choice / consequence_ of unemployment among young people is lack of income.
2 The outcome of such a _choice / decision / situation_ could be that it is even more difficult to find work.
3 Unemployment _triggers / leads to / results_ low self-esteem in many young people.
4 As a _cause / result / consequence_ many young people cannot afford to move out of their parents' homes.
5 In some cases, unemployment can even _cause / outcome / result in_ crime as young people find themselves desperate for money.

◯◯◯

King James School Students Speak Up!

HOME | ARTICLES | FORUM | CONTACT

This month's winning opinion piece comes from Sara Stokes in class 10E – well done to Sara!

These days, many school-leavers are unable to find jobs and at the same time, many employees are overworked, stressed and working increasingly long hours. Personally, I believe that a four-day week would be a great solution that would benefit everyone in this situation. To explain the reasons for my view, it is my intention to explore this issue in terms of work-life balance and employment.

When it comes to productivity, studies show that most people perform best when working between 25–30 hours a week. A four-day week would take advantage of this and this could also lead to employees using their time more efficiently and increasing their output. Undoubtedly, staff would be less stressed and probably have a better work-life balance. As a result, they are likely to be more motivated and creative so I am of the opinion that both employees and employers would benefit.

Another important aspect of this issue is employment. If people worked only four days a week, companies would employ more staff. Young people could then be offered part-time work or job-sharing with experienced staff. Undeniably, this would reduce unemployment among young people and give them valuable work experience to improve their career prospects. Without doubt, companies would also benefit from fresh new talents.

Some people disagree, and argue that a shorter working week would mean people earning less as they would be unable to work more if they wanted to. However, these issues could be solved. Employees could have the option to work overtime, or salaries could be guaranteed, to ensure a good standard of living.

All things considered, I think introducing a four-day week would have tremendous advantages. I would prefer to earn less and have a far better work-life balance, also knowing that I was helping to reduce unemployment. For me, the outcome of working less would mean I was a happier, more enthusiastic and hard-working employee.

Sara Stokes (10E)

5 **Read the task below. Complete the opinion essay with the words in the box.**

> believe   conclusion   consider   examine   this issue
> in terms of   no doubt   ~~personally~~   result in   while

> Many people think schools don't do enough to prepare young people for the world of work. In your opinion, should schools teach more practical and critical thinking skills and give career guidance, or is it better for them to focus on improving students' academic performance?
>
> Write an opinion essay on this topic analysing the advantages or disadvantages of schools teaching work skills and giving career guidance.

Many school-leavers struggle to get a job because businesses are reluctant to employ people they think have few useful skills and cannot think for themselves. _Personally_, I believe schools could do far more to prepare young people for the world of work, and that this should be one of the main purposes of education. To explain the reasons for this opinion, I will ¹_____ the issue ²_____ the advantages of teaching work skills and giving career guidance.

When it comes to preparing for the workplace, there is ³_____ that learning practical and critical thinking skills is part of a good all-round education. Learning to prioritise tasks, cooperate in teams and work to a deadline are skills that students can equally well use with schoolwork. Teaching them at school could also ⁴_____ improved academic performance.

It is also important to ⁵_____ with regard to career guidance. It is often the case that this advice is out-of-date, insufficient or non-existent, and students would really benefit from learning more about how to evaluate and compare information on different careers and study paths.

⁶_____ some people say school standards have dropped in recent years, and using class time to prepare students for work takes valuable time away from studying subjects such as maths or languages, I ⁷_____ this time would be well spent studying transferable life skills. They are just as useful in the classroom as in the workplace and beyond.

In ⁸_____ , I think learning practical and critical thinking skills at school and having better career guidance would be of enormous benefit to students, and not distract them from their learning. Personally, I have found studying these skills has increased my confidence and enabled me to make better-informed choices about my studies and career.

6 **Read the task below. Before you start writing, note down some ideas and plan your work.**

> Recently it has become more difficult for young people leaving school or university to find a job. In your opinion, should all young people do internships or apprenticeships to give them work experience? Write an essay on this topic. In your essay:
> - give your main opinion about the topic,
> - discuss the advantages (or disadvantages) of doing internships and apprenticeships,
> - mention other ways young people can get work experience,
> - describe the effects of long-term unemployment on young people,
> - write your conclusion restating your main opinion and including a final comment.

In my opinion essay:

• I have introduced the topic, stated my main opinion and said which points of view or aspects will be discussed.	⃝
• I have discussed the different aspects, supported my main opinion and given examples.	⃝
• I have acknowledged an opposing opinion and said why I disagree with it.	⃝
• I have used linking phrases and language to express certainty and describe consequences.	⃝
• I have finished by restating my main opinion and included a final comment.	⃝
• I have used a formal style.	⃝
• I have checked my spelling.	⃝
• my handwriting is neat enough for someone else to read.	⃝

VOCABULARY AND GRAMMAR

1 Complete the text with one word in each gap.

Time management at work

How is it that some people manage to get a huge amount done during the working day, while others struggle to work to _deadlines_ and get a job done? If you're serious about increasing your
¹ _____ and achieving your long and short-term work
² _____ , you have to get organised. Here's how:

#1 Write down a daily plan. It should be in detail, including breaks. Note down everything you have to do ³ _____ in, day out, as well as unexpected tasks, like a last-minute report.

#2 Prioritise. Do your biggest and most important tasks first. Don't take on tasks that aren't part of your job. You might have to speak your ⁴ _____ here and learn to say 'no'.

#3 Love what you do. When you care about what you are doing and put your ⁵ _____ into it, then you'll work faster and better.

Follow these simple tips to reach your full potential!
Good luck!

/5

2 Complete the sentences with the correct forms of the phrasal verbs in the box. There is one extra verb.

> burn out   carry out   get down to   keep at
> ~~map out~~   put off   work towards

I've already got my career _mapped out_, so I know what I'll be doing next year, in five years and in 10 years' time.
1 Our office is going to _____ a survey related to the health and welfare of all company staff.
2 It's hardly surprising she _____ , she was working 14-hour days and the weekends as well.
3 Tom's always talking about how much he dislikes his current job. It's high time he _____ looking for a new one!
4 Don't _____ doing new tasks because they seem tricky. Making a start is always the hardest part.
5 I always admire sports stars. You really have to _____ training if you want to succeed.

/5

3 Complete the sentences with the correct forms of the words in the box.

> conscientiousness   ~~enthusiasm~~   knowledge
> overwork   punctuality   single-mindedness

All the staff were _enthusiastic_ about the new project and keen to start work on it.
1 The bus drivers have gone on strike due to their long hours. They're complaining about being _____ .
2 We require all staff at the health centre to be _____ and hard-working.
3 Advertising is a creative industry where being _____ about ideas doesn't work.
4 Being _____ is important in most jobs because being late means lost working time and less productivity.
5 Marie Curie didn't just know a lot about physics, she was extremely _____ about chemistry too.

/5

4 Complete the second sentence so that it reports the first.

'Prepare your CV for the next Friday,' Tim's tutor said.
Tim's tutor _told him to prepare his CV_ for the following Friday.
1 'How long were you looking for a job before you found one?' Leo asked me.
Leo asked me _____.
2 'I'm flying to Canada tomorrow,' Bob told her.
Bob told her that _____.
3 'Don't ask me for a loan,' my mum told my brother.
My mum told my brother _____.
4 'I will have to buy at least two new suits,' Steve said.
Steve said that he _____.
5 'Are you going to commute to Leeds?' he asked me.
He wanted to know _____.

/5

5 Complete the second sentence so that it means the same as the first. Use the word in capitals.

'You must talk to the boss immediately!' Simon said.
URGED
Simon _urged me to talk to the boss_ immediately.
1 'No, Chris. I must prepare the draft copy of the contract myself,' the manager said. **INSISTED**
The manager _____
the draft copy of the contract himself.
2 'Why don't we wear our new jumpers for the charity concert?' Nina said. **THAT**
Nina _____
our new jumpers for the charity concert.
3 'We've been doing research for the new campaign since January,' Rob said. **EXPLAINED**
Rob _____
for the new campaign since January.
4 'I'm sorry. I can't get the report ready in time for the meeting,' Leo said to his boss. **FOR**
Leo _____
the report ready in time for the meeting.
5 'Don't forget, they're decorating the office soon,' Clare said to me. **REMINDED**
Clare _____
the office soon.

/5

6 Choose the correct answers A–C.

Worst mistakes at work

Once, my boss told me _B_ a client in an office block in London. When I got there, the receptionist ¹___ how to get to the office, but I got the directions wrong. I opened a fire door on to the roof and it closed behind me, so I had to walk round the roof to find a way out. To my horror, I walked past a window only to see my colleagues and the client inside the room! The client suggested ²___ to the door, but, in the end, they opened the window for me to climb in! Of course, I apologised ³___ late and all the confusion. Luckily the client found it funny and he assured ⁴___ it wasn't a problem. We got the contract, and when I returned, my boss congratulated ⁵___ making the meeting a success!

	A	B	C
	A visiting	(B) to visit	C that visit
1	A explained	B convinced	C insisted
2	A to go back	B that go back	C going back
3	A for to arrive	B for arriving	C that I arrived
4	A to me that	B me that	C that
5	A me on	B to me	C on

/5

Total   /30

7 Complete the second sentence so that it means the same as the first. Use the word in capitals.

'You need to rest at home,' the doctor said to me.
ADVISED
The doctor _advised me to rest_ at home.

1 'It wasn't me who broke the photocopier in the office,' Sally said.
DENIED
Sally _____ in the office.

2 It seems that I forgot to bring my CV.
HAVE
I appear _____ .

3 'Don't forget to turn off the lights,' the manager told me.
REMINDED
The manager _____
the lights before leaving the office.

4 Why didn't you ask first?
SHOULD
You _____ .

5 It is my intention to explore this issue from the viewpoint of motivation.
TERMS
I will explore this issue _____
_____ .

/5

8 Complete each pair of sentences with the same answer A–C.

If you're a farmer, you need to be accustomed to _A_ work at all hours.
Jem failed the exam because it was extremely _A_ and covered things he hadn't revised.
(A) hard   B manual   C voluntary

1 I'm not enjoying the course. I think I might __ out of it.
You need to carry those boxes carefully or you'll __ one.
A retire   B drop   C keep

2 When are you going to __ round to painting the house? You've been putting it off for ages.
Lisa is nearly forty years older that Ella, but they __ on incredibly well. It's a pretty unusual friendship.
A come   B grow   C get

3 When you work freelance, it's good to have __ well-paid work that you do regularly.
There's been a __ increase in the number of unemployed young people.
A sharp   B marked   C steady

4 Before you choose a career __ , you should look at all your options.
If you want a short-cut to the shops, you can walk along that __ . It only takes a few minutes.
A path   B road   C way

5 I'm sorry to let you down by cancelling at the last moment, but I'll __ up for it, I promise.
If I have time later, I'm going to __ a cake for Joanna's birthday as a surprise.
A prepare   B cook   C make

/5

9 Complete the sentences using the words in capitals and any other necessary words.

Lucia doesn't think the same way as anyone else I know, she is _wired differently_. (WIRED)

1 I can't help you right now because I'm _____ this project, but as soon as I can, I'll phone you. (TIED)

2 I thought Ben would _____ these bad habits as he got older and more sensible, but if anything, they've got worse. (GROW)

3 Mark doesn't really know what he wants to do, but we're confident that he'll _____ and get a job doing exactly what he loves. (NICHE)

4 Sylvia is always starting things and not finishing them. She _____ , but I hope she starts to focus more soon. (PURPOSE)

5 My parents keep reminding me to fill in the job application, but I haven't done it yet. I'll _____ it next weekend. (GET)

/5

10 Read the text and choose the correct answers A–D.

I have always dreamt of working _B_ electronics so when I graduated from university, I immediately got **1**__ to applying for jobs. I applied for one in a multinational corporation whose products mainly target young people. Many of my friends said that getting a post there **2**__ impossible because I was young and inexperienced. However, I wanted to prove them wrong, so I sent my CV together with a covering letter. To my surprise, I was invited to an interview.

The whole procedure took several days. Having been divided into several groups, we were given a number of tasks to complete to test our ability to **3**__ ourselves in stressful situations, work under pressure or within a set time. The task I enjoyed most was the one in which we had to design adverts and commercials promoting new products, but we were told **4**__ any electronic devices. We had to be really creative and resourceful.

I'd describe the selection process as nerve-racking and incredibly stressful. Although I didn't get the job, the experience helped me learn a lot about myself. It certainly didn't make me less **5**__ about working in electronics – I'm still determined to find the perfect job in the industry.

	A on	(B) in	C at	D by
1	A out	B off	C up	D down
2	A will be		B would be	
	C is going to be		D had been	
3	A achieve	B reach	C think for	D work to
4	A don't use	B not use	C to not use	D not to use
5	A enthusiastic		B conscientious	
	C overworked		D knowledgeable	

/5

Total	/20

INTERVIEW ISSUES

Job interviews are certainly stressful for job seekers, but what about the people conducting the interviews? Do they get worried? Four managers share their experiences.

A Paula

The interview that most sticks in my mind is actually the first one I ever did. I'd just been promoted and was interviewing candidates for an IT job. I'd printed out the first candidate's CV and had prepared questions to ask based on his experience. Unfortunately, when he introduced himself I realised I had the wrong CV and had no idea who he was or what his skills were. I panicked and my mind went completely blank. I remember asking him about his summer holiday plans and if he liked dogs. It was awful. I felt so bad for the way I'd treated him that I decided to hire him, and I'm really happy I did. He has worked here for over ten years and was the brains behind our highest selling software. Maybe I should ask him about the interview, but just thinking about it makes me grimace.

B Jeffrey

I was interviewing a man a few years ago in this very high-tech building. We'd just moved in and were getting used to how everything worked. All the doors were operated by key cards and on that particular day I'd forgotten mine. I asked a colleague to open one of the conference rooms for me and had a good interview with a man named Brian. Unfortunately, after thanking Brian for attending I realised we couldn't get out. We were banging on the door for ages. At the end of the interview I wasn't planning on offering him the job, but during the half hour we were trying to get out we talked more and I realised he was the perfect fit for our company. I offered him the job then and there and luckily he accepted. He's worked here ever since.

C Pierre

I interviewed a woman for a sales manager role and I must say it was difficult. She told me she had worked in sales before, but she couldn't come up with any examples of how to actually increase sales. However, she was very happy to speak her mind about why she didn't get on with her previous boss. When she left, I felt very relieved. Unfortunately, when I went to the café next to the office for lunch she was there and immediately came over. She apologised and explained she had been extremely stressed which was why the interview had gone so badly. She wanted to repeat the interview, however, I'd already found someone for the role and I turned her down. I realise interviews are stressful and I try to make people feel at ease, but ultimately it's up to the candidate to behave appropriately.

D Coral

I was new in my job when a senior colleague asked me for a favour. She was stuck on a train and wanted me to conduct an interview for her. I wanted to make a good impression, so I agreed and prepared by printing some really nice interview questions. What I forgot to do was familiarise myself with the role advertised. A really conscientious woman turned up and answered the questions brilliantly. She knew how to focus on her strengths and had her career path all mapped out. It started to go wrong when she asked me detailed questions. Because I was new, I struggled to find answers, especially when she asked company policies and beliefs. It was extremely embarrassing as she knew more than me. She didn't get the job which I thought was strange, but part of me was relieved that I wouldn't have to face her again. I blush just thinking about it.

1 Read the text on page 82. Match sections A–D with statements 1–10. The sections may be chosen more than once.

Which person
1 feels that the candidate was better prepared than they themselves were? ☐
2 refused to give someone a second chance? ☐
3 was surprised a particular person wasn't hired? ☐
4 gave someone a job because they felt guilty? ☐
5 changed their mind about someone they interviewed? ☐
6 was unhappy to meet the interviewee for a second time? ☐
7 was eager to impress their boss? ☐
8 prepared questions for the wrong candidate? ☐
9 realised the candidate was ideal for the job after spending more time with them? ☐
10 thinks interviewees should know how to conduct themselves in an interview? ☐

2 Read each text and put a cross (X) by the missing phrase.

1 | We live in a throw-away society where people buy new mass-produced items every week. To minimise waste, it's important to avoid _____ and shop responsibly.

A impulse purchases ☐
B charity shops ☐
C local brands ☐

2 | The latest exhibition is inspired by nature and the outdoors. All of the paintings in the show are _____ , but you'll have to be prepared to spend a fortune. The cheapest piece costs as much as a small car!

A up for auction ☐
B rolling in money ☐
C available to buy ☐

3 | Successful candidates will be expected to work long hours and be prepared to work abroad. They will also need to _____ the latest developments in the financial sector.

A keep up with ☐
B put up with ☐
C come up with ☐

WRITING

3 Read the writing task and write an opinion essay.

Fast fashion, or producing the latest trends quickly and cheaply, allows everyone to wear fashionable clothing whether they are rich or not. Write an opinion essay in which you discuss the advantages and disadvantages of fast fashion for teenagers.

6 A matter of fact

VOCABULARY

6.1

The media • truth and falsehood
• adjective-noun collocations
• adverbs

SHOW WHAT YOU KNOW

1 Choose the collocation that is not correct in each sentence.

On the way to college, I listen to *podcasts* / *music streaming services* / *social media posts* / *the radio*.

1 Most evenings, I watch *online video clips* / *news blogs* / *reality TV* / *drama series*.
2 The best places to get news from are *reality TV* / *news apps* / *local newspapers* / *social media posts*.
3 Maria loves being up-to-date with what's going on in the world, so she often reads *celebrity twitter feeds* / *newspaper editorials* / *news blogs* / *drama series*.
4 Sam's always online and *posts* / *retweets* / *shares* / *feeds* / *'likes'* lots of things. I don't know how he has time to work!

---

2 Complete each gap with one word from Exercise 1.

Which celebrity Twitter feeds do you follow?
My favourite is Ryan Reynolds. I often *retweet* what he posts, he's so funny.

1 My favourite TV drama _____ was *Game Of Thrones*. I used to write social _____ posts about it all the time.
2 My sister can't stand _____ TV. She thinks it's a waste of time watching people being themselves on a TV show.
3 Have you got any news _____ on your phone or do you read news _____ online?
4 I like knowing what's happening in my area, so I read the _____ newspaper every week. They have some interesting newspaper _____ about issues affecting our town.
5 We sometimes watch music video _____ online, but usually use a music _____ service to download songs.
6 Do you ever _____ interesting things with your friends on social media?
7 Katia made a _____ recently about good books for teenagers. Over a hundred people have listened to it already.

WORD STORE 6A | Truth and falsehood

3 Complete the dialogue. The numbers in brackets show the number of letters in the missing words. The first two letters are given.

Host: Welcome to the programme. Each week on 'Why I decided to be a …' we talk to young people who have recently started their career and ask them to explain their choice. This week, Amy Jones is with us. She studied journalism and now works as a reporter. Amy, what attracted you to this career?

Amy: I wanted to be a journalist because I think it's important to give people authentic stories that don't **di**_*stort*_ (7) the truth so they can form their own opinions. I'm afraid many news agencies these days ¹**mi**_____ (9) the public deliberately and they most likely have an ²**ag**_____ (6) when they do it. Sometimes, they even spread ³**fa**_____ (4) news or ⁴**ta**_____ (6) with photos to support what they write. ⁵**Ma**_____ (12) the media is more common than you would imagine. I think journalists have a responsibility to tell the truth, although I also think readers have a responsibility not to believe everything.

Host: Some interesting points there, Amy. So, what can newsreaders do about these issues?

Amy: Well, when you read any news story, you shouldn't take it at ⁶**fa**_____ (4) value. You should check the ⁷**ac**_____ (8), ⁸**ev**_____ (8) the sources and, of course, double-check the ⁹**fa**_____ (5) yourself. Often when we read a news story, something bothers us about it, but we don't trust our ¹⁰**in**_____ (9). We should! If a story doesn't quite add up, chances are it isn't entirely true.

WORD STORE 6B | Adjective-noun collocations

4 Complete the pairs of sentences with the words in the box.

~~basis~~   commitment   feeling   gain
information   source   story

I watch the news on TV on a daily *basis*.
Do you tend to read newspapers on a regular *basis*?

1 The papers are awash with _____ about the elections.
I feel like I'm constantly being bombarded with _____ , but too little of it is about important issues such as climate change.
2 This paper has a clear _____ to telling the truth, we don't report fake news.
Is it possible to make a long-term _____ to truthful reporting?
3 Don't believe anything you read on that website, it doesn't use any reliable _____ of information or check facts carefully.
I was surprised there were incorrect facts in the editorial as that website is usually a reputable _____ of information.
4 The company made up the story for commercial _____ , but they didn't make any money on it.
It's wrong to spread fake news for political _____ . It should be illegal in my opinion.
5 I've got a gut _____ that this story isn't true.
Matt had a distinct _____ that the interview was going to be a disaster, and he was right!
6 Journalists are always looking for a newsworthy _____ that they can report on.
When I glanced at the headlines, there was an eye-catching _____ about the prime minister.

WORD STORE 6C | Adverbs

5 Choose the correct option.

I almost got in an accident while I was cycling to work yesterday when a car turned *knowingly* / *alarmingly* close to me.

1 It is important to examine the facts in a situation *critically* / *deliberately* before deciding whether something is true or false.

2 Sara is a kind and thoughtful person. She would never *remarkably* / *knowingly* hurt or upset you.

3 In spite of the fact that the town's population has grown, it's a *critically* / *remarkably* peaceful place to live.

4 I've been following the news of the election *alarmingly* / *closely*, because I want to know the results as soon as they are announced.

5 Max *deliberately* / *remarkably* broke his phone, hoping that he would get a new one from the company.

6 Complete the sentences with the adverbial forms of the words in the box.

> alarming   close   critical   ~~deliberate~~
> knowing   remarkable

I was shocked because the politician *deliberately* lied about the facts. He chose to do it and everyone found out.

1 Always look at the facts _____ and don't just believe everything you hear.

2 Too many people can't recognise fake news and are becoming _____ misinformed. It's very worrying.

3 As a journalist, Sam has tight deadlines, but he's always _____ relaxed about them. How can he be so calm?!

4 The ability to think _____ is a necessary skill nowadays. You should first read the information, and then decide your own opinion.

5 I evaluate my sources carefully and I've never _____ written anything false. I would never do that on purpose.

7 Choose the correct answers A–C.

News Not News

Can you spot fake news?

Have you ever checked the <u>B</u> of a story you've read? What made you suspect there was something wrong with it? The Internet is ¹___ with information about everything, but how good are you at spotting fake news? A study of nearly 5,000 people in America had some surprising results. It turns out that people who think the media is trying to ²___ everyone were often the worst at spotting fake news. People with a negative attitude to the word 'news' often thought they needed the least help ³___ sources to check if a story was true or not. In contrast, people who had a more positive view of the news were able to trust their ⁴___ when it came to working out which were fake stories – 82 percent of them spotted the fake ones compared to 69 percent of those who felt more negative about the news. The other factor that helped people spot fake headlines was a higher level of education. The higher the level of education, the less likely people were to take a story at face value, and the more likely they were to think ⁵___ about it.

	A	B	C
	A value	(B) accuracy	C true
1	A awash	B full	C reliable
2	A distort	B spread	C mislead
3	A evaluating	B manipulating	C tampering
4	A feelings	B thoughts	C instincts
5	A remarkably	B critically	C alarmingly

/5

8 Find and correct the mistakes in the sentences.

I read the newspaper on a regular ~~base~~ so I know what's happening around the globe.   *basis*

1 When you look at the images. It obvious someone has tampered on the photos.   _____

2 Pay closely attention to what you read – so many stories distort the truth one way or another.   _____

3 They ran the story to make money. It was all about commercial gaining, not the truth.   _____

4 I couldn't help noticing the catch-eye story about a celebrity on the front page.   _____

5 I think that website has a political agenda, it's always publishing alarmingly stories about the government.   _____

/5

85

GRAMMAR

6.2

Conditional clauses –
alternatives to *if*

SHOW WHAT YOU KNOW

1 Match the beginnings of the sentences with the endings and then choose the correct options.

    You'll miss the end of the film   `e`
1 If you read the instructions,   ◯
2 If you didn't know it was computer animation,   ◯
3 I wouldn't have believed it,   ◯
4 If Pinocchio tells the truth,   ◯

a you *wouldn't* / *would* believe it was real.
b if I *hadn't* / *had* seen it with my own eyes.
c you *won't* / *'ll* be able to do it yourself.
d his nose *doesn't grow* / *grows*.
e if you *stay* / *(don't stay)* awake.

2 ★ Complete the sentences with *unless* or *provided/providing*.

    Don't invest in this risky business *unless* you are willing to lose all your savings.
1 Most cats will be perfectly OK on their own all day _____ you leave them some food.
2 Exams are unfair _____ you can guarantee that no one cheats.
3 _____ the fish actually moves, it is virtually impossible to spot it because of its camouflage.
4 _____ you don't look too closely, you can't tell the watch is a fake.
5 Mike exaggerates, but he's good company _____ you take what he says with a pinch of salt.
6 It's impossible to look so wrinkle-free at the age of 72 _____ you've had plastic surgery.

3 ★ ★ Put the words in the correct order to complete the conditional questions.

    you/imagine/could/a super-power/choose
    Imagine you could choose a superpower, which would you choose?
1 been/suppose/the Apollo moon landings/had/fake

    _____ ,
    could the space shuttle programme really have happened?
2 I/I/said/didn't want/university/to go to/supposing

    _____ ,
    what would you say?
3 imagine/have to/didn't/go to school/we/today

    _____ ,
    what would we do instead?
4 you/been born/had/imagine/fifty years ago

    _____ ,
    how might life be different?
5 you/imagine/any job/could have

    _____ ,
    what would you like to be?

4 ★ ★ Match answers a–e to questions 1–5 in Exercise 3.

a Well, to start with, there'd be no Internet or mobile phones. ◯
b I doubt it. The technology to build it wouldn't have existed. ◯
c We'd stay home and watch films all day. ◯
d I'd ask what you planned to do instead. ◯
e A brain surgeon. Or perhaps an astronaut. ◯

5 ★ ★ ★ Rewrite the sentences using inversion to make them more formal.

    If I had taken what he said at face value, I would have made the wrong decision.
    Had I taken what he said at face value , I would have made the wrong decision.
1 If I should not return, tell my family I love them.

    _____ ,
    tell my family I love them.
2 If Helen wasn't so two-faced, I'd ask for her opinion.

    _____ ,
    I'd ask for her opinion.
3 If the announcement hadn't been so ill-timed, fewer people would have objected.

    _____ ,
    fewer people would have objected.
4 If you should see Meredith, please give her our love.

    _____ ,
    please give her our love.
5 If it wasn't summer, our journey through the mountains would be impossible.

    _____ ,
    our journey through the mountains would be impossible.

SHOW WHAT YOU'VE LEARNT

6 Complete the text using the words in the box. There are two extra words.

> had   imagine   not   provided   should
> ~~supposing~~   unless   were   would

Supposing you were asked to define reality, what would you say? **1**_____ something very strange happened during the night, your world is roughly the same today as it was when you went to sleep yesterday. You are still you, and the past remains unchanged. **2**_____ you looked out of your window this morning, you would have seen the same view as last night and, **3**_____ you didn't develop incredible powers of prediction as you slept, the future is still unknown, just as it was yesterday at this time. To put it another way, you woke up to reality.

However, **4**_____ you curious enough to ask a philosopher or scientist to define reality, you would probably get a rather more complicated answer. **5**_____ it turned out that reality was actually an illusion, how **6**_____ you feel? Well, some deep thinkers believe exactly this, and in his new book Professor Brian Sixsmith attempts to make their ideas accessible to the everyday reader.

         /6

GRAMMAR: Train and Try Again page 176

1 Complete the extract from the dialogue about Banksy with *about, for, on* or *through*. Sometimes more than one option is possible.

Extract from Student's Book recording 🔊 **3.5**

Alice: What are you doing?

Robert: I'm trying to find some information <u>on</u> the Internet [1]_____ my art project. I've got to do an essay [2]_____ artists who raise ethical issues [3]_____ their work.

Alice: Ooh, that sounds interesting. I did a similar module [4]_____ my degree. You should write [5]_____ street artists like Banksy who make statements [6]_____ society [7]_____ graffiti.

Robert: I don't know much [8]_____ him. Do you?

---

2 Complete the next part of the extract by choosing the correct verb forms.

Alice: [...] He's been doing street art for 25 years, but I've no idea how old he was when he started. Actually it's amazing how he's managed [1]*staying / to stay* so enigmatic, but apparently his friends are really loyal and committed to helping him [2]*remain / remaining* anonymous. I don't know much about his background – nobody does – but I can tell you about his murals and his painting techniques if you like.

Robert: Yes, that would be good.

Alice: OK, he started off with traditional painting onto walls and then later he started [3]*using / use* stencils and spray cans to speed up the painting process. When you want your identity [4]*to remain / remaining* a secret you don't want to hang around the streets too long doing something illegal! I mean, he is committing an offence.

Robert: [...] Right. Let me just finish [5]*write / writing* that down. OK, so what's he trying [6]*to achieve / achieving* with all this – what does he believe in?

Alice: Well, he's quite political – he calls himself an activist and he's against authority in general. He has strong beliefs about people and the way we live our lives. ...

Robert: So what other issues is he most interested in?

Alice: He's anti-war, so some of his murals aim [7]*raising / to raise* awareness of the stupidity of war. [...]

REMEMBER BETTER

When you learn a new verb, try to learn the common verb patterns that follow it. As well as the information in Unit 1, 1.5 and in the Grammar Reference in the Student's Book, you will find numerous tables of English verbs and their patterns online.

3 Complete the pairs of sentences with the correct forms of the words in capitals.

STUPID
I think it's *stupid* to fork out 50 euros extra for the same pair of shoes in a different colour.
In the end, his *stupidity* cost him a severe injury and a lengthy prison sentence.

1 FAIR
To ensure [a]_____ , anyone found cheating during the exam will automatically be given a fail grade.
Do you really think it is [b]_____ to steal someone's intellectual property?

2 EQUAL
The Earth belongs to everyone and all people on it should have [a]_____ rights.
Denmark has an impressive record on gender [b]_____ .

3 ANONYMOUS
This is an [a]_____ vote so please do not write your name on the voting paper.
To ensure [b]_____ the famous actor only walked through the city streets late at night.

4 LOYAL
One [a]_____ friend is worth a thousand acquaintances.
The next song I'd like to sing is about the importance of friendship and [b]_____ .

5 MYSTERY
The disappearance of Malaysia Airlines flight 370 will remain a [a]_____ unless the wreckage is found.
The [b]_____ disappearance of Lord Lucan, the aristocrat suspected of murder, has never been solved.

WORD STORE 6D | Collocations

4 Complete the sentences with the missing words. The first letters are given.

Don't give away any personal information online; always **p**r o t e c t your identity.

1 The **u**_ _ _ _ _ _ _ message of the article was that social media spread fake news.

2 The journalist received the information from a source who wished to **r**_ _ _ _ _ anonymous.

3 She claims she is innocent and that she didn't **c**_ _ _ _ _ the offence.

4 You can use the media to **r**_ _ _ _ awareness about important issues.

5 A representative of the company will **m**_ _ _ a statement today at a press conference.

6 He has **s**_ _ _ _ _ beliefs about the way society should be and he won't change his mind.

READING

6.4

Is the news good for you?
• verbs and verb patterns
• photography

1 Read the article and choose the best description.

1 The text aims to persuade people to watch and read less news because it can have an impact on how you feel.

2 The text aims to inform people about the potential negative effects of watching and reading the news and what you can do about this.

3 The text aims to recommend the best way to read or watch the news so that you do not feel anxious or worried.

Is the news good for you?

Keeping up with what is happening in the world is generally seen as an essential part of being a well-informed and educated citizen. Watching, listening to or reading the news can satisfy our curiosity, make us think, help us make choices and even avoid danger. Or at least that was the common view until recently. However, people are increasingly wondering if staying up to date with what is going on is good for us.

The frequency, speed and way we access news has completely changed over the past few decades. Whereas previously most newspapers were published daily and TV and radio news broadcasts were limited, now we are constantly bombarded with news from all sides: we have 24-hour news channels, apps to notify us about stories of interest and social media that expose us to news whether we want to see it or not. Online newspapers are updated many times a day, with 'breaking news' posts that follow events in real time.

The content of news reports is almost always negative. Throughout history, our survival has depended on noticing threats and avoiding danger, so the human brain is hard-wired to seek out information that is frightening or alarming, a concept known as 'negativity bias'*. We pay more attention to negative things because that kept us alive in the past and this is reflected in the news we consume. In addition, because people now use smartphones to record events live, the news we see has become far more graphic and shocking.

Recent studies have shown that our news habits have disadvantages for our physical and emotional health. In one survey, over 50 percent of Americans reported that the news caused them stress and anxiety, often causing tiredness or poor sleep. Research by psychology expert Graham Davey has also proved that watching terrible or sad news on TV can worsen people's moods and make them worry more about their own lives. Clearly, being exposed to this ever-increasing bad news can make us feel less positive and affect our health.

However, there are ways to counteract* this negativity. It is recommended that you limit the number of times you check the news to once or twice a day and avoid looking at news apps before bed in an effort to reduce the amount of negativity you are exposed to. If you notice your mood has changed after hearing or reading the news, try doing activities that improve mood such as exercising, listening to music or watching a funny video clip to make yourself feel better.

Several websites, podcasts and apps, such as DailyGood, the Good News Network and Positive News magazine offer an antidote* to the huge number of bad-news stories in the mainstream news. The Good News Network, for example, has over 20,000 positive news stories in addition to podcasts, showing that there is no lack of good news, but the media simply do not report it. Positive News was established to develop journalism that focuses on progress and solutions. Switching to these news sources could not only make us feel more positive about the world and ourselves, it could simply make us healthier.

While it is true that staying aware and informed is not a bad thing, it is evident that our news habits can have long-term effects on our health. We should not forget that we have a choice, not only about how much news we consume, but equally importantly about the kind of news we want to see.

2 Read the article again. Are statements 1–6 true (T) or false (F)?

1 Nowadays, people are exposed to as much news as they were in the past, but it is more shocking. ☐

2 People pay extra attention to dangerous things because they are more interesting. ☐

3 More than half of Americans who took part in the survey said that the news affected them negatively. ☐

4 Davey's research showed that people usually worry about things they see on TV news shows. ☐

5 The article recommends watching amusing videos if you feel worse after watching the news. ☐

6 The Good News Network reports stories that the mainstream media don't publish. ☐

GLOSSARY

bias (n) – an opinion about whether a person, group or idea which makes you treat them unfairly or differently

counteract (v) – to reduce or prevent the bad effect of something by doing something that has the opposite effect

antidote (n) – a substance that stops the effect of poison, something that helps improve the effects of something bad or negative

3 Complete the sentences with up to five words from the article in the correct form.

1 Not long ago, people thought being up to date with the news was necessary if you wanted to be _____ _____ .

2 In modern times, we are nonstop _____ _____ news stories from all kinds of channels – from newspapers, TV or the radio to social media.

3 Since historically human survival was related to the ability to recognise and react to dangerous situations, our minds are programmed to look for _____ _____ .

4 Information on the media has become more alarming due to _____ made by smartphone users.

5 One survey conducted in the USA proved that negative news stories have a bad influence on our well-being; more than half of the participants complained of news-related _____ _____ , as well as sleeping problems and tiredness.

6 In order to reduce the negative effects of keeping up with what's happening in the world, we are advised to check the news only _____ _____ .

7 In contrast to mainstream media, some sites or apps are dedicated to sharing positive news stories, by e.g. focusing on _____ _____ .

REMEMBER THIS

Compound adjectives can be made with nouns, adjectives, verbs and adverbs. They usually have a hyphen (-) before a noun. The following patterns are common:

number/measurement + noun e.g. *24-hour, half-price*

adjective + noun e.g. *high-speed, low-calorie*

adjective/adverb + -ed / -ing participle e.g. *left-handed, slow-moving*

self + adjective/noun e.g. *self-employed, self-service*

---

4 Read REMEMBER THIS and underline five examples of compound adjectives in the main reading text.

5 Complete the sentences with the compound adjectives in REMEMBER THIS.

If you need something late at night, there's a *24-hour* shop at the end of the road.

1 The TGV is a _____ train which can travel at about 320 km per hour.

2 About 10 percent of the world's population is _____ and only one in a hundred is naturally able to use both hands equally well.

3 We sat for ten minutes waiting for a waiter until we realised it was a _____ restaurant.

4 Don't miss the 50 percent reductions in our _____ Boxing Day sale.

5 One way to lose weight is by following a _____ diet.

6 Reports are coming in of _____ traffic on the M6 motorway between junctions 32 and 33.

---

6 Look at the vocabulary in lesson 6.4 in the Student's Book. Complete the sentences with the correct forms of the words in the box.

become   date   gain   have   make
seek   shake   trigger

Many people post selfies because they are *seeking* to feel part of a group.

1 The earliest mobile phone _____ back to 1973, when the first call was made on April 3.

2 When did tablets and smartphones _____ mainstream?

3 Can selfies really _____ serious illnesses and medical conditions?

4 I can't _____ off the thought that I've forgotten to do something important. What could it be?

5 Ella's just _____ a ridiculous claim – she says she invented the word 'selfie'. Can you believe it?

6 Max _____ a terrible habit of playing with his mobile phone when he's out with his friends.

7 Phone apps using photo filters have steadily been _____ popularity. Everyone's using them now.

WORD STORE 6E | Photography

7 Complete the text with the missing words. The first letters are given.

Using your camera:

Getting that perfect shot

When it comes to **c**apturing a memorable moment, we often end up taking ¹**s**_____ that don't do the occasion justice. Read on for some tips on improving the quality of your photos.

- Before you take a picture, make sure the subject is in ²**f**_____ – you want clear, ³**s**_____ images, not ⁴**b**_____ ones where you can't see the details clearly.

- Make sure you choose the correct ⁵**l**_____ – if you want to take close-ups then you need one that will allow you to ⁶**z**_____ in and take a good picture.

- When taking photos of people, decide if you want them to ⁷**p**_____ for the shot or if you are going to try and take the picture without them noticing so they look natural.

- Once you have your photos, remember you can ⁸**c**_____ them, so for example you can just have a shot of someone's face instead of their whole body. You can also ⁹**r**_____ them to make the colours stronger or get rid of things you don't want.

- You can also ¹⁰**a**_____ photos to remove elements you don't like, or change the colours in the picture.

Happy photographing!

89

GRAMMAR

6.5

Mixed conditionals

SHOW WHAT YOU KNOW

1 Match the conditional sentences to the meanings.

1 If we wait for the sales, we'll probably get the same coat at a discounted price.

2 If you are fair-skinned, you get sunburnt more easily than someone with darker skin.

3 If she had kept the lemons in the fridge, they wouldn't have gone mouldy so quickly.

4 If I had to save all my money, I wouldn't have any fun at the weekend.

a a situation that is always true ⬭
b a possible situation in the future ⬭
c an imaginary situation in the present or future ⬭
d an imaginary situation in the past ⬭

2 ★ Choose the correct options.

1 If Diane hadn't had singing lessons last year, she wouldn't be in the band now.
Diane *had / didn't have* singing lessons last year.
She *is / isn't* in the band now.

2 If I enjoyed playing pool, I'd have met you at the pool hall last night.
I *enjoy / don't enjoy* playing pool.
I *did / didn't meet* you at the pool hall last night.

3 I wouldn't be able to afford to go on holiday if I'd forked out for a new laptop.
I *forked out / didn't fork out* for a new laptop.
I *can / can't* afford to go on holiday.

4 I might have asked Leah to dance if I wasn't so shy.
I *am / 'm not* shy.
I *asked / didn't ask* Leah to dance.

5 If I didn't like you, I wouldn't have invited you to the party.
I *like / don't like* you.
I *invited / didn't invite* you to the party.

3 ★ ★ Complete the dialogues with the correct forms of the verb in brackets.

Kylie: I could trust you if you *weren't* (be) so two-faced.
Aaron: Come on, Kylie! You know I didn't mean it. I was only joking.

1 Alan: If Mr Lancaster _____ (like) football, he might not have given us homework for tonight.
Vic: I know. Doesn't he realise it's the cup final?

2 Allie: We wouldn't be in this situation now if you _____ (keep) quiet about what happened.
Eric: Well, it was your idea to skip class in the first place.

3 Eve: I _____ (have) a D now too if I had copied your essay.
Ben: Oh come on, Eve! You only got a C, which is not much better.

4 Anne: If you weren't so sweet, I _____ (leave) you a long time ago.
Matt: Thanks a lot! Is that a compliment or a threat?

4 ★ ★ ★ Complete the sentences to express imaginary conditions and results. Use short forms where possible.

Harry had an accident – he's got his leg in plaster now.
If Harry *hadn't had an accident*, he *wouldn't have* his leg in plaster now.

1 The photograph was airbrushed – the actor looks 10 years younger.
The actor ᵃ_____ 10 years younger if the photograph ᵇ_____ .

2 Justine isn't eighteen – she can't apply for the vocal workshop without her parents' consent.
If Justine ᵃ_____ eighteen, she ᵇ_____ for the vocal workshop without her parents' consent.

3 Charles is scared of flying – we drove to the Alps.
We ᵃ_____ to the Alps if Charles ᵇ_____ scared of flying.

4 Nick had plastic surgery – he doesn't have a nasty scar any more.
Nick ᵃ_____ a nasty scar if he ᵇ_____ plastic surgery.

5 Fran forgot her passport – she's not in Egypt now.
Fran ᵃ_____ in Egypt now if she ᵇ_____ her passport.

SHOW WHAT YOU'VE LEARNT

5 Complete the sentences using the prompts in brackets.

1 If Helen wasn't so gregarious, _____ _____ (she/not meet) all her friends from camp last summer.

2 If _____ (Stewart/turn) at those traffic lights, he wouldn't be stuck in traffic now.

3 If you had dressed in warmer clothes, _____ _____ (you/not be) ill now.

4 If _____ (I/pass) my driving test when I was eighteen, I wouldn't be on this bus now.

5 If _____ (he/not have) good eyesight, he wouldn't have seen the thief's face in the dim light.

6 If Daisy brushed her teeth properly, _____ _____ (she/not spend) so much on dental treatment last week.

/6

GRAMMAR: Train and Try Again page 176

SPEAKING

Discussing ethical issues

1 Translate the phrases into your own language.

SPEAKING BANK

Beginning your answer

I firmly believe/
I'm not convinced
they do because …

_____

_____

_____

One obvious/clear advantage /
disadvantage is that …

_____

_____

I think I'd emphasise/
explain that/how …

_____

_____

It's absolutely vital / quite
important, I think, because …

_____

_____

As well as (avoiding fur
products), other
(things that can help)
include …

_____

_____

_____

_____

I think the main/one/
a significant reason is that …

_____

_____

**Expressing opinions
tentatively**

It could be argued that …

_____

_____

_____

I don't feel particularly
strongly about …

_____

_____

I don't have a strong
opinion about …

_____

_____

I suppose you could
say that …

_____

_____

2 Complete the statements with comment adverbials. The first letters are given.

Ob_viously_, freedom of speech applies to everyone
including people whose views are generally
disliked by the majority. ⟨U⟩

1 Fr_____ , I'm tired of hearing the same old
arguments from pro-gun campaigners. ◯

2 Sa_____ , the government chose to ignore
nearly half a million protesters. ◯

3 Cl_____ , there is still a lot of work to be
done to change people's attitudes. ◯

4 Re_____ , the company cares more about
making money than it does about protecting
the environment. ◯

3 Label the sentences in Exercise 2 with letters using the following categories:

U – where the speaker is saying something they feel
can easily be noticed or understood.

R – where the speaker is saying what they really think
about something.

W – where the speaker is saying something they wish
wasn't true.

4 Put the words in order to complete statements 1–5, then match them with questions A–E.

1 that / emphasise / I'd / think
I _think I'd emphasise that_ the vast majority of it is
vandalism and has no artistic content at all.

2 obvious / one / is / disadvantage / that
Well, _____
most people throw them away without reading.

3 important / I / quite / because / think
It's _____
without the correct information, young people can't
make sensible decisions.

4 other things / as / well / reducing their energy
consumption, / include
As _____
_____
avoiding wasting food and minimising car travel.

5 don't / a strong / about / have / opinion / I
To be honest, _____
_____ that. This city has bigger
problems to worry about than a few more shops.

A What would you say to those people who insist
that graffiti is art? ⟨1⟩

B What are the drawbacks of handing out leaflets
to highlight ethical issues? ◯

C Don't you think it's terrible that they are building
another shopping centre in the city? ◯

D How important is it to educate young people on
the dangers of drugs? ◯

E What can the general public do to reduce their
impact on the environment? ◯

5 Complete the dialogue with the words in the box.

advantage ~~argue~~ argued explain firmly
obviously regrettably significant suppose

P: On today's 'My View' we are joined by Tom, who
believes that the UK voting age should be reduced
from eighteen to sixteen. Tom, what would you say to
those who might _argue_ that the average sixteen-year-
old is not wise enough to vote in a general election?

T: I think I'd [1]_____ that in my view that is an
unfair generalisation. It could be [2]_____
that many of the people who are currently old enough
to vote don't know enough to make an informed
choice. [3]_____ , a significant number of
voters make their decision based on what someone
looks like or some other irrelevant detail.

P: And do you think a sixteen-year-old could make
a more informed decision?

T: I [4]_____ believe they could. All UK
teenagers attend citizenship classes now and they
often know more about politics than older voters.
[5]_____ , young people are also affected
by the decisions of policy makers. Remember that in
the UK at the age of sixteen you can legally marry,
work full time and join the armed forces.

P: And what other reasons are there in your opinion?

T: Well, I think one very [6]_____ reason is
that a sixteen-year-old who works full time has to pay
taxes and therefore should have a say in how that
money is spent. Another clear [7]_____ of
lowering the age limit would be recognition that young
people's opinions are important. I [8]_____
you could say that, at the moment, they simply feel
completely excluded from politics.

1 ★ Cross out the word which does not form a collocation with the word in bold.

24-hour   service, journey, ~~anchor~~
1 **face**   weather-beaten, sunburnt, weatherproof
2 **knee-high**   water, check, socks
3 **woman**   thin-lipped, kind-hearted, casual
4 **news**   affairs, station, story
5 **green**   sky, lime, screen

2 ★ Write the missing letters to complete the words.

We're still looking for a young, **c** _u r l y_-haired girl to star in the shampoo commercial.
1 The decision to sell the company was premature and ill-**a** _ _ _ _ _ _. They've lost a lot of money.
2 I'd like to work as a translator or a copy **e** _ _ _ _ _ for a well-known publisher.
3 For a blow-by-**b** _ _ _ account of recent events and exclusive interviews, visit our website.
4 I can't decide between this **s** _ _-blue dress and that lemon-yellow skirt. Which is better for a job interview?
5 When she looked through the window, she saw a tall, **b** _ _ _ _-shouldered man standing at the door.

3 ★ ★ Complete the text with the phrases in the box.

> 24-hour   high-quality   mouth-watering   ~~old-fashioned~~   snow-white   state-of-the-art   user-friendly

Home Away from Home
Six Reasons to Stay at the City Retreat Hotel

A great choice for travellers looking for modern, spacious rooms combined with _old-fashioned_ luxury.
1 With our simple _____ app, you can book a room in just under one minute.
2 Our friendly staff at the _____ reception desk are always ready to provide you with information about attractions in the area.
3 All rooms and suites feature _____ furniture, including a queen-size bed, a leather sofa and a working desk.
4 Luxurious bathrooms provide fresh, _____ towels and bathrobes, made with organic cotton.
5 If you want to burn some energy, try our indoor swimming pool or the _____ gym where a qualified personal trainer will prepare a workout for you.
6 The hotel's restaurant offers _____ dishes, prepared by awarded chefs and made with local products.

4 ★ ★ Find and correct the mistakes. Two sentences are correct.

Most people don't pay attention to the old, ~~weather-bitten~~ building, but it's an important example of early 20th century architecture.   _weather-beaten_
1 My father used to work for a company car, but the factory closed when the economic crisis started a few years ago. _____
2 A thirteen-years-old boy is accused of making a phone call to airport security, which resulted in an emergency evacuation. _____
3 The advert promised a state-of-the-play laptop, but all I got was an old computer that shuts down unexpectedly. _____
4 The programme lasts for two hours and twenty minutes, including commercial breaks.
_____
5 With an extensive network of reports, the BBC and CNN can cover broken news from almost any part of the globe. _____
6 Regular health checks can help you identify early symptoms of diseases before it's too late.
_____
7 I don't believe Marcus could have done such a horrible thing – he's a kindly-hearted man.
_____

5 ★ ★ ★ Replace the words in bold with compound nouns or adjectives.

The **person reading the news** finished the interview by apologising for getting the interviewee's name wrong.   _newsreader_
1 I've never been interested in **the relationship between my country and other countries**.
_____ _____
2 Australian airlines hope to start **direct** flights from Sydney to London in a few years' time.
_____-_____
3 His ideas might sound a bit **unlikely** today, but I think it's exactly what'll happen.
_____-_____
4 In the future, I want to work in the film industry and specialise in applying **cosmetics**.
_____-_____
5 When the teacher pointed out my mistake, I was so embarrassed that I became **speechless**.
_____-_____
6 The musician revealed the name of his new album during a radio interview **that was being broadcast live**. _____-_____

6 ★ **Choose the correct answers. Sometimes more than one option is correct.**

Recently (a few)/ a little /(a couple of) famous fashion designers have decided not to use real furs in their collections.

1 Jason promised *calling me* / *to call me* / *that he would call me* as soon as he landed in London.

2 Don't forget to buy the newspaper tomorrow, *aren't you* / *will you* / *wouldn't you*?

3 How would your parents feel *imagine* / *unless* / *if* they found out you had lied to them about an important issue?

4 We have received this story from a person *who* / *that* / *whose* wants to remain anonymous.

5 If you *start* / *started* / *had started* doing some exercise to strengthen your muscles just after the injury, you wouldn't be in pain now.

7 ★ ★ **Choose the correct answers A–D.**

Can success be predicted?

Parents around the world <u>B</u> about their children's future and would love to know ¹__ advance how well their daughter or son will do at school and later in life. Predicting a child's future is an almost impossible task, but for many years, the 'marshmallow test' used ²__ considered one solution to this problem.

In the famous experiment, ³__ was first conducted at Stanford University in the late 1960s, researchers gave small children one marshmallow and ⁴__ to give them another one if they didn't eat it for fifteen minutes. Some years later, the authors of the study got in touch with the children again and found out that those who ⁵__ their marshmallow were doing better at school and work.

However, a more recent study questions the findings of the experiment ⁶__ at Stanford. It now seems that the 'marshmallow test' has little predictive value. In ⁷__ cases, whether the child ate the marshmallow did not determine his or her future.

	A would worry	B often worry
	C have worried	D are always worrying
1	A at	B on
	C from	D in
2	A to be	B be
	C being	D been
3	A who	B what
	C whose	D which
4	A forgot	B promised
	C let	D forced
5	A hasn't eaten	B wouldn't have eaten
	C hadn't eaten	D weren't eating
6	A made up	B carried out
	C dealt with	D led to
7	A each	B any
	C most	D every

8 ★ ★ **Complete the text with one word in each gap.**

MEMORIES

Separating fact <u>from</u> fiction isn't always easy. I'm not talking about things like deciding what's true in news reports or stories, but something ¹_____ closer to home – our own memories. Our memories are ²_____ a big part of the person we are that it's shocking to learn that some things that we remember vividly did not, ³_____ fact, happen.
⁴_____ my aunt not informed me otherwise, I would still believe that I personally witnessed our house on fire when I was about four. I ⁵_____ still see the picture of the burning house in my mind, but I wasn't there! Apparently, I was on holiday with my aunt and uncle at the time. People had ⁶_____ me so much about the fire that I had created my own memory of it. This has started me wondering how many more of our early memories are false. A scary thought! ⁷_____ you check and cross-reference all those memories, who knows which ones the brain has made up itself?

9 ★ ★ ★ **Complete the second sentence so that it has a similar meaning to the first. Use between two and six words, including the word in capitals.**

Teenagers used to watch television more often in the past.
WOULD
Teenagers *would watch television* more often in the past.

1 I don't share news articles if I'm not absolutely sure that they're true.
UNLESS
I don't share news articles _____ that they're true.

2 It is very likely that people will discover the truth even if you try to keep it a secret.
BOUND
People _____ the truth even if you try to keep it a secret.

3 This book sold well because its author is an Internet celebrity.
IF
This book _____ its author weren't an Internet celebrity.

4 'Well done, Sarah! You've won the chess championship,' the man said.
CONGRATULATED
The man _____ the chess championship.

5 It was a mistake that the journalist didn't check the facts.
SHOULD
The journalist _____ the facts.

WRITING

A review of a TV series

1 Complete the tips with the words in the box.

attract~~ characters director influences opinion plot recommendations summarise

A review
• In the introduction, use an interesting opening sentence to *attract* the reader's attention. Then give information such as the stars, ¹_____ and writer as well as details about the setting and obvious ²_____ on the show.
• In the main paragraphs, give more details about the ³_____ (the story) and the ⁴_____ (the people). Say what you liked and didn't like about it and present your ⁵_____ using a variety of adjectives and modifiers.
• In the conclusion, ⁶_____ your review and make any ⁷_____ .

2 Read the tips again and decide in which part of a review you would find the following sentences: the introduction (I), main paragraphs (MP) or conclusion (C).

In season 1, the main character is murdered, and events are told in a series of flashbacks. `MP`

1 I would recommend this series to fans of mystery and drama for its clever plot. ◯
2 Although the show is average at best, the soundtrack is incredible. ◯
3 Written by Eva Acorn, this show is influenced by films such as *X-Men* and *Superman*. ◯
4 All in all, the series offers a fresh, hilarious story about teenagers at high school. ◯
5 The performances by most of the cast are poor, with one exception. ◯
6 The plot explores interesting themes such as poverty, education and friendship. ◯
7 Prepare to be thrilled by this dark sci-fi drama. ◯
8 As far as I'm concerned, it's one of the best series around at the moment. ◯

3 Read the webpage and answer the questions.

1 What is the website about?
2 What do you have to do to enter the competition?

THE BEST SHOWS ON TV

| TV series by genre | Read reviews | **Competition Time** |

What TV shows would you recommend? Send us a review of an outstanding TV show that you think everyone should watch. The best reviews will be published on the website next month and the winner will receive a $50 prize.

4 Read the model review and put paragraphs A–D in the correct order.

◯ **A** The series tells the **g***ripping* story of Barry Allen, who becomes a 'metahuman' with the ability to move at super-human speed after being struck by lightning during a mysterious explosion. After his accident, Barry becomes 'the Flash' and dedicates his life to fighting crime. He travels back and forward in time as well as teaming up with other superheroes to fight villains and save those he loves. *The Flash* is now in its sixth season and the story remains far from ¹**p**_____ .

◯ **B** In conclusion, *The Flash* is a highly original series that viewers will be talking about for years to come. From the ²**o**_____ scene, it draws you in and you feel part of the story. I definitely ³**r**_____ it and look forward to next season's plot, which will no doubt be full of the usual ⁴**t**_____ and turns that make the story so unforgettable.

◯ **C** Journey into an imaginary world with a crime-fighting superhero in the exciting drama series, *The Flash*. This incredible show, developed by Greg Berlanti, Andrew Kreisberg and Geoff Johns, is heavily ⁵**i**_____ by comic book fiction. It combines action, mystery and science fiction to create a ⁶**w**_____ - _____ show that, in my opinion, everyone should see.

◯ **D** The plot of *The Flash* ⁷**e**_____ themes such as friendship, loyalty and time, particularly the consequences of trying to change the past or future. The story has terrifying and exciting moments that will have you sitting on the edge of your seat, but ultimately it is about human relationships. The show doesn't depend heavily on special effects – the confident ⁸**p**_____ of the cast are what make it successful. It is beautifully ⁹**s**_____ and accompanied by an excellent soundtrack.

5 Read the model text again and complete it with the missing words. The first letters are given.

6 Complete each sentence with an appropriate adjective. Use the clues in brackets to help you.

This show is _hilarious_ (very funny) and will make you cry with laughter.

1 For me, the characters were _____ (impossible to forget) because they were so real.

2 Some critics said that the plot was _____ (hard to believe), but I actually thought it was quite realistic.

3 Be warned – this is a _____ (exciting) series that you won't want to stop watching.

4 There are no twists and turns in the plot, which is fairly _____ (easy to guess), but the series is beautifully shot.

5 The first episode takes a _____ (emotional about the past) look at life in a small town in the 1970s.

6 Some scenes in the series are absolutely _____ (very frightening), so if you don't like horror films this is not for you.

7 Although the series was _____ (liked by critics), I thought the special effects were low-quality and the acting was average at best.

7 Read the task and complete the review with the words in the box.

```
●○○
```

Reviews wanted

Do you know a good TV series from a bad one? Could you write a review that makes someone want to watch – or _not_ watch – a series? We're looking for talented writers to create reviews for our new website. We pay 30 euros for each review we publish.

cast   concerned   conclude   ~~creators~~   drama
enough   plot   scenes   set   soundtrack

SHOW WHAT YOU'VE LEARNT

8 Read the task below. Before you start writing, note down some ideas and plan your work.

Write a review of a TV series you have watched or read about. Include these points:

- information about the type of show / stars / director / writer and who / what it was influenced by, and your opinion of it,
- details about the plot and characters,
- what you liked / didn't like about the series,
- your recommendation.

SHOW THAT YOU'VE CHECKED

In my review …

- I have used the opening paragraph to attract the reader's attention, mention the name of the TV show and state my overall opinion of it. ☐
- I have used the main paragraphs to give more details about the plot and characters and say what I liked / didn't like about the show. ☐
- I have summarised my review and made a recommendation in the conclusion. ☐
- I have used a formal style. ☐
- I have checked my spelling. ☐
- my handwriting is neat enough for someone else to read. ☐

```
●○○
```

Glee

Enjoy a ride through high school and beyond with some incredible characters in Fox's musical series _Glee_. Series _creators_, Ryan Murphy, Brad Falchuk and Ian Brennan, have created a hilarious show about life for would-be music stars. As far as I'm ¹_____ , this well-reviewed comedy ²_____ is a must-watch series.

³_____ in the fictional William McKinley High School, the story centres around teacher Will Schuester and his efforts to start and run a competition-winning choir, which school sports coach Sue Sylvester is determined to stop. The twists and turns of the ⁴_____ focus on the members of the choir and their problems with social issues, relationships and teamwork. It ran for six seasons, and from season four onwards it featured some stories about ex-choir members who had already left school.

Glee is a heart-warming series with a brilliant ⁵_____ that mixes pop tunes with classic hits. The plot is a little far-fetched at times, but that's part of its charm, and it's definitely not predictable. It explores themes of friendship, ambition, fame and success for young people at high school and their struggles to find happiness after high school. The ⁶_____ give convincing performances and the musical routines are brilliantly put together.

To ⁷_____ , _Glee_ is an unforgettable series that is by turns funny and sad, and impossible to stop watching. From the opening ⁸_____ , it becomes clear that this is a story that will make you think as well as laugh. I can't recommend it ⁹_____ for fans of music, drama and comedy and am sure it will still be popular in years to come.

6.9 SELF-CHECK

VOCABULARY AND GRAMMAR

1 Choose the correct answers A–C.

Many people who contact the police prefer to
A anonymous.
Ⓐ remain B raise C protect
1 These days, we are __ with information on the Internet twenty-four hours a day.
 A washed B bombarded C given
2 The image in the photo was __ because it was out of focus.
 A blurred B posed C sharp
3 We are waiting for officials to __ a statement about the events.
 A do B say C make
4 A lot of fake news is released for commercial __ .
 A profit B money C gain
5 The picture is too big. Would you mind __ it slightly?
 A cropping B airbrushing C retouching

 /5

2 Choose the correct word to complete the sentences.

It's clear that you take /(have)/ make an agenda in suggesting this because you want it to happen.
1 Do you think big businesses ever try to *tamper / double-check / manipulate* the media for financial reasons?
2 I have a distinct *feeling / thinking / knowing* that someone had tampered with the evidence. I'm sure Martin didn't steal anything.
3 The city council decided to *look into / come across / pick up* the way the mayor was spending public money.
4 When you write something, you should always *mislead / evaluate / distort* your sources.
5 I have very *big / underlying / strong* beliefs that the media shouldn't promote celebrity culture.

 /5

3 Match the beginnings of the sentences with the endings. There is one extra ending.

It's definitely irresponsible to spread   g
1 All in all, I'd say that the underlying
2 They will investigate anyone who commits
3 It seems the article is a deliberate attempt to distort
4 You shouldn't take this story at face
5 Many technology advances, such as mobile phones, have become

a value because it might not be completely accurate.
b mainstream in recent years and they're everywhere now.
c the truth and mislead people into believing false information.
d message of the film is that it's never too late to take action.
e commitment that you will keep at all costs.
f an offence online or attempts to do so.
g fake news stories from the Internet.

 /5

4 Choose the correct answers A–C.

A you woken me up, we wouldn't have missed the flight.
Ⓐ Had B Were C Should
1 __ you saw a UFO in your garden, what would you do?
 A Providing B Supposed C Imagine
2 __ they not competent, they wouldn't have hired you.
 A Were B Should C Had
3 I wouldn't have done it __ I knew it was worth trying.
 A suppose B provided C unless
4 __ revealed his plans to Catherine, we wouldn't have had any idea what he was going to do.
 A Leo had not B Had Leo not C Had not Leo
5 I'd be very happy to help you make a model of the solar system __ you prepare all the bits and pieces.
 A provided B imagine C supposing

 /5

5 Complete the second sentence so that it means the same as the first. Use conditional sentences.

Joshua published the article without consulting the chief editor, so he's in trouble now.
If Joshua *hadn't published the article without consulting the chief editor, he wouldn't be* in trouble now.
1 Mia stayed late because her boss was angry she hadn't finished the report.
 Mia _____ that she hadn't finished the report.
2 Pamela hasn't got a smartphone, and that's why she couldn't download the app.
 If Pamela _____ downloaded the app.
3 I am busy and that's why I didn't send you a reply.
 If I _____ a reply.
4 Neal studied acting, and that's why he's an actor now.
 If Neal _____ an actor now.
5 We were on holiday, that's why we didn't go to the party.
 We _____ on holiday.

 /5

6 Choose the correct words to complete the comments.

Is The Press Too Free?

Unless / Imagine the press was controlled more, would this be a good thing? Comment below!

• The press needs to be free! If it wasn't free, journalists [1]*would / did* only be able to write certain stories. Recently, a newspaper published an article criticising the latest environmental policies. If they hadn't published it, I [2]*knew / wouldn't know* so much about the problem now.
• Freedom of the press is fine as long as they don't encourage violence or crime. After an article about graffiti appeared in the local paper, some teenagers here decided to try it. They wouldn't have done that [3]*provided / if* they hadn't read about it.
• The press should be free but journalists should be reported if they break the law. Too many stories now are badly researched and contain incorrect facts. If they were better written, more people [4]*would read / will read* them!
• Definitely not! The public wouldn't get to know many things if we didn't have freedom of the press. [5]*Had we / We had* not had it over the years, many things would have been covered up from the public.

 /5

 Total /30

7 Choose the correct option to complete the news headlines.

> (Kind) / Cold-hearted woman adopts seven abandoned puppies.

1 'These are *made-up* / *makeup* government claims, because they haven't checked the facts,' say experts.

2 'My fame was short-*faced* / *lived* – I should have won the competition,' complains X-Factor loser.

3 'Consumers ill-*hearted* / *advised* to borrow more money,' says finance minister.

4 'There will be a *crack-down* / *backup* on crime,' police chief promises.

5 *Story* / *News* anchor braves storm to report for TV station!

/5

8 Complete the sentences with the correct form of the words in the box.

> go through   provide   help   ~~not tackle~~
> alarm   change

If you *don't tackle* this problem now, it will be even more difficult to do in the future.

1 I'll lend you my bike _____ you return it by tomorrow.

2 The car was driving _____ close to the wall.

3 I'm sure I'll recognise Maggie unless she _____ a lot since I last saw her fifteen years ago.

4 Imagine you _____ a difficult time in your life, who would you confide in?

5 If Cathy weren't so self-centred, she _____ us with the report which was supposed to be ready last week.

/5

9 Complete the text with the correct form of the words in the box. There is one extra word.

> break   capture   commit   deliberate
> ~~fetch~~   popular   read

April Fool!

There is a tradition in Britain of newspapers publishing silly stories on April Fool's Day (April 1) as a joke for people to spot. People can usually spot them because they are far-*fetched*, but these days, when fake news is everywhere, it can be hard to tell which stories have been published ¹_____ as a joke, and which are actually meant to mislead the public. In recent years, eating food on buses and trains has gained ²_____ , so in 2019 when a story appeared about the British Transport Police (BTP) banning people from eating strong-smelling food on trains and buses, with fines of up to £2,000 for offenders, the reaction was mixed. Some people thought it was ³_____ news and immediately started complaining – they wanted to carry on eating mouth-watering snacks while travelling, even if fellow passengers didn't like it. Others had a more positive reaction and thought this showed the BTP had a clear ⁴_____ to improving the quality of passenger services. Finally, there were those that trusted their instincts and realised that this 'news story' was a joke. If other people ⁵_____ the story more carefully and double-checked facts, they wouldn't have been fooled!

/5

10 Complete the sentences using the prompts in brackets. Do not change the order of the words. Change the forms or add new words where necessary. Use up to six words in each gap.

We won't take legal action *unless the company breaks* (unless/company/break) the contract with us.

1 _____ (Suppose/she/not/tell/we) the truth about the burglary at your house last winter, would you trust her now?

2 If you hadn't forgotten to pay the electricity bill, we _____ (not/sit) in total darkness now.

3 She _____ (never/employ/he) if he weren't a well-respected advisor.

4 They wouldn't believe your version of events _____ (be/you/not/honest) them all the time.

5 If Caroline _____ (have/habit/lie/people), then she will never get on with anybody.

/5

Total /20

SPEAKING

1 **In pairs, ask and answer the questions.**

Talk about the media.

Student A

1 Are you interested in politics? Why?/Why not?
2 Think of the last positive news story you came across. What was it?
3 Do you like discussing the news with your friends? Why?/Why not?
4 Do you think people will still read paper newspapers in the future? Why?/Why not?
5 Have you ever been on a protest? Would you like to go to one?

Student B

1 Should newspapers be free or should we pay to read the news?
2 Would you like to work in a newspaper or television? Why?/Why not?
3 Is it important for young people to follow the news?
4 Is there too much celebrity gossip in the news?
5 What's the most surprising news story you've ever come across?

2 **Look at the diagram. It shows different places where people with flexible jobs can work. In pairs, follow these steps.**

• Talk to each other about the advantages of each workspace.
• Say which workspace would be best for you.

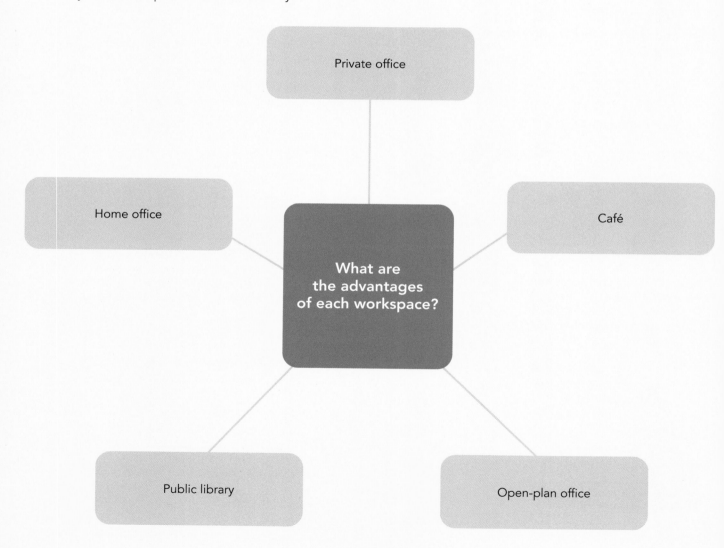

3 In pairs, discuss the questions about work and jobs.

1 What are the advantages and disadvantages of working as part of a large team?
2 Do you think people have a good work-life balance in your country? Why?/Why not?
3 What advice would you give to someone who doesn't know what career path to choose?
4 Should all teenagers be encouraged to do voluntary work abroad before starting their first job? Why?/Why not?
5 What qualities should a good boss have?
6 What are your tips for being successful in a job interview?

4 Do the task in pairs.

Student A
Look at the photos. They show different ways people can express their opinions and beliefs. Compare the photos and say why the people might have chosen these methods.

Student B, do you think graffiti can be considered a form of art? Why?/Why not?

Student B
Look at the photos. They show different ways to access the news. Compare the photos and say how reliable each source is.

Student A, how do you prefer to access the news?

7 It's not rocket science!

7.1 VOCABULARY

Science and scientists • scientific research • prepositions after verbs and nouns • words in science

SHOW WHAT YOU KNOW

1 Complete the words in the encyclopaedia entries. The first parts of the missing words are given.

Heinrich Schliemann was the German **arch**_aeologist_ who discovered Troy, the ancient city of Homer's *Iliad*.

Galileo Galilei, who was an early pioneer in the field of [1]**astro**_____ , was influenced by the work of Nicolaus Copernicus.

The Herbarium at Kew Gardens in the UK contains an impressive collection of around seven million [2]**bot**_____ items.

[3]**Bio**_____ warfare is the deliberate use of bacteria and viruses to harm humans, animals or plants.

Kevlar, a synthetic fibre so strong that it can stop bullets, was invented by a Polish-American [4]**chem**_____ named Stephanie Kwolek.

The Greek [5]**math**_____ Archimedes is supposed to have made an important discovery when he stepped into his bath, causing him to shout, 'Eureka!'

[6]**Phy**_____ is the scientific study of matter and energy and the effect that they have on each other.

WORD STORE 7A | Scientific research

2 Complete the text with the correct forms of the verbs in the box.

> award   coin   gain   ~~make~~   receive
> recognise   see   win

Stephen Hawking

On March 14, 2018, Stephen Hawking lost his long battle with motor neuron disease, and the world lost a scientist who had _made_ an enormous contribution to our understanding of the universe.

Much has been written about Hawking. The scientific community [1]_____ his achievements at an early stage in his career. It was a surprisingly long career if you consider the disease that robbed him of speech and movement. For this reason, he [2]_____ the respect of people around the world for his extraordinary will to live, as well as his brilliant mind.

As a respected scientist, he was often asked for his views on many subjects. Concerning artificial intelligence, he

WORD STORE 7B | Prepositions after verbs and nouns

3 Match the beginnings of the sentences with the endings.

> She's an **expert** [g]
> 1 Hippocrates is often **referred** ☐
> 2 On this project, we are **collaborating** ☐
> 3 Alexander Fleming is **credited** ☐
> 4 If you have an **aptitude** ☐
> 5 The Hubble Space Telescope was **named** ☐
> 6 Only senior students **have access** ☐

a **for** Maths, you can study Science or Engineering.
b **after** a famous American astronomer.
c **to** the department's specialised labs.
d **with** another team of scientists.
e **to** as the 'Father of Medicine'.
f **with** discovering penicillin, the first true antibiotic.
g **in** astrophysics and lectures at a university.

4 Complete the sentences using the correct forms of the phrases in Exercise 3.

NASA scientists _have access to_ top-secret information.
1 Scientists are people who _____ clear and logical thinking.
2 Many planets were _____ gods and goddesses in Greek and Roman mythology.
3 Alessandro Volta is _____ developing the world's first battery.
4 After completing her university course, Lisa became an _____ computer engineering.
5 The word 'lunar' is an adjective that _____ the moon.
6 Fifteen countries _____ each other to maintain the International Space Station.

Great Scientists

[3]_____ the potential and the benefits it could provide, but he was also worried that it could end the human race. Hawking [4]_____ recognition for his work on black holes, which helped to prove the idea of a 'Big Bang' at the birth of the Universe. Interestingly, he was hoping Fred Hoyle, the scientist who had [5]_____ the term 'Big Bang' in the 1940s, would be his PhD supervisor at the University of Cambridge in 1962, but this was not possible as Hoyle already had enough students under his supervision.

What surprises many people is the fact that Hawking was never [6]_____ a Nobel Prize. This is because theoretical scientific discoveries, like Hawking's, have to be established by data before they can be considered for a Nobel. It is impossible to see black holes with current telescopes.

As an icon of popular culture, Hawking [7]_____ many mentions in the press and also appeared on the TV series, such as *The Big Bang Theory*, *The Simpsons* and *Star Trek: The Next Generation*.

5 Read the definitions and complete the puzzle with the words in science.

1 a theory of physics about the relationship between space, time, and energy
2 something you write using mathematical symbols to show that two amounts are the same
3 something such as hydrogen, oxygen, or aluminium
4 the smallest part of a substance that can be part of a chemical reaction
5 the central part of an atom
6 something that you think about and work out mathematically
7 a very small piece of matter that moves around the nucleus of an atom
8 when a substance produces powerful and harmful rays

```
1 [ ] [ ] [ ] [ ] [ ] [ ] V [ ]
              ²E [ ] [ ] [ ] [ ] [ ] [ ]
          3 [ ] L [ ] [ ] [ ] [ ]
        4 [ ] O [ ] [ ] [ ]
      5 [ ] C [ ] [ ] [ ]
  6 [ ] [ ] I [ ]
      7 [ ] [ ] T [ ] [ ] [ ]
8 [ ] [ ] [ ] [ ] [ ] [ ] [ ] Y [ ]
```

6 Complete the extracts from the science books with the words in Exercise 5.

> Uranium is a silvery-grey metal with the symbol *U*. It is the 92nd element in the periodic table. A uranium ^{1}_____ is made up of a ^{2}_____ in the centre and a cloud of 92 ^{3}_____ around it. It was in a sample of uranium that ^{4}_____ was first discovered in 1896. It wasn't known at the time how dangerous it could be and that high levels of it, particularly from X-rays, can kill.

> $E = mc^2$ is possibly the most famous ^{5}_____ in science. Many people recognise it, even though they may not know what it means. It's a central part of Einstein's theory of special ^{6}_____ . It states that energy (E) is mass (m) multiplied by the speed of light (c) squared. In other words, it expresses the relationship between these things.

> How fast something moves in a particular direction is known as its ^{7}_____ . In order to find it, you can do a ^{8}_____ . Here's an example: Usain Bolt's fastest time for the 100 metres race was 9.58 seconds. If the distance in metres is divided by time in seconds, the answer, or his velocity, is 10.43841 m/s.

7 Match the words with the symbols and diagrams.

acid   (g)
1 algorithm
2 base
3 division
4 fraction
5 molecular structure
6 multiplication

a
$$42 \div 7$$

b
$$H-O-H$$

c

d
pH 7.0

e
$$14 \times 3$$

f
½

g
pH 3.0

SHOW WHAT YOU'VE LEARNT

8 Choose the correct answers A–C.

1 Nobel prizes are ___ at ceremonies in Oslo and Stockholm.
  A gained   **B** received   **C** awarded
2 Stella has an aptitude ___ languages and can speak four fluently.
  A in   **B** for   **C** with
3 A half and a quarter are both ___ .
  A fractions   **B** equations   **C** calculations
4 Tim Berners-Lee ___ the term 'world wide web', or 'www'.
  A coined   **B** made   **C** invented
5 Scientists from different countries often collaborate ___ each other on projects.
  A after   **B** by   **C** with
6 Unfortunately, her achievements were not ___ until after her death.
  A made   **B** recognised   **C** won
7 Isaac's parents are scientists and he was named ___ Isaac Newton.
  A at   **B** for   **C** after
8 Be careful when you do experiments with ___ because you can get badly burnt.
  A acids   **B** bases   **C** elements
9 He thinks he's become an expert ___ coding, but actually, he isn't very good at it.
  A at   **B** in   **C** with
10 He wants to study chemistry and ___ a valuable contribution to science.
  A do   **B** have   **C** make

/10

GRAMMAR

7.2

Advanced passive forms

SHOW WHAT YOU KNOW

1 Complete the sentences with a passive form.
Add *by* + agent if necessary.

Luckily, someone showed me how to recover the file I had lost.
Luckily, I *was shown how to recover the file I had lost.*

1 The manufacturer creates these phone cases using a 3D printer.
These phone cases _____

2 Lodge Computers are designing the system.
The system _____

3 By the end of the training session, we were using the software to solve a variety of problems.
By the end of the training session, the software _____

4 Fifty percent of the students have completed the assignment.
The assignment _____

5 We will deliver your order within 48 hours.
Your order _____

2 ★ Read the extract from a sci-fi novel and choose the correct option.

The attack had come from nowhere. They were lucky to be alive. As the badly damaged craft ¹*approached / was approaching* its home planet, it became clear there was a major problem here too. The incoming ship ought to ²*be / have been* contacted by the command centre by now, but so far no message ³*had been / had* received. Even more worryingly, the spaceport's tracking laser should ⁴*be / have been* switched on by the ground crew several minutes earlier, but the battered star cruiser was still ⁵*being / to be* controlled manually by the surviving crew.

Looking out of the forward viewing screen, no lights could ⁶*be / have been* seen on the surface of the planet. What ⁷*had / had been* happened down there? The growing realisation that their home planet may also ⁸*be / have been* attacked filled the crew with horror. Their families! Their homes!

Just when it seemed that all hope was lost, there was a crackle, then a faint voice from the communication system … 'Sorry number 6, we just popped out for a coffee and lost track of time. Is everything OK up there?'

3 ★ ★ Complete the sentences and the questions with the correct passive forms of the verbs in brackets.

Are you aware that you risk *being fined* (fine) if you download files illegally?

1 Courtney hates _____ (tell) to switch her phone off during mealtimes.

2 Tristan hopes _____ (send) somewhere hot as part of the student exchange programme.

3 Now that I'm eighteen, I expect _____ (treat) like an adult.

4 Some scientists worry about the world _____ (take over) by intelligent machines.

5 Lee is keen to avoid _____ (ask) questions during lessons.

6 Stevie refuses _____ (beat) by a simple wooden puzzle!

4 ★ ★ ★ Read the dialogue then complete the sentences below with the correct passive forms.

Harriet: My parents sent me for riding lessons for my sixteenth birthday.

Cynthia: Riding lessons? Bah! My father is buying me a pony.

Jim: A pony? Well, my Mum and Dad are going to give me a horse for my birthday.

Will: A horse? My uncle has promised me a car when I'm sixteen! With some real horsepower!

Brian: Well, guys, listen to this. When I was sixteen, my fairy godmother offered me a unicorn she had taught to fly.

Others: A flying unicorn? No way! You're so lucky!

Brian: Guys … seriously?

Harriet *was sent for riding lessons* for her birthday.

1 Cynthia _____ a pony.

2 Jim _____ a horse.

3 Will _____ a car when he's sixteen.

4 A unicorn _____ when he was sixteen.

5 The unicorn _____ to fly by Brian's fairy godmother.

SHOW WHAT YOU'VE LEARNT

5 Complete the sentences with the correct form of the verb *be*.

Henry finds it difficult to sit still and *be* quiet for more than five minutes at a time.

1 The sound of fireworks could _____ heard all across the town that night.

2 The computer system might _____ damaged when lightning struck the office block.

3 The judge _____ shown all available evidence in court yesterday.

4 At the ceremony, medals _____ given to the heroic firefighters who had helped during the flood.

5 Will you agree _____ examined by a medical professional?

6 The athlete enjoyed _____ massaged before competitions.

/6

GRAMMAR: Train and Try Again page 177

7.3

Phrases to describe products
• phrasal verbs

1 Choose the correct answers to complete the dialogue between Julie and a shop assistant.

Extract from Student's Book recording 🔊 **3.17**

SA: Good afternoon. Can I help you?

J: Oh yes, I'm looking for a new laptop. I've got a budget **1**__ £400. [...]

SA: Well, you won't be looking at a top-of-the-range model for that amount, but I'm happy to come **2**__ with a few options. Let's start here. This one's a basic laptop with 4 gigabytes of RAM and a terabyte of storage.

J: That sounds good.

SA: Well, compared with how computers **3**__ be, it's not bad. If you just want to stick to word processing and social networking, it's a waste of money buying a more powerful computer. But **4**__ you want to go in for gaming and download films and music, you can get a computer with 8GB of RAM and an SSD hard drive for £450, that's just £50 **5**__ .

J: I **6**__ want to download films and music, but do I really need 8GB of RAM?

SA: Well, you need to think about the future. If you want to edit photos and videos, it's well worth **7**__ a bit more. For just £50 you get double the RAM and SSD storage.

J: Hm, I'm not sure. I need to think it **8**__ .

SA: Of course. If it helps you to make a decision, I'll throw in a laptop bag with the more expensive model.

1 A to	B of	C at
2 A out	B over	C up
3 A would	B could	C used to
4 A if	B whether	C when
5 A plus	B more	C over
6 A am	B won't	C do
7 A spending	B to spend	C spend
8 A again	B over	C about

2 Complete the examples in REMEMBER THIS with the adjectives from the extract.

REMEMBER THIS

Retailers use a wide range of adjectives and nouns to describe the price, quality and other details of the products they sell.

A state-of-the-art camera can cost you several thousand pounds.

This one's a **a**_____ *laptop with 4 gigabytes of RAM.*

You won't be looking at a **b**_____ *model for that amount.*

3 Complete the definitions with the words in the box.

branded   custom-made   cutting-edge
~~entry-level~~   mid-range   own brand
premium   user-friendly

	of a lower price/quality	*entry-level*
1	of a medium price/quality	_____
2	of a higher price/quality	_____
3	designed for a particular person	_____
4	produced by a recognised company	_____
5	produced and sold by a shop	_____
6	using the latest design or technology	_____
7	easy to understand or operate	_____

4 Complete the adverts with the most suitable words in Exercise 3.

On a budget? Our *entry-level* laptops do all the basics for a very reasonable price.

With its **1**_____ design, the Talkon 101 makes keeping in touch as simple as 1, 2, 3.

If you are looking for the best sound money can buy, try our
2 _____
range of speakers.

Looking for quality at a reasonable price?
Our **3**_____ phone is similar to the top-of-the-range handset, but it has a plastic case and a smaller screen.

Greenscreen's **4** _____ projectors use the most up-to-date technology available.

Pick Rico's
5 _____
baked beans and
save, save, **save!**

Visit Regency Motors for your 6_____ motorbike. If it has to be uniquely yours, choose Regency.

WORD STORE 7D | Phrasal verbs

5 Complete the sentences with the correct form of the phrasal verbs. There are two extra phrasal verbs.

bring in   carry out   come out   ~~figure out~~
get down to   go in for   talk into
throw in   wind up

I can't *figure out* how to use this camera.

1 He tried to _____ me _____ by interrupting me, but I ignored him.

2 I don't _____ video games – I find them boring.

3 Our school is going to _____ new rules about using mobile phones.

4 The sales assistant managed to _____ me _____ buying the most expensive computer.

5 Whenever a new smartphone _____ , people line up outside shops to buy it.

6 If you buy this printer, we'll _____ two black ink cartridges for free.

READING

7.4

Driverless cars • collocations to do with driving • medical conditions • word families

1 Read the text and label paragraphs A–F with the headings below. There is one extra heading.

Cost ☐	Free time ☐
Traffic ☐	Parking ☐
Environment ☐	Safety ☐
Freedom ☐	

FUTUREPROOF

How driverless cars will change the world

A driverless car with a top speed of 60 mph has recently been revealed by a well-known tech firm. It may not look like it, but this machine and its successors are going to change your life. Today we explain how.

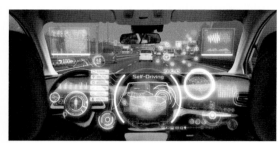

A No matter what we like to believe, humans are unfortunately no good at driving. The fact that 1.2m people are killed every year on roads worldwide is a shocking and sad reminder of that. Unlike us, driverless cars will never drive drunk and will not be able to break the speed limit, take reckless* chances or race their mates away from traffic lights. They will never doze off*, lose concentration or send a text message from behind the wheel. Nor will they get angry, frustrated or competitive. In short, they will be a lot, lot safer than we are.

B Finding a place to park will no longer be our problem – our car will handle it for us. Once we arrive at our destination we will hop out at the front door and leave the car to park itself using its superior parking skills. Later, when we need it, we will be able to summon* it with our smartphone. No more parking tickets, no more multiple attempts at reverse parking and no more endlessly driving in circles looking for an empty parking space.

C Think how much of our time is wasted on driving. Those daily journeys to work or school soon add up to hundreds of hours a year. Sure, driving is occasionally enjoyable – the winding country road on a summer's day or the empty motorway late at night, for instance – but, unless you are a Formula 1 driver, the vast majority of the time you spend behind the wheel is likely to be tedious and frustrating. Why not read a book, watch a film, or chat with family and friends and let the car drive itself instead?

D There are known to be approximately 7.5 billion people on our planet and it is estimated that well over a billion cars crowd our roads. For those who travel regularly on four wheels, it may sometimes seem that all of them are gathered in a never-ending traffic jam between where you are and where you need to be! Using sophisticated technology, driverless cars will be able to travel in convoys, centimetres apart, without the unnecessary braking that slows down traffic and creates jams.

E If we can solve congestion*, perhaps we won't need to continue digging up the country's green spaces to create huge eight-lane motorways which, in turn, encourage even more traffic. The impact of these huge roads on nature does not stop once their construction is complete, of course. Noise and light pollution seriously disturb animal populations and there is of course the danger to both animals and motorists of potential collisions. Not only could the reduction in congestion resulting from driverless cars save vast areas of our countryside, but also huge amounts of money. This money could then be spent on health, education and other more beneficial causes instead.

F One great plus of driverless cars is the freedom to travel that they will bring to those who cannot drive. It is unlikely that a driving licence will be required in order to operate a driverless car, so, theoretically, children could 'drive' themselves to karate practice, Sunday football or school, and Grandma could take herself to have her hair done on a Saturday morning! Provided that a trustworthy and secure system can be developed, the school run could become a thing of the past and parents could find themselves with an extra half hour of 'me-time' every morning.

The world's first large-scale test of driverless cars has already been carried out, but it will be some time before you can actually go to a car dealership and get your hands on one. There are many complex legal issues regarding their security, privacy and safety which need to be resolved first. However, it seems very likely that within our lifetime they will be a common and very welcome sight on our roads. In years to come, rather than saying 'I'm taking the car,' we may find ourselves saying 'The car is taking me!'

GLOSSARY

reckless (adj) – not caring or worrying about the possible dangerous results of your actions
doze off (phr. v) – to fall asleep, especially when you did not intend to

summon (v) – to order someone to come to a place
congestion (n) – overcrowding on the road caused by too much traffic

2 **Read the text again and answer the questions.**

1 What causes of traffic accidents could be eliminated thanks to driverless cars?

_____

_____

2 What technology would car owners use to get their vehicles back after parking?

_____

_____

3 What activities could people spend time on instead of driving?

_____

_____

4 How can driverless cars reduce traffic congestion?

_____

_____

5 What impact could driverless cars have on green areas?

_____

_____

6 Which groups of people could benefit most from these cars?

_____

_____

7 What issues need to be solved before driverless cars become commonly available?

_____

_____

3 **Complete the collocations to do with driving with words from the article.**

drive after consuming alcohol –
drive _drunk_ / drunk driving
1 drive faster than the law permits – _____ the speed limit
2 driving a motor vehicle – _____ the wheel
3 reversing into a parking space – _____ parking
4 driving round and round because you are lost or looking for a parking space – driving in _____
5 small countryside roads with lots of bends – _____ country roads
6 very wide roads used to travel long distances – _____ motorways
7 a place where cars are sold – a car _____
8 a document that states you are legally qualified to drive – a driving _____
9 a regular car journey to take children to school or bring them home – the school _____

4 **Complete the sentences with the most suitable collocations in Exercise 3 in the correct form.**

People are often caught _driving drunk / drunk driving_ the next morning after a big party.
1 Finally, we made it! We've been _____ for half an hour looking for your house.
2 My handset connects with the car stereo and I can talk while I'm _____ .
3 We need to see some official ID, please, your _____ or passport.
4 I don't see the point in owning a huge 4x4 vehicle if the only driving you do is _____ twice a day.
5 What do you think of the new car? My dad helped me choose it from the local _____ .
6 Some of these _____ are not wide enough for two cars to pass.
7 Do you know why I have stopped you, sir? No? Well, you were _____ and drove past one of our speed cameras.
8 _____ are actually safer than smaller roads as there is room for faster vehicles to overtake slower traffic.
9 For me, _____ is definitely the hardest thing to master when you are learning to drive.

VOCABULARY PRACTICE | Medical conditions

5 **Look at the vocabulary in lesson 7.4 in the Student's Book. Complete the sentences. The first letters are given.**

Too much junk food in your diet can lead to **o**_besity_ .
1 After Max lost his job, he suffered from **d**_____ for a while.
2 Ella got a chest **i**_____ and had to take antibiotics for two weeks.
3 Some people can't eat peanuts because they have an **a**_____ to them.
4 He became sick because his **i**_____ **s**_____ was very weak.
5 The child has difficulties in communicating due to **a**_____ .
6 There's too much sugar in her blood, so she's taking medication to control her **d**_____ .
7 He occasionally has trouble breathing because of his **a**_____ , especially when he becomes stressed.

WORD STORE 7E | Word families

6 **Choose the correct option.**

Clean / (Cleanliness) is very important in hospitals.
1 What are some of the _medicinal_ / _medicine_ uses of honey?
2 The patient's _respond_ / _response_ to the new treatment was very good.
3 It is _advice_ / _advisable_ not to go swimming after having a heavy meal.
4 All manufacturers must obey the government's new safety _regulations_ / _regulatory_.
5 Radiation can be very _harm_ / _harmful_ to human health.
6 It would _beneficial_ / _benefit_ your health greatly to take up a sport and improve your diet.
7 Eating fruit is supposed to be good for your _digestion_ / _digestive_ system.

SHOW WHAT YOU KNOW

1 Choose the most appropriate verbs to complete the sentences.

1 The judge *expected / told / felt* that community service was more appropriate than a prison sentence in this case.
2 Scientists *think / know / regard* we are the only intelligent beings in this universe.
3 The police *understand / argue / believe* an escaped prisoner is hiding in his home village.
4 The IT managers *believed / agreed / thought* to meet again after the Christmas break.
5 I can't believe people *expect / know / feel* me not to be angry after the way I was treated.

2 ★ Complete the radio news headlines with *it* or *there*.

Welcome to the midday news on Radio RMN. Here are the headlines. It is thought that the Prime Minister will announce the date of the next general election later on today. ¹_____ is believed to be great pressure on her from members of her own party to go to the polls as soon as possible.

²_____ was announced at the International Climate Change Conference taking place in Rio this week that global pollution reduction targets for 2020 are now unrealistic. ³_____ was suggested by the chairman of the conference that the US and Russia are largely to blame by failing to meet their own countries' targets.

⁴_____ is reported to have been a major explosion at a power plant near Paris, the French capital. ⁵_____ is not yet known how many people may have been killed or injured.

3 ★ ★ Complete the rewritten sentences from Exercise 1 with the phrases in the box. There are two extra phrases.

> am expected to be   am expected not to be
> it is thought that   it was agreed by   ~~it was felt that~~
> there is believed to be   we are thought to be

It was felt that community service was more appropriate than a prison sentence in this case.

1 _____
we are the only intelligent beings in this universe.
2 _____
an escaped prisoner hiding in his home village.
3 _____
the IT managers to meet again after the Christmas break.
4 I can't believe I _____
_____
angry after the way I was treated.

4 ★ ★ ★ Read text 1 and complete text 2 with passive reporting structures.

Text 1

Insomnia – a cultural history

Medical historians think that insomnia is a relatively modern problem. Of course, they know that medieval Europeans woke in the night frequently, but they don't believe they were particularly worried about it. These days, we understand there to be around 100 million Europeans who suffer from some kind of sleep disorder. Psychologists consider stress to be the most common reason that people find it difficult to sleep. Additionally, we think that eating too late in the evening causes many cases of sleeplessness. Some experts also say that changes in our living environment or work schedule can cause insomnia.

Text 2

It is thought that insomnia is a relatively modern problem. Of course, medieval Europeans ¹_____ in the night frequently, but they ²_____ particularly worried about it. These days ³_____ around 100 million Europeans who suffer from some kind of sleep disorder. Stress ⁴_____ the most common reason that people find it difficult to sleep. Additionally, ⁵_____ many cases of sleeplessness ⁶_____ eating too late in the evening. ⁷_____ changes in our living environment or work schedule can cause insomnia.

SHOW WHAT YOU'VE LEARNT

5 Find and correct the mistakes.

~~There~~ was agreed that the new handset was more attractive than the old one. *It*
1 It has not currently been known exactly how big the Internet is. _____
2 Some companies thought to have been using sophisticated hacking techniques to protect their interests. _____
3 There was known to be several computer viruses within the system at the time. _____
4 The troubled company was understood that have invested heavily in wearable technology. _____
5 People are said to be many negative consequences of inactive lifestyles. _____
6 The Saturn Explorer craft is believed to passing Mars as we speak. _____

/6

GRAMMAR: Train and Try Again page 177

SPEAKING

Clarification

1 Translate the phrases into your own language.

SPEAKING BANK

Signalling confusion

Sorry, I'm not with you. _____

_____

I'm not sure I follow (you). _____

I'm afraid you've lost me there. _____

I don't know what you mean by … _____

_____

Checking your understanding

So, in other words … _____

Are you saying …? _____

If I understand correctly, you mean …, right? _____

Giving clarification

Yes, precisely/exactly. _____

Yes, (that's) pretty much (it). _____

No, that's not (quite) what I meant. _____

_____

What I meant was … _____

_____

2 Choose the correct words to complete the phrases.

So, in other *thoughts* / *ways* / *words* … (U)

1 Sorry, I'm not *with* / *follow* / *understand* you.

2 *What* / *How* / *That* I meant was …

3 I'm not sure I *lost* / *follow* / *mean* (you).

4 No, that's not (quite) what I *meant* / *knew* / *understood*.

5 I'm afraid you've *meant* / *lost* / *known* me there.

6 If I *understand* / *know* / *think* correctly, you mean …, right?

7 I don't know what you *mean* / *saying* / *tell* by …

8 Yes, *precise* / *precisely* / *precision*.

9 Yes, (that's) *pretty* / *quite* / *almost* much (it).

10 Are you *meaning* / *saying* / *following* …?

3 Mark the phrases in Exercise 1 as S for signalling confusion, U for checking your understanding or C for giving clarification.

4 Put the words in order to make phrases and then use them to complete the dialogues.

1 A mean / you / what / know / I don't / by
   I don't know what you mean by
  B sure / I / I'm / follow / not / you
   _____
  C it / yes / exactly / that's _____

Henry: Make sure you save it on the thingy as well.
Flora: Er … A 'thingy'.
Henry: You know, on the … thingy! What is it called?
Flora: Do you mean the external hard drive?
Henry: ¹__ ! The extra hand drive.
Flora: What? It's called an EXTERNAL HARD drive.
Henry: Yes, you said that.
Flora: But that's not what you said.
Henry: Er … ²__ any more.
Flora: Henry, you said … Oh, never mind.

2 A meant / I / was / what _____
  B you / saying / are _____
  C quite / not / meant / that's / I / what
   _____
  D with / I'm / you / not _____

Lucas: What's up, Mum?
Mum: The computer, look.
Lucas: Oh no. It's the BSOD.
Mum: Sorry, ³__ .
Lucas: The BSOD. The blue screen of death!
Mum: Er … so the computer has died?
Lucas: Probably not. That's just what they call it.
Mum: So what should I do?
Lucas: Just reboot it.
Mum: Do what? ⁴__ I should … hit it?
Lucas: What? No Mum, ⁵__ . Please don't hit it.
   ⁶__ restart it.
Mum: Ah-ha! OK, I see … how do I do that?

3 A it / that's / much / pretty _____
  B lost / there / afraid / me / I'm / you've
   _____
  C understand / I / correctly / you / if / mean
   _____
  D other / words / in _____

Kim: Are you coming to my New Year's Eve party?

Ally: Yes, I am.

Kim: Good. Can't wait to see you ☺

Ally: So, ⁷__ , you want us to start the year together?

Kim: Yes, ⁸__ ☺ You're my best friend! I want to mug you at midnight.

Ally: Er what? … ⁹__ , Kim. ¹⁰__ 'hug' right?

Kim: Oh no! Stupid auto-correct. Yes, hug.

Ally: That sounds much better! ☺

1 ★ **Choose the correct answers A–C.**

If I were on a _C_ island, I wouldn't survive for long. I wouldn't have anything to eat!
A deserted   B dessert   C desert

1 Have you been to the gym __ ? There is some new weight training equipment.
A later   B late   C lately

2 We can't let Grandma spend New Year's Eve __ . We'll cook dinner and invite her over.
A lone   B alone   C lonely

3 Since I lost weight, these trousers have become far too __ . I need to buy a new pair.
A lose   B loose   C loser

4 Please don't interrupt the teacher. __ your hand if you would like to ask a question.
A Raise   B Rise   C Arise

5 The exam __ of four written papers and an oral test. You will take all parts of the exam on the same day.
A comprises   B includes   C consists

6 The __ reason you are here is … Happy birthday! I hope you like your surprise.
A really   B present   C actual

2 ★ ★ **Complete the words with the missing letters.**

A: Can I give you some **advi**_ce_ that might help you to swim faster?

B: Yes, please. I've been ¹**pract**_____ but …

A: Well that's good; ² '**practi**_____ makes perfect' they say, but I think you are lifting your head too high when you ³**breat**_____ . It's ⁴_____**ffecting** the way your body moves through the water by slowing you down.

B: OK, so what would you ⁵**ad**_____ me to do instead?

A: Well, perhaps try taking a ⁶**breat**_____ just as your lips break the surface of the water. I guarantee you'll notice a positive ⁷_____**ffect** immediately.

B: OK, thanks a lot!

3 ★ ★ **Choose the correct option.**

What's today's (date)/ data? Is it the first of October?

1 The government will introduce major _economic_ / _economical_ reforms before the next election.

2 Today will be remembered as a _historic_ / _historical_ day by all those interested in space exploration.

3 The patient is no longer _conscientious_ / _conscious_ and his heart rate is dropping rapidly.

4 The King's Day celebration in Amsterdam is a truly memorable _opportunity_ / _occasion_ for all involved.

5 It's impossible to get my homework done with these _continual_ / _continuous_ interruptions.

4 ★ ★ **Replace the expressions in bold with the words in the box.**

~~actually~~   complements   compliment   currently
eventually   fantastic   possibly

I pretend I enjoy our family meals, but **in fact** I'd rather eat watching TV. _actually_

1 **At the moment** I'm reading a collection of short stories by an American writer. _____

2 I'm not sure that red top **goes well with** those orange trousers. _____

3 **In the end,** you'll get the hang of driving; it just takes time. _____

4 Couldn't you just **say something nice about** me for once, instead of your constant criticism? _____

5 My first bungee jump was a **great** experience. I'd highly recommend it. _____

6 Could you **maybe** lend us your sat-nav for the weekend, Dad? _____

5 ★ ★ **Complete the text with the correct form of the words in the box. There are two extra words.**

advise   depend   economy   ~~invent~~   late
practice   see   sure

Satellite Navigation is not a recent _invention_ by any means, as the first portable navigation system became available in the Netherlands in 2004. However, since then the cost of purchasing one has decreased considerably and today it's possible to find a device at a very ¹_____ price. It's no surprise that more and more drivers decide to follow the step-by-step instructions they hear, without having to check the map.

For me, the popularity of sat-nav systems is further proof that we are becoming too ²_____ on technology. In the past, most people were able to read maps, but ³_____ , I think most people have lost this ability. What is even more worrying is the fact that some people seem to be losing their common sense too.

Every summer I read articles about people who got into trouble because they had blindly followed the ⁴_____ of their sat-nav, for example, the tourists who drove their rental car into the ocean just because their device told them to drive ahead. Driving requires focus – you can't lose ⁵_____ of where you're going. Road and traffic signs are just as important as your sat-nav.

6 ★ ★ Complete the text with the correct form of the words in brackets.

Robots in the kitchen ——————

It's very rare that a week can pass without some new _technological_ (**TECHNOLOGY**) advance making the headlines, and ¹_____ (**LATE**) a kitchen robot has been appearing in the news. At a technology fair last month, the world's first robo-chef was announced.

A top chef has been working with a robotics engineering company to ²_____ (**SURE**) that the machine can measure and add ingredients and cook a meal like an expert professional. In ³_____ (**REAL**), the robo-chef is a pair of metal arms which have been programmed to copy a real chef's ⁴_____ (**MOVE**) when mixing, stirring etc., so that it can cook perfect meals again and again.

An obvious ⁵_____ (**ADVANTAGE**) of the robo-chef is that, unlike a real person, it cannot taste the food it cooks! However, a good result might be a ⁶_____ (**REDUCE**) in the number of repetitive injuries that chefs can suffer from.

Will the robo-chef revolutionise cooking? As this branch of science progresses over the next decade, robots will ⁷_____ (**DENY**) invade our kitchens to some extent. But, at the current cost of £10,000, today's robo-chef is ⁸_____ (**LIKE**) to be found in the average household just yet.

7 ★ ★ Complete the second sentence so that it has a similar meaning to the first. Use the word in capitals.

'I didn't copy any answers from Janet,' he said.
DENIED
He _denied copying any answers_ from Janet.

1 An American scientist has been given this award for the first time ever. **TO**
This award _____
an American scientist for the first time ever.

2 We've arranged to meet Paula at the conference venue. **ARE**
We _____
at the conference venue.

3 If the engineer hadn't made a mistake in the algorithm, he wouldn't have made a great discovery. **UNLESS**
The engineer wouldn't have made a great discovery _____ a mistake in the algorithm.

4 'Next week we will learn about numbers in other cultures,' explained the teacher. **THE**
The teacher explained that _____ _____ about numbers in other cultures.

5 Why didn't you pay attention to the experiment in Science class? **OUGHT**
You _____
attention to the experiment in Science class.

6 It is believed that Columbus was born in Liguria, in Italy. **TO**
Columbus _____
born in Liguria, in Italy.

8 ★ ★ Choose the correct answers A–D.

We're watching you!

Parents constantly worry about their children and their concerns _B_ once the child is old enough to drive. Teenagers ¹__ to have the freedom to go where they want, but should their driving still be monitored when they have passed their driving test? A new app has been developed to allow parents to ²__ an eye on their teenagers' driving habits and location even when they are not with them.
It's linked to a ³__ which is installed in the car and allows parents ⁴__ to all types of information, from the speed of the car, how often and hard the driver brakes, to how far the car has travelled and where it's been. ⁵__ parents see it as a way to reduce accidents, but as you can imagine, not all teens welcome the idea ⁶__ and are concerned about privacy issues. It's possible they ⁷__ into having the system, as it can considerably reduce the cost of insurance. However, I would have been appalled ⁸__ my parents ever suggested anything similar!

	A raise	B⃝increase	C develop	D progress
1	A look up	B can't wait	C look forward	D can't stand
2	A meet	B keep	C make	D get
3	A drive	B device	C screen	D data
4	A access	B connection	C view	D control
5	A Much	B Plenty	C Each	D Most
6	A to follow		B to be followed	
	C of following		D of being followed	
7	A may be talked		B won't be talked	
	C must have been talked		D might have been talked	
8	A had	B should	C were	D would

9 ★ ★ ★ Complete the sentences using the prompts in brackets. Do not change the order of the words. Change the forms or add new words where necessary. Use between two and five words in each gap.

We _have just run out of_ (just/run) an important chemical at the lab, which means we can't carry out any more experiments this week.

1 I _____ (not/graduate) university by the end of next year.

2 If I weren't so busy at school, _____ (I/definitely/look) a part-time job a long time ago.

3 When her photos appeared in a gossip magazine, the actress _____ (blame/mother/leak) them to the press.

4 It's important that you get on well with _____ (people/you/work) with.

5 When I went to university, my uncle asked me a lot of questions and _____ (want/know/student) still had lectures with Professor Green.

6 All participants of the reality show _____ (make/hand over) their mobile phones and personal items when it started.

1 Decide where these features go in a narrative. Write B for the beginning, M for the middle or E for the end.

Use a variety of verbs to report speech. Ⓜ
1 Write about a lesson learned. ⬭
2 Use a dramatic opening sentence. ⬭
3 Use narrative tenses to describe the action. ⬭
4 Write about a twist. ⬭
5 Use shorter sentences to add drama. ⬭
6 Give characters a voice with direct speech. ⬭
7 Say where and when the story takes place. ⬭

2 Read the story quickly. How would you describe the tone?

3 Read the story and match the underlined sentences to features 1–7 in Exercise 1. Write the numbers in the boxes next to each sentence.

<u>Jake looked at the screen in shock and rubbed his eyes.</u> ②

ᵃ<u>It was late and he was in his room, playing his favourite football game.</u> ⬭ He really shouldn't have been doing that – he needed to be up early the next day to attend a lecture. 'Never mind,' thought Jake, and kept playing.

He had just scored a goal when the game suddenly stopped. ᵇ<u>What was worse, the screen had gone black.</u> ⬭ 'Well, that's annoying,' sighed Jake. He hoped the computer wasn't broken. Not being very good with technology, he wasn't sure what to do. As it was nearly 2 a.m., he decided to go to bed. 'I'll deal with it in the morning,' he thought. He put on his pyjamas and turned off the light. But, closing his eyes, he heard something. Voices? ᶜ<u>Jake was terrified!</u> ⬭ He was sure someone was in his room!

Now the voices were louder! ᵈ<u>'Wake him up!' someone yelled.</u> ⬭ 'Throw water on him,' giggled another. 'What the …?' gasped Jake. He turned on the light and … froze! Standing in the room were the players from the game. 'What … what's happening?' Jake whispered. 'There's nothing wrong with your computer. Just restart it!' said one of them. 'We want to play!'

Was he dreaming? Was he going crazy? 'Um … sure, just a second,' replied Jake. He restarted the computer and loaded the game. 'OK, it's ready,' he said, looking up from the keyboard. But they were gone! ᵉ<u>And there, on the screen, were the players!</u> ⬭ ᶠ<u>'I really need to stop gaming at night,'</u> <u>Jake said to himself and went to bed.</u> ⬭

4 Choose the correct option.

Lionel *got* / *(was getting)* into bed when a weird noise stopped him.
1 Jackie took out her keys and *unlocked* / *was unlocking* the front door.
2 It was strange. He never *came across* / *had never come across* anything like it before.
3 He read the note again, but it *didn't make* / *hadn't made* any sense.
4 They *looked* / *were looking* for someone, but they wouldn't say who.
5 Max *wasn't working* / *hadn't been working* there long when he found a little red book.
6 She said that she *can't* / *couldn't* remember where she'd bought the ring.
7 He began yelling and said he *will* / *would* never go back there again.

5 Complete the sentences with the correct form of the verb in brackets.

She wondered where she *had seen* (see) the strange blue liquid before.
1 The sun _____ (shine) and the birds were singing, but Lucy felt no happiness that day.
2 First, they shook the box and then, curious about its contents, they _____ (open) it.
3 The adults _____ (not watch) as one boy, and then another, walked into the cave.
4 They _____ (walk) for miles when they saw a house in the distance.
5 After typing in his question, an answer _____ (appear) on the screen, 'Get out!'
6 _____ (it/hide) behind the door? He couldn't be sure, but he was too scared to look.
7 The creature was terrifying, but Jo stayed calm and she _____ (not panic).
8 They _____ (not see) such a strange object before and decided to examine it.

6 Choose the correct option.

William *(gasped)* / *snapped* when a ghostly face appeared at the window.
1 She *yelled* / *whispered* because she didn't want to be heard.
2 They *screamed* / *giggled* in terror and ran out of the house.
3 He was *yelling* / *sighing* my name, but I didn't hear a thing.
4 She was *giggling* / *sobbing*, so it was obvious she was very sad.
5 He *snapped* / *sighed* at the children because they refused to keep quiet.
6 I *screamed* / *sighed* in relief when they returned home and were safe.
7 We could hear them *giggling* / *snapping* as they looked at the funny old photos.

7 Read the story in Exercise 8 and put the events in the correct order.

A Robbie went in search of a place that he could explore. ⃝
B Robbie was bored because he had nothing to do. ⃝
C Robbie had a terrifying experience. ⃝
D Robbie was told about an interesting place. ⃝

8 Read the task and the story. Then add inverted commas, commas, full stops, question marks or exclamation marks where necessary in the second and third paragraphs.

> Write a narrative about a strange event. Write when and where the narrative takes place, and who the main characters are. Decide what happens and how the story ends.

1

'What a boring day!' sighed Robbie, sitting in the lobby of his hotel. He'd been looking forward to his holiday on the island, but it wasn't much fun there on his own. He'd already explored the place by jet pack the previous day. As he flew over the beaches and the villages, he live-streamed it to his sister back in the UK.

2

He picked up a brochure about a cave. You should visit it suggested the owner, who knew the island well. What is there to see asked Robbie. There are strange wall paintings and some writing in a language no one understands he replied. Wow said Robbie. Suddenly, he was interested. He was studying ancient languages at university and was excited by the idea of the mysterious writing. He decided to go the next day.

3

Early in the morning, Robbie set off. After hiking up a mountain, he eventually found the entrance to the cave. As he approached, he saw a young woman there. Hi. Have you been inside yet he asked her. Why are you here she snapped. Robbie was shocked. Err ... umm ... I just want to see the cave he said. Go away she yelled at him. This is my home and I have come back after many centuries she continued.

4

Centuries? What was she talking about? Robbie looked at her closely then and realised she had live snakes instead of hair! 'You're a monster!' he gasped. He turned and ran like the wind down the mountain. Robbie left the island that day, but sometimes he wonders what would have happened if he'd stayed.

9 Choose the correct answers A–C.

He didn't know how they <u>A</u> escape from the locked room.
(A) would   B will   C can

1 'Hurry up! __ time,' shouted Max.
   A We waste   B We're wasting   C We'd wasted

2 They __ all day and were hopelessly lost.
   A could walk   B have walked   C had been walking

3 I asked him about the old house and he __ me not to go there.
   A warned   B was warning   C had warned

4 Hearing the scream, he broke down the door and __ inside.
   A was rushing   B had rushed   C rushed

5 She told them she was terrified, but they __ .
   A weren't listening   B haven't listened
   C hadn't listened

6 'Where __ the treasure?' Leila yelled at them, but they refused to reveal its location.
   A had you hidden   B have you hidden
   C were you hiding

SHOW WHAT YOU'VE LEARNT

10 Read the task below. Before you start writing, note down some ideas and plan your narrative.

> Write a narrative about a strange person in a scary place.
> • Write when and where the story takes place, and who the main characters are.
> • Decide what happens and how the story ends.

SHOW THAT YOU'VE CHECKED

In my narrative:

- I have used the beginning to get the reader's attention and to set the scene by introducing the time, place and characters of the narrative. ⃝
- I have used narrative tenses, shorter sentences, language that appeals to the senses, reported speech and direct speech in the middle of the narrative. ⃝
- I have concluded the story with a twist, a lesson learned, a decision taken or a later event linked to the narrative. ⃝
- I have used correct punctuation for direct speech. ⃝
- I have checked my spelling and punctuation. ⃝
- my handwriting is neat enough for someone else to read it. ⃝

VOCABULARY AND GRAMMAR

1 Choose the most suitable word.

We can really *find* / *make* / (*see*) the true potential of wind and solar farms in this country.

1 The American continent was *suggested* / *called* / *named* after the Italian explorer Amerigo Vespucci.

2 Although Elena had done all the research, one of her colleagues was credited *with* / *by* / *for* the discovery.

3 A Czech writer named Karel Čapek *made* / *coined* / *discovered* the term 'robot' in a play he wrote in 1920.

4 She was very proud when she *received* / *gained* / *recognised* a mention in the press for her work on the project.

5 You don't need to become an expert *at* / *in* / *for* environmental science to realise the planet is in trouble.

/5

2 Complete the sentences with the most appropriate words. The first and last letters are given.

This **a**lgorith**m** is easy to follow as it only has four steps.

1 Charles Darwin made a huge **c**_____**n** to biology and the science of evolution.

2 In his talk on radioactive elements, the chemist made **r**_____**e** to the work of Marie Curie.

3 Here is a diagram of the **m**_____**r** structure of water – as you can see, it's quite a simple substance.

4 My department at the university would like to **c**_____**e** with other scientists on this project.

5 Henry doesn't have much of an **a**_____**e** for languages, but he's very good at maths.

/5

3 Complete the sentences with the correct form of the phrasal verbs in the box.

> bring in   come out   go in for   talk into
> throw in   ~~wind up~~

My brother *winds* me *up* all the time and it's really annoying!

1 Because I bought the most expensive phone, the salesman _____ a free case.

2 I can't wait for the next Jason Bourne film to _____ . I've loved all of them so far.

3 Alex doesn't _____ physical sports. He prefers to play games like chess.

4 Unless the government decides to _____ tougher laws against pollution, air quality won't improve.

5 My friend _____ me _____ going to the science museum with him, and I actually enjoyed it.

/5

4 Correct the underlined parts of the sentences.

The physicist believed that the theory <u>couldn't tested</u> *couldn't be tested* without more data.

1 I enjoyed <u>to be showing</u> _____ the new computer lab by my colleagues yesterday.

2 All children need <u>to encourage</u> _____ by their parents and teachers to reach their full potential.

3 Aristotle <u>know to write</u> _____ on a wide range of topics, but many of his texts have been lost.

4 More girls <u>estimate to study</u> _____ science and engineering now than ever before.

5 <u>It could argue</u> _____ the wheel was the most important invention of all.

/5

5 Complete the sentences with the correct passive form of the verbs in brackets.

This type of photocopier needs *to be serviced* (service) after about 10,000 copies.

1 My sister hates _____ (force) to limit her hours in front of a computer to two a day.

2 The battery should _____ (charge) last night, but now it's flat and we can't use the equipment.

3 Before the screen went blank, I accidentally opened a strange email which I _____ (send).

4 New solar panels are going _____ (install) tomorrow to make our house more energy efficient.

5 Maria gets very tired of _____ (criticise) by her parents for her choice of career.

/5

6 Complete the second sentence so that it means the same as the first.

It is believed that Aristarchus presented the earliest model of the universe with the Sun at the centre.
Aristarchus *is believed to have presented* the earliest model of the universe with the Sun at the centre.

1 In the past, people thought that computers would never become popular and widely available.
In the past, it _____ computers would never become popular and widely available.

2 Many say that Einstein had problems at school because of his reluctance to learn everything by heart.
Einstein _____ problems at school because of his reluctance to learn everything by heart.

3 According to the latest estimate, last year over 200 pupils aged 13–16 failed Maths in our town.
Last year there _____ over 200 pupils aged 13–16 that failed Maths in our town.

4 Doctors claim that obesity causes depression.
Obesity _____ depression.

5 It is known that penicillin revolutionised medicine.
Penicillin _____ medicine.

/5

Total   /30

7 Choose the correct answers A–D.

For a coachload of kids from a <u>A</u> primary school it was supposed ¹__ a pleasant day trip to a newly-opened theme park. Unfortunately, the journey turned out to be an unpleasant lesson for everybody, but especially for the driver, who relied on his sat-nav to ²__ the shortest route.

As a result, the kids and their teachers ³__ found themselves stuck between two walls for nearly three hours since the driver's sat-nav had sent his vehicle down an impassable country lane. It took over two hours for the fire brigade to free the coach and its passengers, who ⁴__ to be quite anxious by then.

It seems that although the system has many advantages and provides information about one's exact location, distance and best routes, it is still more ⁵__ to just use your own judgement.

	(A) local	B	regional
	C country	D	areal
1	A to being	B	to have been
	C had been	D	have been
2	A bring in	B	wind up
	C go in for	D	figure out
3	A actually	B	likely
	C lately	D	after all
4	A have been reported	B	were reported
	C have reported	D	were being reporting
5	A conscious	B	conscientious
	C sensible	D	sensitive

/5

8 Complete the sentences using the prompts in brackets. Change the forms or add new words where necessary. Use up to six words in each gap.

Is English still spoken (English/still/speak) by the largest number of people in the world? Or is it Chinese?

1 Alan Turing, a famous cryptologist,_____
_____
(expect/not/reveal) any details of his work on Enigma during World War II.

2 I know that the conference is today. But where _____ (it/hold)?

3 At least fifteen people _____
_____ (know/apply) for the post of manager of IT department at the moment.

4 Emily _____
(not/stand/remind) to switch off the equipment every single night.

5 I can't believe how silly I was! Last week, I _____
_____
(talk/buy) an all-in-one piece of equipment that was supposed to be very efficient, but is actually useless.

/5

9 Complete the text with the correct form of the words in brackets.

To spy or not to spy?

It's a question that most parents *eventually* (**EVENTUAL**) ask themselves when it comes to monitoring their kids' texts, emails or posts on social networking sites. Some parents are so concerned about their children's activities that they unplug the Internet router at a certain time in the evening to ¹_____ (**REGULAR**) screen time or demand access to their kids' messages and social media accounts. But does this approach have a ²_____ (**BENEFIT**) effect on their relationship? Psychologists generally believe that restricting and monitoring technology isn't ³_____ (**HARM**) to the parent-child relationship if there is a set of rules for everybody to follow. They agree that both parents and children should respect each other's ⁴_____ (**PRIVATE**), but at the same time it might be a good idea to place a computer in a family area and occasionally talk about potential dangers connected with the Internet. Obviously, with rapid ⁵_____ (**TECHNOLOGY**) progress, adults need to keep up to date with any new gadgets or ways of communicating that the kids might want to use. Parents definitely need to know what their kids are doing online, but they should also trust them and try to be discreet.

/5

10 Complete the second sentence so that it means the same as the first.

The headmaster is just announcing the winner.
The winner is *just being announced*!

1 It is said that Steve Jobs designed one of the most powerful and yet beautiful computers.
Steve Jobs _____
one of the most powerful and yet beautiful computers.

2 Every year the company sells the employees several new products at a discount.
Every year, several new products _____
_____ at a discount.

3 I don't want you to inform me about changes in the programme of our meetings at such short notice.
I would prefer _____
about changes in the programme of our meetings at such short notice.

4 Most teenagers don't like it when they are monitored all the time.
Most teenagers can't _____
_____ all the time.

5 I would advise you to establish what gadgets are currently popular among teenagers before you decide what to invest in.
Before you decide what to invest in, it's
_____ what
gadgets are currently popular among teenagers.

/5

Total /20

FAKING it on social media

With endless photo sharing apps and online platforms enabling teenagers to publicise their lives, it's no wonder that some young people start to question their own experiences and body image, and start to feel inadequate. In fact, some of these sites have been associated with poor mental health, bullying, lack of sleep and depression, and are considered dangerous by many health professionals. However, since we live in a world of fake news and distorted truths, it's not surprising that much of what is shared on these profiles by celebrities, influencers and normal people is also very often manipulated, or just plain untrue. Here we reveal some of the scary truths of online photo sharing.

We all know the feeling: we upload our latest holiday snaps, a photo with our best mates or a carefully planned out selfie, then wait to see just how many likes it will get. The more likes, the better we feel. But some people seem to get way more than anyone else. It could be that they have a lot of friends, or alternatively, they could have subscribed to one of many free services that promise unlimited likes. They're usually free, all you have to do in return is a simple social action, such as sharing their website on your page, or completing an online survey. Repeating the action, which you can usually do every twenty-four hours, leads to more likes; and if that's not enough, you can even buy more.

There are similar ways to accumulate followers, although you usually have to pay for them. Influencers – people with popular accounts who promote particular products or brands – are often guilty of doing this. These people are usually paid in relation to the size of their audience, so more followers results in higher fees. There are ways to identify suspicious accounts, for example usernames that include a lot of letters and numbers, and accounts that follow a lot of people, but have no followers of their own.

Then there's the issue of the photos themselves which tend to blur reality with fantasy. Many people feel the need to add the hashtag 'no filter' to photos that have not been enhanced in some way, and yet those that don't feature filters are also often not what they seem. Every time you see a photo of a perfect room, or someone posing in front of a fabulous view, remember that you're only seeing a small slice of real life. Zoom out and you see that in fact, the rest of the house is a mess and whilst the photo makes it look like the person is alone in nature enjoying the view, they are actually surrounded by tourists and litter, it's just a clever camera angle. Unfortunately, this leads many people to believe others are living the perfect life, and feel inadequate in comparison.

So what can be done? Firstly, don't take the information you find on these platforms too seriously. Much of what you see has been staged and edited. Experts are encouraging social media sites to make all information about likes and followers private, or even disable these functions. They are also campaigning for signals where images have been airbrushed. Alternatively, you could deactivate your social media accounts, although that is admittedly a little bit too drastic, even for me!

1 Read the article on page 114 and complete the sentences with up to five words from the article in the correct form.

1 It's not surprising that teenagers may _____ when they compare their own lives to the lives of the people they follow online.

2 Some websites offer unlimited likes to subscribers who carry out _____ .

3 Influencers get _____ if they have more followers.

4 One _____ is by looking at how many people are following them.

5 People feel the need to signal when their images _____ .

6 Many of the photos you see online only show a _____ .

7 Social media sites have been encouraged to limit access to information about _____ .

8 _____ is another way to avoid the negative aspects of photo sharing apps.

2 Read the article again and answer the questions.

1 What can be the consequences of spending too much time looking at online photo sharing apps?

_____

_____

2 Why is the writer not surprised that we see things that are not true online?

_____

_____

3 How can you increase the number of likes your posts or photos get?

_____

_____

4 Why do influencers sometimes spend money on increasing the number of followers they have?

_____

_____

5 What does having a lot of letters and numbers in your username suggest?

_____

_____

6 Why do people feel the need to use the 'no filter' hashtag?

_____

_____

7 What examples are given in the text of using photography skills to make things seem better than they are?

_____

_____

8 What changes would experts like to see on photo sharing platforms?

_____

_____

WRITING

3 Read the writing task and write a narrative.

Write a narrative that starts with the following line:

I couldn't believe what I was seeing – was it a dream?

- Write when and where the story takes place, and who the main characters are.
- Decide what happens and how the story ends.

8 Costing the earth

VOCABULARY

8.1

Nature • environmental issues • landscapes • animals

SHOW WHAT YOU KNOW

1 Complete the text with the missing words. The first letters are given.

Every country aims to create **ec**_onomic_ **gr**_owth_ because it brings more jobs and better living conditions for its population. However, this kind of development is often bad news for the environment. For example, when more factories are built, there is more employment, but air pollution from manufacturing leads to [1]**gl**_____ **wa**_____ , a phenomenon that is increasing temperatures around the world. This [2]**cl**_____ **ch**_____ causes problems for farmers because when it's hotter and there isn't enough rain, [3]**wa**_____ **sh**_____ mean animals have nothing to drink and food crops die. In addition, warmer temperatures destroy areas where animals live and we now have many [4]**en**_____ **sp**_____ that could die out completely.

There needs to be a balance between economic growth and protecting the environment. Governments should invest in [5]**re**_____ **en**_____ such as wind farms and make it affordable for homes and businesses to install [6]**so**_____ **pa**_____ on roofs. Some countries make sure all homes have [7]**re**_____ **bi**_____ for their household waste, too. Glass, paper and aluminium can be reused, which is great for the environment.

WORD STORE 8A | Environmental issues

2 Match the two statements. Use the words in bold to help you.

Try to avoid buying **single-use plastics**. ☐F

1 It's important that all of our waste is **biodegradable**. ☐

2 **Contamination** of the air by dangerous gases is a serious problem. ☐

3 People who don't believe in climate change think **eco-warriors** are wrong. ☐

4 Our actions are doing **irreparable damage** to the Earth. ☐

5 Removing just one species from the **food chain** destroys the whole system. ☐

A That's why we need to find different forms of energy for our cars.

B So if smaller fish die, larger ones will starve, and so on.

C However, who else is fighting to protect the natural world?

D Otherwise, we can't get rid of it and it's with us forever.

E For instance, polar bears could die out if Arctic ice melts due to global warming.

F Instead, use glass, paper or aluminium containers that can be recycled.

3 Complete the text with the words in bold in Exercise 2.

One of the biggest threats to the quality of the natural environment is _single-use plastic_ such as drinks bottles, bags, straws and packaging. Unlike paper packaging, plastic is not [1]_____ , so it stays on the ground and in the oceans for many, many years and causes [2]_____ of land and water.

When plastic is in the ocean, sea creatures mistake it for food, eat it and die. These deaths affect the [3]_____ in terrible ways as it means there is less for other animals to eat. We should produce less plastic and get rid of plastic waste more responsibly to stop the [4]_____ that it causes. It isn't enough for us to depend on [5]_____ to fight for the environment. Everyone has a duty to protect the planet.

WORD STORE 8B | Landscapes

4 Complete the missing words. The first letters are given.

A **d**_itch_ can be at the side of a road or a field, and it holds or carries away water.

1 A **s**_____ is a small narrow river.

2 A **p**_____ is a large flat area of land with very few trees on it.

3 A **b**_____-_____ **a**_____ has many homes, roads and businesses.

4 An **o**_____ is an area of land where fruit trees are grown.

5 A **f**_____ is at the bottom of a mountain.

6 A **m**_____ is an area of land which has grass and flowers in it.

5 Complete the email with the words in the box.

> built-up area   ditch   ~~foothills~~   meadow
> orchard   plain   ploughed field   stream

To: Emily

From: Anna

Hi Emily,

We're having a great time. I didn't think I'd enjoy hiking, but I've changed my mind! We're staying in a village in the _foothills_ of the mountains. It's far away from any ¹_____ , so it's nice and quiet. Our accommodation is on a farm and it's such a pretty place.

On our first day, the farmer showed us around. First, he took us to the ²_____ where we picked cherries from the trees. The following day, we had a picnic in a ³_____ with soft grass and colourful wildflowers. After we ate, Andy and Lou decided to play football. Bad idea! The ball rolled into a grassy ⁴_____ and when Andy went to get it, he slipped on the grass and hurt his foot. Luckily, it wasn't serious, but the next day he couldn't hike with us.

Do you like the photo I've attached? That's the view from my room. The ⁵_____ belongs to the farmer. He got it ready yesterday and he's going to grow some vegetables there. Nearby you can see a ⁶_____ – the water is so clear that you can drink it!

Today we're going hiking again. There's a flat ⁷_____ not far from here and Andy won't have any problems walking there. So, I'd better get my boots on and join the others!

Bye for now,

Anna

WORD STORE 8C | Animals

6 Complete the biologist's notes with the words in the box. There are two extra words.

> breeding grounds   extinction   hatch   ~~in captivity~~
> migration   natural habitat   on the loose
> release into the wild   thriving populations

Common name: Loggerhead Sea Turtle
Scientific name: _Caretta caretta_
Lives for: 50+ years in the wild,
33+ years _in captivity_
Body length: around 90 cm
Weight: 70–170 kg
¹_____ : Oceans all around the world, except in the coldest seas
Diet: Clams, crabs, mussels; also some softer foods including jellyfish, fish and seaweed
²_____ : Every two or three years they may travel over 12,000 km
³_____ : They return to the same beach where they were born to lay their eggs. It takes 46–80 days for the eggs to ⁴_____ , depending on the temperature.
Threat of ⁵_____ :
Numbers are declining and there are no ⁶_____ . Considered to be an endangered species due to capture in fishing equipment, water pollution, plastic waste and destruction of beaches by development.

7 Choose the correct option.

Scientists release animals into the _loose_ / (_wild_) if they believe that they can survive there.

1 Areas that are _thriving_ / _breeding_ grounds for animals should be protected.

2 When just a few members of a species are left, the only way to save them is to keep them in _captivity_ / _the wild_, where they will be safe.

3 It's our fault that some species are facing _migration_ / _extinction_ and could disappear forever.

4 As soon as they _hatch_ / _release_, baby loggerhead turtles head towards the sea.

5 A lion has escaped from the zoo and is _in_ / _on_ the loose in the city!

6 It's amazing how far some animals travel during their _migration_ / _population_ from one place to another.

7 The Amazon jungle is the _wild_ / _natural_ habitat of thousands of plant and animal species.

8 There used to be a _breeding_ / _thriving_ population of dodos on Mauritius, but the species died out.

SHOW WHAT YOU'VE LEARNT

8 Choose the correct answers A–C.

1 I like to imagine that animals feel great happiness when they are released into the __ .
  A captivity   B habitat   C wild

2 In the past, farmers had to dig their __ by hand, but now they use tractors to plough them.
  A fields   B plains   C meadows

3 __ is the worst thing that can happen to any plant or animal species on the planet.
  A Extinction   B Breeding   C Migration

4 Brightly coloured flowers filled the __ and we saw deer eating the grass.
  A ditch   B meadow   C stream

5 The fence around the field broke during the storm and now the cows are __ the loose.
  A at   B in   C on

6 __ plastics have created huge 'garbage patches' in the Pacific Ocean.
  A Only-time   B Single-use   C Once-used

7 Global warming has caused __ to fish populations, which are dying in great numbers.
  A endangered species   B climate change
  C irreparable damage

8 A __ chain shows what each living thing eats, and how energy is passed from creature to creature.
  A species   B diet   C food

9 In __ areas, there are many homes as well as services such as schools and hospitals.
  A ploughed   B built-up   C thriving

10 Unless the energy we use is clean and __ , we will continue to pollute the planet and damage life.
  A renewable   B biodegradable   C recycled

/10

GRAMMAR

8.2

Unreal past and regrets
• *wish, if only, it's time*
and *would rather*

SHOW WHAT YOU KNOW

1 Complete the sentences with the correct form of the verbs in brackets.

I wish I *had* (have) a longer attention span but, I … Oh, er sorry, what was I saying?

1 If only there _____ (be) a pill people could take to get rid of serious illnesses quickly.
2 Sarah wishes her friends _____ (not upload) photos of her to social media sites without asking first.
3 I wish I _____ (not suffer) from insomnia before tests and exams.
4 If only my parents _____ (buy) a sat-nav, we might not get lost so often.

2 ★ Choose the correct option to explain the meaning of each sentence in italics.

1 *If only I had taken on the new role at work.*
The speaker *did / didn't* take on the new role at work.
2 *I wish the living expenses in this city weren't so high.*
The living expenses in the speaker's city *are / aren't* high.
3 *I wish I'd performed better at the interview.*
The speaker *did / didn't* perform well at the interview.
4 *If only my job wasn't so monotonous.*
The speaker's job *is / isn't* monotonous.
5 *I wish my contract hadn't expired.*
The speaker's contract *has / hasn't* expired.

3 ★ ★ Complete the second sentence so that it has a similar meaning to the first.

I think you should go home now.
It's time *you went home.*

1 I would like you to drive instead of me today.
I'd rather you _____ today.
2 I really should have set my alarm for 6 a.m. instead of 7 a.m.
If only _____ my alarm an hour earlier.
3 You haven't bought your girlfriend flowers for at least six months.
It's high time _____ flowers.
4 I regret that I didn't learn to swim when I was a child.
I wish I _____ when I was a child.
5 I'd prefer not to sit at the table right next to the entrance.
I'd rather _____ at the table right next to the entrance.

REMEMBER THIS

We never say I wish I would.

I wish I ~~would~~ could stay a bit longer.

4 ★ ★ Change the underlined words so that the tense is correct in the second sentence.

If only I was more outgoing.
If only I *had been more outgoing* when I was at school.

1 I wish I could go on holiday.
I wish I _____ last summer.
2 If only we lived in a big city now.
If only we _____ when we were children.
3 I wish I hadn't lived alone at university.
I wish I _____ now.
4 If only I hadn't been so tired that night.
If only I _____ now.

5 ★ ★ ★ Complete the messages with the correct forms of the words in the box.

| begin   can   ~~explore~~   invest   make   spend |

If you love the sea, then **Ocean Fans** is the website for you.

Sea not Space – jellyfish99 writes:

It's high time we explored the world's oceans more thoroughly. Amazingly, 95 percent of our waters remain unseen by human eyes. I would rather governments ¹_____ in this than in developing weapons, for example. I wish we ²_____ concentrate on learning more about what is here on Earth and how to preserve it. The answer to many of our environmental problems could lie beneath the waves – if only we ³_____ the effort to look.

1 Reply – ocotboy8 writes:

I couldn't agree more, jellyfish99. I wish we ⁴_____ the billions it took to fight the wars of recent years on preserving the planet and its oceans instead. If only we ⁵_____ developing clean energy alternatives earlier, the Earth might now be in a much better state.

SHOW WHAT YOU'VE LEARNT

6 Find and correct the mistakes.

I wish you ~~are~~ nicer to me. *were*

1 If only you remembered to lock the car properly last night. _____
2 It's highly time you started taking responsibility for your actions. _____
3 I wish I would remember what Tom said he wanted for his birthday. _____
4 I'd rather of stayed at home than spend two hours in a traffic jam. _____
5 I wish it is Christmas already – I need a break!
_____
6 If only you had liked seaweed, we could go for sushi now. _____

/6

GRAMMAR: Train and Try Again page 178

LISTENING LANGUAGE PRACTICE

8.3
Interview about intelligent animals
• word building

1 Complete the interview with Dr Matthews with the appropriate forms of the words in brackets.

> *Extracts from Student's Book recording* 🔊 **3.36**
>
> P: Welcome to Animal World, the series in which we examine animals' *behaviour* (behave) in their
> ¹_____ (NATURE) habitats. This week,
> we're turning our attention to some of the smartest animals on the planet. Here to deliver today's three-minute lecture is wildlife expert and animal rights ²_____ (CAMPAIGN) Dr Roger Matthews. Thank you, Dr Matthews.
>
> DM: Thank you. When you think of intelligent animals, no doubt chimpanzees come to mind. Chimpanzees share ninety-eight percent of the same genes as humans and they resemble humans in many ways. […] They experience adolescence and develop ³_____ (POWER) mother and child bonds. They are also similar to humans in that they attack and kill rival gangs of chimpanzees when they want to extend their territory.
>
> The notion of chimpanzees being aggressive is pretty ⁴_____ (SHOCK), but it's even harder to imagine dolphins being anything other than affectionate, ⁵_____ (PLAY) and intelligent. Dolphins are undoubtedly ⁶_____ (EXTREME) intelligent. They have large brains and a number of things in common with humans and chimpanzees. […] Also like humans, they are totally ⁷_____ (DEPEND) on their parents during ⁸_____ (CHILD). But they're also good at defending themselves and can be quite competitive, even ⁹_____ (AGGRESSION), particularly when they want to keep other males away from a female.
>
> But I'd like to move nearer to home and consider farm animals. Which do you think are the least intelligent: cows maybe, or sheep? It's true that sheep have a reputation for being stupid because they ¹⁰_____ (MIND) follow the crowd and frankly, they don't look very bright. However, scientific research shows that they've been seriously undervalued. […]

REMEMBER THIS

The word **mind** is widely used in collocations with verbs and adjectives, as well as in a large number of useful phrases.

When you think of intelligent animals, no doubt chimpanzees **come to mind**. *(verb + mind)*
Despite his physical disabilities, Stephen Hawking had one of the most **brilliant minds** *of his generation.* (adjective + mind)
There is no doubt in my mind *that you are the right person for the job.* (phrase with *mind*)

---

2 Read REMEMBER THIS. Complete the collocations using the words in the box.

> back   closed   enquiring   fresh
> ~~lose~~   on   out of

lose **your mind**   become crazy
get sb or sth ¹_____ **your mind**
   stop thinking about somebody or something
a ²_____ **mind**
   with very fixed opinions; unwilling to change your ideas
an ³_____ **mind**
   curious, wanting to find out new things
there is no doubt in sb's mind
   used when someone feels certain about something
at the ⁴_____ **of your mind**
   used when you are aware of something but you don't really want to think about it
sth is ⁵_____ **in sb's mind**
   someone remembers something clearly
sth is ⁶_____ **sb's mind**
   someone worries about something or thinks about it a lot

3 Complete the sentences with the words and phrases in Exercise 2. Change the form if necessary.

> *At the back of* John's mind he had a strange feeling he'd been to this house before.

1 I will clearly _____ my mind if you keep asking me about your birthday surprise over again!
2 With yesterday's fall _____ in his mind, Tim skied slowly and carefully.
3 _____ minds are always hungry for knowledge.
4 Jenny couldn't sleep because she had the next day's exam _____ her mind.
5 Kelly couldn't get the eccentric physicist she had met that morning _____ her mind.
6 The politician complained that the voters had _____ minds when it came to the new environmental laws.

WORD STORE 8D | Word building

4 Complete the sentences with the correct form of the word in brackets.

> It is commonly believed that owls are wise, but appearances can be *deceptive* (deception).

1 There is a strong _____ (resemble) between donkeys and horses, but donkeys have longer ears.
2 It is a _____ (conceive) to think that English bulldogs are aggressive – they're really very friendly.
3 Any dog owner will tell you that dogs are _____ (doubt) more loyal than cats.
4 _____ (competitive) for food and water can be observed between a lot of different species.
5 Animal charities do great work and their contribution should not be _____ (value).
6 Anita is a volunteer for a _____ (reputation) organisation that aims to protect natural habitats.
7 Are _____ (adolescence) chimpanzees as playful as baby ones?

Endangered species
• severe weather and natural disasters
• collocations

1 Read the texts. What is the common topic of all four?

1 Population
2 Extinction
3 Large creatures

(A) The Tasmanian devil is found on the island of Tasmania, but it once had thriving populations on the Australian mainland* too, where it was <u>widespread</u>. The devil's extinction there 3,000 years ago was likely due to increasingly dry conditions with little rain to support plant and animal life. The Tasmanian population survived because of the wetter conditions and also because the dingo – a native* Australian wild dog – was unable to reach the island and hunt the Tasmanian devil.

Early European settlers* considered Tasmanian devils a danger to their farm animals and, in 1830, a plan was introduced to remove them from the island. For over 100 years, devils were caught and killed, and their extinction was <u>imminent</u>. But the population recovered after a 1941 law began to protect them. For over fifty years, all was well, until a disease epidemic* had a <u>severe</u> impact on the population, causing it to <u>shrink</u> considerably. The Tasmanian devil is now an endangered species, and as the disease cannot be cured, there are serious concerns about its continued survival.

Earth News

(B) The world's largest bee, thought to be extinct, has been discovered by scientists in a group of Indonesian islands. Now, there is some hope for the survival of the species. However, it is threatened by deforestation – the region where the bees live lost seven percent of its trees between 2001 and 2017.

Part of the funding for the expedition* to find the bee was provided by Global Wildlife Conservation. In 2017, this organisation began a worldwide search for twenty-five species that have been 'lost' for at least a decade, including a pink-headed duck and a tree kangaroo.

Though it is an exciting discovery, scientists worry that there may be a new threat. In 2018, a sample of the bee was sold on eBay for $9,100. They are concerned that people may attempt to find the bees for profit. To protect them, the exact location of the discovery has not been <u>revealed</u>. The team plans to return to the island to do more research soon.

(C)

Prehistoric Giant Revealed

An <u>enormous</u> species of dinosaur, which weighed more than a Boeing 737, has been found by scientists, who claim the beast was so large it would have 'feared nothing'. Named *Dreadnoughtus Schrani*, after the dreadnought battleships of the early twentieth century, the <u>herbivore</u> would have done little other than eat in order to support its vast* body. Measurements of its fossilised bones suggest that the long-extinct creature measured twenty-six metres in length and weighed about sixty-five tonnes.

The <u>ancient</u> remains unearthed in Argentina represent by far the most complete skeleton ever recovered of a super-massive herbivore from a group known as the titanosaurs. Although <u>partial</u> skeletons of potentially larger cousins have previously been found, the find makes *Dreadnoughtus* the largest land animal for which a body size can be accurately estimated. Examination of the 77-million-year-old specimen* suggests it may not even have been fully grown at the time it died.

(D) The red squirrel has been almost entirely driven out of almost all of England and Wales after the introduction of the grey squirrel from North America in the nineteenth century. Environmentalists and nature lovers are calling for a nationwide reduction in the number of grey squirrels in order to prevent the total extinction of the native red. There are estimated to be just 15,000 reds left in England, compared to a massive 2.5 million grey squirrels. Although experts once believed that the aggressive grey squirrel was able to out-compete the gentler red in the battle for food and habitats, many are now convinced that the decisive factor in their disappearance was actually a viral-like infection carried by the greys and passed on to the reds. The virus is probably responsible for the decline of the red squirrel over a long period of time and now the race is on to see whether environmental groups and scientists can save what remains of the population.

GLOSSARY

mainland (n) – the largest part of a country separate from the islands around it

native (adj) – plants or animals that are from a particular area and were not brought there

settler (n) – a person who goes to live in a new country or colony

epidemic (n) – a disease that affects a large number of people/animals and spreads quickly

expedition (n) – a journey made for a particular purpose

vast (adj) – extremely large

specimen (n) – a single plant or animal which is an example of a particular species

2 Match statements 1–9 with texts A–D. You can choose each text more than once.

This text ... explains the impact of the introduction of a foreign species. ☐ D
1 reports the discovery of a record-breaking extinct species. ☐
2 gives an example of a link between climate and extinction. ☐
3 talks about the man-made destruction of a natural habitat. ☐
4 explains what has happened to two groups of the same species. ☐
5 talks about a misconception concerning a threatened species. ☐
6 explains the meaning of a species' name. ☐
7 explains that a rival species is responsible for the problem in question. ☐
8 talks about a species that has faced extinction twice. ☐
9 reports on a selfish reason to find a particular species. ☐

3 Read the texts again. Are statements 1–8 true (T) or false (F)?

The Tasmanian devil lived in different parts of Australia. ☐ T
1 Wild dogs are currently threatening the Tasmanian devil. ☐
2 It is unlikely that the Tasmanian devil will survive. ☐
3 The bee's natural home in Indonesia has been almost completely destroyed. ☐
4 For the survival of the bee, people shouldn't find out where it lives. ☐
5 The *Dreadnoughtus* dinosaur probably ate very little considering its enormous size. ☐
6 Other *Dreadnoughtus* dinosaurs might have been bigger than the one discovered in Argentina. ☐
7 The red squirrel has no hope of surviving. ☐
8 The grey squirrel does not die from the illness it carries. ☐

4 Match the words with underlined opposites in the texts. Use a dictionary if necessary.

eventual/distant _imminent_
1 local/limited _____
2 whole _____
3 tiny/minuscule _____
4 slight/mild _____
5 hidden _____
6 carnivore _____
7 grow _____
8 modern/recent _____

5 Match the words in Exercise 4 with the definitions.

happening after a long period of time _eventual_
1 existing or happening in many places _____
2 serious or extreme _____
3 extremely small _____
4 meat eater _____
5 incomplete or unfinished _____
6 become smaller _____
7 from long ago _____
8 not hidden _____

6 Look at the vocabulary in lesson 8.4 in the Student's Book. Complete the missing words. The first letters are given.

Between 1981 and 1984, Africa suffered a deadly **d**_rought_ with over a million lives lost to the dry conditions.
1 The Galveston **h**_____ of 1900, with wind speeds of up to 235 km an hour, was the deadliest natural disaster in the history of the United States.
2 Most **w**_____ are due to human carelessness, such as throwing away cigarettes.
3 Severe weather has been affecting the country's transport networks for days, bringing ice, **b**_____ and strong winds.
4 Residents of the city were woken by shaking buildings as a level 5.3 **e**_____ hit, causing widespread damage.
5 Locals and tourists on the island ran to higher ground following an urgent warning that a **t**_____ was approaching.
6 Trees were brought down and roofs were ripped from buildings as **g**_____ **w**_____ tore through the area.
7 Search teams are trying to locate skiers who have been missing since the **a**_____ happened.

WORD STORE 8E | Collocations

7 Complete the sentences with the words in the box.

> agony   ascent   conditions   ~~demanding~~   injuries
> note   overboard   poverty   storm   tale

Cross-country skiing is a physically _demanding_ activity for only the fittest of athletes.
1 The sailor was swept _____ by a massive wave and was rescued by the rest of the crew.
2 I highly recommend this book. It's a gripping _____ of survival in the jungle.
3 When the climbers began their _____ , they were all looking forward to reaching the top of the mountain.
4 The long drought destroyed the village's crops and the people faced extreme _____ .
5 It's a sad story, but it ends on a positive _____ when the animals are rescued.
6 This winter has been unusually hard. Unfortunately, the severe weather _____ will continue.
7 The cyclist suffered life-threatening _____ when he was hit by a car while riding.
8 The captain of the ferry boat decided not to sail because a _____ was brewing.
9 Can you imagine the _____ suffered by the parents before their children were safely found?

121

GRAMMAR

8.5

Emphasis – cleft sentences
and inversion

SHOW WHAT YOU KNOW

1 Add one of the phrases in the box to each sentence
to make it more emphatic.

> absolutely   at all   on earth   own
> so   the question is

It's your fault you are busy now. You should've done
more work last week. _own_

1 If you don't do any exercise, I'm not surprised you
feel unwell so often. _____

2 I'm sorry I was rude to you. I've had a difficult day.
_____

3 Are you going to do it again? _____

4 I don't know why you didn't call me first to check.
_____

5 I am convinced she is telling the truth. _____

2 ★ Complete the text with phrases a–f.

The Rosetta Mission

_d_ such an exciting space project as the Rosetta mission.
Just in case you missed the news. ¹___ land a spacecraft on
a comet travelling at 24,600 miles per hour 511 million km
from Earth. ²___ an opportunity to study a comet in such
detail. ³___ the journey to the comet take ten years, but it cost
over a billion pounds. ⁴___ the unimaginably distant comet is
only 2.5 miles wide. Scientists have compared the task to
trying to land on a speeding bullet. ⁵___ remind us how
advanced science has really become.

a It's these kinds of achievements that
b Never before has there been
c Not only did
(d) Rarely has there been
e What is most amazing is that
f What scientists managed to do was

3 ★ ★ Choose the correct option to complete the
sentences.

1 What *was happened / happened was* that I forgot to
log out of Facebook and Jo posted this comment.

2 Never *have I / I have* been so humiliated in all my life.

3 *It's / What's* people like him that should be given
the most responsible tasks.

4 What I find most unbelievable *that is / is that* no one
saw Becky leaving the party.

5 All *we are / are we* saying is please give us a chance
to explain what happened.

6 What *he did was / did he was* wander around the
streets hoping he would recognise his hotel.

7 Rarely *the temperatures have / have the
temperatures* fallen so low in September.

8 Not only *do you / you do* ask me for a lot of money,
but you lie about why you really need it.

4 ★ ★ ★ Rewrite the story using the words in brackets.

Ryan lost track of time. (happened)
What happened was that Ryan lost track of time.

1 He was distracted by a documentary about a man
snowboarding on an iceberg. (it)
_____
_____

2 The film crew flew out to the North Atlantic by
helicopter. (did) _____
_____

3 They dropped the man onto the top of the huge
iceberg. (happened) _____
_____

4 The man only rode down it for about half a minute,
but the shots were amazing. (all)
_____
_____

5 Ryan hadn't ever seen anyone snowboarding in such
an unusual place. (never) _____
_____

6 He found the effort that the whole team went to most
impressive. (what) _____
_____

SHOW WHAT YOU'VE LEARNT

5 Choose the correct answers A–C.

1 ___ cheapest holiday they had ever been on,
but also the best.
A Not was it only the   B It was only not
C Not only was it

2 ___ identify stress as a major cause of insomnia.
A What they did was   B It's what they did that
C What happened was

3 ___ I liked her old hairstyle better and next thing she
was in tears.
A Rarely had I   B All I said was   C Not only did

4 ___ boys like him who break young girls' hearts.
A What's   B What   C It's

5 Rarely ___ visit their grandparents, and then only for
a very short time.
A they do   B do they   C are they

6 ___ was the coffee and cake they served during
the break.
A What I liked most   B What liked I most
C What most I liked

/6

GRAMMAR: Train and Try Again page 178

8.6 SPEAKING

Giving a presentation

1 Translate the phrases into your own language.

SPEAKING BANK

Introduction

Have you ever thought about/considered/wondered how/why/what, etc. …? _____

During my/this presentation, I plan to tell you about … _____ _____ _____

You may be wondering why I've chosen to talk about … today. Well, let me explain … _____ _____ _____ _____

Introducing familiar information

You are (probably) all familiar with … _____ _____

You may be aware that … _____

You may already know that … _____ _____ _____

Perhaps you have heard of/about … _____

Introducing surprising information

Most people aren't aware/don't realise … _____ _____ _____

… but, did you know that …? _____

You might not know that … _____

Finishing your presentation

OK, that's all from me. _____

Thank you for listening. _____

I hope you found the presentation interesting. _____ _____

If anyone has any questions, please feel free to ask now. _____ _____

2 Complete the advice with the words in the box. There are two extra words.

> contact   forget   invite   involved   notes
> speed   stand   questions

Speak with a clear voice at a natural _speed_.
1 Make eye _____ with the audience.
2 Ask the audience questions to keep them _____ .
3 Have some _____ with you, but don't read them.
4 If you _____ something, keep going. Nobody knows what you were planning to say anyway!
5 When you finish, thank the audience for listening and _____ questions.

3 Put the words in order to complete the extracts from presentations. Then match them to the next thing that is said.

you / how / ever / about / thought / have
Have you ever thought about how your mobile phone actually works? [f]

1 why / to talk about / you / wondering / may / be / I've chosen _____ _____ British electronic music today. Well, let me explain … ◯

2 probably / all / are / familiar / we / with _____ _____ the Apollo moon landing of 1969. ◯

3 that / might / know / not / you _____ _____ , according to astronauts returning from space walks, space smells like 'hot metal'. ◯

4 all / from / that's / me _____ _____ . Thank you all for listening. ◯

5 to ask now / feel free / please / questions / any / anyone / has / if _____ _____ . ◯

a Some of you may also know that certain groups believe the whole mission was faked.
b I hope you have learnt a few new things about your own amazing brain today.
c Thanks for an interesting presentation. I want to ask what your personal opinion on music piracy is.
d Many of the most influential electronic musicians of the last thirty years actually come from the UK.
e The odour has also been compared to frying steak.
f How is it possible that this little machine in your pocket can connect you with any place or person in the world?

4 Put the extracts from the beginning and the ending of a presentation in a logical order.

Beginning
A Have you ever tried holding your breath for more than a minute? It's not easy, is it? Well, today [1]
B but did you know that the world record holder is able to hold his breath for almost ten minutes? ◯
C get going. Now, perhaps some of you have heard of an extreme sport called free diving. ◯
D I plan to explain how we can all train ourselves to easily hold our breath for longer. So, let's ◯
E You may be aware that free divers are able to stay under water for several minutes at a time, ◯

Ending
A OK everyone, that's [1]
B please feel free to do so now. ◯
C for listening, and I hope ◯
D If you would like to ask any questions ◯
E all from me. I'd like to thank you ◯
F that you found the presentation interesting. ◯

USE OF ENGLISH

8.7
Prefixes

1 ★ **Form opposites by adding correct prefixes.**

(dis- il- im- in- ir- un-)

*il*legal

1 ___regular
2 ___possible
3 ___able
4 ___agree
5 ___believe

6 ___responsible
7 ___literate
8 ___accurate
9 ___conscious
10 ___mature

2 ★ ★ **Complete the definitions with words formed by adding prefixes to the words in capitals.**

after the WAR		*post-war*
1	the opposite of ALLOW	_____
2	having many COLOURS	_____
3	BEHAVE badly	_____
4	PAID too little	_____
5	in favour of DEMOCRACY	_____
6	WORK too much	_____
7	against NUCLEAR	_____
8	before the ELECTION	_____
9	extremely SENSITIVE	_____
10	not PERFECT	_____

3 ★ ★ ★ **Complete the words in bold with the correct prefixes.**

The effects of the drought seem to have been *under***estimated** – the current situation is much worse than we initially thought.

1 If you insist on behaving so _____**responsibly**, David, it is impossible for me to treat you like an adult.
2 My Grandma remained _____**married** for 65 years before she finally met John and they decided to become husband and wife.
3 If you _____**cook** meat, there is a risk that dangerous bacteria are left in the areas that don't get hot.
4 Warning: Your anti-virus programme has been _____**abled** and your computer could be at risk.
5 The government has been criticised by environmental organisations for being _____**willing** to spend more on protecting marine wildlife.
6 Are you sure this is a reliable website? In my opinion, the author is just spreading _____**information** to attract more readers.

4 ★ ★ ★ **Complete the sentences with the correct forms of the root words in brackets.**

Refugees who have entered the country *illegally* (legal) are currently treated as criminals.

1 With the correct training techniques, even the most _____ (obey) dogs can be taught to behave.
2 Our English teacher says my essay will have to be _____ (write) because he can't read my handwriting.
3 I _____ (understand) the care instructions for my shirt and shrank it in the washing machine.
4 I managed to delete most of the unnecessary apps that came _____ (install) on my phone.
5 If there is even the smallest _____ (perfect) in one of our products, this software will detect it.
6 Speaking no fewer than five languages, Pierre is truly _____ (lingual).
7 If you suffer from skin problems, try our new _____ (acne) face wash for instant results.
8 Our neighbour's cat is so skinny that I think they must be _____ (feed) it.
9 This paragraph of your essay is completely _____ (relevant), so I think you should delete it.

5 ★ ★ ★ **Complete the comments with the correct forms of the root words in capitals.**

◯◯◯

Is it too late to stop climate change now? What's your opinion?

Some people think that with global warming the climate in their country will improve, but this is extremely unlikely. The weather will probably be more *unpredictable* (PREDICT) and more extreme, with little rain and winds strong enough to
¹_____ (TURN) cars. We might have to ²_____ (BUILD) our homes so such winds cannot destroy their roofs.

³_____ (NEW) energy sources, such as solar or wind power, simply cannot produce enough power to meet our current needs. Now we have become accustomed to having air-conditioning and central heating, nobody wants to live without them in ⁴_____ (STANDARD) conditions, so we'll probably keep burning fossil fuels for a long time.

It's obvious that our lifestyle is causing ⁵_____ (REPAIR) damage to wildlife, and the environment cannot recover fast enough. Do you need more proof? Well, have a look at the number of ⁶_____ (DANGER) species. Soon the list of extinct animals will have become much longer.

124

6 ★ **Choose the correct answers A–C.**

I'm sick and tired of _C_ in traffic every single morning.
A stick   B was stuck   Ⓒbeing stuck

1 Rarely __ such a beautiful sunset – the colours were spectacular.
A had I seen   B I had seen   C seen I had

2 Don't forget to buy some sugar-free biscuits for Dan, __ ?
A do you   B can you   C will you

3 The expedition would have been a success if we __ better for the extreme weather conditions.
A prepared   B have prepared   C had prepared

4 Some dog owners don't understand that chewing and barking is __ normal behaviour for dogs.
A deeply   B supremely   C perfectly

5 Helen __ to comment on the rumour her cousin was spreading about her.
A urged   B declined   C denied

7 ★ ★ **Complete the second sentence so that it has a similar meaning to the first. Use no more than six words, including the word in capitals.**

Having spent a few weeks working outdoors, he was tanned.
BEEN
He was tanned because he _had been working_ outdoors for a few weeks.

1 Please don't eat anything in here.
RATHER
I _____ eat anything in here.

2 I'm tired this morning because I worked very late last night.
IF
I wouldn't be so tired this morning _____
_____ very late last night.

3 They studied a herd of elephants in the wild.
DID
What _____ a herd of elephants in the wild.

4 I intend to start my own design company before I'm thirty years old.
HAVE
By the time I'm thirty years old, I _____
_____ my own design company.

5 They think that the explosion was caused by a gas leak.
THOUGHT
The explosion _____ caused by a gas leak.

6 We stayed at the best hotel and it was very cheap!
ONLY
Not _____ at the best hotel, but it was very cheap too.

8 ★ ★ **Complete the text with one word in each gap.**

Do chimps smile?

Being able to laugh and smile is important when it _comes_ to communication between human beings and this ability is thought to ¹_____ developed more than five millions years ago. Smiling is a complicated procedure and involves ²_____ of facial movements. Humans can smile both silently and when we laugh, and this is one of the things ³_____ set us apart from other animals. However, research now tells us that chimps and humans laugh and smile in a very similar way. Scientists ⁴_____ to think that, although chimps laughed when they were playing, they didn't smile silently at ⁵_____ other like we do. Recent studies analysed the facial impressions of forty-six different chimps from several wild colonies. The results showed very subtle changes in the chimps' facial movements, which compare to human silent smiles. ⁶_____ this implies is that, like us, chimps use smiling as a communication tool. Scientific research continues ⁷_____ provide us with evidence that chimps and humans have a lot more ⁸_____ common than anyone had ever thought!

9 ★ ★ ★ **Complete the sentences using the prompts in brackets. Do not change the order of the words. Change the forms or add new words where necessary. Use up to six words in each gap.**

You sister didn't finish the project on time because she _spent too long looking for_ (spend/long/look) information online.

1 My brother's thinking of changing his job because he _____ (not/stand/criticise) by his boss.

2 She _____ (should/complain) the waiter when she realised there was a mistake on the bill. Now it's too late.

3 The beach won't become clean _____
_____ (unless/everyone/stop/drop) litter.

4 There are two famous trees in this forest – _____ (both/think/be) at least 500 years old.

5 I _____ (wish/we/not/live) so far from the seaside when I was a child.

6 My parents _____ (insist/take/I) to hospital after I was stung by a bee.

125

8.8 WRITING

A letter to an editor

1 Change the underlined words and phrases to make the introduction to a letter to an editor more formal. There may be more than one way to do this.

> [1]Hi there,
>
> [2]I'm [3]getting in touch after reading the article in your [4]paper last Thursday about the positive effects of tourism on a country's economy. I [5]want to tell you that tourism can do terrible damage to the environment and areas of natural beauty.

1 *Dear Editor / Dear Sir or Madam*
2 _____
3 _____
4 _____
5 _____

2 Match the advice on achieving a formal style to your corrections in Exercise 1.

Begin with a formal greeting. ☐ 1
1 Avoid contractions.
(e.g. *can't, he's, should've*, etc.) ☐
2 Avoid informal language.
(e.g. thanks = *thank you*) ☐ & ☐ & ☐
3 Avoid overusing phrasal verbs and colloquial expressions. (e.g. carry on = *continue*) ☐

3 Choose the correct words and phrases to complete the rest of the letter in Exercise 1.

> (Having recently spent) / I have recently spent a week on holiday in a resort town, I have personally seen the effects of development for tourism. As [1]the / a result, more and more high-rise hotels have been built. In addition, roads, an airport, shops and restaurants support the increased demands for transport and services. The outcome [2]of / with such development is that beautiful landscapes and natural habitats have become irreparably damaged.
>
> There is [3]no / without a doubt that tourist facilities consume massive amounts of water and electricity. At a time when global warming is making the planet hotter and drier, water resources should not be wasted, as this could [4]result / lead to shortages. Furthermore, burning fossil fuels to generate electricity contributes to global warming. Unless hotels and businesses use renewable energy, they add to this ever-growing problem.
>
> Holidays are now [5]so / such an affordable that record numbers of people are travelling and the negative impacts of tourism can only become worse. To my mind, [6]in spite of / even though tourism has led to economic growth, it has also played a major role in the destruction of the environment and will continue to do so in the future.
>
> Yours faithfully,
>
> Dean Robertson

4 Complete the sentences with the words in the box.

> although ~~as~~ being despite having in so such without

As a consequence of global warming, sea levels are rising and coastal areas are in danger.

1 Climate change is _____ a terrible threat that we need global cooperation to fight it.
2 _____ gathered all of my old newspapers and magazines, I put them into the recycling bin.
3 The people of the village are very generous, _____ the fact that they have very little.
4 _____ an important part of the food chain, bees must be protected so that they can continue to pollinate plants.
5 Our responses to the climate crisis are _____ inadequate that I wonder how long it will be before humans can no longer live on Earth.
6 The use of solar panels results _____ lower energy costs for homes and businesses.
7 _____ a doubt, a great deal is being done by zoos to protect endangered species.
8 _____ the conditions were dangerous, the climbers continued their ascent of the mountain.

5 Complete the second sentence so that it has a similar meaning to the first. Use the words in brackets.

Because holidays are so affordable, more people are travelling. (so)
Holidays *are so affordable that* more people are travelling.

1 People are forbidden to wash their cars because there is a serious water shortage. (such)

_____
people are forbidden to wash their cars.

2 The beach is a breeding ground for turtles, but a bar has been built there. (even)
A bar has been built on the beach _____ .

3 You can't deny that climate change is caused by global warming. (leads)
You can't deny that _____ .

4 Although there was a severe drought, the farmer's animals survived. (spite)
The farmer's animals survived _____ .

5 The decision means that the trees will not be cut down. (result)

_____
the trees will not be cut down.

6 Areas of natural beauty will definitely be protected from development by new laws. (doubt)

_____
will protect areas of natural beauty from development.

7 There was an earthquake and half the village was destroyed. (consequence)
There was an earthquake. _____ .

6 Choose the correct words to complete the sentences.

Some habitats have been destroyed, (whereas) /
nevertheless others have not.

1 It is wrong to keep animals in captivity. *That said /
Saying that*, zoos do an important job.
2 *Actually / While* some species have disappeared,
many others have survived.
3 It may seem too late to save the planet,
nevertheless / whereas we must try.
4 In spite of the hunters in the area, the tiger *yet / actually*
managed to escape.
5 Many people object to zoos. *While / Having said this*,
they remain major attractions.
6 Solar energy can solve many problems, *yet / actually*
not enough people are using it.
7 Some solutions are not perfect; *even so / while*,
they are better than doing nothing.

7 Read the task and the letter. Then complete the letter
with the words in the box.

actually   nevertheless   that said
whereas   ~~while~~   yet

The Daily Sentinel Environment Section

We would like our readers' views on zoos.
- Do you think it is wrong to keep animals in zoos?
- Are there any good reasons to keep animals in captivity?

Send your letters to the editor.

Dear Sir or Madam,

I am writing to you in response to your request for views about
zoos. *While* I understand that keeping animals in captivity can
be cruel, I would like to point out that for many species,
zoos [1]_____ offer their only hope for survival.

Having been a volunteer at a zoo, I have personally seen how
they work to protect endangered species. Animals in the
wild face many dangers, [2]_____ wildlife in captivity
is safe from threats that can lead to extinction. One of these
is the loss of natural habitats. With nowhere to live or breed,
species cannot survive. Another danger is disease, which can
spread quickly and greatly reduce a population. Hunters are
also a threat, [3]_____ despite this, they continue to kill
for profit in many places.

Zoos often play a very important role in saving a species
from extinction. Experts in different fields can contribute
to our knowledge of animal habits and behaviour and help
zoos create breeding programmes. Whenever possible,
bred animals are released back into the wild, where they are
monitored.
[4]_____ , not all programmes are successful, but they
are worth trying.

It may be considered wrong to keep animals in zoos, [5]_____ , it is undeniable that zoos provide a safe place for animals to live
and breed. Perhaps more importantly, they give endangered species a chance to survive. To my mind, zoos have become increasingly
necessary as natural habitats are destroyed and more species become extinct.

Yours faithfully,

Emma Dixon

---

8 Read the task below. Before you start writing, note
down some ideas and plan your piece of writing.

The Daily Sentinel Environment Section

We would like our readers' views on climate change.
- How serious is it?
- How can we stop it from causing more damage to the
environment?
- Is there hope for the future?

Send your letters to the editor.

In my letter:

• I have begun with a formal greeting (e.g. *Dear Editor*).	☐
• in the first paragraph I have explained my reason for writing and expressed my view.	☐
• in the main paragraphs I have supported my point of view, given further opinions and examples.	☐
• in the last paragraph, I have summarised my opinion.	☐
• I have used an appropriate formal ending (e.g. Yours faithfully).	☐
• I have used formal language.	☐
• I have not used contractions (e.g. that's, there's, we're).	☐
• I have checked my spelling.	☐
• my handwriting is neat enough for someone else to read.	☐

VOCABULARY AND GRAMMAR

1 Choose the correct words to complete the text.

Dear Editor,

I am writing to express my concern about the air and water pollution and the natural *ground /* (*habitat*) */ plain* of the animals living in the area.

Firstly, it must be emphasised that factories continue to release high levels of dangerous gases into the atmosphere and the ¹*extinction / migration / contamination* is terrible. Once in the air, the gases react with water molecules and fall onto the ground in the form of acid rain. This rain can destroy farmers' crops and kill fruit trees in the ²*meadows / orchards / foothills*. We must stop this before it causes ³*irreparable / reputable / undervalued* damage.

Another serious problem is the ⁴*single-use / once-used / only-time* plastic which has found its way into our river. This has killed many fish, disrupting the food ⁵*species / connection / chain* and it must stop!

I hope that all these problems can be solved promptly.

Yours faithfully,

Michael Preston

/5

2 Complete the sentences with the phrases in the box.

> breeding ground   built-up areas   extreme hunger
> ploughed fields   thriving population   ~~water shortages~~

Due to the drought, there are serious *water shortages* in the area which have affected crops and animals.

1 The farmer spent all day in the sun preparing the land for growing crops and, by evening, the _____ were ready.
2 The river water in this remote area is so clean that there is a _____ of fish.
3 Most job opportunities are in cities and other _____ , so many people must live and work there.
4 So little food is grown in the area that the people suffer from _____ and something must be done to help them.
5 There are strict laws to protect the _____ of the turtle so that it may continue to lay eggs there.

/5

3 Complete the sentences with the missing words. The first letters are given.

Residents in the local villages have been told to stay indoors while a tiger is on the l o o s e .

1 Trees were brought down by **g** _ _ _-**f** _ _ _ _ winds and many roads were blocked during the storm.
2 A sailor was swept **o** _ _ _ _ _ _ _ by huge waves, but luckily, he was saved by a rescue team.
3 I wonder how animals feel when they are kept in **c** _ _ _ _ _ _ _ _ and aren't allowed to be free.
4 The surfer sustained life-threatening **i** _ _ _ _ _ _ _ when he was attacked by a shark.
5 When zoos or other animal organisations release animals into the **w** _ _ _ , they monitor them.

/5

4 Complete the sentences with the correct forms of the verbs in brackets. Use short forms where possible.

I wish Joe *didn't bring* (not/bring) stray animals home. Instead, he should ring an animal shelter.

1 In my opinion, it's high time the factory _____ (stop) polluting our city. Actually, it should be closed down.
2 If only you _____ (not/throw out) the old books. They could have all been recycled.
3 I'd rather Maria _____ (plant) more roses in the front garden this spring. They'll look really nice.
4 David wishes he _____ (not/sell) his tent because he can't go camping now.
5 Don't you wish you _____ (install) solar panels when you built your new house?

/5

5 Find and correct the mistakes in the sentences.

We had to decide what to do at the weekend. And it was the dog show ~~what~~ we chose in the end. *that / which*

1 Under any circumstances are you allowed to leave your children unattended at the zoo. _____
2 Not before have we experienced worse weather conditions on our skiing holiday than last winter. _____
3 It's not serious. All happened was that Kim forgot to ask someone to water her plants while she was away. That's why she is upset. _____
4 There was James who rescued the cat. He's an animal lover and does all he can to help them. _____
5 If only have you left all the lights on, but you've also forgotten to turn the TV off. _____

/5

6 Complete each sentence with one or two words.

What an awful day it is today! If only it *wasn't* so cold and wet.

1 Island holidays are nice, but I _____ we went hiking in the countryside like we did last summer.
2 I wish I _____ volunteer to help at the local animal shelter, but I'm too busy these days.
3 _____ I find annoying is that the local council provides so few recycling bins.
4 _____ is the planet getting warmer, but the air and the oceans are becoming more polluted.
5 _____ have I read a more gripping tale! You really must read it when you get the chance.

/5

Total   /30

7 Complete the text with the correct forms of the words in brackets.

Watch out – a bear!

For years, Kate and I used to go camping by a lake not too far from where we lived. But last year, we both thought we should _reconsider_ (CONSIDER) and go on a journey further afield. We chose to spend a fortnight in a tent in the Sequoia National Park, which is famous for its amazing trees and black bears.

When we arrived at the campsite, we were warned about an
1 _____ (USUAL) high number of black bears in the area. It was explained to us that the bears are **2** _____ (SENSITIVE) to food smells and that we should hide food in the boot of our car or a metal box on the site. We were also told not to behave **3** _____ (RESPONSIBLE) and to avoid certain paths. We didn't take the instructions that seriously, but we tried to follow the ranger's advice. For the next two weeks everything went smoothly, with no bears in sight. We felt safe and it seemed **4** _____ (PROBABLE) that we would come across any bears. We had a great time hiking and enjoying nature.

However, on the last night, we suddenly heard a bear roar right outside our tent. At first, I was so shocked that I was completely **5** _____ (CAPABLE) of moving or thinking. I wished I had paid more attention to the ranger's advice about what you're supposed to do in this situation. Then I remembered to throw a jumper in the air and make a lot of noise. A ranger heard the bear as well and he came to our rescue. It was the most terrifying experience ever.

/5

8 Choose the correct answers A–D.

○○○

According to the National Weather Service, we can expect severe weather _D_ , with a very dry and hot summer this year. Therefore, a number of warnings are being issued.
First of all, expect southern parts of the country to suffer serious **1** ___ because rainfall has been the lowest ever in that region. **2** ___ have we seen such dryness in recent decades. It will definitely have a substantial impact on the ecosystem and agriculture, **3** ___ in the affected region, but the rest of the country too. Experts are very concerned. **4** ___ worrying them in particular is that a large number of young animals may die because of possible starvation. Dry weather is also likely to contribute to a greater incidence of wildfires because they can easily spread to other areas. **5** ___ the emergency services can do now is to monitor those forests which are rarely visited and not very well-documented. People are requested to notify the police or fire brigades about any visible smoke.

	A expressions	B situations
	C changes	Ⓓ conditions
1	A hurricanes	B drought	C blizzards	D tsunamis
2	A Not	B Hardly	C None	D Rarely
3	A not only	B if only	C although	D in addition
4	A It's	B There's	C What's	D That's
5	A Despite	B All	C Though	D However

/5

9 Complete the sentences with one word in each gap.

What they wanted to present to us was actually a revolutionary idea on how to save energy.

1 If _____ our hens would lay more eggs, we could have omelettes for breakfast every morning.
2 What a terrible wildfire; never _____ I seen so much destruction.
3 I think it's_____ time the government limited tourism in areas of outstanding beauty because it's causing too much damage.
4 Not _____ did Matt reject my proposal to raise money for the animal shelter, he also suggested ending all of our support.
5 During our visit to the zoo, my daughter decided that pandas are so loveable _____ she wanted me to get her one right away.

/5

10 Complete the second sentence so that it has a similar meaning to the first. Use the words in capitals, but do not change their form.

Despite leaving early in the morning, we didn't get very far because of a traffic jam.
THOUGH
Even _though we left_ early in the morning, we didn't get very far because of a traffic jam.

1 Mark needs to feed the baby gorilla first thing in the morning.
WHAT
_____ is feed the baby gorilla first thing in the morning.
2 We regret we didn't preserve the nesting areas by the river.
WISH
We _____ the nesting areas by the river.
3 I would like you to think about the problems of living in a remote place before you move there.
RATHER
I _____ about the problems of living in a remote place before you move there.
4 It's a pity we can't join you on your expedition to Greenland. It sounds very interesting.
ONLY
If _____ on your expedition to Greenland. It sounds very interesting.
5 We have never dumped any rubbish in the forest.
WE
Never _____ any rubbish in the forest.

/5

Total /20

SPEAKING

1 **In pairs, ask and answer the questions.**

Talk about science and technology.

Student A

1 Tell me about a time you had to manage without technology.
2 Why do you think some people are afraid of new technology?
3 What's the biggest change you've seen in technology in your lifetime?
4 Would you like to work as a scientist? Why?/Why not?
5 In what ways can technology help the environment?

Student B

1 What apps are the most important in your life? Why?
2 Why do some people choose to live a simple life without technology?
3 Should teenagers be able to do more science experiments during science lessons? Why?/Why not?
4 What are the advantages of e-books over paper books?
5 Tell me about a time you used technology to solve a problem.

2 **Read the instructions on your card and role-play the conversation.**

Student A

The situation:

You and Student B are discussing a suggestion that phones and computers or tablets should be banned at school. Explain to Student B why you think this is a good idea. Think about mental health, addiction to screens and improving face-to-face communication.

Your goal:

Persuade Student B that a ban on technology is a good idea.

Student B

The situation:

You and Student A are discussing a suggestion that phones and computers or tablets should be banned at school. Explain to Student A why you think this is a bad idea. Think about access to information and the skills needed to get a good job in the future.

Your goal:

Persuade Student A that a ban on technology is a bad idea.

3 Look at the photos and answer the questions.

Student A
Look at the two photos showing different environments where people live. What can you see in the photos? What impact does each environment have on health? Which of these places would you rather live in?

Student B
Look at the two photos showing ways to reduce pollution in cities. What can you see in the photos? What are the advantages and disadvantages of each form of transport? Which one would you like to see more of in your country?

4 Discuss this statement together. 'Some people think that the way we eat now is unsustainable and in the future we will have to become vegan or start eating insects.' What do you think?

VOCABULARY BANK

Translate the phrases into your own language.

People

Life stages

adolescence _____
adolescent _____
come of age _____
_____
earliest memory _____
_____
elderly _____
grow out of _____
_____
have a clear memory of _____
_____
have a distant memory of _____
_____
have a vague memory of _____
_____
have a vivid memory of _____
_____
life expectancy _____
turn eighteen _____
upbringing _____

Character features

(be) full of oneself _____
adventurous _____
affectionate _____
agile _____
agreeable _____
argumentative _____
attentive _____
bird-brained _____
brainy _____
bursting with confidence _____
_____
carefree _____
cautious _____
character trait _____
clumsy _____
competitive _____
conscientious _____
daring _____
determined _____
enterprising _____
enthusiastic _____
fair-minded _____
flake _____
_____
free spirit _____
_____
genial _____
gentle _____
good-natured _____
highly intelligent _____
honest _____
hopeless _____
humble _____

hyperactive _____
_____
hypersensitive _____
imaginative _____
_____
immature _____
impolite _____
insecure _____
_____
intellectual _____
irresponsible _____
kind-hearted _____
_____
laid-back _____
level-headed _____
_____
loner _____
modest _____
moody _____
neat and tidy _____
neurotic _____
overactive _____
painfully shy _____
pay attention to detail _____
_____
perceptive _____
_____
perfectly normal _____
_____
personality _____
playful _____
protective _____
punctual _____
reliable _____
reputable _____
self-centred _____
self-conscious _____
self-critical _____
self-obsessed _____
_____
sense of humour _____
sensible _____
sensitive _____
short-tempered _____
_____
single-minded _____
_____
slob _____
sociable _____
spontaneous _____
strong-willed _____
_____
supportive _____
supremely confident _____
_____
tactful _____
the life and soul of the party _____
_____
thorough _____
trusting _____
vivid imagination _____
weakness _____
well-behaved _____

wise _____
witty _____

Feelings and emotions

agonizing _____
alarming _____
alarmingly _____
annoying _____
appeal to _____
appear _____
astonishingly _____
astonishment _____
astounding _____
attract sb's attention _____
_____
awe-inspiring _____
based on _____
be concerned about _____
be the centre of attention _____
_____
bitterly disappointed _____
_____
bloodcurdling _____
brighten _____
_____
burst into tears _____
can't be bothered to do sth _____
_____
captivating _____
_____
certainly _____
certainty _____
clearly _____
comforting _____
compassionate _____
complain about _____
confused _____
convinced _____
cope with _____
deceptively _____
deeply depressed _____
_____
deeply disappointed _____
_____
definitely _____
delight _____
delighted _____
desirable _____
develop a desire _____
disgusting _____
distinct feeling _____
_____
doubt _____
draw sb's attention to _____
_____
embarrassing _____
embarrassment _____
_____
envy _____
experience _____
expression _____
fancy _____
feel/get an urge _____

feel left out _____
feel offended _____
feel strongly about sth _____

firmly _____
frankly _____
funnily _____
gut feeling _____
hard to be sure _____
have a hairy moment _____

have a laugh _____

heartwarming _____

hideous _____
humiliated _____
incidentally _____

irresistible _____
irritability _____
it's a pity / it's a shame _____
judging by _____
keep a cool head _____

keep your wits about you _____

kick back _____
knowing _____
larger than life _____
letdown _____
look miserable _____

lose your temper _____

make an impression _____
make sb feel at ease _____
memorable _____
mind-blowing _____
miraculous _____
miserable _____

obvious _____
obviously _____
off-balance _____
off-colour _____
off-putting _____
on a positive note _____

on the edge of your seat _____
ordeal _____
out of the blue _____
overnight _____
overreaction _____
overwhelmed _____
piercing _____
please _____
predictably _____

regrettably _____
relieved _____
remarkable _____
remarkably _____

ridiculous _____
risky _____
roar with laughter _____

roller coaster ride _____

scary _____
self-doubt _____
smile politely _____

steadily _____
strong feeling _____
suffer agony _____
tempting _____
thrilled _____
treat yourself to _____

tremulous _____
trust your instincts _____

unaware _____
uncertainty _____
uncharacteristically _____
uncomfortable _____
unearthly _____
unexpectedly _____
unwanted _____
unwilling _____
upset _____
violent _____
wind sb up _____
worn out _____

Appearance
alike _____
broad-shouldered _____
contorted _____
curly-haired _____
cute _____
decent _____
defect _____
differ _____
duck-face _____

dye your hair _____
faint _____
flat-footed _____
glamorous _____
long-legged _____
resemblance _____
resemble _____

rosy-cheeked _____

shaggy _____
slobbery _____
solidly built _____
sunburnt _____
thin-lipped _____

unkempt _____
weather-beaten _____

Body parts
at arm's length _____
breath _____
cell _____
chest _____
developed _____
digestive system _____
facial _____
fingerprint _____
from the corner of your eye _____

gut _____
handedness _____

hemisphere _____
immune system _____

knuckle _____
left-handed _____
left-hander _____
nerve cell _____
nervous system _____
respiratory system _____

sight _____
waist-high _____

Physical and mental actions
acknowledge _____
add _____
adjust _____
adrift _____
approach _____
arise _____

assume _____
assure _____
bend _____
bother _____

break off _____
bring about _____
burst into flames _____

chase _____
check up on _____
comprise _____
conceive _____

confirm _____
crouch down _____
curl up _____
cut down on _____

dash _____
declare _____
demolish _____
determine _____
drag _____
embrace _____
emerge _____
emphasise _____

VOCABULARY BANK

Translate the phrases into your own language.

ensure _____
explain _____
express _____
flicker across _____

flinch _____
float _____

float away _____
gasp _____
gather _____
gaze _____
get hold of _____
get the message _____
giggle _____
give a wave _____
glance _____
glimpse _____
grimace _____
grip _____
have a go _____
have sth on the brain _____

hesitate _____
hold sth up _____
hug _____
identify _____
ignite _____
include _____
insist _____
intend to _____
knock sb out _____

leap out _____
let out a groan _____
look out for _____
manipulate _____
overturn _____
peep _____
peer _____
permit _____
position _____
precede _____
push through _____
put sb in a headlock _____

rack your brains _____
raise _____
recall _____
reckon _____
reconsider _____

reinforce _____
reject _____
reveal _____
rise _____
roam _____
scream _____
seek _____
shake sth off _____
shrug your shoulders _____

sigh _____
skip _____

slip down _____
snap _____
sob _____
spill _____
spot _____
squirt _____
stare _____
stiffen _____
straighten _____
substitute _____
suggest _____
swallow _____
swap _____
take effort _____
take sth into account _____

tangled up _____
tilt _____
tousle _____
trigger _____
twist your mouth _____
undo _____
whisper _____
wink _____
wonder _____
yell _____

Clothes and accessories

blood-red _____
bracelet _____
charcoal-grey _____

collarless _____
fashion _____
fashionable _____
frill _____
garment _____
lemon-yellow _____
lime-green _____
loose _____
nut-brown _____
old-fashioned _____
on trend _____
ornament _____
personal belongings _____

scrubs _____
second-hand clothes _____

sky-blue _____
snow-white _____
sportswear _____
streetwear _____
stripe _____
synthetic fabric _____
vibrant colour _____

Skills and interests

acquire a skill _____
be an expert in _____

be of interest to _____

be passionate about _____

be the brains behind sth _____

bowling alley _____
capable of doing sth _____

carve wood _____
catch the bug _____
competent user of _____

curious about _____
enable _____
excellent command of _____

focus on your strengths _____

get the hang of _____

go in for _____
have a passion for _____

have an aptitude for _____
have no clue _____
inclined towards _____
it's worth a try _____
jack of all trades, master of none _____

multipotentialite _____

natural inclination _____

not be everyone's cup of tea _____

perception _____
pick up a new skill _____

polymath _____

proven ability to _____

range of interests _____

recognition skills _____

sharpen a skill _____
sharpness _____
step out of your comfort zone _____

take sth up _____

tend to do sth _____

think outside the box _____

thrive _____
transferable skills _____

valuable _____
well suited _____

well-developed _____

Sense of identity

background
be second nature to sb

broad accent
identity
privacy
sense of community

tribe

Personal values

achieve a goal
attitude
balance
be bound to
be obliged to

choice
common sense
confidently
conscientiousness
enthusiasm
equally important
ethical values
evaluate
face a challenge

for the common good

generosity
genuine
in equal measure
justify
lack purpose
loud and clear
meaning of life
meet the requirements

miss an opportunity

on balance

on second thoughts
opt for

outweigh
pleasure
pluck up the courage

poorly
practise what you preach

pros and cons

punctuality
purpose
purposeful

put a lot of effort into

put your heart into sth

quiet life
reach your full potential

responsible attitude

responsibly
self-awareness
self-esteem

self-sacrifice
set high standards

single-mindedness
speak your mind

strong belief
take on a challenge
think for yourself

unconditional

Home

Home and vicinity

at the town hall
bachelor pad
built-up area
bustling
cobbled street
co-housing

communal house
convenient
crack
cramped
demolish

domestic chore

drainage system

fence
flourish
get a facelift
halfway across town

hall of residence
home town
homeowner
household
household rules

housing development

in decline
in the city centre
in the park
in the suburbs
multi-storey car park

on the outskirts

pull down

quaint (backstreet / town /
    neighbourhood)

reliable network

rent
rental price
resident
residential area

run-down
second home

self-contained flat

shabby
site
smart house

smooth
snug
social housing
tarmac
tower block
underground car park

urban
urban development

vibrant

within 500 metres

within easy reach

within walking distance

Rooms, furniture and equipment

axe
basement
bin bag
blanket
bric-a-brac
central heating

chopping board
cleaning solution
cleanliness
clear-out
clutter
cushioned
damp
domestic
draughty
drawer
en suite bathroom

fireplace
fitted kitchen
footrest

VOCABULARY BANK

Translate the phrases into your own language.

furnished
glow
go out
household appliance

keyhole
kitchen facilities

laundry basket
light fixture
lock
mantelpiece
peaceful
pile
running water
sanitation

share a room
sheepskin
solar panel
spacious
spare room
spotless
surface
tasteful
trunk
wood burner

wool throw

School

Educational system

academic training

drop out of
drop-out

educationalist
fee
get a degree
get a scholarship

get expelled (from school)

graduate

illiterate
kindergarten
major in

pre-schooler
scholar
school-leaver
supervisor

write a dissertation

School life and learning

accessible
accurately
acquire

announcement
assembly hall
association
attend a lecture

attend a workshop

be up to your eyes in

brainstorm

cite
come up against

come up with

consist of
core
counsellor

deepen your knowledge

design
disruptive
disturb
dyslexic

engaging
enrol on a course

enter a competition

excel in
exchange student

exchange trip
fall behind
fidget
full-time course

get out of
get round to
get top marks

gifted
give a lecture / a speech

give up on

go into
go on to

hand in

handwriting
have a brainwave
have a day off

have a good memory for

have a love of learning

have a memory like a sieve

have a photographic memory

have a terrible memory for

have an impact on
improve your memory

in a nutshell
keen to do sth

keep quiet
keep up with
learning disorder

leave sth out
lenient
level of commitment

make up
memorise
mess up
narrative
omit
pay attention in class

postpone

put sth off
recall
request
run a seminar

scrape through

self-disciplined
settle down

sit an exam
strict
succeed in

swot
visualise

Work

Jobs

attendance in the office

be in charge

butcher
childcare
coordinate
copy editor
entrepreneur
financial advisor
have a vocation

have one true calling

lead a team
minder

miner _____
novelist _____
number theorist _____

nun _____
park warden _____
screenwriter _____
security guard _____
supervise _____
supervisor _____

work in the field of _____

Career

approval _____
at a rapid rate _____
be suited to _____
be wired differently _____

burn out _____
career guidance _____

career path _____
career prospects _____

carry out _____
combine _____
commit to _____

considerable _____
dedicated member of _____

diversity _____
do an apprenticeship _____

find your niche _____

fulfil an objective _____
gain work experience _____

get down to _____
goal _____
high-powered job _____

intersection _____

keep at _____
keep your options open _____

knowledge _____
knowledgeable _____

leadership skills _____

make a successful living _____

map sth out _____
objective _____
on a day-to-day basis _____
outline _____

practical experience of _____

pursue a career _____

quitter _____

reflect the need _____

set sth out _____

settle on _____

stick to _____
trainee _____
unrelated _____
welcome an opportunity _____

work placement _____

Working conditions and employment

adaptable _____

apply for a position _____

at your convenience _____

be at risk _____
be tied up with _____
be unchanged _____
benefit _____
commute to work _____

commuter _____

company car _____
covering letter _____
daily commute _____

distracted _____
distraction _____

do sth day in, day out _____

employment policy _____

employment possibilities _____

enter the job market _____

flexitime/flexible working _____

freelancer _____
fulfilling _____
handle sb _____
health and safety regulations _____

improve your career prospects _____

in response to _____
increase your output _____

interview _____
job-sharing _____

lucrative _____
meet deadlines _____

overpaid _____
overwork _____
overworked _____
part-time job _____

part-timer _____

pressure _____
recruit _____
references _____
rejection _____
relevant _____
replace _____
require _____
required _____
rigid _____
secure _____
self-employment _____

sit in _____
skilled _____
split the work _____
stable _____
staff _____
staff entrance _____
struggle to do sth _____

summer job _____
take sth over _____

tedious _____
time management _____

to-do list _____

understaffed _____

unemployment _____
volunteer _____

work alongside _____
work flexibly _____

work to a deadline _____

work towards _____

workforce _____
workplace _____

Family and social life

Family and friends

casual acquaintance _____

VOCABULARY BANK

Translate the phrases into your own language.

dependant

dependent
family counselling
family ties
firstborn
get-together
have a baby
host family
in honour of
neighbourly
on behalf
reception
roommate
sibling
soulmate
spoilt brat

welcome party

Relationships

adore
alone
appreciate
be attracted to
be madly in love with

be obsessed with

bond
boss sb around

bring sb up
common
competition
drift apart

fall for
fall in love with
fancy
find common ground

get on with

go out with

good company
gossip
have nothing in common

heartbreak
heartbroken

hold sb's attention

interact with sb

late
leave sb behind

like-minded

lone
lonely

long-distance relationship

look down on

look up to

lose touch
love at first sight

make up for

propose to sb
refuse
relationship
rely on
remain
remarry
reputation
see sb

separate from sb
share an interest

split up with
talk sb into
turn sb down

undivided attention
widowed
worship

Everyday activities

alteration
answer the phone
be up to sth

coincidence
early hours
greet
hang around

hang out
have a shower
hold
lay
lie
lose
maintain order
make an effort

nap
on a daily basis
on a regular basis
oversleep
party
rinse
run out of

sleep badly
small talk

speak up

turn up

Conflicts and problems

abandon
accusation
accuse sb of
address
agree
argue for/against sth

assure
be banned from

beg
blame
claim
clarification
compromise
confusion
convincing
course of action
deal with
demand
deny
disallow
disapprove
disbelieve
dismiss sb as

downside/drawback
equally

excuse
figure sth out

gender-based stereotype

get yourself into
have a narrow escape

ill-advised
interfere
jog your memory

kick sb out

meet halfway
mindlessly
misbehave
misconception
misjudge
neglected
nightmare
object
on purpose
outdo
overestimate
put up with
reach an agreement

reason with
reconsider

relax the rules

reprimand

solution _____
solve a problem _____
stand up for _____
tackle a problem _____

take a chance _____

tell sb off _____
threaten _____
treat sb unfairly _____

unable _____
underestimate _____
undervalued _____
urge sb to do sth _____

voluntarily _____
witness _____
work things out _____

Food

Meals and their preparation

carbohydrates _____
dessert _____
ginger beer _____
jar _____
leftover _____
mouth-watering _____
raw _____
refreshments _____
rotten food _____
stale _____

Eating habits

fussy eater _____
inn _____
locally grown _____

nutrition _____
starving _____

Shopping and services

Selling and purchasing

affordable _____
antiques market _____
auction house _____
average _____
bar code _____
bargain price _____
bid _____
bid for sth (in an auction) _____

car boot sale _____

chain store _____

come up for auction _____

delivery _____
enter your PIN _____
exchange _____
fetch _____
flea market _____
get a discount _____
go bargain-hunting _____

high street _____

hold an auction _____
impulse purchase _____

in advance _____
in demand _____
market stall _____

money-off voucher/coupon _____

online auction _____
online shopping _____

open-air market _____

order sth online _____

pay out _____
pick-up _____
place a bid _____
pre-owned goods _____

price range _____
put sth aside _____
put sth up for sale _____

reasonably-priced _____

receipt _____
reduced _____
reduction in the price _____

resell _____
retail _____
send sth back _____
shop around _____

shop locally _____
split the cost _____
stallholder _____
stock of _____
sufficient _____
take sth back _____

throw sth in _____
used goods trade _____

value _____
winning bid _____

Advertising

consumer behaviour _____

eye-catching _____

hyped _____
label _____
latest _____
leaflet _____
limited edition _____
publicity stunt _____

Finance

afford to do sth _____

allowance _____
average cost _____
a penny saved is a penny earned _____

be broke _____
be loaded _____
be on a limited budget _____

be rolling in money _____

be short of money _____

be well-off _____

bills _____
charge royalties _____

disadvantaged _____

disposable income _____

economic _____
economical _____
financial support _____

find it hard to make ends meet _____

fund _____
funding _____
gain _____
go halves _____
guidance _____
have money to burn _____

increase (your) earnings _____

interest on a loan _____

live from hand to mouth _____

luxurious _____
make a fortune _____
make a profit _____
make money _____
open a bank account _____

pocket money _____
profitable _____
save for a rainy day _____

save up for _____
savings account _____

VOCABULARY BANK

Translate the phrases into your own language.

sum of money _____
transfer money _____
waste money _____
winnings _____

Travelling and tourism

Sightseeing, trips and excursions

(be) swept overboard _____

_____

ancient _____
armour _____
battered _____
begin the ascent/descent _____

blazing _____
campsite _____
canvas camp bed _____

checked bag _____
cultural heritage _____

custom _____
destination _____
embark on _____

enjoy your own company _____

facilities _____
famed for _____
flint and steel _____
guided tour _____

historic _____
historical _____
inaccessible _____

kit _____
look up directions _____

lost property _____
lounge _____

medieval _____
natural beauty _____
on the border _____
on the coast _____
path _____
picturesque _____
popular with _____
remote _____
route _____
run wild _____

set off _____
shrine _____
sunbed _____
supplies _____
tourist resort _____
tourist spot _____

unclaimed _____
voyage of a lifetime _____

Means of transport

boot _____
commercial aircraft _____

delivery truck _____
dock _____
flat tyre _____
fuel _____
moped _____
submarine _____

Traffic

at the roundabout _____
at the traffic lights _____
cycle lane _____
exit _____
motorway _____
on-street parking _____

pedestrian _____
pedestrian zone _____

pedestrianisation _____

pull out _____
roadside _____
roundabout _____
speedboat _____
turn around _____

Culture

Artists and their work

cult following _____

entertainer _____
exhibition _____
form a band _____

music industry _____
paintbrush _____
stencil _____

Film, theatre, books

audience _____
box-office success _____
come out _____
disaster movie _____
fictional character _____
genre _____
gripping tale _____
hero _____
movie set _____
on-stage _____
opening scene _____
passage _____
plot _____
rehearse _____
screen _____

shoot _____
soundtrack _____
spoiler _____

stage _____
subtitles _____
twists and turns _____
villain _____

Media

accurate _____
airbrush _____
awash with information _____

background _____
backup _____
believable _____
binge-watch _____

blow-by-blow _____
blurred _____
bombarded with information _____

breaking news _____

broadcast _____
capture a memorable moment _____

check the accuracy _____

clear commitment _____

close _____
closely _____
commercial break _____

critical _____
critically _____
crop images _____

deliberate _____
deliberately _____
distort the truth _____

double-check facts _____

evaluate sources _____
examine sth closely _____

eye-catching story _____

fact-checker _____

fake news _____
falsehood _____
far-fetched _____
green screen _____

have an agenda _____
high-quality _____
in focus / out of focus _____

inaccurate _____

invent a story _____
knowingly _____
lens _____
made-up _____
manipulate the media _____

mislead/misinform people _____

misleading _____

morning show _____
news anchor _____
news station _____
news story _____
newsreader _____
newsworthy story _____

nonstop _____
not take a story at face value _____

on-air _____
overview _____
pose for a photo _____

post a video _____

present-day _____
print-based media _____

question facts _____
reliable/reputable source _____

report on _____
retouch images _____
sharp _____
snap _____
snap a selfie _____
spread fake news _____

superimpose _____

take _____
take a snap _____
tamper with photos _____

zoom in/zoom out _____

Description

appeal _____
appealing _____
average _____
dark _____
date back to _____

geometric pattern _____

gripping _____
heavily influenced _____

hilarious _____
minimalist _____
nostalgic _____
origin _____

originate _____
predictable _____
terrifying _____
unforgettable _____
well-reviewed _____

youth culture _____

Sport

Doing sports

physically demanding _____

post-match _____
raft _____
warm-up _____
whitewater rafting _____

Health

Lifestyle

accustomed to _____
carer _____
develop a habit _____
harmful _____
harmless _____
have a habit of _____
healthy lifestyle _____
nasty habit _____
strike a balance _____

sunscreen _____

Illnesses, symptoms and treatment

addiction _____
advice _____
advisable _____
advise _____
allergy _____
apply _____
archaea _____

asthma _____
autism _____
bang on the head _____
be found unconscious _____

be hit/struck by lightning _____

be left unconscious _____

beneficial _____

blind _____
body dysmorphic disorder _____

brain damage _____
breathe _____
come out of a coma _____

compensate for _____
_____
condition _____
deaf _____
dental patient _____
depression _____
diabetes _____
digest _____
digestion _____
disability _____
disabled _____
exposed _____
exposure _____

fall into a coma _____
feeble _____
fight off _____
first aid course _____
fungi _____
genetic factor _____
germ _____
harm _____
health check _____
infection _____
instant _____
irritant _____
life-threatening injuries _____

lose consciousness _____
lose your memory _____
lung condition _____
makeup _____
medicate _____
medicinal _____
medicine _____
mental health problem/condition _____

microbe _____
microbiome _____
neurotransmitter _____
nurture _____
nutrients _____
obesity _____
operating theatre _____
pathogen _____

perform an operation _____

pollen allergy _____
range of movement _____
rash _____
recover from an injury _____

regain consciousness _____

regulate _____
regulation _____
regulatory _____
respond _____
response _____
responsive _____
risk of infection _____
robotic surgeon _____
routinely _____

VOCABULARY BANK

Translate the phrases into your own language.

rub _____
saliva _____
sanitiser _____
savant syndrome _____

_____
strengthen _____
suffer an injury _____

surgical unit _____
thoroughly _____
treat _____
unhurt _____
vision _____
wheelchair _____

Science and technology

Using technical devices and IT technology

battery _____
bleep _____

_____
chart _____
diameter _____
fully-automated _____

image editing software _____
locate _____
measure _____
payphone _____
provider _____
pull the plug / unplug _____

receiver _____
remote _____
sat-nav _____
shredder _____
spare parts _____
state-of-the-art _____
storage _____
store _____
switch sth on/off _____

take sth apart _____

telephone exchange _____

top-of-the-range _____
unlock _____
user-friendly _____

voice command _____
voice recognition _____

wire _____
word processing _____

Scientific discoveries

account for _____
acid _____

addition _____
advance (v) _____
advance (n) / advancement _____

_____
affect _____
algorithm _____
applied science _____
artificial intelligence _____

_____
atom _____
award a prize _____
base _____
be made up of _____
breakthrough _____
calculation _____
carry out research _____

chemical composition _____

coin a term _____
collaborate with _____
collect _____
complex _____
credit sb with _____

decompose _____
dense _____
derived _____
detach _____
division _____
electron _____
element _____
equation _____
essential _____
essential part _____
essentials _____
exact _____
examine/explore an issue _____

excessive _____
exclusively _____
fellow scientists _____
fossil _____
fraction _____
gain recognition _____
hidden away _____
illogical _____
in terms of _____

intention _____
invent _____
lead to _____
limited _____
linked back to _____
make a contribution _____

make reference to _____

medical advances _____

molecular structure _____

multiplication _____

name sth after sb _____

nucleus _____
numeral _____
odd/even number _____

outcome _____
outer space _____
periodic table _____

periodically _____
principle _____
question _____
radiation _____
radioactivity _____
receive a mention _____

recognise an achievement _____

relativity _____
release _____
remain a mystery _____

remarkable _____
rough _____
see the potential _____

solve a mystery _____
source of gravity _____
stimulating _____

subtraction _____
survey _____
theory of relativity _____

undeniably/undoubtedly _____

unlimited _____
valued _____
velocity _____
viewpoint _____

volume _____
win the respect _____
with regard to _____

The natural world

Landscape

cave/cavern _____
coastline _____
countryside _____
current _____
deep sea _____
desert _____
diverse landscape _____

foothill _____
ice cap _____
leafy _____
meadow _____
natural wonder _____

orchard _____
patch _____
plain _____
ploughed field _____
rolling hills _____

soil _____
spark _____
stream _____
summit _____
wilderness _____

Plants and animals

animal cruelty _____

animal rights _____
breeding ground _____
bush _____
domesticate _____
establish a community _____

extend a territory _____

extinct _____
extinction _____
food chain _____
grow in number _____
hatch _____
in captivity _____
lay eggs _____
marine reptile _____
migrate _____
migration _____
natural habitat _____

nesting beach _____

on the loose _____
predator _____
prey _____
release into the wild _____

reunite _____
set free _____
tern _____
thorny _____
thriving population _____

trapped _____
treatment of animals _____

tweet _____

The weather

blizzard _____
downpour _____
gale-force winds _____
gust of wind _____
hurricane _____
pour with rain _____
pre-storm _____
raindrop _____
rainfall _____

severe weather conditions _____

snowfall _____
storm is brewing _____

weatherproof _____

whiteout _____

Environmental protection

alternative energy _____

biodegradable _____
biodiversity _____

carbon dioxide _____
carbon emission _____

contamination _____
creature _____
deforestation _____

discard _____
ditch _____
do harm _____
drain _____
eco-warrior _____

electricity-generating _____

emission _____
environmental impact _____

fumes _____
fur _____
fur trade _____
greenhouse effect _____

harness _____
irreparable damage _____

landfill _____
litter _____
noise pollution _____
nuclear testing _____

particle _____
plastic waste _____

pollute _____
polluter _____
preserve _____
renewable _____
single-use plastics _____

sustainable _____

sustainable tourism _____

textile waste _____
trash _____
water tank _____

wildlife protection _____

wind turbine _____
windmill _____

Natural disasters

avalanche _____
drought _____
earthquake _____
flood _____
tsunami _____
wildfire _____

State and society

Social events and phenomena

acceptance speech _____

annual _____
anonymity _____
authenticate _____
awareness-raising campaign _____

become mainstream _____

cause _____
civilian _____
coincidence _____
come down to _____

commitment _____
community _____
conscious _____
consist of _____
contribute to _____

data _____
date _____
donate _____
effect _____
emigrate _____
engage with _____
equality _____
ethical issue _____
eventually _____
fairness _____
for the sake of _____

fundraise for charity _____

gain popularity _____
general public _____
hand out leaflets _____
immigrate _____
insure _____
involvement _____
long-term commitment _____

make a claim _____
make a difference _____

VOCABULARY BANK

Translate the phrases into your own language.

make a statement _____
_____
make your point _____
_____
member of the public _____
multicultural _____
multipurpose _____
_____
occasion _____
outnumber _____
peaceful protest _____
peacefully _____
petition _____
principal _____
_____
proceed _____
_____
promote awareness _____
_____
protect your identity _____
_____
protest march _____
protestor _____
public figure _____
raise awareness _____
raise money _____
_____
recognised _____
refer to _____
remain anonymous _____
_____
security _____
step in _____
time-consuming _____
unconfirmed rumour _____
_____
underlying message _____
_____
unusual _____
upturn _____

The problems of the modern world

aftermath _____
anti-nuclear _____
anti-social _____
ban _____
break the law _____
bully _____
_____
commit an offence _____
_____
crack down on _____
_____
crackdown on _____
deception _____
deceptive _____
devastating scene _____
discriminate against sb _____

downturn _____
extreme poverty _____
famine _____
fine sb _____
_____
gender gap _____
go missing _____
harsh reminder _____
_____
have access to _____
human trafficking _____
illegal _____
improbable _____
inadequate _____
incapable _____
incident _____
injustice _____
irrelevant _____
limit _____
make a complaint _____
_____
misinformation _____
offence _____
offender _____
out of reach _____
prevent from _____
receive criticism _____
replace _____
riot _____
robbery _____
run low on sth _____
_____
security measures _____
_____
short-lived _____
sub-standard _____
sue sb _____
_____
take advantage of _____
take notice of _____
_____
take priority _____
take sb to court _____
_____
theft _____
throw-away society _____
_____
_____
_____
uncontrollable _____
_____
unheard-of _____

Politics and economy

(be) on the rise _____
available _____
bring in _____
business empire _____
car company _____
clothing industry _____

decreasing _____
double _____
figure _____
for commercial gain _____
_____
for political gain _____
_____
foreign affairs _____
_____
generate _____
gradual drop/decline (in) _____
_____
gradual rise/increase (in) _____
_____
growing number _____
have a bad reputation _____
_____
headquarters _____
increasing _____
industrialisation _____
industry _____
lifetime supply _____
local brands _____
management _____
marked rise/increase (in) _____
_____
mass-produced product _____
_____
provide _____
rapid drop/decline (in) _____
_____
remain constant _____
_____
sharp drop/decline (in) _____
_____
sharp rise/increase (in) _____
_____
spring up _____
steady drop/decline (in) _____
_____
steady rise/increase (in) _____
_____
support local producers _____
_____
take off _____
_____
target _____
_____
vital _____
withdraw _____

Authorities

authority _____
mayor _____
policy _____
pre-election _____
pro-democracy _____

Culture of English-Speaking Countries

Ada Lovelace (1815–1852) an English mathematician, the daughter of the poet Lord Byron; she contributed to the development of C. Babbage's first computer called the Analytical Engine; she is said to be the first female computer programmer in history

the Appalachian Mountains a mountain range in the northeast region of North America

Bangor University a university in Wales, established in 1884

Bangor a city in northwest Wales; it is the oldest city in Wales and one of the smallest in the United Kingdom; Bangor University is located there

Banksy an anonymous British street artist; he displays his work on city walls and uses a stencilling technique; in his works he usually comments on current social and political problems

Barbara Kingsolver (b. 1955) an American novelist, essayist and poet

BBC the British Broadcasting Corporation – a British public service broadcaster

Beefeaters a popular name for traditional guards at the Tower of London, officially known as Yeomen Warders

Bernard Silver (1924–1963) an American engineer who together with N. Joseph Woodland created the first barcode

Bilbo Baggins an imaginary character and protagonist of *The Hobbit*, a novel by J.R.R. Tolkien

Bill Gates (b. 1955) an American computer programmer and businessman who started the Microsoft company, one of the richest men in the world; he is also well-known for donating money to charity through the Bill & Melinda Gates Foundation

Birmingham the second largest city in the UK, located in the West Midlands of England; in the past it was known as a major industrial city, but now it is also recognised as a centre of art and education

Bob Brown (b. 1944) an Australian politician and environmentalist, former parliamentary leader of the Australian Greens

Brian Acton (b. 1972) an American computer programmer and entrepreneur, the co-founder of WhatsApp

Britney Spears (b. 1981) an American singer

Bruce Lee (1940–1973) a Hong Kong-American actor famous for his martial arts skills; he appeared in films such as *Enter the Dragon* and *Return of the Dragon*

Byron Company a New York photography studio in Manhattan, established in 1892 and still working; thousands of pictures taken by photographers working for the studio are now kept in the museum of the City of New York as part of a collection depicting the history of the city

Camden Town a borough in North London, famous for unusual clothes shops, night clubs and markets, one of which is Camden Lock

Cape Town the largest and the oldest city in South Africa, located near the Cape of Good Hope; it is built around Table Mountain; South Africa's parliament building is there

Captain America an imaginary character, the superhero of the *Captain America* comic books published by Marvel Comics

the Ceremony of the Keys a traditional ritual of locking and unlocking of the gates of the Tower of London; the ceremony takes place every evening, at 9:53 p.m., and the way it is done hasn't changed for seven centuries; it is said that during that time, the ritual was disturbed only once – in December 1940, when the tower was under aerial bombardment

Charles Babbage (1791–1871) a British mathematician and inventor who designed projects of calculating machines, including the Analytical Engine, which modern computers are based on

Charles Dickens (1812–1870) a British novelist, the most popular British writer of the 19th century, whose novels are still popular today; his books show life in Victorian England, especially how hard it was for poor people and children; his most famous works include *The Pickwick Papers, David Copperfield, Oliver Twist, Great Expectations, A Christmas Carol* (a short story) and *A Tale of Two Cities*

Chiwetel Ejiofor (b. 1977) a British actor and director, famous for his role of Karl Mordo in the *Doctor Strange* series as well as writing, directing and starring in *The Boy Who Harnessed The Wind*

Daniel Radcliffe (b. 1989) a British actor who is best known for playing the role of Harry in the *Harry Potter* films

Desmond Morris (b. 1928) a British zoologist and anthropologist; he has made many television programmes and written popular books about human and animal behaviour, including *The Naked Ape*

Donna Strickland (b. 1959) a Canadian physicist who was awarded the Nobel Prize in Physics in 2018

Dorothy Hodgkin (1910–1994) a British biochemist who was awarded the Nobel Prize in Chemistry in 1964

the Duffer Brothers Matt and Ross Duffer – American film and television writers, directors and producers, creators of the series *Stranger Things*

Ebenezer Howard (1850–1928) the English founder of the garden city movement, which influenced the development of two cities – Letchworth (1903) and Welwyn (1919)

Ed Yong (b. 1981) a British science journalist, the author of the blog *Not Exactly Rocket Science* and the book *I Contain Multitudes: The Microbes Within Us and a Grander View of Life*; his articles have been published by *National Geographic, New Scientist* and *Nature*

Essex a county in southeast England, between East London and the North Sea

Ewan McGregor (b. 1971) a Scottish actor, famous for his role as the young Obi-Wan Kenobi in the *Star Wars* prequel trilogy; he also played in *Shallow Grave, Trainspotting, Moulin Rouge, The Ghost Writer* and *The Impossible*

George Laurer (1925-2019) an engineer at IBM; in 1973 he developed the Universal Product Code, commonly known as the bar code, by improving and developing Silver and Woodland's original idea of the code

Girl with Balloon a series of murals in London created by Banksy, depicting a young girl with her hand extended towards a red heart-shaped balloon carried away by the wind

Grace Hopper (1906–1992) an American computer scientist and mathematician, one of the first female programmers; she influenced the development of computer programming and served in the US Navy

Harry Potter the main fictional character in British writer J. K. Rowling's books and their film adaptations

The Hobbit a very popular children's book by J. R. R. Tolkien, which is also read by adults; it describes the exciting and magical adventures of Bilbo Baggins, who is a hobbit, in a place called Middle Earth; *The Lord of the Rings* continues the story of *The Hobbit*

IBM a very large international computer company, based in the US; it produces both hardware and software, especially for business users

James Bond also called 007; a fictional character in novels by Ian Fleming; Bond is a Secret Service agent who works for the British government; he became more famous when the stories were made into popular films; the part of James Bond has been played by several actors including Sean Connery, Pierce Brosnan, Roger Moore and Daniel Craig

Jan Koum (b. 1976) a Ukrainian-American computer programmer and entrepreneur, a co-founder of WhatsApp

Jocelyn Bell Burnell (b. 1943) a British astrophysicist, the first person to observe radio pulsars; the discovery was awarded a Nobel prize, however, even though Burnell was the person who discovered the pulsars, she was not one of the recipients of the prize

Joe Woodland (1921–2012) an American inventor who together with Bernard Silver created the first barcode

John Gray (b. 1951) an American relationship counsellor and writer, author of the long-term best seller – *Men Are from Mars, Women Are from Venus*

Jojo Moyes (b. 1969) a British journalist and author of romantic novels

Ken Robinson (b. 1950) a British author, speaker, specialist and advisor to government and non-governmental organisations on creativity and education in the arts; his TED talk *Do Schools Kill Creativity?* is one of the most watched in history

Liverpool a city in the northwest of England, on the River Mersey; the famous music group the Beatles began there; currently, it is the home of two famous football clubs, Liverpool and Everton

Manhattan an island and borough of New York City, between the Hudson River and the East River

Mark Twain (1835–1910) an American writer best known for his novels *The Adventures of Tom Sawyer* and *The Adventures of Huckleberry Finn;* his real name was Samuel Langhorne Clemens

Mary Anning (1799–1847) one of the first English palaeontologists and fossil collectors

Meryl Streep (b. 1949) an American film actress, known for her versatility, often described as the best actress of her generation; she has won three Oscars, for *Kramer vs. Kramer*, *Sophie's Choice* and *The Iron Lady*

Naomi Watts (b. 1968) an English actress and film producer; nominated for an Oscar for her roles in *21 Grams* and *The Impossible*

Notting Hill a well-off area of London, famous for the Notting Hill Carnival – a colourful street parade taking place every August – and the Portobello Road Market

Oxford a city on the River Thames in southern England, the home of the University of Oxford, the oldest university in the English-speaking world; because of its well-preserved architecture, especially the university buildings, Oxford is frequently featured in film productions

Paris Hilton (b. 1981) an American celebrity, actress and singer

Portobello Road Market a street market on Portobello Road in London; every Saturday it sells antiques and collectibles

Rob Knight (b. 1976) a scientist and biologist from New Zealand known for his research into the human microbiome; a co-author of *Dirt is Good* and *Follow Your Gut*

Robert Cornelius (1809–1893) an American pioneer of photography and a lamp manufacturer; his self-portrait from 1839 is thought to be the first preserved selfie

Robert Pattinson (b. 1986) a British actor, famous for his role in the *Twilight* series

Ronald Reagan (1911–2004) an American Republican Party politician, the president of the US from 1981 to 1989; before Reagan became president he was a film actor and the governor of California; during his presidency, Reagan supported anti-communist movements worldwide

Rosalind Franklin (1920–1958) a British chemist, biophysicist and crystallographer; she studied X-ray radiation as well as the molecular structures of DNA

Sheffield a city in the north of England, famous for making tools and cutlery; Sheffield has two universities and two football teams

Stephen King (b. 1947) a popular US writer of horror stories, the author of *The Shining*, *Salem's Lot* and *The Green Mile;* he has received many awards for his contribution to literature; many of his books have been adapted into films

Steven Spielberg (b. 1946) one of the most successful film directors and producers in the history of US cinema; he won Oscars for *Schindler's List* and *Saving Private Ryan;* his other films, known especially for their special effects, include *Jaws, Raiders of the Lost Ark, E.T.* and *Jurassic Park;* he is a co-founder of the film studio called DreamWorks

Table Mountain a high mountain in South Africa standing behind the city of Cape Town; it is also a symbol of that city

TED Technology, Entertainment and Design – conferences designed to promote 'ideas worth spreading'; presentations are in the form of short talks and are available on the Internet for free

Tim Berners-Lee (b. 1955) a British computer scientist who invented the World Wide Web (WWW) in 1991 and made his idea freely available to everyone; he has been the director of the W3C (World Wide Web Consortium) since 1994; currently Berners-Lee is a professor of computer science at the University of Oxford and the Massachusetts Institute of Technology (MIT)

The Tower of London a fortress in London by the River Thames, built in the 11th century; in the past it was the home to kings and queens, and it also served as a prison; it is now a museum, where the Crown Jewels are kept; the Tower of London is guarded by the Beefeaters, who also look after the ravens; according to the legend if the ravens ever leave the Tower of London, the British monarchy will end

The US Department of Defense the US government department responsible for the military forces

University of California in San Diego one of ten campuses forming the University of California, famous for achievements in science

Will Smith (b. 1968) an American film actor and singer, who starred in *Independence Day* and the *Men in Black* series

Winston Churchill (1874–1965) a British politician who was prime minister during World War II and again from 1951 to 1955; famous for the many speeches he made during the war, especially on the radio, encouraging British people to believe that they would eventually win; he won the Nobel Prize in Literature and in 2002 was voted the greatest Briton ever in a BBC poll

The World Health Organization an international organisation that is part of the UN (United Nations), concerned with international public health

VOCABULARY BANK

PEOPLE

1 Complete the text with the words in the box. There are three extra words.

> background   blood-red   ~~childhood~~   coffee   elderly   garment   jack   frills   master   memory   passionate   second-hand   soul   star   tea   upbringing

'I remember my _childhood_ well. My parents were both musicians, so I don't think I had a standard ¹_____ . I was raised by music. My earliest ²_____ is of my mother singing while I was eating my lunch. I wasn't the same as other kids my age. Their parents seemed ³_____ and boring, while mine were glamorous musicians, who took me to gigs. Even their clothes were amazing. They were both from a poor ⁴_____ and didn't have much money, so everything they wore was ⁵_____ . Nevertheless, they looked like pop stars. I remember when they came to school once to talk to the principal; my mother was dressed in a very smart, ⁶_____ dress and my dad was wearing a collarless shirt with ⁷_____ on the sleeves. Their music wasn't everyone's cup of ⁸_____ , but they were so talented. They could play anything, and my dad was a real ⁹_____ of all trades. I suppose I take after him in that respect, but I'm more the ¹⁰_____ of none. My parents were always the life and ¹¹_____ of the party, but they always had time for me as well. I think it's fair to say that my love for music grew out of these experiences. They taught me to be ¹²_____ , something I didn't feel I was learning at school.'

2 Complete the sentences with the missing words. The first letters are given.

I have a vivid **m** _e m o r y_ of falling off the swing and breaking my arm.

1 My sister is so good at music and she knows it. She's bursting with **c** _ _ _ _ _ _ _ _ _ .
2 In dangerous situations, it's important that you keep a cool **h** _ _ _ and make good decisions.
3 My aunt is so funny. She literally makes me roar with **l** _ _ _ _ _ _ _ .
4 My mother hates it when she asks me a question and I just shrug my **s** _ _ _ _ _ _ _ _ .
5 I'm doing a revision test, and I'm really racking my **b** _ _ _ _ _ for the answers.
6 I know I need to push myself and step out of my comfort **z** _ _ _ .
7 I love my best friend but he is a bit annoying at parties. He always has to be the **c** _ _ _ _ _ of attention.
8 That lecture was so interesting. I was on the **e** _ _ _ of my seat.

3 Choose the correct answer A–D.

I hate meeting up with Tara. She's not very _A_ so I always have to sit by myself for ages.
(A) punctual   B supportive
C sociable   D trusting

1 My brother is so ___ . He'd say black was white if it meant he could disagree with me.
A attentive   B argumentative
C competitive   D perceptive

2 My friend is always falling over. She's so ___ .
A genial   B daring   C cautious   D clumsy

3 Tom is lovely. He's just so kind and ___ . You can't not like him.
A enterprising   B short-tempered
C good-natured   D conscientious

4 I really like hanging out with Bob. He's so ___ nothing bothers him.
A bird-brained   B single-minded
C strong-willed   D laid-back

5 I love Sarah, but she is ___ shy and quiet. It's so hard to have a conversation with her.
A perfectly   B highly   C painfully   D bitterly

6 My brother is such a ___ . He never cleans up after himself.
A flake   B slob   C loner   D free spirit

7 I don't come from a very ___ family. We never hug and I've never seen my parents kiss.
A affectionate   B gentle
C kind-hearted   D sensitive

8 You can't say anything to my mother without her taking offence. She is ___ .
A hyperactive   B hypersensitive
C humble   D honest

9 She's kind, funny and beautiful but she just keeps talking about all of her faults. She's so ___ .
A self-conscious   B self-centred
C self-obsessed   D self-critical

10 He's very detail-focused and can help with every aspect of the project. He's really ___ .
A moody   B thorough   C witty   D tactful

4 Match the words in boxes A and B to make eight compound nouns.

A

> curly   fair   ~~good~~   level   nut   self   thin   well

B

> behaved   brown   haired   headed   lipped   minded   ~~natured~~   obsessed

good-natured, _____
_____
_____
_____

5 Complete the text with the correct form of the words in the box.

> astonish   aware   clear   dare   feel   ~~final~~
> firm   hair   imagine   risk

Stephen was _finally_ home. He came in and shut the door ¹_____ behind him. Weird … it was not locked. His mum always complained about him not locking the door – this time it had ²_____ been her that had forgotten. He went into the kitchen to get something to eat. He could hear his mother upstairs, but she was ³_____ he had returned. 'She must be back from doing the shopping already,' he thought. He opened the fridge, but the shelves were practically empty. Weird. If she was still out doing the shopping, who was upstairs? 'It's only my vivid ⁴_____,' he thought. 'Maybe I've watched too many movies?' She could have decided not to do the shopping today. Maybe she was just cleaning the wardrobe? Or doing that big clear-out she'd promised to do? But that was a lot of 'maybes' and he had a gut ⁵_____ that it wasn't her. The question was: what should he do now? He could leave by the front door again but that was too ⁶_____ . Whoever it is might hear him. 'I'm not so ⁷_____,' he thought. He eventually came to a decision. He took his phone and, trying to keep his voice steady, he called the police. Then he hid in the toilet. They arrived within minutes and caught the man trying to steal everything they owned. As they put him into the car, there was a look of ⁸_____ on his face. He couldn't believe they had caught him. When they drove off, Stephen thought that this had been one of those ⁹_____ moments he would never forget.

6 Are the statements true (T) or false (F)? Correct the false statements.

If you glance at something, you look at it for a long time.   [F]

1 If you caught a glimpse of something, you only saw it for a moment.   ⃝
2 When you hesitate, you do something immediately.   ⃝
3 You sob when you are happy and full of joy.   ⃝
4 When you peep, everyone knows you are looking.   ⃝
5 When you swallow, you make a movement as if something is going down your throat.   ⃝
6 When you whisper, you speak clearly and loudly.   ⃝
7 When you grip something, you hold it lightly.   ⃝
8 Yelling involves speaking quietly and calmly.   ⃝
9 A wink is when you close one eye and open it again quickly.   ⃝
10 You giggle when you are sad and things are not going well.   ⃝
11 You flinch when you think someone or something might hit you.   ⃝
12 You might gasp if you hear some shocking news.   ⃝

HOME

1 Find the words in the text that match the definitions below.

She walked into her new house; it was a bit run-down, so there was a lot to do if she was going to turn it into a home. First of all, it was freezing; the high ceilings and old windows meant that it was quite draughty. Those windows also made her worry about damp, the walls did feel quite cold and a little wet. She'd definitely need new windows and perhaps a wood burner to heat the place up. That would give it the right atmosphere. For now, she would just have to do some cleaning. She'd brought a bucket full of cleaning solutions, but first she was going to give the house a good clear-out, as the previous owners had left a lot of their old clutter behind. She tested the taps, at least there was running water; nothing else seemed to work. The lock on the door was broken and the old solar panels the previous people had installed no longer seemed to create any electricity at all. 'Don't worry,' she thought to herself. 'By the time I'm finished with it, it will be absolutely spotless.'

Adjective: the windows and doors are not of a high quality and allow cold air to enter the house _draughty_
1 Adjective: completely tidy and clean   _____
2 Adjective: in a poor state, that needs fixing   _____
3 Noun: you put a key in this to keep a door shut   _____
4 Noun: a heater that is fuelled by wood   _____
5 Noun: liquids for cleaning the house   _____
6 Noun: water that comes from a tap   _____
7 Noun: a collection of untidy things   _____
8 Noun: these are usually on the roof of a house and turn sunlight into electricity   _____

2 Do the crossword.

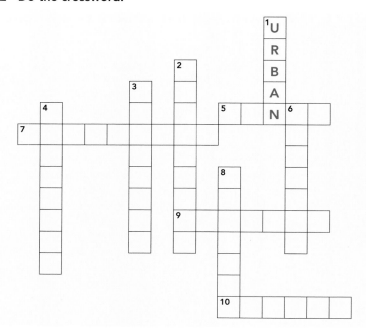

Down

1 Related to cities or in a city (e.g. area, development).
2 A special place in a wall of a room where you can make fire.
3 A room in a building that is under the level of the ground.
4 Full of activity, busy (e.g. market square).
6 That doesn't have enough space (e.g. about a room).
8 An area where people live which is away from the centre of a town or city.

Across

5 A wooden or metal structure between two properties.
7 Containing furniture.
9 Paved with large stones that are difficult to walk on.
10 In poor condition due to lack of care.

3 Choose the correct answer A–D.

He turned up the _B_. It was starting to get a bit cold now that the summer was over.
A fireplace   B central heating
C glow   D household appliance

1 Her husband was a slob. He never put his dirty clothes in the __ .
A laundry basket   B pile
C spare room   D trunk

2 He couldn't find his keys. He was sure he had left them in the __ . He opened it, but there was nothing there.
A mantlepiece   B keyhole
C bin bag   D drawer

3 She took a wool throw and pulled it on. She hated staying in her mother's old and __ house.
A snug   B draughty
C spacious   D cushioned

4 She had piles of clothes everywhere. She needed to have a __ and get rid of some of it.
A blanket   B clear-out
C sanitation   D cleaning solution

5 She opened her wedding present. 'Great!' she thought. 'Another kitchen __ I don't need.'
A appliance   B fence
C facility   D drawer

6 The house came with a __ kitchen. It had all the appliances you could want, including an oven and a fridge-freezer.
A en suite   B spare
C fitted   D self-contained

7 There was a warm glow coming from the __ . It made the house feel like a home.
A keyhole   B fireplace   C basement   D light fixture

8 There were a lot of poorer people in the area so the government decided to build some more __ housing.
A multi-storey   B development
C communal   D social

SCHOOL

1 Match the words 1–8 with a–i to make phrases.

give	c	a	an exam
1 deepen		b	attention
2 enrol		c	a lecture
3 hand		d	on a course
4 pay		e	off writing an essay
5 put		f	in your homework
6 scrape		g	through your final exams
7 sit		h	up with the rest of the class
8 keep		i	your knowledge

2 Complete the sentences with the correct forms of five of the phrases in Exercise 1.

My teacher _gave us a lecture_ on the environment last week. It was very interesting.

1 I know I have to _____ in class, but sometimes I get distracted, especially if I am tired.

2 Biology and Chemistry are my favourite subjects. I even watch videos on these topics in my free time. I think it's good to _____ my _____ in areas I'm interested in.

3 I _____ two weeks ago, but the teacher hasn't checked it yet. I'm a bit angry: I spent the whole weekend on it!

4 My friend hasn't done any studying lately. He is quite smart though, so if he's lucky he might _____ .

5 I missed a lot of important lessons when I broke my leg, but I've been studying hard so I can _____ .

3 Complete the text with the words in the box. There are three extra words.

> degree   dissertation   drop out   ~~education~~
> enrol   exchange student   fees   graduate
> kindergarten   major   pre-schoolers   scholarship
> school-leavers   supervisor   swot

In the US, children usually start their _education_ at the age of five when they join ¹_____ . Before this, they would be known as ²_____ . There are 12 grades in the US and they are divided into 3 schools: elementary school, middle school and high school. Students usually ³_____ from high school when they are 17 or 18 years old. However, some students may choose to ⁴_____ and start work before that point.

After graduating, many will apply to universities to continue their education. Unfortunately, as school ⁵_____ are quite high in the US, some people may not be able to receive a higher education. Students who cannot afford university may choose to apply for a ⁶_____ , but they will need to study hard and be a bit of a ⁷_____ if they hope to be accepted.

At university, students will choose a subject to ⁸_____ in. This is the subject that they will write a ⁹_____ in. This large essay will serve as their final test and will take them much of their final year. Luckily, they are not alone and will have a ¹⁰_____ who can help them along the way. If they pass, they will receive a ¹¹_____ and then it's time to find a job.

4 Choose the correct option to complete the dialogue.

– Did you hear about Tony?

  – No, what happened?

– He (got expelled) / dropped out from university for cheating.

  – Seriously? That's crazy. Why did he do that? He always ¹gets top marks / falls behind in his tests. He's such a ²swot / educationalist!

– I know. He has a good memory ³for / to facts, so he didn't need to cheat, but he did.

  – Wow, he's really ⁴messed up / let it out. I always thought he'd ⁵go on to / go into graduate with a great degree.

– Yeah, I know. Maybe they will be ⁶lenient / strict with him and let him back in.

  – It will be too late. He'll miss the final exam. Hopefully, if he speaks to his supervisor, they will be able to come up ⁷with / against a solution.

– Well, they might let him retake the exam this year, but he will definitely have to pay ⁸a fee / attention. It won't be free this time.

WORK

1 Complete the email with the words in the box. There are four extra words.

> apprenticeship   basis   ~~copy editor~~   deadline
> experience   interview   in the field   novelist
> objective   part-time   placement   position
> references   self-employment   suited

Dear Sir / Madam,

I am writing to apply for the position of _copy editor_ in your publishing house which was advertised online.

I have worked ¹_____ of writing for many years, first as a published ²_____ and later as a screenwriter. I feel I'm perfectly ³_____ for this job because I've been writing and editing texts on a day-to-day ⁴_____ . I have worked as a freelancer for many years, but now I would prefer to move to a more stable ⁵_____ .
The advertisement also appealed to me as it said it was a ⁶_____ job, which would mean I could continue screenwriting in my spare time as well.

Having gained considerable ⁷_____ as a writer and a screenwriter, I'm both creative and conscientious. I'm also good at time management and I can work to a ⁸_____ .

Please find attached my CV. I am available for an ⁹_____ either in person or by video call any day this week between the hours of 9 and 5. Should you require ¹⁰_____ or any further information, please do not hesitate to contact me.

Yours faithfully,
John Denver

2 Match the words with their definitions.

increase your output	_h_	6 find your niche ◯
1 employment policy ◯		7 keep your options open ◯
2 flexitime ◯		8 freelancer ◯
3 diversity ◯		9 lucrative ◯
4 career path ◯		10 tedious ◯
5 burn out ◯		11 quitter ◯

a   variety
b   a series of jobs in the same profession
c   rules and regulations for employee and employer rights
d   not commit to one job
e   someone who often leaves positions; who doesn't finish what they started
f   become physically or emotionally tired because of overwork
g   boring
h   produce more products or services
i   find the job that suits you perfectly
j   a person who is self-employed
k   producing a lot of profit
l   work hours that are not fixed

3 Choose the correct option to complete the text.

> Radio 1 has a brand new competition. We would like to come into your *rooms* / (*offices*) and provide lunch and drinks for your whole team. To enter the competition, leave a comment below telling us why you love your job.
>
> **Deirdre:** I work with children so my job is extremely [1]*fulfilling* / *considerable*. Every day when I go home, I know I've made a difference. I can see it in their smiles.
>
> **John:** I'm [2]*a trainee* / *an apprenticeship* in an office. What I love about my job is that my boss treats us all equally.
>
> **Jo:** I love my daily [3]*commuter* / *commute* to work. I work from home so it's only a few short steps to my desk. LOL!
>
> **Anna:** My job allows us to do [4]*it day in, day out* / *job-sharing*, which is great for me as I am a new mother.
>
> **Vic:** I [5]*work part-time* / *volunteer* at a charity so I don't get paid but I love my job anyway because my co-workers are the best.
>
> **Jen:** Ugh, I don't love my job. I HATE my job. We are [6]*overworked* / *overpaid* and I struggle to pay my bills. We are under a lot of [7]*workforce* / *pressure* to meet our deadlines but they never congratulate us when we do. It's terrible! I don't want to win the competition.
>
> **James:** @Jen, my [8]*job market* / *workplace* is the same. We constantly have to work harder and harder to increase our output but there are no [9]*benefits* / *goals*.

FAMILY AND SOCIAL LIFE

1 Complete the phrasal verbs connected with relationships with the correct prepositions.

bring somebody *up* – educate / raise (e.g. a child)

1 get _____ with somebody – have a good relationship with somebody
2 look _____ on somebody – think that you are better than somebody
3 split _____ with somebody – finish a relationship with somebody (e.g. boyfriend or girlfriend)
4 put _____ with somebody – tolerate somebody even though they annoy you
5 tell somebody _____ – speak angrily to somebody because they have done something wrong
6 look _____ to somebody – admire somebody
7 go _____ with somebody – have a romantic relationship with somebody
8 turn somebody _____ – refuse (e.g. an offer, an invitation)
9 hang _____ with somebody – spend time with somebody socially
10 stand _____ for somebody – defend somebody

2 Complete the dialogues with one word in each gap. The first letters are given.

A: Are you and Anna dating?
B: No, no. She's just a casual a*cquaintance*. Not even a good friend.

1
A: Are you going to see Tony again?
B: Yes, I think so. He's really good c_____ . I just enjoy being around him. We have a lot in common.
A: Yes, you do share an i_____ in photography.
B: Exactly. So much to talk about.

2
A: Where are you staying when you go on your course in London? A hotel?
B: No, my parents have organised a h_____ family. They seem really nice and they make you breakfast and dinner every day, which is great because I can't cook.

3
A: Are you listening to me, Mark?
B: Of course. You have my u_____ attention.

4
A: Do you have any plans for the weekend?
B: Nothing much. I think I'll just h_____ around my area. There's an event on in the park so I might go there. You?
A: Oh we're throwing a w_____ party for John. He's just moved into our flat.

5
A: You should go out with Jo. She really likes you.
B: I don't know. What if we don't get on well?
A: Go on, take a c_____ ! What have you got to lose?
B: But I don't know anything about her.
A: Oh, I'm sure if you talk to her for long enough, you can find some c_____ ground.

3 Complete the text with the words in the box.

> drift apart   fancied   fell for   ~~fell in love with~~
> firstborn   have a baby   long-distance relationship
> love at first sight   proposed

'I met your mother when we were very young. We were at university together and I *fell in love with* her immediately. I would like to say that it was [1]_____ for her as well, but unfortunately, it took her a little bit longer to decide she [2]_____ me. We were good friends though and that was enough.

Eventually, she agreed to go out with me so I took her to a restaurant and then we went for a romantic walk in the park. I think that was when she [3]_____ me. We stayed together all through university, but then she was offered a job in London. We talked about having a [4]_____ but we were worried we might [5]_____ . Fortunately, it worked well.

She eventually moved back here and I [6]_____ to her. We got married a year later, and then we decided to [7]_____ . That was you, our [8]_____ daughter. And we've never been happier.'

FOOD

1 Are the statements true (T) or false (F)? Correct the false statements.

You usually eat your dessert after your starter. `F`
1 Eggs and fish contain a lot of carbohydrates. ◯
2 Buying locally grown food is good for the environment. ◯
3 If food is rotten, it's safe to eat it. ◯
4 A fussy eater is happy to eat anything. ◯
5 If you are starving, you are extremely hungry. ◯
6 An inn is similar to a pub. ◯
7 Jam usually comes in a jar. ◯
8 If food is mouth-watering, it is disgusting. ◯
9 Raw chicken is safe to eat. ◯

SHOPPING AND SERVICES

1 Match the words with the definitions.

online shopping `d`
1 flea market ◯
2 high street ◯
3 online auction ◯
4 open-air market ◯
5 chain store ◯
6 antiques market ◯
7 car boot sale ◯
8 auction house ◯

a an outdoor market where people can sell their unwanted goods (usually from the backs of their cars)
b a public market outside where you can buy fresh locally grown food and other goods
c a street market selling second-hand goods, e.g. old books, cutlery, old CDs, clothes
d buying goods on a website
e a company that allows you to bid in person against other people for items, e.g. works of art
f a market where you can buy old, valuable goods, e.g. furniture
g a series of shops with one owner in which they sell the same goods
h the main street of a town where you will find most of the shops
i when you bid for items on a website against other people

2 Complete the sentences with the correct forms of the verbs in the box. There are three extra verbs.

> afford   be   burn   have   live   meet   make
> need   open   save   transfer   want   waste

John has no money. He _is_ absolutely broke.
1 I'd love to go on holiday this year, but I had to pay for my wedding so I just can't _____ to go.
2 Jo got her bonus and now she's buying presents for everyone. She has money to _____ .
3 My son has just turned two, so we went and _____ a bank account for him. We put in a little every month, just to _____ for a rainy day.
4 I never buy bottles of water. I hate _____ money when I can get it for free from the tap.
5 Did you hear the news? Tony sold his online company. He's _____ a lot of money on this deal.
6 A lot of families in the UK are earning the minimum wage. They barely have enough food to live. They are _____ from hand to mouth.
7 Since I lost my job, I've been finding it hard to make ends _____ . By the end of the month, I have to borrow money to pay my rent.
8 Jenny, can you _____ some money to my account? I have to pay the bills.

3 Complete the text with the correct form of the words in capitals.

◯◯◯

Saving starts early – hot saving tips for teens

You might think your pocket money is never enough. But no matter how big your monthly or weekly _allowance_ is, you can still save a little money. Here's how:

• Buy a piggy bank, or find an old jar and label it 'savings'. Put one third of your pocket money inside, and if you have a summer job, one third of your [1] _____ (EARN).

• If you get money from your parents for new trousers, or a mobile phone, look for [2] _____ (REDUCT) in the prices.

• If you get something you don't like as a present, [3] _____ (CHANGE) it for something you need.

• If you want to buy something extremely expensive, like the latest [4] _____ (LIMIT) edition trainers, stop and consider if it's worth it. Is it [5] _____ (AFFORD)? That is: wouldn't it cost you too much?

• Avoid impulse purchases. Marketing specialists studying consumer [6] _____ (BEHAVE) know that most of what we buy we don't really need. It's just a question of advertising it well.

• Be [7] _____ (ECONOMY). Look for cheaper train tickets, offers, sales. Do you really need this coffee? Can't you drink one at home?

• If you see a deal in the supermarket, e.g. three for the price of two, ask yourself, does it make [8] _____ (FINANCE) sense? You only needed one so why pay for two?

VOCABULARY BANK

TRAVELLING AND TOURISM

1 Complete the text with the words in the box. There are two extra words.

> beauty   camp   campsite   coast   company
> ~~cruises~~   destinations   directions   facilities
> tourist   path

Oh my goodness! What a pack of lies. I went on one of these Caribbean *cruises* with my family last year, and it was an absolute disaster. They mentioned making new friends. Well, unfortunately, everyone on the cruise was incredibly rude, including the staff. I suppose if you enjoy your own [1]_____ , this might be the holiday for you. The [2]_____ on board were terrible, the pool was always dirty and the rooms were small and cramped. The films they offered on board were ancient. When we got to our 'family' room, there were only three beds for four of us so my son had to sleep on a [3]_____ bed they brought in. It felt like being in a tent on a [4]_____ . We probably should have had a camping holiday; it would have been much cheaper!

And then we got to one of the 'ports', one of the 'picturesque' [5]_____ we had been promised. Well, it was a tiny dock on the [6]_____ of some island I'd never heard of with a dirt [7]_____ that led up to a few little cafés and restaurants and nothing else. So much for taking in the local culture! We tried to look up [8]_____ to a nearby village, but there was no wi-fi on board, which did not make my 10-year-old son very happy.

My advice? Just stay at home and clean the house, it would be more relaxing than this!

2 Complete the text with the missing words.

ADVENTURE *OF* A LIFETIME!

Are you tired of the hustle and bustle of everyday life? Are you ready for the *voyage* of a lifetime? Why not [1]e_ _ _ _ k on a cruise around the Caribbean, [2]f_ _ _ d for its clear seas and beautiful beaches? Along the way, you can stop at various ports and have a [3]g_ _ _ _ d tour of the city or just go and visit the [4]h_ _ _ _ _ _ c sites yourselves to take in their [5]c_ _ _ _ _ _ l heritage. If that's not your thing, you can visit the local [6]t_ _ _ _ _ t spots or just sit on a [7]s_ _ _ _ d by the pool, making new friends and looking out at the [8]p_ _ _ _ _ _ _ _ e scenery and watching the world go by. Whatever holiday you're looking for, you'll find it with Caribbean Cruises.

3 Complete the dialogue with the correct prepositions.

– Hi, I think I'm going to be late. I'm stuck in traffic.

– Oh no! What's up? I've only just set [1]_____ so I won't be on time, either.

– There's been an accident [2]_____ the motorway.

– What happened? John and I are just [3]_____ the roundabout in the city centre. He's meeting a friend, so agreed to drop me off on the way. Should we turn [4]_____ now?

– We were [5]_____ the traffic lights waiting to get onto the motorway and a moped pulled [6]_____ in front of us and went through the lights. I think you should keep on going, they might have sorted it out by the time you get there.

– That's crazy. Mopeds aren't supposed to go there. Did they crash?

– Yeah, but it wasn't bad. Everyone is fine, but it stopped traffic until the police arrived. At least you're running late too.

– Yes, I'll ring the restaurant and tell them we will be another half an hour.

– Thanks. Can you ask if they have [7]_____-street parking available there?

– I know they don't but there is some parking down the road. It's [8]_____ walking distance of the restaurant so I usually park there.

– Perfect. OK, I'll see you when you get there. Don't forget, this is a fancy restaurant. I hope you've dressed up.

– Don't worry. I've got my heels [9]_____ the boot. LOL! See you soon.

CULTURE

1 Match the words in the two columns to make common collocations related to media.

~~post~~	~~a video~~
mislead	anchor
out of	facts
crop	at face value
morning	show
double-check	focus
print-based	media
news	the people
take a story	images

post a video, _____
_____
_____
_____

2 Choose the correct answer A–D.

The story was totally <u>B</u> and we soon realised it was just fake news.
A believable   (B) unbelievable
C believably   D unbelievably

1 The celebrity sued the newspaper. She claimed the facts were totally __ .
A inaccurate   B accurate
C inaccurately   D accurately

2 They always listened to him because he was a __ source.
A disreputable   B reliable
C well-reviewed   D made-up

3 The photographer managed to capture the __ moment of the two politicians shaking hands for the first time in decades.
A memorable   B gripping
C catching   D reliable

4 His actions were __ . He listened in on the phone conversation and printed it in his newspaper.
A fictional   B average   C deliberate D appealing

5 It was a __ newspaper, but this one time, they printed the lies that led to the impeachment.
A fake   B misleading
C newsworthy   D reputable

6 It was a clearly __ story and it was obvious that none of it was true.
A high-quality   B made-up
C out-of-focus   D accurate

7 To increase their viewing numbers, they printed the article and __ their readers on purpose.
A misinformed   B distorted
C blurred   D bombarded

8 The story was __ and people were talking about it for years to come.
A forgettable   B unknowing
C knowing   D unforgettable

3 Choose the correct option to complete the text.

SUPERHERO SUCCESS

It's finally (come) / gone out and early [1]audiences / characters are not disappointed. This is the most hotly anticipated blockbuster of the summer and let me tell you, it promises to be an absolute box-office [2]success / disaster. Watch out though, if you keep reading, [3]subtitles / spoilers will follow. You've been warned.

The opening [4]scene / stage sets the tone for the entire movie. Everyone's favourite hero suffers his greatest defeat yet, which causes him to retreat to his homeworld, where he must face the truth that he is not the most powerful being in the universe. The [5]genre / plot revolves around this acceptance and his redemption. But don't worry, while this film is definitely [6]darker / blacker and more character driven than its prequel, there is plenty of action and numerous [7]twists and turns / passages, which make for quite a [8]gripping / predictable tale. The real treat of this second instalment in the trilogy, however, is that the [9]villain / hero is finally revealed and we are not disappointed. She will be a formidable enemy for the finale.

On top of amazing writing, acting and direction, this film also features an incredibly powerful [10]soundtrack / movie set. Set in the 90s, the music is heavily influenced by all of the [11]nostalgic / hilarious classics, which really help to place us in that period.

This film is not to be missed. Go forth and watch!

SPORT

1 Are the statements true (T) or false (F)? Correct the false statements.

Whitewater rafting is done on a cruise ship. (F)
1 If a sport is physically demanding, you need to be quite fit. ☐
2 A raft is a large boat. ☐
3 Post-match discussions usually happen before a match. ☐
4 You do a warm-up during a game of tennis. ☐

HEALTH

1 Match the words 1–8 to a–i to make phrases.

perform	(i)	a	unconscious
1 fight	☐	b	your memory
2 fall into	☐	c	off an illness
3 hit/struck by	☐	d	on someone
4 risk	☐	e	a disease
5 be found	☐	f	lightning
6 treat	☐	g	a coma
7 operate	☐	h	of infection
8 regain/lose	☐	i	an operation

2 Complete the conversation below with the missing words. The first letters are given.

A: My father has an u _n h e a l t h y_ lifestyle. He has a [1]h _ _ _ _ of sunbathing without any [2]s _ _ _ _ _ _ _ _ . He says the sun is good for him and he needs to soak up its nutrients, which I think is just an excuse because he likes to look good.

B: Oh no, that is a [3]n _ _ _ _ habit. I mean, I like to tan but I think you need to strike a [4]b _ _ _ _ _ _ between safety and beauty.

A: I completely agree. I think he has a bit of an [5]a _ _ _ _ _ _ _ though. He just can't stop. He knows how [6]h _ _ _ _ _ _ it can be, but he does it anyway.

B: You should send him for a health [7]c _ _ _ _. He might listen if he hears it from a doctor.

3 Do the crossword.

Across

4 ___ is a condition that requires you to take insulin.
6 ___ is a breathing issue that is usually linked to allergies (e.g. to pets, dust or smoke).
7 ___ is the condition of being dangerously overweight.
8 A ___ limits a person's movements or senses.
9 A serious accident can cause you to fall into a ___ and not wake up for a period of time.
11 He got hit in the head and was found ___ .

Down

1 When you cannot see, you are ___ .
2 If you feel extremely sad, you might suffer from ___ .
3 If you cannot hear, you are ___ .
5 A very serious injury that could result in death would be called a life-___ injury.
10 Red marks on your skin, usually because of an allergy, are called a ___ .

SCIENCE AND TECHNOLOGY

1 Complete the sentences with the correct forms of the words in capitals.

The scientists were shocked. The rock's chemical _composition_ did not seem to be from this planet. (COMPOSE)

1 The _____ of the Internet has changed the world completely. (INVENT)
2 The problem with baby wipes is that they can take up to two hundred years to _____ . (COMPOSE)
3 It is important that doctors carry out thorough _____ . Otherwise they might miss something. (EXAMINE)
4 _____ is the giving off of radiation. (RADIOACTIVE)
5 Scientists have made great _____ in the fight against cancer. (ADVANCE)
6 He works in _____ sciences but was originally a medical doctor. (APPLY)
7 Marie Curie gained worldwide _____ for her work. (RECOGNISE)
8 He was awarded a Nobel prize because he made a huge _____ to medicine. (CONTRIBUTE)

2 Complete the text with the words in the box. There are two extra words.

> battery   break   image   locate   parts   range
> sat-nav   ~~smartphone~~   storage   store   switch
> take   unplug

The Payphone is Dead, Long Live the Smartphone!

Gone are the days of searching through your pocket for some spare change to make a phone call in the street, hoping to catch your friend before they leave the house.

The latest _smartphone_ from the Pear Company has been released and it's a winner in all areas.

Lost on the long drive home at night? Don't worry, this phone has in-built ⁱ_____ to help you find your way.

Unhappy with the photo you took last night? Worry not, it comes equipped with ²_____ editing software to help you remove those red eyes. And you can make as many different versions as you like because this phone lets you ³_____ up to 240GB.

Lost your tablet? Not an issue. This phone can help you ⁴_____ any of your devices.

Forgot to ⁵_____ the charger and worried your house will burn down? Worry no more, you can ⁶_____ off any plug socket in your house remotely as long as it's linked to your phone.

This truly is a top-of-the-⁷_____ phone. With all of these features you would expect the ⁸_____ life to suffer, but thankfully that is not the case. It lasts a full 24 hours without needing a charge. And, if you do need to replace it, this phone is fully customizable, meaning you can ⁹_____ it apart and buy spare ¹⁰_____ easily online.

3 Match the words with the definitions.

	fossil	e				
1	acid	◯	5	algorithm	◯
2	velocity	◯	6	electron	◯
3	nucleus	◯	7	breakthrough	◯
4	outcome	◯	8	viewpoint	◯

a a set of rules to help in solving a calculation
b chemical substance with a PH of less than 7
c the result, consequence of a process
d it moves around the nucleus
e a shape or shell of an animal (e.g. a dinosaur) that has been preserved in rock for a long time
f a new and very important discovery
g the speed something is moving
h a particular way of thinking about a problem
i the centre of an atom

THE NATURAL WORLD

1 Choose the correct answer A–D.

His house was located on the <u>A</u> so they went fishing regularly.

(A) coast   B deep sea
C countryside   D seaside

1 In Devon, in the south-west of England, you can find __ full of apple trees for making English cider.
    A meadows   B orchards   C plains   D bushes

2 In springtime, you can see all sorts of birds collecting sticks and mud, and __ in the trees.
    A rolling   B thriving   C nesting   D breeding

3 In the winter months, many birds will leave Britain. They will __ to warmer climates and return later in the year.
    A migrate   B domesticate
    C release   D establish

4 Foxes are a common __ found in the UK. They often hunt birds and smaller animals like rats and mice.
    A prey   B predator   C reptile   D tern

5 When eggs __ , the mother will always be there to feed her babies.
    A lay   B tweet   C set   D hatch

6 When you reach the __ , you will have a beautiful view of the countryside.
    A stream   B current   C summit   D soil

7 The __ landscape in the UK means that you can see a lot of different types of wildlife.
    A rolling   B diverse   C ploughed   D leafy

8 His family had owned this __ of land for centuries and he was delighted to give it to his son.
    A patch   B foothill   C coastline   D desert

2 Complete the leaflet with the correct words.

Looking to become

the next eco-w <u>a r r i o r</u> ?

Check out these top tips for reducing your environmental ¹**i** _ _ _ _ _ .

- Reduce your carbon ²**e** _ _ _ _ _ _ _ _ by walking or cycling instead of driving.

- Don't buy any clothes that are made from real ³**f** _ _ . Save the animals!

- ⁴**P** _ _ _ _ _ _ waste is one of the biggest issues. Try finding more ⁵**s** _ _ _ _ _ _ _ _ _ options. For example use paper bags or get a bamboo toothbrush.

- Reduce your water usage, for example take a short shower not a bath and get a water ⁶**t** _ _ _ for your back garden and use rain water for your plants.

- Fossil fuels are destroying our planet. Try out ⁷**a** _ _ _ _ _ _ _ _ _ energy. These days you can get wind energy created by wind ⁸**t** _ _ _ _ _ _ _ or install solar panels on a roof.

---

3 Are the statements true (T) or false (F)? Correct the false sentences.

Downpour means light rain.   ☐ F

1 A hurricane is a storm with violent wind.   ☐
2 Gale-force winds are very light.   ☐
3 If a storm is brewing, it has happened recently.   ☐
4 If something is waterproof, it is OK to take it in the swimming pool.   ☐
5 A whiteout is when there has been a light dusting of snow.   ☐
6 An earthquake is when the wind gathers dust into a dust cloud.   ☐
7 A gust of wind is a sudden heavy wind.   ☐
8 Drought means there is a lot of water.   ☐

STATE AND SOCIETY

1 Complete the dialogue with the words in the box. There are two extra words.

> awareness   charity   commitment   ~~difference~~
> figures   fundraising   identities   leaflets
> members   peaceful   statement

A: The world is being destroyed and it's our job as young people to do something about it. We need to make a _difference_.

B: I know, but what can we do? We need public ¹_____ to help us, like actors or politicians. We're just teenagers. We can't do anything.

A: Oh, but we can. We can raise ²_____ through a protest.

B: A protest? We could get in trouble.

A: Not if it was a ³_____ protest.

B: That's true! We could stand outside the supermarket and protest against plastic bags. And maybe we would get ⁴_____ of the public to donate, just normal people as they come out of the shop.

A: Yes but what effect will that have? I think if we're collecting money, we should fundraise for a ⁵_____ . An organised group with a specific cause.

B: That's a good idea. There are many that work to reduce plastic.

A: Yes, it's a great idea. We could make posters for our protest and hand out ⁶_____ to let people know of the dangers. We will have to do this every weekend if we want to make a difference. This is a long-term ⁷_____ . Are you ready?

B: Yes! This is brilliant. Let's get started. I'll buy the masks.

A: Masks!!! Why?

B: To protect our ⁸_____ .

A: Maybe I'll just do this by myself …

2 Choose the correct option to complete the sentences.

The minister for (foreign)/ abroad affairs travelled to China to discuss a new trade deal.
1 There has been a sharp *increase / decrease* in the levels of crime in many areas because of cuts to the police budget.
2 New problems are springing *up / down* all over the world. As soon as one is finished with, the next arises.
3 We need to support our local *producers / makers* of fruit and vegetable.
4 There is a *gaining / growing* number of politicians discussing fake news, which is extremely worrying.
5 Some politicians sell stories about their rivals to the media for *commercial / political* gain.
6 The clothing *company / industry* as a whole needs to make some drastic changes and ensure their workers are being paid fairly.

3 Match the words with the definitions.

extreme poverty 〔e〕
1 famine ▢   5 misinformation ▢
2 gender gap ▢   6 riot ▢
3 human trafficking ▢   7 robbery ▢
4 throw-away society ▢   8 antisocial behaviour ▢

a the practice of illegally transporting people from one country to another and exploiting them
b a violent disturbance by a crowd
c the difference between how men and women are treated (e.g. in pay)
d a consumerist society, constantly replacing and buying new products instead of repairing them
e a condition characterised by severe deprivation of basic human needs (e.g. food, health, education)
f false information intended to keep the truth away from the public
g extreme lack of food leading to starvation and death
h behaviour which is violent or harmful to other people in a society
i the crime of stealing money or other things from a bank or shop often using violence

CULTURE OF ENGLISH-SPEAKING COUNTRIES

1 Are the statements true (T) or false (F)? Correct the false statements.

The Appalachian Mountains are in central Europe. 〔F〕
1 Manhattan is an island in the UK. ▢
2 Essex and Sheffield are both located in Scotland. ▢
3 The Beatles are from Manchester. ▢
4 Notting Hill is quite a poor area in London. ▢
5 Portobello Road Market is quite a good place to buy antiques. ▢
6 Hobbiton is in Australia. ▢
7 Bangor is a small university town in Wales. ▢
8 Oxford is a city on the River Thames. ▢

2 Match the people with their descriptions.

James Bond 〔g〕
1 Captain America ▢   4 Meryl Streep ▢
2 Jojo Moyes ▢   5 Robert Pattinson ▢
3 Rosalind Franklin ▢   6 Stephen King ▢

a a British actor, famous for his role in *Twilight*
b a US film actress, known for her versatility, often described as the best actress of her generation
c an imaginary character, a superhero of American comic books published by Marvel Comics
d a British chemist who contributed to the discovery of the molecular structure of DNA
e a popular US writer of frightening stories
f a British journalist and author of romantic novels
g also called 007, a fictional character in novels by Ian Fleming

3 Choose the correct answer to complete the sentences.

Ada Lovelace worked on the 'Analytical Engine' together with
A Jan Koum.   (B) Charles Babbage.
1 Mary Anning was a
A palaeontologist.   B historian.
2 Ewan McGregor and Naomi Watts are actors in the film
A *Everest*.   B *The Impossible*.
3 Joe Woodland created the first
A barcode.   B QR code.
4 *The Hobbit* was written by
A J. R. R. Tolkien.   B Stephen King.
5 One of Banksy's murals is called
A *Girl with Balloon*.   B *Girl with a Pearl Earring*.
6 Ebenezer Howard started a movement which influenced the development of two cities. It was called
A the garden wall movement.
B the garden city movement.
7 The actor who played Harry Potter is
A Daniel Day Lewis.   B Daniel Radcliffe.
8 The actor known for his skills in martial arts was
A Bruce Lee.   B Bruce Banner.

4 Write the correct answers below.

This is a borough in London where you can buy unusual clothes. *Camden Town*
1 This is the largest city in South Africa. _____
2 This is the name of the guards at the Tower of London. _____
3 She was an English mathematician and daughter of Lord Byron. _____
4 He is the lead character of *The Hobbit*. _____
5 This is the traditional ceremony of locking the Tower of London. _____
6 This is a famous Netflix series created by the Duffer Brothers. _____
7 He was an actor and later became president of the US. _____

Present tenses – review

Present Simple

We use the **Present Simple**:

- to talk about actions which are repeated regularly:
  *I always **drive** to work.*
- to talk about states and permanent situations:
  *The chef **doesn't come** from Italy.*
- with verbs expressing emotions (*hate, like, love,* etc.), states of mind (*believe, know, need, prefer, remember, seem, think, understand, want,* etc.) or senses (*feel, hear, see,* etc.):
  ***Do** you **prefer** Indian or Chinese food?*

Present Continuous

We use the **Present Continuous** to talk about:

- actions happening at the time of speaking:
  *Most of the guests **are sitting** on the outdoor patio at the moment.*
- temporary situations:
  *I'**m working** at Tuco's bar during the summer break.*

Present Perfect Simple

We use the **Present Perfect Simple** to talk about actions and situations which:

- finished in the past and have a result in the present (and we don't know or it's not important when exactly they happened):
  *I'**ve made** coffee. Would you like some?*
- started in the past and continue into the present:
  *How long **have** you **owned** this restaurant?*

Present Perfect Continuous

We use the **Present Perfect Continuous** to talk about actions which:

- started in the past and continue into the present:
  *Zoe **has been sleeping** since two o'clock.*
- lasted for some time (and possibly still continue) and whose result we can still see now:
  *I'm tired because I'**ve been cleaning** the house all day.*

Present Perfect Simple vs Present Perfect Continuous

We use the Present Perfect Continuous to focus on the action or process (which may or may not be complete):
*I'**ve been baking** biscuits all morning.*

We use the Present Perfect Simple to focus on the result of a finished action:
*I'**ve baked** 200 biscuits.*

---

1 Complete the dialogues with the correct forms of the verbs in brackets.

1. A: *I'm following* (follow) the seafood diet at the moment.
   B: The seafood diet? I ᵃ_____ (never/hear) of that one.
   A: It's pretty easy really. Whenever I ᵇ_____ (see) food, I ᶜ_____ (eat) it.
2. A: What ᵃ_____ (you/do), Julia?
   B: I ᵇ_____ (make) some lunch for us, Dave. It shouldn't be long. ᶜ_____ (you/think) these eggs will be hard-boiled yet?
   A: Well, I don't know. How long ᵈ_____ (you/boil) them for?
   B: About an hour.
   A: An hour? I ᵉ_____ (think) they might be done, yes. In fact, we might have trouble eating them unless you've got a hammer!

2 Make questions using an appropriate present tense. Then ask and answer the questions in pairs.

ever / try / spicy Thai food?
Have you ever tried spicy Thai food?

1. food prices / go up / at the moment?
   _____
2. ever / cut your finger / preparing food?
   _____
3. How often / cook a meal / for the family?
   _____
4. How long / go to this school?
   _____
5. How long / know your best friend?
   _____

3 Complete the sentences and questions with the correct form of the verbs in brackets.

She *goes* (go) for a run a few times a week, but she *'s thinking* (think) of giving it up.

1. I _____ (think) this coffee _____ (taste) bitter. I _____ (not like) it.
2. My grandma _____ (bake) a lot. She _____ (probably make) a cake right now.
3. My dad _____ (not see) why young people _____ (love) fast food so much.
4. What _____ (you/look) for? _____ (you/lose) your glasses again?
5. I _____ (do) some cooking all morning. That's why it _____ (smell) of onions here!

4 Correct the mistakes. There is one mistake in each sentence.

What ~~are you thinking~~ about buying this software?
do you think

1. You're out of breath. Do you run? _____
2. Guess what! I'm becoming a vegetarian since we last met. _____
3. Ken hasn't cooked every evening because he usually gets home very late. _____
4. Shelly and Nick don't work today because they've both got food poisoning. _____
5. Excuse me, waiter. We're waiting for our desserts for half an hour now. _____

5 Complete the sentences with the correct forms of the verbs in the box.

> cook   not make   not see   prefer
> read   take   think   write

I'm really tired. I've been cooking all day.

1 I _____ Margaret recently. How is she?

2 She _____ she'd like the steak, but she _____ up her mind yet.

3 My daughter _____ a lot about Mexico lately. That's where she wants to go on her holiday, I guess.

4 I'm watching my weight, so I _____ a vegetarian diet at the moment.

5 The meeting _____ place upstairs today because of the flood damage on the ground floor.

6 Margaret _____ all the reports. Can you take them up to Mr Jones?

Past tenses – review

Past Simple

We use the **Past Simple** to talk about:

- actions and situations which started and finished in the past. We often say when they happened:
  We **bought** this house in 2013.

- a series of actions that happened one after the other:
  Messi **kicked** the ball, and it **flew** into the net.

Past Continuous

We use the **Past Continuous**:

- to talk about actions which were in progress at a particular time in the past:
  'What **were** you **doing** at eight yesterday evening?'
  'I **was watching** a football game on TV.'

- to talk about an action which was in progress when another action took place (for the shorter action, which happened while the longer action was in progress, we use the Past Simple):
  When she **was skiing** down the slope, another skier **crashed** into her.

- to describe background states for other events:
  On the day of the match, the sun **was shining**, and a light breeze **was blowing**.

Past Perfect Simple

We use the **Past Perfect Simple** to talk about an action that happened before a particular time in the past or before another past action (for the action that happened first, we use the Past Perfect):

The party **had finished** by midnight.

Owen **had scored** two goals before the coach **decided** to substitute him.

1 Complete the sentences and questions with the correct forms of the verbs in brackets.

I went ice-skating last weekend – it was the first time I had tried it.

1 Sheila _____ (come) home and _____ (lock) herself in her room.

2 I couldn't open the door because I _____ (leave) my keys at home.

3 Sorry, we _____ (talk) about something else. Could you repeat that, please?

4 I broke a bone once. I _____ (ride) my bike and crashed into a tree.

5 _____ (he/ever coach) a basketball team before he took on the school team?

2 Complete the text with the correct forms of the verbs in brackets.

> Yesterday, two British climbers completed (complete) one of the most difficult climbing routes in the world. Over 4 million people ¹_____ (watch) live on the Internet when the brave pair ²_____ (reach) the top of 'Old Major', a rock face in Yellowstone National Park. By the time they completed their adventure, they ³_____ (climb) over 900 metres through all kinds of weather. Luckily, there were no weather problems yesterday – the sun ⁴_____ (shine) brightly when the exhausted climbers finally ⁵_____ (pull) themselves over the top of the rock face at exactly 15.37.

3 Complete the sentences with the correct past forms of the verbs in the box.

> make   never beat   not bring
> score   skate   train   watch

Tom slipped on the ice and broke his leg when he was skating.

1 It was 2–2. Then Joe _____ the winning goal in injury time.

2 We fell asleep while we _____ a film.

3 Beth couldn't do PE because she _____ her PE kit.

4 Jack was ecstatic. He _____ his brother before.

5 Tess didn't realise she _____ so many mistakes!

6 Lucy _____ for a triathlon when she twisted her ankle.

4 Correct the mistakes. There is one mistake in each sentence.

It ~~snowed~~ heavily when the marathon began. _was snowing_

1 We got stuck in traffic on the way to the game and, by the time we got there, our team was already scoring three baskets. _____

2 Had you remembered to take an extra racket for Tom yesterday? _____

3 The golfer who missed the vital shot was throwing his club into the lake after the game. _____

4 We weren't allowed in the pool because we were forgetting our swimming caps. _____

5 They didn't listen to the radio, so I turned it off. _____

6 Had you watched when the rider fell off his horse? _____

5 Complete the extract from a successful football player's biography with the correct past forms of the verbs in the box.

> be ~~do~~ like look forward to
> not understand score study win

I've always been a very competitive person. At school, I _did_ a lot of athletics, and later while I ¹_____ at university, I played football on the first team. I was never truly satisfied unless I was the one who ²_____ the goals. It wasn't enough to beat the opponent, I had to be the absolute best at whatever I did. By the time I was twenty-three, I ³_____ several awards and I ⁴_____ a successful football career. To be honest, not many people ⁵_____ me, because of my attitude, but I couldn't help it at that time. If I ⁶_____ more mature, I would have realised that winning wasn't the most important thing in life. I ⁷_____ then why other people were satisfied with keeping fit or going cycling, or even just throwing a ball around for fun, but now I do.

6 Make sentences and questions using an appropriate past tense.

We / meet / long before / we / start / high school.
We had met long before we started high school.

1 I / not know / how to make a cake / when / I / be ten.
_____
_____

2 it / rain / when / you / go to school?
_____

3 by the time / we / arrive / at the party / everyone / already leave.
_____
_____

4 We / talk about her / when / she / call.
_____

5 She / never feel / so happy / before / she / meet him.
_____

Future tenses – review

Present Simple

We use the **Present Simple** for schedules, timetables and future events whose dates have been officially planned:

Lunch break **starts** at 12:30 and **finishes** at 13:30.
What time **does** our train **leave**?

Present Continuous

We use the **Present Continuous** for future plans and arrangements, usually with a time reference:

I**'m leaving** tomorrow, so I can't go to the cinema with you.

be going to

We use **be going to** + **infinitive** for:

* intentions and future plans which may change:
  What **are** you **going to prepare** for lunch?

* predictions about the future based on what we know and can see now:
  Look at the time! We**'re not going to get** to the station on time.

Future Simple

We use **will** + **infinitive** for:

* decisions made at the time of speaking:
  Wait for me! I**'ll help** you with the shopping.

* predictions about the future based on opinions, intuition or experience:
  You can borrow my dictionary, but I**'ll** probably **need** it back next week.
  Do you think Poland **will beat** Italy?

We use **shall** for questions with _I_ and _we_, offering help and making suggestions:

These bags look heavy. **Shall** I **carry** them for you?
**Shall** we **have** a barbecue this evening?

Future Continuous

We use the **Future Continuous** to talk about actions which will be in progress at a particular time in the future:

We **will be making** a cake at 5 p.m.

Future Perfect

We use the **Future Perfect** to talk about actions or situations which will be completed before a particular time in the future:

I **will have cooked** all the dishes by 3 o'clock.

Future time clauses

In sentences referring to the future, we use the **Present Simple** after the following conjunctions:

- **if** → If you **don't have** breakfast at home, you will feel hungry very soon.
- **when** → We will cook the pasta **when** Luigi **arrives**.
- **unless** → You won't lose weight **unless** you **eat** fruit and vegetables every day.
- **before** → I'll brush my teeth **before** I **go** to bed
- **after** → We'll have some coffee **after** we **get** back home.
- **until** → I'll wait for you **until** you **finish** your homework.
- **as soon as** → I'll call you **as soon as** I **finish**.
- **as long as** → I'll make breakfast **as long as** you **do** the washing-up.

1 Match the sentences with their functions.

I think I'll go for a walk today. ☐ j

1 Jill loves cooking and she's going to become a chef. ☐
2 Will you show me how to use the new oven? ☐
3 We have Biology class every Monday at 11. ☐
4 The students will have received their results by Friday. ☐
5 The planet will become warmer in the future. ☐
6 Dad's so tired that he's going to fall asleep on the sofa. ☐
7 Shall we go out for dinner tonight? ☐
8 I'll be meeting Sam at the station at two o'clock. ☐
9 We're going away next weekend. ☐

a an action in progress at a future time
b an event that will happen before a specific future time
c a prediction based on evidence
d a scheduled event based on a timetable
e a suggestion
f an intention
g a prediction
h a future plan or arrangement
i a request
j a decision taken at the moment of speaking

2 Choose the correct option to complete the sentences.

Hang on a minute. *I get /* I'll get my jacket and then we can leave.

1 Tom *will have left / will be leaving* by 3 p.m. tomorrow.
2 Technology *will make / will be making* life easier in the future.
3 Josh and Kate *are returning / will return* from their holiday tomorrow.
4 *Shall / Will* I make you a cup of tea, Grandma?
5 Slow down! *You're going to have / You're having* an accident!
6 Don't forget to meet Jim at the station; his train *will arrive / arrives* at 3:45 p.m.
7 *Do they finish / Will they have finished* painting their house by next week?
8 You can call Alice in the evening. She *won't be working / isn't going to work* then.

3 Choose the correct answers A–C.

By this time tomorrow, he _A_ for Scotland.
Ⓐ will have left B will be leaving C is leaving

1 On Sunday at 12 o'clock, I ___ my friends in the country.
   A will visit   B will have visited C will be visiting
2 By the time we get to the stadium, the match ___ .
   A will start   B will have started
   C is going to start
3 I ___ you tomorrow at school.
   A will see   B see   C will be seeing
4 We ___ Stan at the café at two thirty today.
   A meet   B are meeting   C will meet
5 Where ___ for your summer holiday this year?
   A are you going to go B do you go
   C shall you go
6 You must be hungry. ___ you a sandwich?
   A Am I going to make   B Will I be making
   C Shall I make
7 Look at those dark clouds. It ___ soon.
   A rains   B is going to rain   C is raining
8 I promise I ___ out too late.
   A won't be staying   B am not going to stay
   C won't stay

4 Read Ben's schedule for university tomorrow. Then complete the sentences with the Future Continuous or the Future Perfect forms of the verbs in brackets.

8.00	leave the house	1.00	have lunch
8.30	arrive at university	2.00	lab experiment
9.00	lecture starts	5.00	leave lab
11.00	lecture finishes	5.30	arrive home

By 8.15, he *will have left* (leave) the house.
1 At 8.45, he _____ (wait) for the lecture to start.
2 By 9.15, the lecture _____ (start).
3 At 10.30, he _____ (sit) in the lecture hall.
4 By 2.00, he _____ (eat) his lunch.
5 At 3.00, he _____ (do) a lab experiment.
6 By 5.15, he _____ (finish) the experiment.
7 By 6.00, he _____ (arrive) home.

5 Complete the sentences with the correct forms of the verbs in brackets.

Our coach thinks we *will win* (win) the match, but I'm not so sure.

1 This time next month, he _____ (sail) in the Mediterranean.
2 When _____ your music lesson _____ (start)?
3 We _____ (go) to the concert on Friday, but we haven't bought tickets yet.
4 I _____ (have) a dinner party tomorrow night, so I need to go shopping today.
5 The phone's ringing; I _____ (answer) it.
6 _____ I _____ (bring) you the newspaper, Dad?
7 The Smiths _____ (not move) into their new house by the summer.
8 Don't walk to the station; I _____ (drive) you there.

6 Correct the mistakes in bold.

If you **will work** hard, you'll do well in your exams. _work_

1 Look at Sally! She **will be winning** the race! _____

2 Do you think humans **shall ever live** on other planets? _____

3 Tomorrow, we **will be having** a picnic in the park. _____

4 The film **is starting** at 6:30, so let's meet outside the cinema at 6:15. _____

5 I **will go** swimming tomorrow morning. Why don't you come with me? _____

6 This time next year, I **study** at university. _____

7 I'll buy the cinema tickets, as long as you **will pay** for dinner. _____

8 By the time I finish this novel, I **will be reading** three other books. _____

7 Complete the second sentence so that it means the same as the first. Use the word in capitals.

What's your prediction for the World Cup?
WIN
Who do you think _will win_ the World Cup?

1 I'm going to the beach tomorrow and I'm going to play volleyball.
WHEN
I'm going to play volleyball _____ to the beach tomorrow.

2 Hurry up, or we'll get to the stadium after the match starts.
WILL
Hurry up, or by the time we get to the stadium, the match _____ .

3 You must speak to your teacher before you can leave.
UNTIL
You can't leave _____ to your teacher.

4 Their party is on Saturday night.
HAVING
They _____ on Saturday night.

5 I'm going to play tennis at six, so I can't meet you then.
PLAYING
I can't meet you at six because I _____ tennis then.

6 After you cook the pasta, serve it immediately.
SOON
You must serve the pasta _____ it.

7 What are your plans for the summer?
DO
What _____ in the summer?

8 If you don't want to go out tomorrow night, we won't.
UNLESS
We won't go out tomorrow night _____ to.

First Conditional

- We use **First Conditional** sentences (**if** + **Present Simple**, **will/could/might** + **infinitive**) to talk about things which will happen in the future under certain conditions:

  If you **leave** a message, they**'ll call** you back.

  You **might get lost** unless you **take** a map with you.

Second Conditional

- We use **Second Conditional** sentences (**if** + **Past Simple**, **would/could/might** + **infinitive**) to talk about present or future situations or states which are impossible or unlikely:

  Would you **tell** him the truth if he **asked** you?

  I'm sure you **could do** that if I **showed** you how.

Third Conditional

- We use **Third Conditional** sentences (**if** + **Past Perfect**, **would have** + **Past Participle**) to talk about events in the past that did not happen:

  If you **had accepted** my help, you **would have avoided** a lot of trouble.

wish and _if only_

- We use **wish/if only** + **Past Simple** to express regret and dissatisfaction with a present situation:

  John **wishes** he **didn't have to** sell the house.

  If only I **could** help you.

- We use **wish/if only** + **would** + **infinitive** to express annoyance about a present situation that we would like to be different. It usually refers to things we can't change or control:

  I **wish** they**'d stop** playing loud music in the evenings.

  If only you**'d come back** earlier.

- **Wish** and **if only** have a similar meaning, but **if only** is more emphatic. It expresses a greater degree of regret.

1 Complete the sentences with the correct forms of the verbs or phrases in the box.

> buy ~~explode~~ know never remember
> not behave see sit

Careful! If you shake up the lemonade, it'_ll explode_ (explode) when you open it.

1 Three hours with nothing to eat! I _____ a sandwich for the journey if there'd been time.

2 You _____ all the important stuff if you don't take notes during lectures.

3 Kids in horror films are silly. If I _____ an old house in the woods, I wouldn't go anywhere near it.

4 If I _____ how difficult this book was going to be, I wouldn't have started it in the first place.

5 The cat's shy, but he will come to you if you _____ still and keep quiet.

6 If you really respected me, you _____ so horribly towards me all the time.

2 Write sentences with *wish* or *if only* to show that you would like the situations (S) or behaviour (B) to be different. Which wishes are true for you?

I don't live abroad. (S) *I wish/If only I lived abroad*.

1 I can't read music. (S)
   _____

2 My sister doesn't help around the house. (B)
   _____

3 My dad has to work very long hours. (S)
   _____

4 My sister doesn't let me use her laptop. (B)
   _____

5 My brother is very annoying. (S)
   _____

6 My mum always embarrasses me in front of visitors. (B)
   _____

3 Complete the second sentence to show you would like the situation or behaviour to be different.

My parents are so strict.
If only my parents *weren't* so strict.

1 Mum makes such a fuss if I'm slightly late.
   If only _____ such a fuss when I'm slightly late.

2 I don't have a photographic memory.
   If only _____ a photographic memory, I wouldn't need to do any revision.

3 My girlfriend hasn't called me yet today.
   I wish _____ me before bedtime.

4 There is no snow in the mountains.
   If only _____ snow in the mountains, we could go skiing.

5 I don't want to be here. I'd rather be anywhere else.
   I wish _____ here. I'd rather be anywhere else instead.

6 Kerry taps her pen on the desk. It's annoying.
   I wish _____ her pen on the desk. It's annoying

4 Write the correct forms of the verbs in brackets.

I can't go out now. If I *don't help* (not help) my mother around the house, she *won't let* (not let) me use the Internet tomorrow.

1 If I _____ (can) meet anyone, dead or alive, I _____ (choose) to meet John Lennon.

2 I'm a big fan of opera. I wish my boyfriend _____ (love) opera too.

3 You _____ (never/be able) to buy a new laptop last year if I _____ (not lend) you the money.

4 I'd love to visit Barcelona one day. If only I _____ (can) afford to go.

5 Jane's little brother is so spoilt.
   If you _____ (not give) him what he wants, he _____ (get) really angry.

6 If you _____ (be) a teacher, _____ (you/accept) friend requests from your students on Facebook?

7 Jake has a scooter, but he wishes he _____ (have) a motorbike.

5 Make sentences and questions using correct verb forms.

My grandma died when she was seventy-six. I / wish / she / live to be eighty. *I wish she had lived to be 80.*

1 I don't understand what he's saying. If / I / know Arabic / I / talk to him. _____
   _____ .

2 She can't do it herself. If only / I know / how to help her. _____
   _____ .

3 if / the weather in Poland / be better / last year / we / not go abroad on holiday. _____
   _____ .

4 you / ask her to dance / if / she / come to your party tomorrow? _____
   _____ .

5 he / wish / his sister / not come into his room all the time _____
   _____ .

6 She / not be late every day / if / she / live closer.
   _____
   _____ .

Modal verbs for speculation

- When speculating about present or future situations, we use *must/might/may/could/might not/may not/can't* + **infinitive**.
- When speculating about past situations or events, we use *must/might/may/could/might not/may not/can't* + **have** + **past participle**.

must + infinitive/perfect infinitive

- ***Must*** expresses a strong belief (bordering on certainty) that something is or was true:
  There **must be** something wrong with the engine.
  She **must have made** a mistake in her calculations.

might/may/could + infinitive/perfect infinitive

- ***Might***, ***may*** and ***could*** express a possibility that something is, will be or was possible or probable:
  This **might/may/could be** the article I'm looking for.
  Scientists disagree on what **might/may/could happen** to the Earth in the future.
  Some people say that life on Earth **might/may/could have originated** from another planet.
- ***Might not*** and ***may not*** express a weak possibility that something is not, will not be or was not true:
  Life on other planets **might not/may not** exist at all.
  Here are some facts you **may not/might not have heard** about.

can't/couldn't + infinitive/perfect infinitive

- ***Can't/couldn't*** expresses a strong belief (bordering on certainty) that something is not or was not true:
  He **can't be** English; his accent is too strong.
  This book **can't/couldn't have been written** by an expert.
  Peter **can't/couldn't have gone** home.

1 Complete the second sentence so that it means the same as the first.

It's possible space exploration will lead to the discovery of other life forms.
Space exploration _might lead_ to the discovery of other life forms.

1 I'm sure he's very intelligent.
He _____ very intelligent.

2 I don't know if all the explorers understood the significance of their discoveries.
Many explorers _____
the significance of their discoveries.

3 I'm sure early computer analysts didn't imagine how important the Internet would become.
Early computer analysts _____
how important the Internet would become.

4 I'm sure that documentary was very interesting.
That documentary _____
very interesting.

2 Rewrite the sentences. Use the words in capitals.

I'm sure it isn't true that your cousin saw a UFO land on the school football field. (CAN'T)
Your cousin can't have seen a UFO land on the school football field .

1 It is possible that human beings will visit the Moon again one day. (MAY) _____

2 I am sure it's true that there is life somewhere else in the universe. (BE) _____

3 It is possible that life arrived on Earth when an asteroid crashed into the planet. (HAVE)
_____

4 It's possible we didn't land on the Moon in 1969. (MIGHT) _____
_____

3 Complete the sentences with an appropriate modal structure and the verb in brackets. Sometimes more than one answer is possible.

They _can't have come_ this way because there are no footprints in the snow. (not/come)

1 All the other passengers got off, but Vicky wasn't there. She _____ the train. (miss)

2 Derek still isn't here. I suppose he _____ stuck in traffic, or got lost on the way. (get)

3 We _____ there yet. It's 400 km away, and we only left home 90 minutes ago. (be)

4 I _____ late if the traffic is bad, so please start without me if I'm not there by nine. (arrive)

5 I know you are worried that the parcel has got lost, but they _____ it yet. (not even/post)

6 Diane's shoes are still here, so she _____
_____ yet. (leave)

4 Think of alternatives for the underlined verb structures. Use *can't*, *could*, *may*, *might* and *must* and an infinitive or perfect infinitive. Use each modal verb once.

According to a recent UK survey, many people still believe that aliens _may/might/could have visited_ (have possibly visited) Earth. When people report sightings of Unidentified Flying Objects (UFOs), they usually describe strange lights and shapes. Other people say aliens [1] _____ (definitely haven't approached) our planet because otherwise there would be some proof. They believe that all 'sightings' of UFOs [2] _____ (are definitely) either natural weather events or man-made, i.e. aircraft, Chinese lanterns or even hoaxes.
But certain government officials think that aliens
[3] _____ (have possibly been) to Earth for military reconnaissance, scientific research or tourism and
[4] _____ (will possibly continue) to do so in future.

5 Rewrite the comments using the verbs in capitals.

I'm sure you're very pleased. (MUST)
You must be very pleased.

1 It's possible that she is in her room. (MIGHT)
_____

2 What?! I'm sure she isn't that old. (CAN'T)
_____

3 It's possible that he hasn't received it yet. (MAY NOT)
_____

4 I'm certain you left it at home. (MUST)
_____

5 I'm sure you're not serious. (CAN'T)
_____

6 It's possible that you don't want to hear this. (MIGHT NOT)
_____

7 It's possible that they overheard what we said. (COULD)
_____
_____

FOCUS 3 GRAMMAR REVIEW

Reported speech

Statements

To report another speaker's words, we often use verbs such as **say** or **tell** (or other reporting verbs) and the pronoun **that** (which can be omitted). The verb **tell** takes an object:

'I bought a bunch of flowers for my wife.' → He **said / told me (that)** he had bought a bunch of flowers for his wife.

We make the following changes in Reported Speech:

* tenses:

Direct Speech	Reported Speech
Present Simple Rose: 'I do the shopping at weekends.'	**Past Simple** Rose said (that) she did the shopping at weekends.
Present Continuous Rose: 'I am doing the shopping.'	**Past Continuous** Rose said (that) she was doing the shopping.
Present Perfect Rose: 'I have already done the shopping.'	**Past Perfect** Rose said (that) she had already done the shopping.
Past Simple Rose: 'I didn't do the shopping this morning.'	**Past Perfect** Rose said (that) she hadn't done the shopping that morning.
Past Perfect Rose: 'I hadn't done any shopping before the party.'	**Past Perfect** Rose said (that) she hadn't done any shopping before the party.
can/can't Rose: 'I can't do the shopping.'	**could/couldn't** Rose said (that) she couldn't do the shopping.
will/won't Rose: 'I won't do the shopping on my own.'	**would/wouldn't** Rose said (that) she wouldn't do the shopping on her own.
be going to Rose: 'I'm going to do the shopping on Saturday.'	**was/were going to** Rose said (that) she was going to do the shopping on Saturday.

* time expressions and words referring to places (depending on the context):

Direct Speech	Reported Speech
now	at that time / then
today	that day
tonight	that night
yesterday	the day before / the previous day
two hours ago	two hours earlier / before
tomorrow	the next day / the following day
here	there

* demonstrative pronouns, personal pronouns, object pronouns and possessive adjectives (depending on the context):

Direct Speech	Reported Speech
this/these	that/those
I/we	he/she/they
me/us	him/her/them
my	his/her
our	their

Questions

To report questions, we use verbs and phrases, such as **ask**, **enquire** or **want to know**, and make the same changes as in reported statements (tenses, pronouns, time expressions, words referring to places, etc.). The word order in reported questions is the same as in affirmative sentences (the subject comes before the verb).

* To report yes/no questions, we use **if** or **whether**:

*'**Can** I speak to the manager?'* → The customer asked **if/whether** he **could** speak to the manager.

*'**Will** you talk to Jen tonight?'* → I asked him **if/whether** he **would talk** to Jen that night.

* To report wh- questions, we keep the question word (e.g. what, who, how, where, when):

*'**How many** bottles of cola **did** you **buy**?'* → I asked my son **how many** bottles of cola he **had bought**.

*'**When are** you **coming** back?'* → Dorothy wanted to know **when** I **was coming** back.

Imperatives

To report imperatives (orders or requests), we use verbs, such as **ask** or **tell** or other reporting verbs, an object and **(not)** + **to infinitive**:

'Please refund my money.' → The customer **asked** the manager **to refund** his money.

*'**Don't apply** the cream more than twice a day.'* → The shop assistant **advised** the customer **not to apply** the cream more than twice a day.

1 Read the article about advertising slogans. Rewrite the journalist's notes with one word in each gap.

Do products live up to their advertising claims?

By Monica Smith

I asked three people <u>if they ever bought those</u> products and <u>whether they believed</u> their claims. Here are their reactions.

1 This cream will make you look ten years younger.

One woman said that <u>she'd started using anti-ageing cream a few months before</u>, but she knew that it <u>would require</u> more than a cream to keep <u>her</u> young.

2 This chocolate spread is a healthy breakfast for children.

A mother said that <u>her children loved</u> chocolate spread. She said that <u>she had hidden the jar away</u> because it <u>was</u> full of sugar and fat. She asked me <u>when they were going to invent</u> healthy chocolate!

3 You can avoid colds and flu if you use our mouthwash every day.

One man I spoke to was a doctor. He told me that it <u>was impossible</u> for a mouthwash to prevent illness. He told me <u>not to believe</u> everything I read in adverts.

---

1 Questions: <u>Do</u> you ever buy _____ products?
_____ you believe their claims?

2 Woman: I _____ using anti-ageing cream
a few months _____ , but I know that it _____
require more than a cream to keep _____ young.

3 Mother: _____ children _____ chocolate
spread. I _____ hidden it away because it _____
full of sugar and fat. When _____ they going to
invent healthy chocolate?

4 Doctor: It _____ impossible for a mouthwash to
prevent illness. _____ believe everything you
read in adverts.

2 Rewrite the direct speech as reported speech.

I'll meet you at half past two tomorrow.
I remember she said *she would meet me at half past two the next day.*

1 The manager will be here tomorrow if you could
come back then.
The assistant said _____
_____ .

2 The advertising executives are arriving tonight.
It was last Thursday morning that she said _____
_____ .

3 I saw the new advert on TV for the first time today.
He told us _____
_____ .

4 They are going to open the new branch of their
coffee shop next week.
Three weeks ago, the staff member told me _____
_____ .

5 I'm sorry, but your doctor's appointment for today
has been cancelled.
The receptionist called me and told me that _____
_____ .

6 I can't promise anything right now.
She said _____
_____ .

3 Report the questions and imperatives.

Did you buy the product because you saw the advert?
They asked me if *I had bought the product because I had seen the advert.*

1 Taste the drink and then describe the flavour.
She asked me _____
_____ .

2 Would you like to try our service for free for a month?
He asked me _____
_____ .

3 Contact us and let us know what you think.
They told me _____
_____ .

4 Have you ever thought of trying a different brand of
lipstick?
They asked me _____
_____ .

5 Don't forget to take one pill before breakfast and the
other one before bed.
The pharmacist told me _____
_____ .

6 Who is going to pay for the damage to my computer?
She asked _____
_____ .

4 Complete the reported statements, questions and imperatives.

'Our bus left two hours ago,' they told us.
They told us *(that) their bus had left two hours earlier/before* .

1 'Are you from this part of town?' the stranger asked
Greg.
The stranger asked Greg _____
_____ .

2 'Do you like going to the cinema?' asked Pauline.
Pauline asked me _____
_____ .

3 'Please don't play in the kitchen,' Barbara told the
children.
Barbara told the children _____
_____ .

4 'You need to get the assignment back to me by 4 p.m.
tomorrow,' said Mr Roberts.
Mr Roberts said _____
_____ .

5 'Pick me up some of my special toothpaste from the
chemist's,' asked Sylvia.
Sylvia asked me _____
_____ .

6 'I have never bought anything because of an
advertisement,' said Patrick.
Patrick said _____
_____ .

7 'Is your sister going to visit us this weekend?', asked
Vanessa.
Vanessa asked _____
_____ .

8 'Will you be so kind as to show me this photo?',
asked Mrs Brown.
Mrs Brown asked _____
_____ .

FOCUS 3 GRAMMAR REVIEW

Passive forms; *have something done*

The Passive

- We use the Passive when we are more interested in the action itself than the person (the agent) performing it:

  *The presidential election **will be held** in July.*

- If we want to say who performed the action, we use the word *by*:

  *The telephone **was invented** in 1876 **by** Alexander Graham Bell.*

- We form the Passive with an appropriate form of the verb **to be** and the **past participle** of the main verb.

Present Simple → *Coffee **is grown** and **exported** by over fifty developing countries.*

Present Continuous → *The report **is** still **being examined**.*

Past Simple → *When **was** the Willis Tower **built**?*

Past Continuous → *At 11 p.m. the suspect **was** still **being questioned**.*

Present Perfect → *A new community centre **has** just **been opened** in my town.*

Past Perfect → *I found out that my application **hadn't been accepted**.*

will → *Over 1,000 companies **will be affected** by the new regulations.*

be going to → *You're **going to be informed** about the results by email.*

have something done

We use **have** + **object** + **past participle** to talk about actions that someone else (typically an expert or a contractor) does at our request.

Compare the two sentences:

*After the burglary the Jacksons **changed** their locks. (They did it themselves.)*

*After the burglary the Jacksons **had** their locks **changed**. (They hired a locksmith to do it.)*

Present Simple → *We **have** the office **cleaned** twice a week.*

Present Continuous → *Why **are** you **having** your windows **replaced**?*

Past Simple → *We **had** all the installations **checked**.*

Past Continuous → *Last year in June, my neighbours **were having** their house **painted**.*

Present Perfect → ***Have** you ever **had** your nails **done**?*

will → *When **will** you **have** your tyres **changed**?*

be going to → *I'm **going to have** a burglar alarm **installed**.*

We can usually replace the verb **have** with the verb **get**:

*We **had** the documents **translated**. = We **got** the documents **translated**.*

---

1 **Complete the passive sentences. Use *by* + agent if necessary.**

> They have never searched me at the airport.
> I *have never been searched* at the airport.

1 Nobody will ask for my opinion, anyway.
   I _____ for my opinion, anyway.

2 After his first English lesson, his teacher told him that he spoke with an American accent.
   After his first English lesson, he _____ that he spoke with an American accent.

3 Today in the café, they added milk to my cup of tea.
   Today in the café, milk _____ to my cup of tea.

4 My parents sent me to the USA for the summer to learn English.
   I _____ for the summer to learn English.

5 My American friend is meeting me at the airport in New York.
   I _____ at the airport in New York.

6 People will always remember me as the only American in my school.
   I _____ as the only American in my school.

7 When they were painting the walls, they found this hole.
   This hole _____ when the walls _____ .

8 They are going to post our letters soon.
   Our letters _____ soon.

2 **Read some trivia facts about the USA and the UK. Rewrite the sentences in the Passive, using *by* only if it is necessary.**

> Most people think that Christopher Columbus discovered America.
> *Most people think that America was discovered by Christopher Columbus* .

1 Every year in the USA, judges send around 60,000 teenagers to prison. _____
   _____

2 In 1811 in Britain, parents named nearly a quarter of all girls Mary. _____
   _____

3 People in the UK drink more tea than in any other country. _____
   _____

4 French people built the Statue of Liberty in France.
   _____
   _____

3 Complete the sentences with the correct passive forms of the words in brackets.

Will he be invited (he/invite) to their wedding? I don't think he will.

1 My purse _____ (just/steal)!
2 The new shopping centre _____ (not/build) until 2022.
3 I was in the office when the windows _____ _____ (clean).
4 I'm afraid your computer _____ _____(not/repair) yet.
5 Whose documents _____ (print) at the moment?
6 When _____ (they/tell) that they were going to be fired?
7 New magazines _____ (order) every month.
8 Who _____ (this film/direct) by? Did James Cameron direct it?

4 Rewrite the sentences and questions using the correct form of *have something done.*

The millionaire built a ski-lift in his back garden.
The millionaire *had a ski-lift built* in his back garden.

1 Have you fixed your phone yet, Peter?
Have you _____ , Peter?
2 George doesn't cut his hair very often.
George _____ very often.
3 Lena didn't whiten her teeth because it was too expensive.
Lena _____ because it was too expensive.
4 Gina paints her toenails with the American flag every Thanksgiving.
Gina _____ with the American flag every Thanksgiving.
5 Liam is removing the tattoo next week.
Liam _____ next week.
6 Aneta cut her hair extremely short last summer.
Aneta _____ extremely short last summer.

5 Write questions from the prompts. Use the structure *have something done.*

Have you ever / repair / a bicycle?
Have you ever had a bicycle repaired?

1 When did you last / test / your eyes?
_____
2 Will you ever / colour / your hair?
_____
3 Are you going to / redecorate / your bedroom?
_____
4 Have you / pierce / your ears?
_____
5 When did you last / take / a passport photo?
_____

Articles

Indefinite article *(a/an)*

We use *a/an* with singular countable nouns:

- when we mention something for the first time:
  *There is **a** piano in the school hall.*
- when we refer to one of many things:
  *I need **a** new laptop.*
- when we talk about someone's job:
  *Brad is **an** actor.*
- in expressions with the verb *have* (e.g. *have a chat / a walk / a sleep / a talk / a think*):
  *Let's have **a** look around.*
- in expressions about time, frequency, speed and price per amount:
  *twice **a** year*
  *100 miles **an** hour*
  *£1.50 **a** kilo*

Definite article *(the)*

We use *the* with singular and plural nouns and uncountable nouns:

- to refer to something that we have mentioned before:
  *There is a piano in the school hall. **The** piano is very old.*
- to refer to something that both the speaker and the listener know:
  *Let's go to **the** restaurant we went to last week.*
- to refer to something unique or one of a kind:
  ***The** sun sets at 7 p.m.*
  *Who is **the** music director of La Scala?*
- with theatre, cinema and radio:
  *I love going to **the** theatre.*
  *I heard it on **the** radio today.*
- with *morning, afternoon, evening* (but not *noon*):
  *Let's watch a DVD in **the** evening.*
- with musical instruments, when referring to someone playing them:
  *Jane plays **the** flute and **the** trumpet.*
- with the superlative form of adjectives:
  ***the** most famous*
- with ordinal numbers:
  ***the** third*
- with certain names of countries (if the name is in plural form or includes a common noun):
  ***the** Netherlands*
  ***the** United States*
  ***the** United Kingdom*
  ***the** Czech Republic*

169

- with mountain ranges, rivers, seas, oceans, archipelagos and deserts:
  - *the* Himalayas
  - *the* Thames
  - *the* Red Sea
  - *the* Bahamas
  - *the* Sahara

Zero article

We do not use an article:

- with uncountable nouns or plural countable nouns when we are talking about something in general:
  - *Music* is very important in my life.
  - Pete loves *ice cream*.
  - *Pop stars* are often demanding and self-centred.
- with meals:
  - Let's have *dinner*.
- with the names of continents, most countries, cities (exception: *the Hague*), lakes, islands and mountains:
  - Europe
  - Great Britain
  - Manchester
  - Lake Superior
  - Easter Island
  - Mount Everest

1 Correct the mistakes. There is one mistake in each sentence.

Would you like to buy a programme for ~~festival~~?
the festival

1 My favourite place in the city is the park. It's a place where I met my girlfriend.
_____

2 I dream of becoming the famous actor one day.
_____

3 For a lunch today we are having lasagne and green salad.
_____

4 I don't have enough change to pay the parking fee. Do you have the pound coin?
_____

5 Swimming pool in our town is old and scary.
_____

6 Is this only music you've got on your phone? Don't you have anything else?
_____

2 Complete the text with *a/an*, *the* or Ø (no article).

PRE-SHOW RITUALS

In theatres all over Ø London, artists are getting ready to perform. Most of them are too nervous to have ¹ _____ dinner before the show, so how do they spend the few hours before the show begins? Here, three performers talk about their pre-show rituals.

TINIE TEMPAH is ² _____ singer.
He prepares for a gig in the same way ³ _____ athlete gets ready for ⁴ _____ big event. About an hour before the gig, he does a lot of stretching. Sometimes he has ⁵ _____ massage.

STEPHEN MANGAN is ⁶ _____ actor.
After six months of doing the same show eight times ⁷ _____ week, ⁸ _____ biggest challenge is getting himself into exactly the same mental state every night. He comes to ⁹ _____ theatre, and sometimes he doesn't want to be there. But the fact that people are waiting to see him is ¹⁰ _____ great motivating factor.

SARA PASCOE is a comedian.
She always gets nervous before a gig. She looks at ¹¹ _____ script, and tries not to think about the things that could go horribly wrong. She tells herself ¹² _____ positive things.

3 Complete the sentences with *a/an*, *the* or Ø (no article).

I'm going to *the* cinema tomorrow. Would you like to come?

1 Did you know that ___ smallest town in Britain is Llanwrtyd Wells?
2 I just saw ___ cat with really short, silvery fur. Is that what they call a Russian Blue?
3 What time do you want to have ___ lunch?
4 I've decided I'm going to have ___ haircut. I'm tired of having long hair.
5 Isn't he ___ actor that's in that new soap opera?
6 Did you know that ___ capital of ___ Syria is Damascus?
7 It's ___ third time you have been late this week.

1.2 Present and past habits
1.5 Verb patterns

1 Complete the second sentence so that it has a similar meaning to the first. Use the words in capitals.

1 When she was a child, they would take her to the local park every Sunday afternoon. **USED**
   When she was a child, _____ .

2 Sophie never allowed her children to stay up late during the week. **WOULD**
   Sophie _____ .

3 Did you enjoy going to school when you were younger? **USE**
   Did you _____ ?

4 Thanks to the new computer lab, we can take part in IT competitions for schools. **ENABLES**
   The new computer lab _____ .

5 Jenny has an irritating habit of chewing gum in class. **ALWAYS**
   Jenny _____ .

6 Remind me to call the vet. **FORGET**
   Don't let _____ .

7 Why can't you make him tell the truth? **FORCE**
   Why can't you _____ ?

8 'You should start a new hobby, Ms Dodgson,' the doctor said. **ADVISED**
   The doctor _____ .

Summative Practice   Unit 1

2 Complete the text with the correct form of the verbs in brackets.

A lazy wolf lived in a jungle. There was a small lake near his house where other animals ¹_____ (come) to drink fresh water. The wolf ²_____ (always/sit) nearby, hoping ³_____ (get) fresh food easily. This really annoyed the animals but there was no other pond. One day, the wolf found a dead bull. 'What good luck!' he thought. While he ⁴_____ (eat) the bull, he ⁵_____ (realise) that another animal might pass by. The wolf fancied ⁶_____ (eat) the bull all by himself and because he refused ⁷_____ (share) his meal, he began ⁸_____ (chew) on the meat more quickly.

Because he ⁹_____ (eat) so fast he didn't notice a small bone. This got stuck deep in his throat and was really painful. 'Ooooh, this hurts! What now?' thought the wolf. Luckily, he remembered that a crane lived nearby and so he ¹⁰_____ (find) the crane and begged him to remove the bone. 'I ¹¹_____ (give) you a present if you help me,' he promised.

The crane was a friendly creature and told the wolf ¹²_____ (open) his jaws wide. The crane reached into the wolf's mouth and with its long beak managed ¹³_____ (pull) the bone free. The wolf was relieved but when the crane asked for his present he responded: 'I don't remember ¹⁴_____ (promise) anything.'

'You said that if I removed the bone, you ¹⁵_____ (give) me a present,' said the crane with obvious disappointment.

The wolf, who ¹⁶_____ (already/begin) walking away, stopped ¹⁷_____ (say): 'You put your head into my mouth and are still alive. Is that not a present?'

The crane at that moment decided ¹⁸_____ (not help) any other creatures in the future.

3 Find the mistakes and correct the sentences. There may be more than one mistake in a sentence.

1 When Joe was in college, he was used to study hard.
   _____

2 Last year, he used to study very hard.
   _____

3 We can't afford buy a new car right now.
   _____

4 During the meeting, we stopped calling Ms Thomson: we didn't want to waste time to discuss things we didn't know anything about.
   _____

5 Did she used to fall behind with her homework?
   _____

6 Kate couldn't log in because she forgot the password.
   _____

7 If your boyfriend would forget your birthday, will you make a big fuss?
   _____

8 The clock must be stopped. It's six o'clock now!
   _____

4 Read the jokes and choose the correct option.

1 **Q:** What *are you getting* / *do you get* when you cross a fish and an elephant? **A:** Swimming trunks.

2 **Q:** Why did the traffic light turn red? **A:** You *will* / *would* too if you *had to* / *have to* change in the middle of the street!

3 **Q:** Why do seagulls fly over the sea? **A:** Because if they *flow* / *flew* over the bay they *would be* / *will be* bagels!

4 **Q:** Which is the *longer* / *longest* word in *the* / *–* dictionary? 'Smiles', because there is *–* / *a* mile between each 's'!

5 **Q:** Why did Johnny have the clock *threw* / *thrown* out of the window? **A:** Because he wanted to see time *to fly* / *fly*!

5 Complete the sentences with the correct form of the words in brackets. Make any changes necessary, but do not change the order of the words.

1 We _____ (use/have/swim) at least once a day when we were at the seaside.

2 Lily gave up her job because she _____ (can't/stand/work/office).

3 Can you _____ (remember/pay/fine) today, please?

4 Why _____ (you/always/complain/food)? Next time I'd like you to make dinner.

5 I'm sure Bill _____ (not/intend/hurt/you) when he talked to you like that.

6 Do you know if Sue has finished tidying up? I _____ (see/she/clean/floor) an hour ago, and I'm not sure if she can talk to me right now.

2.2 Past Perfect Simple and Continuous
2.5 Relative clauses

1 Complete the sentences with one word in each gap.

1 At last week's party, she met people she _____ not seen for ages.
2 Paul hadn't _____ sleeping for long when he heard a terrible noise.
3 When he finally proposed to Jane, they _____ been going out for three years.
4 We were embarrassed to admit we had _____ heard that name before.
5 She lost touch with her best friend, _____ made her really sad.
6 That's the dog _____ bit the child.
7 My neighbour, _____ husband is Dutch, moved to Holland last week.

Summative Practice   Units 1–2

2 Find the mistakes and correct the sentences.

1 Before meeting Phil, that idea has never come to my mind.
   _____
2 She was trying to call John for some time when she realised she was dialling the wrong number.
   _____
3 Ally and Mark split up, what surprised everybody.
   _____
4 Would you recognise the man stopping you?
   _____
5 In August 2011, I used to live in Boston.
   _____
6 Children bringing up in large families tend to be more independent.
   _____
7 Unfortunately, Dave failed passing his driving test.
   _____

3 Choose the correct option.

Despite record rainfall, one young couple didn't let the bad weather [1]*to stop / stopping / stop* their wedding plans.

A young Chinese couple who [2]*had been planning / planned / was planning* a large ceremony with up to 300 guests were bitterly disappointed when only ten people [3]*were turning up / had turned up / turned up*. The severe weather conditions [4]*whose / that / what* made travelling so dangerous in the Xinxiang region meant that most guests [5]*were unable to / had been unable to / were not used to* attend.

The bride and groom, however, [6]*were not deciding to / had not decided to / decided not to* postpone the wedding. The bride announced on a popular social media platform that the only important thing was to have her groom present, [7]*which / that / what* made thousands of people respond.

People [8]*impressed / who impressed / impressing* with her declaration sent emotional messages citing the value of true love.

Not everybody was so positive though. Some comments [9]*had attacked / attacked / had been attacking* the many guests who failed to attend the couple's wedding. Indeed, many posts encouraged [10]*having / them having / them to have* a 'proper wedding.'

4 Complete the sentences with one word in each gap.

1 We got to the top after we'd _____ walking for hours.
2 She was really thirsty. She _____ not drunk anything since lunch.
3 This is the person _____ we got the news from.
4 Mr Dawson's letter, _____ arrived this morning, is on your desk.
5 My neighbour's children are _____ playing loud music when they're alone.
6 Did they _____ to love sleeping late at the weekend when they were students?
7 When my little sister was younger, she _____ cry every time she lost in a game.

5 Complete the second sentence so that it has a similar meaning to the first. Use the words in capitals.

1 We had to wait for over one hour before the bride finally arrived. **WAITING**
   We _____ for over one hour when the bride finally arrived.
2 I wasn't invited to the wedding reception by anybody. That's why I didn't go. **HAD**
   I didn't go to the wedding reception because nobody _____ go.
3 I have a sister who is married to a French man. **MY**
   The man _____ to is French.
4 I found it really annoying that Kate was showering James with praise. **ANNOYED**
   Kate was showering James with praise, _____ me.
5 Janet won't ever forget the first time she met Simon. **NEVER**
   Janet _____ Simon for the first time.
6 We were late for the wedding because we stopped and bought some flowers. **BUY**
   We were late for the wedding because _____ some flowers.
7 My parents complain all the time about the way I dress. **ALWAYS**
   My parents _____ the way I dress.

6 Complete the sentences with the correct form of the words in brackets. Make any changes necessary, but do not change the order of the words.

1 I came home late yesterday, and when I got back, my neighbour complained my dog _____ _____ (be/bark/hours).
2 My friend, _____ (who/mum/be/mathematician), agreed to help me.
3 _____ (you/parents/use/put) on a big birthday party for you when you were kids?
4 You are always arriving late! I _____ _____ (can't/stand/wait/you) every time!
5 George denied eating the chocolate although his sister _____ (see/he/eat/it). There was nothing left for her.
6 Look! The man _____ (play/saxophone/be) my dad.

3.2 Future forms including the Future Perfect Continuous
3.5 Quantifiers

1 Match beginnings 1–10 with endings a–j to make sentences.

1 She hopes she will have
2 This time next year, they will
3 By 8 p.m. we will have
4 Will you have
5 Should I be worried if most of my friends
6 Every house on that street
7 She said goodbye to each
8 She always says goodbye to all
9 There are a few apples left,
10 There are only few bananas left,

a student as they left the room.
b looks quite the same.
c already built her own house by the time she is forty-five.
d have girlfriends and I don't?
e of the students as they leave the room.
f finished your work by the deadline?
g have opened the shopping mall.
h been working on our school project for four hours!
i we'd better go and buy some.
j I don't think we need to buy any today.

Summative Practice   Units 1–3

2 Choose the correct option.

1 *None of the / Neither / All* parent is coming to the school meeting.
2 *All / Every / Both* student receives a certificate.
3 You can call me at work at 8 a.m. I *will have arrived / will be arriving / will arrive* at the office by 8.
4 This is the town *that / which / where* he would spend his summer holidays.
5 *I'll still be working / I'll have been working / I'll have worked* in the garden when you arrive so I may not hear the doorbell. Just let yourself in, will you?
6 How long *will they be building / will they have built / will they have been building* the sports centre by the end of year? It should be ready now!
7 My parents didn't immediately agree *let / letting / to let* me go on holiday with my friends.
8 She *was waiting / had been waiting / waited* for almost an hour when she was finally served some food.
9 By the end of June, I *will have been saving / will be saving / will have saved* for a new bike for five months.
10 Plans *making / made / which made* in a hurry may prove not to be well-thought-out.

3 Complete the text with the words and phrases in the box.

> a little   both   deal of   every   few   great deal
> had been   is   little   most   most of   much
> number of   was   where   which (2x)

Tea is consumed in ¹_____ country around the globe. But did you know that ²_____ it is drank in India?

Indian tea ³_____ initially grown only for export purposes. In fact, very ⁴_____ of it was actually consumed in India meaning that very ⁵_____ locals enjoyed the results of their hard work. Once production increased and prices became affordable, however, a large ⁶_____ Indians too began drinking the tea which they ⁷_____ producing for a long time. And like the British, they served their teas with ⁸_____ milk and sugar – not a ⁹_____ , but just enough to make the bitter liquid smoother to drink.

Over time, however, the Indians' natural inclination was to seek a brew ¹⁰_____ was inspired by their own Eastern tastes. Masala chai was created and was brewed to be ¹¹_____ stronger and milkier than the tea ¹²_____ of us are familiar with. As well as being so strong, it is also made with great amounts of sugar, ¹³_____ results in a vastly thicker consistency.

Expert masala chai makers may even add a good ¹⁴_____ ginger to the mix and then finish it off with crushed cardamoms, cinnamon or even chilli pepper for extra spice. There are now plenty of places over the whole of India ¹⁵_____ this tasty brew ¹⁶_____ served. Indeed, Indians and tourists ¹⁷_____ enjoy this increasingly popular sweet and spicy tea.

4 Complete the sentences with the correct form of the words in brackets. Make any changes necessary, but do not change the order of the words.

1 _____ (you/go) to the shop later today? Can you buy some milk, please?
2 After they had finished playing, Jenny _____ _____ (encourage/she/niece/put) all her toys in the box.
3 By the time they leave for Mars, she _____ _____ (train/ten/year).
4 _____ (none/we/move) out from our parents' homes by then.
5 I don't know if we _____ _____ (finish/whole/book) by next Friday.
6 _____ (several/people/live/our neighbourhood) are planning to sell their houses.
7 They _____ (wait/door) for half an hour but the shop had not yet opened.
8 Most students are going home for Christmas, so this time next week only very _____ _____ (few/we/stay) on campus.
9 _____ (there/be/number/thing) you need to consider before choosing a college.
10 Her weird behaviour has been attracting _____ _____ (great/deal/attention) recently.

173

4.2 Question tags and reply questions
4.5 Present and past modal structures

1 Choose the correct option.

1 When the party was over, she realised she *didn't need to cook / didn't have to cook / needn't have cooked* so much food as most of it was untouched.

2 No one saw him, *did he / did they / didn't they*?

3 It's never too late, *isn't it / has it / is it*?

4 It was his day off yesterday. That's why he *didn't need to get up / shouldn't get up / needn't have got up* early.

5 You *needn't have called / had better not call / didn't have to call* him after 10 p.m. He'll have gone to bed.

6 A: My parents never let me go to concerts.
B: *Don't they / Do they / Did they*? What a shame!

7 There's no homework for tomorrow, *is there / has there / isn't there*?

8 My sister *ought to / had better / had to* go to bed early because she had an exam the next day.

Summative Practice   Units 1–4

2 Find the mistakes and correct the sentences.

1 You had not better spend so much on sweets.
_____

2 We must go to the doctor's last night because my sister had a terrible rash.
_____

3 There were lots of people in front of the theatre last night, weren't they?
_____

4 Do you have others types of sandwiches?
_____

5 There's only few furniture in the house.
_____

6 By then they'll be shopping for five hours.
_____

7 This is an online course which teaching you how to play chess.
_____

8 Can you imagine to spend the whole afternoon with him?
_____

3 Match the beginnings 1–7 with the endings a–g.

1 I find it very annoying that ☐
2 She can't stand ☐
3 I liked the lecture, ☐
4 She will have ☐
5 Apart from golf, he has very few ☐
6 Everyone will be asked to say something, ☐
7 I think you shouldn't ☐

a hobbies and interests.
b have said anything to Sally.
c wearing a school uniform.
d won't they?
e been studying Japanese for three years at the end of August.
f he's always telling the same joke.
g which I found useful and really thought-provoking.

4 Choose the correct option.

1 He *would / used to* love doing all kinds of sports when he was younger. He doesn't seem *to do / doing* any exercise now.

2 A: Which pair of jeans did you buy, the black one or the blue one?
B: *Both. / All.* Luckily, *either / neither* of them was expensive.

3 There's *none of / no* excuse for being dishonest, is *there / it*?

4 We decided to go to the same restaurant that John *had been to it / had been to*.

5 Mum, *will you be using / will you have used* your laptop this evening? I have online homework to do.

6 A: She ate *all / the whole* cake.
B: *Didn't / Did* she? It was huge!

7 You have hardly ever talked to him, *have you / haven't you*?

8 She had forgotten *buying / to buy* the envelope for the letter she had to send.

5 Complete the sentences with one word in each gap.

1 When Josh joined the team he had _____ working on the project for some time, _____ meant he didn't _____ to waste time being trained.

2 Before accepting that position I was rather worried as it meant _____ of responsibility and hard work. But soon after I _____ begun working with _____ others I realised I needn't _____ worried too much.

3 They were looking _____ to leaving for California. That was the journey they _____ been planning for ages.

4 He _____ given up going out with friends for some time, _____ made his parents worry.

5 When travelling abroad they _____ always complaining about food.

6 Why do you keep _____ him that question? You ought _____ know he's not the right person to answer it.

6 Complete the sentences with the correct form of the words in brackets. Make any changes necessary, but do not change the order of the words.

1 Are you looking for your son? _____ (that/be/he) over there, isn't it?

2 I _____ (not/use/ like/get) up early to go to school when I was a kid.

3 He had forgotten the title of the song, but he _____ (can remember/hear) it before.

4 Thank you for this beautiful vase, but you _____ _____ (need/not/spend) so much.

5 You've got a cold, haven't you? You _____ _____ (better/not/go out) today at all.

6 I think that by 10 o'clock they _____ _____ (already/leave) for the seaside.

5.2 Reported speech
5.5 Reporting verbs

1 Complete the second sentence so that it means the same as the first.

1 'My dad travels on business so often that our dog hardly recognises him,' says Greg.
Greg says _____ .

2 'I didn't break the glass. Gill did it!' said Michael.
Michael denied _____
and accused Gill _____ .

3 'Why didn't you tell me that you had been fired?'
Sam asked Lucy.
Sam asked Lucy why _____ .

4 'Are you happy with the final score?' my mother wanted to know.
My mother wanted to know _____ .

5 'You shouldn't say anything to Jane!' Bob suggested.
Bob suggested _____ .

6 'You mustn't be late,' my dad warned me.
My dad warned _____ .

7 'We're leaving early tomorrow,' he insisted.
He insisted _____ .

8 'We might be late for dinner tonight,' they said.
They informed me _____ .

9 'Did you go to the interview last week?'
Tracy asked Sonia.
Tracy asked Sonia _____ .

10 'Could I borrow your mobile, Bill?' asked Sue.
Sue asked Bill _____ .

Summative Practice   Units 1–5

2 Complete the text with one word in each gap.

Dog helps boy lost in mountains stay alive

A 14-year-old boy [1]_____ got lost in the Sierra Madre Oriental mountain range spent nearly two days surviving in the wilderness before rescuers [2]_____ to locate him. Fortunately for Juan, a Labrador Retriever by the name of Max, a wandering dog he [3]_____ only met a short time before, refused [4]_____ leave him alone during his traumatic ordeal.

Juan Heriberto Trevino, from Galeana, Mexico, had become separated from his summer camp group [5]_____ he went in search of firewood. Although he had assured the camp leaders [6]_____ he would be careful, he accidentally slipped and fell down the mountainside.

After recovering from his fall, it took Juan only a [7]_____ time to realise that his new friend Max had followed him down into the ravine. As night time fell, the boy took cover under a tree and cuddled the dog to stay warm. Although he admitted [8]_____ pretty frightened at the time, the presence of the dog also convinced [9]_____ that he would eventually be safe.

When the pair was eventually located by a search party forty-four hours later, the authorities claimed the role of the dog had [10]_____ vital in helping the boy survive the cold night temperatures.

3 Choose the correct option.

My first (and only ever!) job interview was about six months ago. It was only for part-time work in a local music store but I remember [1]*to spend / spend / spending* hours getting ready for it. Obviously I was a little nervous as I [2]*was hoping / had been hoping / had hoped* to get the job. I'm a bit of an amateur photographer and I [3]*saved up / had saved up / was saving up* for a new camera at the time. There was a school photography competition that term, [4]*what / that / which* I was really keen to take part in and show my talents off.

Anyway, my parents [5]*advised / convinced / recommended* me not to dress up too smartly, but I believed that I knew better. I sometimes think I [6]*should have listened / didn't need to listen / must have listened* to them because I felt a little over-dressed when I arrived. And when the manager came out wearing jeans and a T-shirt, I nearly died. I explained to him that I [7]*didn't expect / hadn't been expecting / wasn't expecting* an informal meeting. Fortunately, he was really cool and he [8]*criticised / congratulated / praised* me for making an effort.

This time next week, I [9]*will work / will have been working / will be working* there for half a year. Oh, and I bought my camera and came first in the school competition – so everything [10]*was working out / had worked out / worked out* really well in the end.

4 Find the mistakes and correct the sentences. There may be more than one mistake in a sentence.

1 He told him that he was ill and that was why he can't come to work the following day.
_____

2 The clerk asked what was her email address.
_____

3 He used to travelling a lot when he was younger. He doesn't seem do that now.
_____

4 You ought not have taken up this post.
_____

5 We decided to go to the same restaurant that John had been to it.
_____

5 Complete the second sentence so that it has a similar meaning to the first. Use the words in capitals.

1 Martin's parents said they wouldn't pay for his studies. **REFUSED**
Martin's parents _____ .

2 His two flatmates didn't blame him for losing the keys. **NEITHER**
_____ for losing the keys.

3 Sooner or later everybody argues with the boss, isn't that right? **THEY**
Sooner or later everybody argues with the boss, _____ ?

4 Her contract expires in June. **BY**
Her contract _____ June.

5 I've seen him several times, but I can't remember his name. **NUMBER**
I've seen him _____ , but I can't remember his name.

6.2 Conditional clauses – alternatives to *if*
6.5 Mixed conditionals

1 Choose the correct option.

1 If she *didn't have / doesn't have / won't have* so much to do, she would have gone to the beach with her friends.

2 He *won't come / hadn't come / wouldn't have come* by bus if he could drive.

3 We *might go / might have gone / would go* for a walk yesterday if it hadn't been raining.

4 If I *would be / were / am* in her shoes, I wouldn't have resigned from this job.

5 *Imagine / Unless / Providing* you were going to dinner with your favourite actor, how would you feel?

6 If you had gone to bed earlier, you *weren't / would be / wouldn't be* so exhausted today.

7 He *won't still be / wouldn't still be / weren't still be* jobless if he'd answered that ad.

8 If *you remembered / you'd have remembered / you'd remembered* to bring a map, we wouldn't be lost now.

9 *Unless / If / When* Tom fails the test again, he will get his driving licence next month.

10 *Should she let me know / Would she have let me know / Had she let me know*, I would have met her at the station.

Summative Practice — Units 1–6

2 Complete the text with one word in each gap.

How two apples explained the effects of bullying

When one teacher decided to tackle bullying in her school, very ¹_____ people would have imagined that she could present the physical and emotional damage it causes via a couple ²_____ mouth-watering apples.

Rosie Dutton, from Tamworth, brought the juicy red apples into the classroom and the children quickly agreed ³_____ they would be delicious to eat. What Rosie failed to tell them at this point, however, was that she ⁴_____ dropped one of the apples on the floor and it was badly bruised.

When the teacher held the dropped apple up for all to see and described it as disgusting and nasty the children were confused. She then encouraged ⁵_____ to pass the apple around the class and to abuse it, ⁶_____ the majority of children began to do: Aren't you ugly? You taste horrible, ⁷_____ you? One girl, however, objected to ⁸_____ unkind things like her classmates.

Rosie then passed ⁹_____ other apple around and the children in the class this time ¹⁰_____ urged to show kindness and say compassionate things to the apple. Rosie then held up ¹¹_____ of the apples and recalled the positive and negative things the children had said. But both apples looked alike.

What Rosie did then was intended ¹²_____ bring about a sharp moment of realisation to the class of young pupils. She cut the apples open.

Rosie drew the children's attention to how the abused apple was all damaged inside. She explained: people ¹³_____ are bullied feel terrible but we often don't see the damage. We wouldn't know how much pain we have caused the apple ¹⁴_____ we looked on the inside.

3 Choose the correct option.

Coffee is good – but how good?

¹*Unless / Suppose / Provided* you woke up in the morning to discover you were out of coffee. Would you immediately run to the shops?

Many people claim that coffee is the only thing ²*who / – / that* gets their bodies working and their minds functioning every morning. For ³*another / the other / others* it's a loyal friend essential in helping to make it through the day.

Fortunately, for those of us that can't get enough of this bitter-tasting bean, it has ⁴*many / few / plenty* beneficial effects on our health too. Back in 2006, for example, one research project ⁵*assured / suggested / urged* that drinking just one cup of coffee a day could prevent a certain liver disease.

A later study revealed that people who drank between three and five cups of coffee a day greatly reduced the chances ⁶*to / - / of* developing Alzheimer's or dementia. Furthermore, neurological studies ⁷*insist / convince / warn* that drinking coffee can also prevent depression.

If you prefer ⁸*to not drink / drinking / not to drink* coffee, however, don't worry. Because, in fact, you ⁹*shouldn't / don't have to / mustn't* even drink it to feel the effects. Scientists now believe that the smell of the hot drink itself has positive influence on brain activity.

So, ¹⁰*unless / providing / imagine* you don't need to go to sleep anytime soon, I'd recommend grabbing a coffee right now!

4 Complete the second sentence so that it has a similar meaning to the first. Use the words in capitals.

1 Mark hung around the park all afternoon, so he has to do his homework now. **WOULD**
   If Mark hadn't hung around the park all afternoon,
   _____
   _____ .

2 They'll come with us, but you have to invite them yourself. **PROVIDED**
   They'll come with us _____
   _____ .

3 Stephen is very shy and that's probably why he didn't win the school talent show. **MIGHT**
   If Stephen weren't so shy, _____
   _____
   the school talent show.

4 Most of my friends were on holiday so it was silly of me to invite them to my party. **NEEDN'T**
   Most of my friends were on holiday so I _____
   _____ to my party.

5 The band is just starting to play and it will take us another half an hour to get to the concert hall! **HAVE**
   By the time we get to the concert hall, the band
   _____
   half an hour!

7.2 Advanced passive forms
7.5 Passive reporting structures

1 Rewrite the sentences in the Passive.

1 The teacher made us switch off our mobiles.
_____

2 Nobody can solve that problem.
_____

3 Have they sent the letter to Ms Johnson?
_____

4 They will have given her the news by now.
_____

5 The police must have already caught the robber.
_____

6 People say that prices have risen dramatically.
_____

7 I hate people asking my age.
_____

8 She wanted them to invite her to the party.
_____

9 People expect the chairman to resign next week.
_____

10 Experts are suggesting that the situation won't improve.
_____

Summative Practice   Units 1–7

2 Choose the correct option.

Solo Yachtswoman missing

Air-sea rescuers, who [1]*had been searching / were searching / have been searching* for missing yachtswoman Mary Unwin, have finally managed [2]*to have found / to find / to be found* the remains of a boat off the coast of Cornwall.

The wreckage, which is thought [3]*of being / to be / it was* Mary's yacht, [4]*was found / is found / found* close to Sennen Cove.

Coastguards [5]*admitted / informed / assured* that they were amazed to discover that the highly experienced yachtswoman [6]*had decided / had been deciding / was deciding* to launch in what [7]*was describing / was being described / had been described* as 'treacherous' weather.

The police agree that Unwin [8]*needn't have / shouldn't have / didn't have to* set sail in such dangerous conditions. Indeed, the alarm [9]*raised / was raised / has been raised* barely twenty-six hours after Unwin's vessel [10]*left / was left / was leaving* port.

Mary Unwin, [11]*who / — / that* was sailing solo on a 200 km trip along the Atlantic coast, is still to be found. Official reports state that investigations [12]*are carried on / are being carried on / were carried on* and coastguards are [13]*warning / insisting / suggesting* sailors to be more responsible.

The harsh reality is that if Unwin [14]*didn't launch / hadn't launched / wouldn't launch* in such dangerous weather, she [15]*couldn't be / won't be / wouldn't be* missing now. In fact, coastguards advise anyone who [16]*will have sailed / will have been sailing / will be sailing* in the next few days to consider delaying their departure.

3 Find the mistakes and correct the sentences.

1 They were questioning by the police last week.
_____

2 The opportunity should not have been given them.
_____

3 The Prime Minister has thought to be planning a trip to the flooded area.
_____

4 If I wouldn't have taken the pill, I would still be sick.
_____

5 How long had they been marrying when they bought a new house?
_____

4 Complete the text using the words in brackets. Add any other words as necessary.

If you [1]_____ (fancy/lose) a little weight, but are like me and [2]_____ (not/stand/tell) by weight loss experts to change your diet, what are you going to do? Well, inventors from Thailand [3]_____ (claim/come up) with just the thing you and I need.

The AbsorbPlate, which [4]_____ (invent) by an advertising agency in collaboration with the Thai government, [5]_____ (promise/remove) excessive grease from food – while you eat!

The people behind the unique plate [6]_____ (insist/meals/can/reduce) by up to 30 calories simply by serving them on the AbsorbPlate. And while the inventors admit it won't remove all of the fat from your meal, they do boast that some of it at least [7]_____ (remove) by the time you finish eating.

How does it work? Quite simply, in fact. The plate has holes that collect fat from the food which is [8]_____ (eat). It has been compared to the way in which a sponge works.

Unfortunately, this unique product [9]_____ (not/expect/enter) the market any time soon. For now, its makers [10]_____ (urge/we/limit) our fat intake in more traditional ways.

5 Complete the second sentence so that it has a similar meaning to the first. Use the words in capitals.

1 They report that there have been many car accidents caused by sat-nav errors recently. **REPORTED**
There _____ many car accidents caused by sat-nav errors recently.

2 I'm very lazy, so I didn't prepare a good presentation. **BETTER**
If I weren't so lazy, I _____ .

3 You won't be allowed to take part in the meeting if you don't learn to respect the rules. **UNLESS**
You won't be allowed to take part in the meeting _____ .

4 Donald was sorry he had left that early. **LEAVING**
Donald _____ that early.

5 'Have you ever taken part in a job interview before this?' they asked me. **IF**
I was asked _____ in a job interview before that.

6 It was a bad decision not to tell your friends. **SHOULD**
You _____ .

8.2 Unreal past and regrets
8.5 Emphasis – cleft sentences and inversion

1 Complete the second sentence so that it means the same as the first.

1 My brother wanted success.
What my brother _____ .

2 I don't want you to keep annoying her.
I'd rather you _____ .

3 We've never seen such careless work.
Never _____ .

4 He never seemed to realise how important the discussion was.
At no time _____ .

5 This must not leak out to the press.
Under no circumstances _____ .

6 She only wants to know your time of arrival.
All she _____ .

7 I shouldn't have gone on that trip with them.
I wish _____ .

8 Julia is sad because she forgot to invite Richard to her birthday party.
If only Julia _____ .

9 It's a pity that camera is so expensive.
I wish _____ .

Summative Practice   Units 1–8

2 Complete the sentences with the words in the box.

> accepting   all   does   didn't   hadn't   should
> to accept   whole   would

1 _____ I be late, start without me.
2 Rarely _____ it rain so much in one day.
3 Can we afford not _____ their offer?
4 I can't imagine _____ his invitation.
5 He said he _____ finish the report on time.
6 Peter did an amazing job on that project, _____ he?
7 If only we _____ missed the performance.
8 I spent the _____ evening lying on the sofa and calling _____ my friends.

3 Complete the second sentence so that it has a similar meaning to the first. Use the words in capitals.

1 I advise you to take your cat to a vet. **BETTER**
You _____ .

2 I'm sure somebody stole my keys. **MUST**
My keys _____ .

3 The President is opening the new hospital tomorrow afternoon. **OPENED**
The new hospital _____ .

4 What a shame. There is no coffee left! **WISH**
I _____ .

5 Get out immediately, or I will call the police. **UNLESS**
I'll call _____ .

6 People think that Harry did it on purpose. **THOUGHT**
Harry is _____ .

4 Choose the correct option.

Small changes make a difference

Below are a number of small changes you [1]*should / ought / better* make in order to be more environmentally friendly.

We all want to contribute to saving the planet on [2]*that / where / which* we live, but this can often appear like too much hard work. Furthermore, one person's efforts [3]*are often thought / often think / don't often think* not to be important. It's exactly [4]*that kind of / those kinds of / kind of these* comments, I would argue, that prevent us from making a bigger positive impact. So, what can we do?

Recycling food waste

You [5]*don't have to / can't / shouldn't* live in the countryside to make compost. Composting, which means [6]*to recycle / recycling / recycle* food waste back into the ecosystem, is possible even if you don't have [7]*little / much / few* space in your garden.

Eco-friendly packaging

If you must buy products in packaging, [8]*you check / you'll check / check* the label and opt for those [9]*made / who were made / which made* from recyclable resources.

Take your own shopping bag

The Great Pacific Garbage Patch, also [10]*knows / is known / known* as the Pacific Trash Vortex, is a major threat to [11]*a / – / the* sea life. If more people had gone shopping with a reusable bag, we [12]*wouldn't be / couldn't have been / won't be* responsible for creating the world's largest floating rubbish dump.

5 Complete the sentences with the correct form of the words in brackets. Make any changes necessary, but do not change the order of the words.

1 _____
(never/before/they/realise) the problem was so serious.

2 It's high time _____
(something/be/do) for the environment in this area too.

3 The tornado _____
(be/say/cause) much damage in the last few hours.

4 He _____
(never/be/give) the answer he has been waiting years for.

5 He wouldn't be able to play basketball so well if he
_____
(not/start/when/he/be) still a schoolboy.

6 After what we had done, he _____
_____ (threaten/never/talk) to us again.

7 We _____
(not/need/tell/he) because John had already done it before.

8 _____
(All/we/need/be/healthy/be) a clean environment.

Accepting suggestions

That sounds fantastic!

I'd love to (go).

Well, it's worth a try.

I suppose it'll work.

Agreeing with opinions

I (completely) agree that/with …

I couldn't agree more that/with …

That's fine with me.

I think so too.

I agree it is true that …

I am of the same/a similar opinion because …

He's absolutely right.

He has a point.

Apologising

Informal phrases

I'm really sorry (that) …

Sorry for bothering you.

Sorry to bother you.

Sorry for any trouble.

Sorry I didn't write earlier, but I …

Sorry I haven't written for so long. / Sorry for not writing for so long.

I'm writing to tell you how sorry I am to … (about) …

It will never happen again.

Neutral phrases

I apologise for …

Please accept my apology …

Article

Introduction

Did you know that …?

Have you ever wondered why/how …?

What would you do if …?

Introducing opinions

It seems/appears that …

It would seem/appear that …

It is believed/recognised that …

There is little/no doubt that …

There is some doubt …

People often believe that …

Some people say that …

Cause and result

In such countries, financial difficulties are common, so people have fewer children.

People spend most of their time online today. As a result/Consequently, many people are losing the ability to tell fantasy from reality.

Before the era of antibiotics, more soldiers died due to/because of disease than were killed in action.

Introducing opposing opinion

On the one hand, the park is extremely popular with elderly people, but on the other (hand), they are not the ones who buy tickets.

Some people feel it is wrong for advertising to be aimed specifically at children, while/whereas others do not share this view.

Mark was not an exceptionally talented man nevertheless/nonetheless he applied for the job and, to everyone's surprise, was offered the post in the IT department.

However, many people say that action should be taken straight away.

Even though/Although many residents support the mayor and his policy, he also has many enemies.

In spite of/Despite winning in the local election, his real ambition was to work for one of the EU institutions.

But all this may be about to change.

Ending

What will the future of … be?

What are (Mark's) plans?

Let's hope (they succeed).

Hopefully, …

For those reasons, I am with those who think …

Perhaps in the future …

WRITING BANK

Closing formulas: emails and letters

Informal phrases

Bye for now / See you!

Love, / Take care! / All the best,

Neutral phrases

Best wishes,

Regards,

Formal phrases

(Dear Mr/Mrs/Miss/Ms Brennon)
    Yours sincerely,

(Dear Sir or Madam / Editor)
    Yours faithfully,

Complaining

Describing problems

I wish to express my strong dissatisfaction with …

I am writing to complain about …

I'm afraid I have to make a complaint.

I am writing to express my concerns about …

I would like to complain about …

Suggesting solutions

One possible way to solve this problem is to …

An alternative solution to this issue is …

Declining suggestions

It doesn't sound very good.

I don't think I fancy it.

I'm sorry, but I can't join you.

I'm not really into …

I've got some doubts about it.

I don't see how it could work.

Actually, I would prefer not to.

Describing a person

The first thing you notice about (him/her) is …

(He/She) is special for a number of reasons.

He/She is the kind of person who …

The most unusual/interesting person I've ever met is …

Height   of medium height, tall, fairly short, long-legged

Build   muscular, well-built, overweight, skinny, slim, thin

Age   in his teens, middle-aged, in her late forties, elderly

Facial features   round, oval, freckles, dimples, scar, mole, wrinkled, almond-shaped eyes, pale, tanned, a crooked nose, moustache, beard

Hair   balding, short, shoulder-length, long, wavy, curly, thick

She dresses casually/smartly/well/in black/fashionably.

He always wears scruffy/stylish clothes.

Describing an object

It is/was…

Size   huge/tiny/35 cm x 25 cm big

Shape   round/rectangular/square/narrow

Colour   white/red and brown/light/dark green

Material   made of leather/plastic/linen

Age   new/young/old/six years old/modern/ancient

It has/had (two handles/a leather strap/a blue cover/two pockets/short sleeves).

Disagreeing with an opinion

I disagree that/with … / I don't agree that/with …

I am totally against …

I see what you mean but …

I see your point of view but …

I'm afraid I can't agree with …

I'm not convinced about/that …

I don't think it's the best solution …

I must say I do not agree / strongly disagree with …

I am of a different/the opposite opinion because …

Contrary to popular belief …

Ending an email / a letter

Informal phrases

It was good to hear from you.

Email me soon.

I'd better get going. / I must go now. / Got to go now. / I must be going now.

Bye for now.

Looking forward to your news / to hearing from you again.

Say hello to …

Give my love/my regards to (everyone at home).

Have a nice (trip).

See you (soon/in the summer).

Write soon.

Keep in touch!

Neutral phrases

I look forward to hearing from you / your reply.

I hope to hear from you soon.

Formal phrases

I look forward to your prompt response/reply.

I wonder what other readers think about …

I hope you will publish more articles about this problem.

I would be grateful if you could publish my letter.

Expressing doubt

I have read the advert/about your services and/but I am not quite sure if …

I cannot understand if …

It is not clear to me if …

Expressing interest

I am interested in … / I have been looking for …

I am planning to … and that is why I found this advertisement/offer/text interesting/important.

I was very interested in your … (article/editorial/ presentation).

Expressing opinion

I believe/think/feel (that) …

I really/do believe …

In my opinion/view,

From my point of view, / The way I see it,

It seems/appears to me (that) …

To my mind,

My opinion is that …

As far as I am concerned,

To be honest,

People often claim that …

Some people argue that …

Expressing preferences

I really enjoy/like/love … because …

I prefer … to …

I'd like to … / I hope to …

… is great because …

I find … boring/dull.

I don't like / I can't stand / I really hate …

It's not really my thing.

For and against / Opinion essay

Introduction – for and against essay

What are the arguments for and against this idea?

What are the benefits and drawbacks of such a solution?

What are the advantages and disadvantages of …?

This idea can be said to have both advantages and disadvantages.

Let us consider the advantages and disadvantages of …

Introduction – opinion essay

Personally, I believe (that) …

In my opinion, / To my mind, …

In this essay, I am going to argue that …

(Today) Many people believe that …

Let me explain why I agree with this view.

WRITING BANK

Introducing various points of view

The first (dis)advantage for (the young adult) is …

From the (teachers') point of view …

Giving arguments

First and foremost,

One (dis)advantage is that …

It is also often hoped that (the event) will …

It is also important/vital to consider …

Another benefit/drawback is that …

Another downside is the …

Expressing your own opinion

In my opinion, / To my mind, / In my view, (the advantages outweigh the disadvantages).

As far as I am concerned,

Conclusion

In conclusion, / To conclude, / To sum up, / All in all, / On balance, / On the whole,

All things considered, / Taking everything into account, …

For all these reasons, I am convinced that …

Giving advice

You should / ought to …

You'd better …

If I were you, I would …

It might be a good idea (for you) to …

Why don't you …?

Have you thought of/about …?

It's better (not) to do …

Make sure that …

Remember (not) to do …

It's (not) worth (doing) …

I (don't) think it's a good idea.

I don't think you should …

Giving examples

For example, / For instance,

Like … / Such as …

Especially / In particular / Particularly

Giving reasons for opinions

I think so because …

In fact,/Actually,

The reason why I believe so is …

Introduction: emails and letters

Informal phrases

It was good to hear from you.

I hope you're doing well / you're fine / you're OK.

How are you (doing)?

I'm writing to tell you …

Thanks for your letter.

I wonder if you remember / have heard …

I wanted to tell you about …

Neutral and formal phrases

I am writing in order to …

I am writing to thank you for …

I would like to express my …

I am writing in connection with … (the article/editorial/ report) …

I have just read … (the article) titled … in Saturday's paper / last month's edition of …

I am writing to ask/enquire about …

I read/found your advertisement in … and would like to …

Listing arguments

First argument

First of all,

First/Firstly,

To begin with,

The main/major argument in support of … is that …

On the one hand, / On the other hand,

One argument in favour of … is that …

Successive arguments

Secondly,

Thirdly,

Then/Next,

Another (dis)advantage is that …

In addition, / Additionally,

Also,

Apart from this,

Moreover, / What is more, / Furthermore,

Most importantly,

Last argument

Finally,

Last, but not least,

Making recommendations

Positive opinion

You'll love it!

If you like love stories, you should definitely read it.

It is a must!

I think it's worth reading because…

I was impressed by …

I couldn't put it down.

It's a classic. / It's a masterpiece of its kind.

The plot is believable/entertaining/thought-provoking.

It's a highly entertaining read.

It will change the way you see …

If I were you, I wouldn't hesitate to …

I highly recommend (reading) it.

I recommend it to everyone.

Negative opinion

One weakness (of the book/film) is that …

It is rather long/boring/confusing/slow.

The cast is awful/unconvincing.

The script is dull.

It is poorly/badly written.

Adjectives

Positive   brilliant/spectacular/striking/impressive/
powerful/convincing

Negative   violent/predictable/unconvincing/far-fetched/
dull/bland/disappointing

Neutral   slow/sentimental/serious

Making a request

Informal phrases

Can you …, please? / Could you …?

Do you think you could …?

Let me know if you can (come).

Could you tell me …?

Neutral phrases

Would it be possible for you to …?

I'd be grateful if you could …

I wonder if I could ask you to/for …

I'm writing to ask for your help/advice …

Making suggestions

I think I/you/we should …

Perhaps I/you/we could …

What do you think about …?

What about …? / How about …?

How do you feel about …?

Would you like me to …?

Why don't we (go) …?

Let's (go to) …

Shall we (go) …?

Do you fancy (going to the cinema)?

I (would) suggest/recommend organising …

You should pay more attention to …

It would be a good idea to …

WRITING BANK

Review

Introduction

The film/book tells the story of …

The film/story is set in …

The book/novel was written by …

The film is directed by …

It is a comedy/horror film/love story.

This well-written/informative/fascinating book …

It is based on real events / on a true story / on a book.

It has been made into a film.

Plot description

The story concerns / begins / is about …

The plot is (rather) boring/thrilling.

The plot has an unexpected twist.

The plot focuses on …

The film reaches a dramatic climax …

Starting an email / a letter

Informal phrases

Dear Margaret,

Hi Anne,

Neutral and formal phrases

Dear Mr and Mrs Edwards,

Dear Miss/Ms Brennon,

Dear Mr Brennon,

Dear Sir or Madam,

Dear Editor,

Telling a story

It all happened some time ago.

It all started when …

It was three years ago.

No sooner had we … than …

While I (was playing),

Just as I was watching…

As soon as

First,

Then,

Finally,

After a little while,

Suddenly / All of a sudden,

Unfortunately,

Fortunately,

It was the best/worst time ever.

We had a great/awful time when we were …

I'll never forget …

Thanking

Informal phrases

I'm writing to thank you for …

Thank you so much.

It was so/really/very kind of you to …

Neutral phrases

I really appreciate your help.

Thank you for sending it back to me.

I am really grateful for your help.

It's very kind of you.

I hope it's not too much trouble for you.

Thank you for doing me a favour.

1.9 Self-check

Vocabulary and Grammar

Exercise 1
1 consciousness 2 disruptive
3 expelled 4 struck 5 brainy

Exercise 2
1 B 2 A 3 C 4 C 5 A

Exercise 3
1 scholarship 2 acquire 3 dissertation
4 major 5 sieve

Exercise 4
1 ~~will walk~~ – would walk
2 ~~always were disturbing~~ – were always disturbing
3 ~~used~~ – use
4 correct
5 ~~don't used~~ – didn't use

Exercise 5
1 to go 2 let him choose
3 avoid revising
4 remind your brother to give
5 remember visiting

Exercise 6
1 B 2 C 3 A 4 C 5 B

Use of English

Exercise 7
1 singing
2 brainwave
3 will
4 scraped
5 urge

Exercise 8
1 deepen 2 unconscious
3 photographic 4 achievements
5 proven

Exercise 9
1 advised me to study
2 remember hitting the tree
3 spent all day reading books
4 is always messing around
5 used to attend

Exercise 10
1 to 2 used 3 always
4 brains 5 will

2.9 Self-check

Vocabulary and Grammar

Exercise 1
1 full 2 intellectual
3 hesitated 4 crouched
5 perceptive

Exercise 2
1 glanced
2 fell
3 gazed
4 swallowed
5 grimaced

Exercise 3
1 short-tempered
2 split up
3 life and soul of the party
4 self-centred
5 at ease

Exercise 4
1 had already started
2 had been snowing
3 had been working
4 talked 5 had known

Exercise 5
1 ∅ 2 which 3 whose 4 ∅ 5 ∅

Exercise 6
1 B 2 C 3 C 4 B 5 A

Use of English

Exercise 7
1 vivid 2 let 3 think 4 reach 5 wave

Exercise 8
1 interesting 2 unforgettable
3 insecure 4 obsessed 5 predictably

Exercise 9
1 the film had already started
2 she hadn't been listening
3 had known
4 had won
5 I hadn't been learning

Exercise 10
1 been 2 self-conscious 3 which/that
4 love 5 with

3.9 Self-check

Vocabulary and Grammar

Exercise 1
1 housing 2 vibrant 3 medieval
4 bustling 5 scenery

Exercise 2
1 on 2 of 3 within 4 In 5 at

Exercise 3
1 A 2 B 3 A 4 C 5 C

Exercise 4
1 will/'ll have been working
2 will/'ll be enjoying
3 will/'ll have owned
4 will/'ll be fitting
5 will/'ll have arrived

Exercise 5
1 either 2 no 3 none
4 deal 5 plenty

Exercise 6
1 few 2 every 3 the others
4 the whole 5 another

Use of English

Exercise 7
1 will have finished the housing development
2 in spite of reminding/in spite of having reminded
3 will be building the garage
4 will have been teaching children
5 a great deal of stuff

Exercise 8
1 home 2 reliable 3 running
4 wild 5 household

Exercise 9
1 will have escaped 2 the others
3 will be living 4 a couple of ideas
5 either of them

Exercise 10
1 cup 2 on 3 number/lot 4 Another
5 have

4.9 Self-check

Vocabulary and Grammar

Exercise 1
1 ~~response~~ – reputation 2 ~~up~~ out
3 ~~fly~~ flea 4 correct 5 ~~key~~ chain

Exercise 2
1 fortune 2 broke 3 support
4 to shop 5 burn

Exercise 3
1 ends 2 belongings 3 impulse
4 sale 5 products

Exercise 4
1 Does he 2 Is she 3 hasn't she
4 will you 5 didn't he

Exercise 5
1 didn't need to / have to hire
2 mustn't use / can't use
3 shouldn't have kept / ought not to have kept
4 had to cancel
5 needn't have brought

Exercise 6
1 obliged 2 certain 3 banned
4 unlikely 5 succeeded

Use of English

Exercise 7
1 have 2 myself 3 out/much
4 should 5 had

Exercise 8
1 had better not spend
2 needn't have paid
3 ought to have gone
4 are not allowed to park
5 are bound to go

Exercise 9
1 haven't they
2 needn't have used
3 banned from going
4 another one
5 ought to have bought

Exercise 10
1 C 2 A 3 D 4 B 5 D

5.9 Self-check

Vocabulary and Grammar

Exercise 1
1 output 2 goals 3 day 4 mind
5 heart

Exercise 2
1 carry out 2 burnt/burned out
3 got down to 4 put off 5 keep at

Exercise 3
1 overworked 2 conscientious
3 single-minded 4 punctual
5 knowledgeable

Exercise 4
1 how long I had been looking for
  a job before I (had) found one
2 he was flying to Canada the following day
3 not to ask her for a loan
4 would have to buy at least two new suits
5 whether/if I was going to commute
  to Leeds

Exercise 5
1 insisted on preparing
2 suggested that we (should) wear
3 explained (that) they had been doing
  research
4 apologised for not being able to get
5 reminded me that they were
  decorating

Exercise 6
1 A 2 C 3 B 4 B 5 A

Use of English

Exercise 7
1 denied breaking the photocopier
2 to have forgotten my CV
3 reminded me to turn off
4 should have asked first
5 in terms of motivation

Exercise 8
1 B 2 C 3 C 4 A 5 C

Exercise 9
1 tied up with 2 grow out of
3 find his niche 4 lacks purpose
5 get round to

Exercise 10
1 D 2 B 3 C 4 D 5 A

6.9 Self-check

Vocabulary and Grammar

Exercise 1
1 B 2 A 3 C 4 C 5 A

Exercise 2
1 manipulate 2 feeling 3 look into
4 evaluate 5 strong

Exercise 3
1 d 2 f 3 c 4 a 5 b

Exercise 4
1 C 2 A 3 C 4 B 5 A

Exercise 5
1 wouldn't have stayed late if her boss
  hadn't been angry
2 had a smartphone, she could have
3 I weren't/wasn't busy, I would have
  sent you
4 hadn't studied acting, he wouldn't be
5 would have gone to the party if we
  hadn't been

Exercise 6
1 would 2 wouldn't know 3 if
4 would read 5 Had we

Use of English

Exercise 7
1 made-up 2 lived
3 advised 4 crack-down 5 News

Exercise 8
1 providing/provided
2 alarmingly
3 has changed
4 were going through
5 would have helped / would help

Exercise 9
1 deliberately 2 popularity
3 breaking 4 commitment
5 had read

Exercise 10
1 Suppose she hadn't told us
2 would not be sitting
3 would never have employed him
4 were you not honest with
5 has a habit of lying to people

7.9 Self-check

Vocabulary and Grammar

Exercise 1
1 named 2 with 3 coined
4 received 5 in

Exercise 2
1 contribution 2 reference
3 molecular 4 collaborate
5 aptitude

Exercise 3
1 threw in 2 come out 3 go in for
4 bring in 5 talked me into

Exercise 4
1 being shown
2 to be encouraged
3 was known to have written
4 are estimated to be studying
5 It could be argued that

Exercise 5
1 being forced
2 have been charged
3 had been sent
4 to be installed
5 being criticised

Exercise 6
1 was thought that
2 is said to have had
3 were estimated to be
4 is claimed to cause
5 is known to have revolutionised

Use of English

Exercise 7
1 B 2 D 3 A 4 B 5 C

Exercise 8
1 was expected not to reveal
2 is it being held
3 are known to be applying
4 can't stand being reminded
5 was talked into buying

Exercise 9
1 regulate 2 beneficial
3 harmful 4 privacy
5 technological

Exercise 10
1 is said to have designed
2 are sold to the employees
3 not to be informed
4 stand being monitored
5 advisable to establish

8.9 Self-check

Vocabulary and Grammar

Exercise 1
1 contamination 2 orchards
3 irreparable 4 single-use
5 chain

Exercise 2
1 ploughed fields
2 thriving population
3 built-up areas
4 extreme hunger
5 breeding ground

Exercise 3
1 gale-force 2 overboard
3 captivity 4 injuries 5 wild

Exercise 4
1 stopped 2 hadn't thrown out
3 planted 4 hadn't sold
5 had installed

Exercise 5
1 any – no 2 Not – Never
3 All – What 4 There – It 5 If – Not

Exercise 6
1 would rather 2 could
3 What 4 Not only 5 Never

Use of English

Exercise 7
1 unusually 2 hypersensitive
3 irresponsibly 4 improbable
5 incapable

Exercise 8
1 B 2 D 3 A 4 C 5 B

Exercise 9
1 only 2 have 3 high
4 only 5 that

Exercise 10
1 What Mark needs to do
2 wish we had preserved
3 'd/would rather you thought
4 only we could join you
5 (before) have we dumped

Present tenses – review

Exercise 1
1a 've never heard
1b see
1c eat
2a are you doing
2b 'm making
2c Do you think
2d have you been boiling
2e think

Exercise 2
1 Are food prices going up at the moment?
2 Have you ever cut your finger preparing food?
3 How often do you cook a meal for the family?
4 How long have you been going to this school?
5 How long have you known your best friend?

Exercise 3
1 think, tastes, don't like
2 bakes, 's probably making
3 doesn't see, love
4 are you looking, Have you lost
5 've been doing, smells

Exercise 4
1 ~~Do you run?~~ – Have you been running?
2 ~~'m becoming~~ – 've become
3 ~~hasn't cooked~~ – doesn't cook
4 ~~don't work~~ – aren't working
5 ~~'re waiting~~ – 've been waiting

Exercise 5
1 haven't seen
2 thinks, hasn't made
3 has been reading
4 prefer
5 is taking
6 has written

Past tenses – review

Exercise 1
1 came, locked
2 had left
3 were talking
4 was riding
5 Had he ever coached

Exercise 2
1 were watching
2 reached
3 had climbed
4 was shining
5 pulled

Exercise 3
1 scored
2 were watching
3 hadn't brought
4 had never beaten
5 had made
6 was training

Exercise 4
1 ~~was already scoring~~ – had already scored
2 ~~Had you remembered~~ – Did you remember
3 ~~was throwing~~ – threw
4 ~~were forgetting~~ – had forgotten
5 ~~didn't listen~~ – weren't listening
6 ~~Had you watched~~ – Were you watching

Exercise 5
1 was studying
2 scored
3 had won
4 was looking forward to
5 liked
6 had been
7 didn't understand

Exercise 6
1 I didn't know how to make a cake when I was ten.
2 Was it raining when you were going to school?
3 By the time we arrived at the party, everyone had already left.
4 We were talking about her when she called.
5 She had never felt so happy before she met him.

Future tenses – review

Exercise 1
1 f
2 i
3 d
4 b
5 g
6 c
7 e
8 a
9 h

Exercise 2
1 will have left
2 will make
3 are returning
4 Shall
5 You're going to have
6 arrives
7 Will they have finished
8 won't be working

Exercise 3
1 C
2 B
3 A
4 B
5 A
6 C
7 B
8 C

Exercise 4
1 will be waiting
2 will have started
3 will be sitting
4 will have eaten
5 will be doing
6 will have finished
7 will have arrived

Exercise 5
1 will be sailing
2 does … start
3 are going to go
4 am having
5 will answer
6 Shall … bring
7 won't have moved
8 will drive

Exercise 6
1 is going to win
2 will ever live
3 are going to have / are having
4 starts
5 am going
6 will be studying
7 pay
8 will have read

Exercise 7
1 when I go
2 will have started
3 until you speak/have spoken
4 are having a/their party
5 will be playing
6 as soon as you cook
7 are you going to do
8 unless you want

First, Second and Third Conditionals, *wish* and *if only*

Exercise 1
1 would've bought
2 'll never remember
3 saw
4 'd known
5 sit
6 wouldn't behave

Exercise 2
1 I wish/If only I could read music.
2 I wish/If only my sister would help around the house.
3 I wish/If only my dad didn't have to work long hours.
4 I wish/If only my sister would let me use her laptop.
5 I wish/If only my brother weren't/wasn't annoying.
6 I wish/If only my mum wouldn't embarrass me in front of visitors.

Exercise 3
1 Mum wouldn't make
2 I had
3 my girlfriend would call
4 there was/were
5 I wasn't/weren't
6 Kerry wouldn't tap

Exercise 4
1 could, 'd choose
2 loved
3 'd never have been able, hadn't lent
4 could
5 don't give, gets/will get
6 were, would you accept
7 had

Exercise 5
1 If I knew Arabic, I'd talk to him.
2 If only I knew how to help her.
3 If the weather in Poland had been better last year, we wouldn't have gone abroad on holiday.
4 Will you ask her to dance if she comes to your party tomorrow?
5 He wishes his sister wouldn't come into his room all the time.
6 She wouldn't be late every day if she lived closer.

Modal verbs for speculation

Exercise 1
1 must be
2 may/might not have understood
3 can't/couldn't have imagined
4 must have been

Exercise 2
1 Human beings may visit the Moon again one day.
2 There must be life somewhere else in the universe.
3 Life could/might/may have arrived on Earth when an asteroid crashed into the planet.
4 We might not have landed on the Moon in 1969.

Exercise 3
1 must/might/may/could have missed
2 might/may/could have got
3 can't be
4 might/may/could arrive
5 might/may not even have posted
6 can't/couldn't have left

Exercise 4
1 can't/couldn't have approached
2 must be
3 may/might/could have been
4 may/might/could continue

Exercise 5
1 She might be in her room.
2 She can't be that old.
3 He may not have received it yet.
4 You must have left it at home.
5 You can't be serious.
6 You might not want to hear this.
7 They could have overheard what we said.

Reported speech

Exercise 1
1 these, Do
2 started, ago, will, me
3 My, love, have, is, are
4 is, Don't

Exercise 2
1 the manager would be there the following/next day if I could come back then
2 the advertising executives were arriving that night
3 he had seen the new advert on TV for the first time that day
4 they were going to open the new branch of their coffee shop the following/next week
5 she was sorry, but my doctor's appointment for that day had been cancelled
6 she couldn't promise anything right then

Exercise 3
1 to taste the drink and then describe the flavour
2 if/whether I would like to try their service for free for a month
3 to contact them and let them know what I thought
4 if/whether I had ever thought of trying a different brand of lipstick
5 not to forget to take one pill before breakfast and the other one before bed
6 who was going to pay for the damage to her computer

Exercise 4
1 if/whether he was from that part of town
2 if/whether I liked going to the cinema
3 not to play in the kitchen
4 (that) I/we needed to get the assignment back to him by 4 p.m. the following/next day
5 to pick her up some of her special toothpaste from the chemist's
6 (that) he had never bought anything because of an advertisement
7 if/whether my/our sister was going to visit us that weekend
8 if/whether I would be so kind as to show her that photo

Passive forms; *have something done*

Exercise 1
1 won't be asked
2 was told (by his teacher)
3 was added
4 was sent to the USA (by my parents)
5 am being met (by my American friend)
6 will always be remembered
7 was found, were being painted
8 are going to be posted

Exercise 2
1 Every year in the USA, around 60,000 teenagers are sent to prison.
2 In 1811 in Britain, nearly a quarter of all girls were named Mary.
3 More tea is drunk by people in the UK than in any other country.
4 The Statue of Liberty was built in France.

Exercise 3
1 has just been stolen
2 won't be built
3 were being cleaned
4 hasn't been repaired
5 are being printed
6 were they told
7 are ordered
8 was this film directed

Exercise 4
1 had your phone fixed yet
2 doesn't have his hair cut
3 didn't have her teeth whitened
4 has her toenails painted
5 is having the tattoo removed
6 had her hair cut

Exercise 5
1 When did you last have your eyes tested?
2 Will you ever have your hair coloured?
3 Are you going to have your bedroom redecorated?
4 Have you had your ears pierced?
5 When did you last have a passport photo taken?

Articles

Exercise 1
1 a place – the place
2 the famous actor – a famous actor
3 a lunch – lunch
4 the pound coin – a pound coin
5 Swimming pool – The swimming pool
6 only music – the only music

Exercise 2
1 Ø 2 a 3 an 4 a
5 a 6 an 7 a 8 the
9 the 10 a 11 the 12 Ø

Exercise 3
1 the 2 a 3 Ø 4 a
5 the 6 the, Ø 7 the

Unit 1

Exercise 1
1 they used to take her to the local park every Sunday afternoon
2 would never/wouldn't allow her children to stay up late during the week
3 use to enjoy going to school when you were younger
4 enables us to take part in IT competitions for schools
5 is always chewing gum in class
6 me forget to call the vet
7 force him to tell the truth
8 advised Ms Dodgson to start a new hobby

Exercise 2
1 came/would come
2 was always sitting
3 to get   4 was eating
5 realised   6 eating
7 to share   8 chewing/to chew
9 was eating   10 found
11 will give   12 to open
13 to pull   14 promising
15 would give   16 had already begun
17 to say   18 not to help

Exercise 3
1 ~~was~~ used to study – used to study
2 ~~used to study~~ – studied
3 afford ~~buy~~ – afford to buy
4 stopped ~~calling~~ – stopped to call, ~~to discuss~~ – discussing
5 ~~used~~ – use
6 ~~forgot~~ – had forgotten
7 ~~would forget~~ – forgot, ~~will~~ – would
8 ~~be~~ stopped – have stopped

Exercise 4
1 do you get   2 would, had to
3 flew, would be   4 longest, the, a
5 thrown, fly

Exercise 5
1 used to have a swim
2 couldn't stand working in an/the office
3 remember to pay the fine
4 are you always complaining about the food
5 didn't intend to hurt you
6 saw her cleaning the floor

Unit 2

Exercise 1
1 had   2 been   3 had   4 not/never
5 which   6 which/that   7 whose

Exercise 2
1 ~~has~~ never come – had never come
2 ~~was~~ trying – had been trying
3 ~~what~~ – which
4 ~~stopping~~ – who/that stopped
5 ~~used to live~~ – lived
6 ~~bringing up~~ – brought up/who are brought up
7 ~~passing~~ – to pass

Exercise 3
1 stop   2 had been planning
3 turned up   4 that   5 were unable to
6 decided not to   7 which   8 impressed
9 attacked   10 them to have

Exercise 4
1 been   2 had   3 who/that   4 which
5 always   6 use   7 would

Exercise 5
1 had been waiting
2 had invited me to
3 (that) my sister is married
4 which really annoyed
5 will never forget meeting
6 we stopped to buy
7 are always complaining about

Exercise 6
1 had been barking for hours
2 whose mum is a mathematician
3 Did your parents use to put
4 can't stand waiting for you
5 saw / had seen him eat(ing) it
6 (who is) playing the saxophone is

Unit 3

Exercise 1
1 c   2 g   3 h   4 f   5 d
6 b   7 a   8 e   9 j   10 i

Exercise 2
1 Neither
2 Every
3 will have arrived
4 where
5 I'll still be working
6 will they have been building
7 to let
8 had been waiting
9 will have been saving
10 made

Exercise 3
1 every   2 most of   3 was   4 little
5 few   6 number of   7 had been
8 a little   9 great deal   10 which
11 much   12 most   13 which
14 deal of   15 where   16 is
17 both

Exercise 4
1 Will you be going / Are you going
2 encouraged her niece to put
3 will have been training for ten years
4 None of us will have moved
5 will have finished the whole book
6 Several people living in our neighbourhood / Several people who live in our neighbourhood
7 had been waiting at the door
8 few of us will be staying
9 There is/are a number of things
10 a great deal of attention

Unit 4

Exercise 1
1 needn't have cooked
2 did they   3 is it
4 didn't need to get up
5 had better not call
6 Don't they?   7 is there
8 had to

Exercise 2
1 ~~not better~~ – better not
2 ~~must~~ – had to
3 weren't ~~they~~ – weren't there
4 ~~others~~ – other
5 ~~few~~ – a little
6 they'll ~~be~~ – they'll have been
7 ~~which~~ teaching – teaching / which ~~teaching~~ – which teaches
8 ~~to spend~~ – spending

Exercise 3
1 f   2 c   3 g   4 e   5 a   6 d   7 b

Exercise 4
1 used to, to do
2 both, neither
3 no, there
4 had been to
5 will you be using
6 the whole, Did
7 have you
8 to buy

Exercise 5
1 been, which, have/need
2 plenty/lots, had, the, have
3 forward, had   4 had, which
5 are/were   6 asking, to

Exercise 6
1 That's him
2 didn't use to like getting
3 could remember hearing
4 needn't have spent
5 had better not go out
6 will have already left

Unit 5

Exercise 1
1 (that) his dad travels on business so often that their dog hardly recognises him
2 breaking the glass, of doing that
3 she hadn't told him that she had been fired
4 if/whether I was happy with the final score
5 not saying anything to Jane / (that) we shouldn't say anything to Jane
6 me not to be late
7 on (our) leaving early the following day / that we should leave early the following day
8 they might be late for dinner that night
9 if/whether she had been to the interview the week before
10 if/whether she could borrow his mobile / to lend her his mobile

Exercise 2
1 who
2 managed
3 had
4 to
5 when/after
6 that
7 little/short
8 being/feeling
9 him
10 been/proved

Exercise 3
1 spending
2 was hoping
3 was saving up
4 which
5 advised
6 should have listened
7 hadn't been expecting
8 praised
9 will have been working
10 worked out

Exercise 4
1 ~~can't~~ – couldn't
2 ~~what was her email address~~ – what her email address was
3 to ~~travelling~~ – to travel, ~~seem do~~ – seem to do
4 ~~ought not have taken~~ – ought not to have taken
5 that John had been to ~~it~~ – that John had been to

Exercise 5
1 refused to pay for his studies
2 Neither of his flatmates blamed him
3 don't they
4 will have expired by
5 a number of times

Unit 6

Exercise 1
1 didn't have
2 wouldn't have come
3 might have gone
4 were
5 Imagine
6 wouldn't be
7 wouldn't still be
8 you'd remembered
9 Unless
10 Had she let me know

Exercise 2
1 few   2 of   3 that   4 had   5 them
6 which   7 don't   8 saying   9 the
10 were   11 both/each   12 to
13 who   14 unless

Exercise 3
1 Suppose   2 that
3 others   4 many
5 suggested   6 of
7 insist   8 not to drink
9 don't have to   10 providing

Exercise 4
1 he would not have to do his homework now
2 provided you invite them yourself
3 might have won
4 needn't have invited them
5 will have been playing for

Unit 7

Exercise 1
1 We were made to switch off our mobiles (by the teacher).
2 That problem can't be solved.
3 Has Ms Johnson been sent the letter?/Has the letter been sent to Ms Johnson?
4 She will have been given the news by now. / The news will have been given to her by now.
5 The robber must have already been caught (by the police).
6 Prices are said to have risen dramatically.
7 I hate being asked my age.
8 She wanted to be invited to the party.
9 The chairman is expected to resign next week.
10 It is being suggested (that) the situation won't improve.

Exercise 2
1 have been searching
2 to find   3 to be
4 was found   5 admitted
6 had decided   7 had been described
8 shouldn't have   9 was raised
10 left   11 who
12 are being carried on   13 warning
14 hadn't launched   15 wouldn't be
16 will be sailing

Exercise 3
1 were ~~questioning~~ – were questioned
2 ~~given them~~ – given to them
3 ~~has~~ thought – is thought
4 ~~wouldn't have~~ taken – hadn't taken
5 been ~~marrying~~ – been married

Exercise 4
1 fancy losing
2 can't stand being told
3 claim to have come up
4 was invented / has been invented
5 promises to remove
6 insist that meals can be reduced
7 will have been removed
8 being eaten / to be eaten
9 is not expected to enter
10 urge us to limit

Exercise 5
1 are reported to have been
2 would have prepared a better presentation
3 unless you learn to respect the rules
4 regretted leaving
5 if I had ever taken part
6 should have told your friends

Unit 8

Exercise 1
1 wanted was success
2 stopped annoying her / didn't annoy her anymore / didn't keep annoying her
3 have we seen such careless work
4 did he seem to realise how important the discussion was
5 must this leak out to the press
6 wants to know is your time of arrival
7 I hadn't gone on that trip with them
8 Julia had invited / had not forgotten to invite Richard to her birthday party
9 that camera was/were cheaper/less expensive / wasn't/weren't so expensive

Exercise 2
1 Should   2 does   3 to accept
4 accepting   5 would   6 didn't
7 hadn't   8 whole, all

Exercise 3
1 'd better take your cat to a vet
2 must have been stolen
3 is being opened tomorrow afternoon (by the President)
4 wish there was/were some coffee left
5 the police unless you get out immediately
6 thought to have done it on purpose

Exercise 4
1 should
2 which
3 are often thought
4 those kinds of
5 don't have to
6 recycling
7 much
8 check
9 made
10 known
11 –
12 wouldn't be

Exercise 5
1 Never before had they realised
2 something was done
3 is said to have caused
4 has never been given
5 hadn't started when he was
6 threatened never to talk
7 didn't need to tell him / needn't have told him
8 All we need to be healthy is

Pearson Education Limited
KAO Two
KAO Park
Hockham Way,
Harlow, Essex,
CM17 9SR England
and Associated Companies throughout the world.

www.english.com/focus

© Pearson Education Limited 2020

Focus 4 Second Edition Workbook

The right of Daniel Brayshaw, Angela Bandis, Bartosz Michałowski, Beata Trapnell, David Byrne and Amanda Davies to be identified as authors of this Work has been asserted by them in accordance with the Copyright, Designs and Patents Act 1988.

First published 2020
Eleventh impression 2024

ISBN: 978-1-292-23411-3

Set in Avenir LT Pro
Printed in Slovakia by Neografia

Acknowledgements

The publishers and authors would like to thank the following people and institutions for their feedback and comments during the development of the material:
Humberto Santos Duran
Anna Maria Grochowska
Beata Gruszczyńska
Inga Lande
Magdalena Loska
Barbara Madej
Rosa Maria Maldonado
Juliana Queiroz Pereira
Tomasz Siuta
Elżbieta Śliwa
Katarzyna Ślusarczyk
Katarzyna Tobolska
Renata Tomaka-Pasternak
Beata Trapnell
Aleksandra Zakrzewska
Beata Zygadlewicz-Kocuś

The publishers are grateful to the following for permission to reproduce copyright material:

Text

© **Telegraph Media Group Limited:** Extract on page 72 adapted from Paper rounds dying out as children 'too lazy', The Telegraph, 05/06/2008 (Alleyne, Richard), Extract on page 104 adapted from Ten ways that driverless cars will change the world, The Telegraph, 28/05/2014 (Sparkes, Matthew), Extract on page 120 adapted from New dinosaur seven times bigger than T. rex discovered in Argentina, The Telegraph, 04/09/2014 (Collins, Nick)

Images

123RF.com: Antonio Guillem 35, 88, Cathy Yeulet 35, 77, conneldesign 131, Matyas Rehak 131, nerthuz 131, rawpixel. com 35, scanrail 52; **Alamy Stock Photo**: Artem Varnitsin 99, dpa picture alliance 8, Hemis 67, Ian McDonald 61, Kristina Kokhanova 99, Matthew Wakem 67, South West Images Scotland 48, Trevor Chriss 56; **Pearson Education Ltd: Studio 8** 14; **Shutterstock.com**: AleksKapa 111, Anton27 69, Bertrand Benoit 24, Bulltus_casso 70, Daisy Daisy 72, David Carillet 120, David Herraez Calzada 120, Dean Drobot 20, 30, DGLimages 5, DisobeyArt 31, Diyana Dimitrova 67, Dragon Images 5, 107, fizkes 71, 106, FloridaStock 116, FLX2 118, FotoKina 124, frantic00 127, garetsworkshop 62, gephoto 32, Graphite and Charcoal 153, Iakov Filimonov 11, inrainbows 40, 40, Intellistudies 5, JR-stock 46, kalen 149, kosmos111 47, LCAT Productions 120, Leszek Czerwonka 17, metamorworks 104, MicroOne 102, Milan Ilic Photographer 28, MPH Photos 72, MYP Studio 74, nd3000 33, Nednapa 101, Neil Burton 120, Neil Lockhart 27, Nejron Photo 79, NicoElNino 67, Pavel Islam 77, Peterfz30 56, Photology1971 49, Podis 150, ppa 40, Pressmaster 92, r.nagy 56, Rawpixel.com 13, Ruslan Huzau 47, Ryan DeBerardinis 131, Sergey Uryadnikov 125, Shunevych Serhii 41, Simon Mayer 99, Stockfotografie 6, Syda Productions 4, 79, Tero Vesalainen 99, travellight 37, VGstockstudio 7, wavebreakmedia 35, 63, 94, 108, Zoomstudio 76

Illustrations
Illustrated by Ewa Olejnik: pp. 10, 23, 43, 85, 90, 97, 110, 122.

All other images © Pearson Education Limited.

Every effort has been made to trace the copyright holders and we apologise in advance for any unintentional omissions. We would be pleased to insert the appropriate acknowledgement in any subsequent edition of this publication.